GW01607091

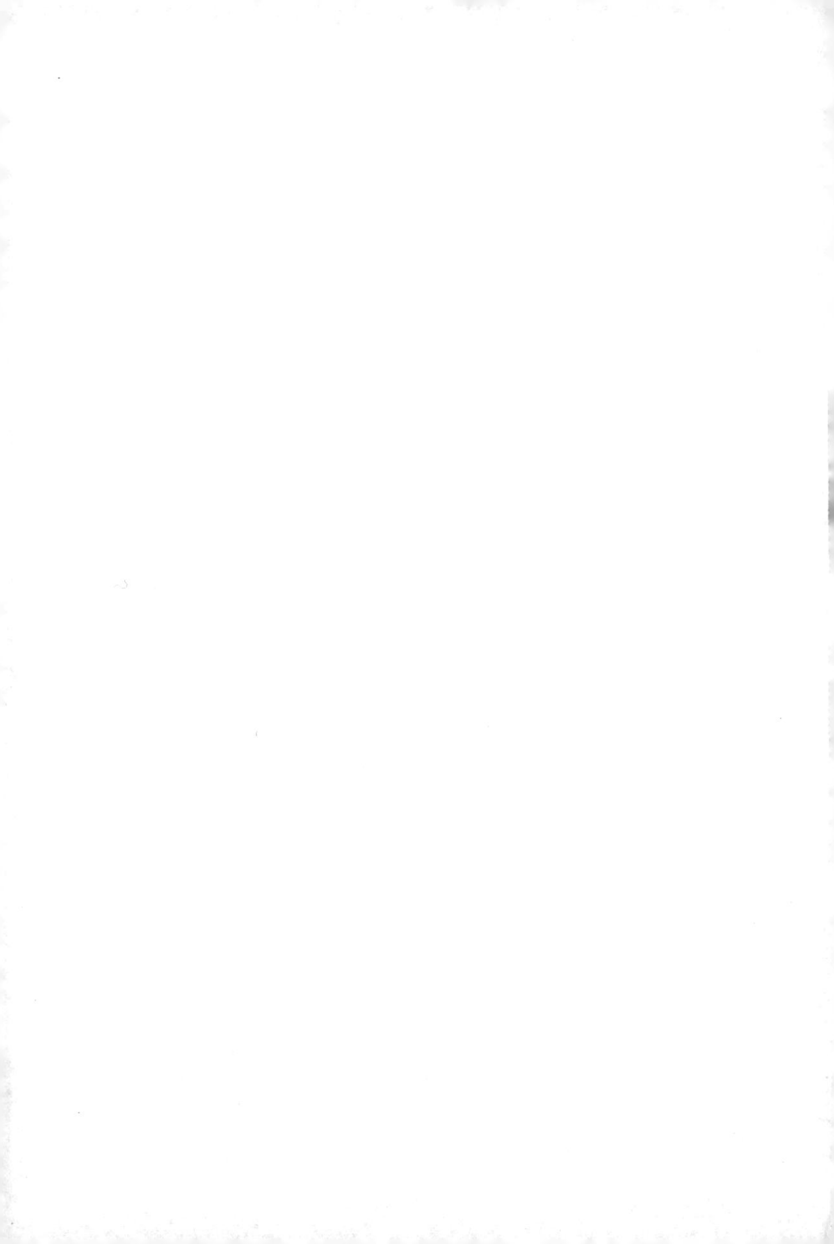

Mrs

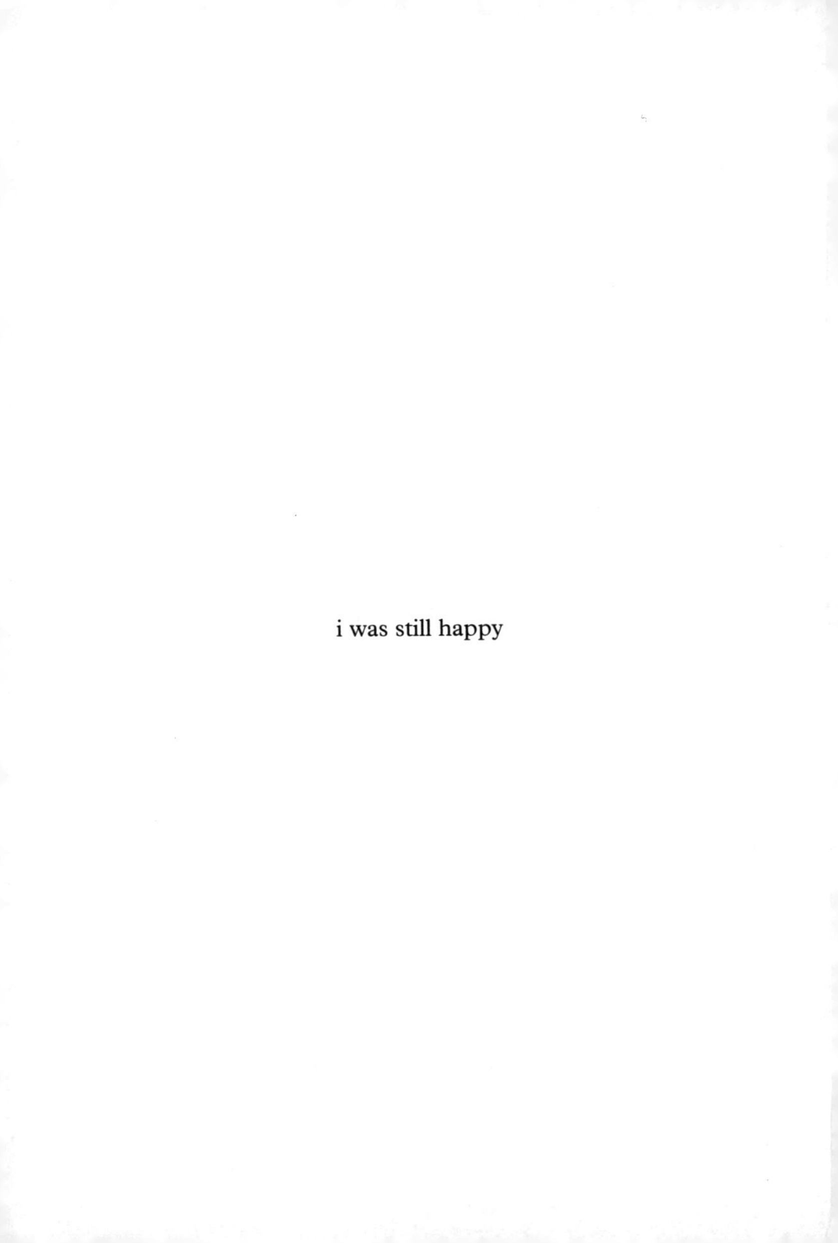

i was still happy

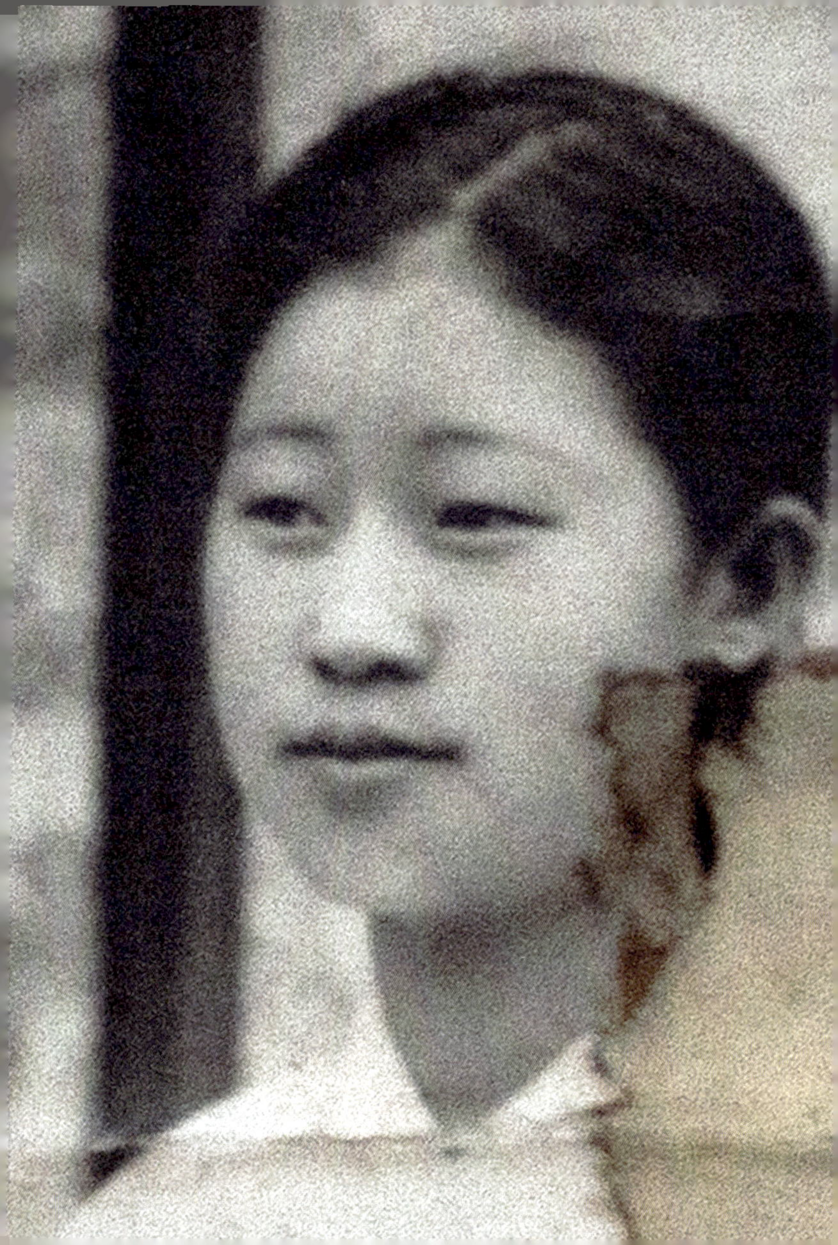

i could not miss out

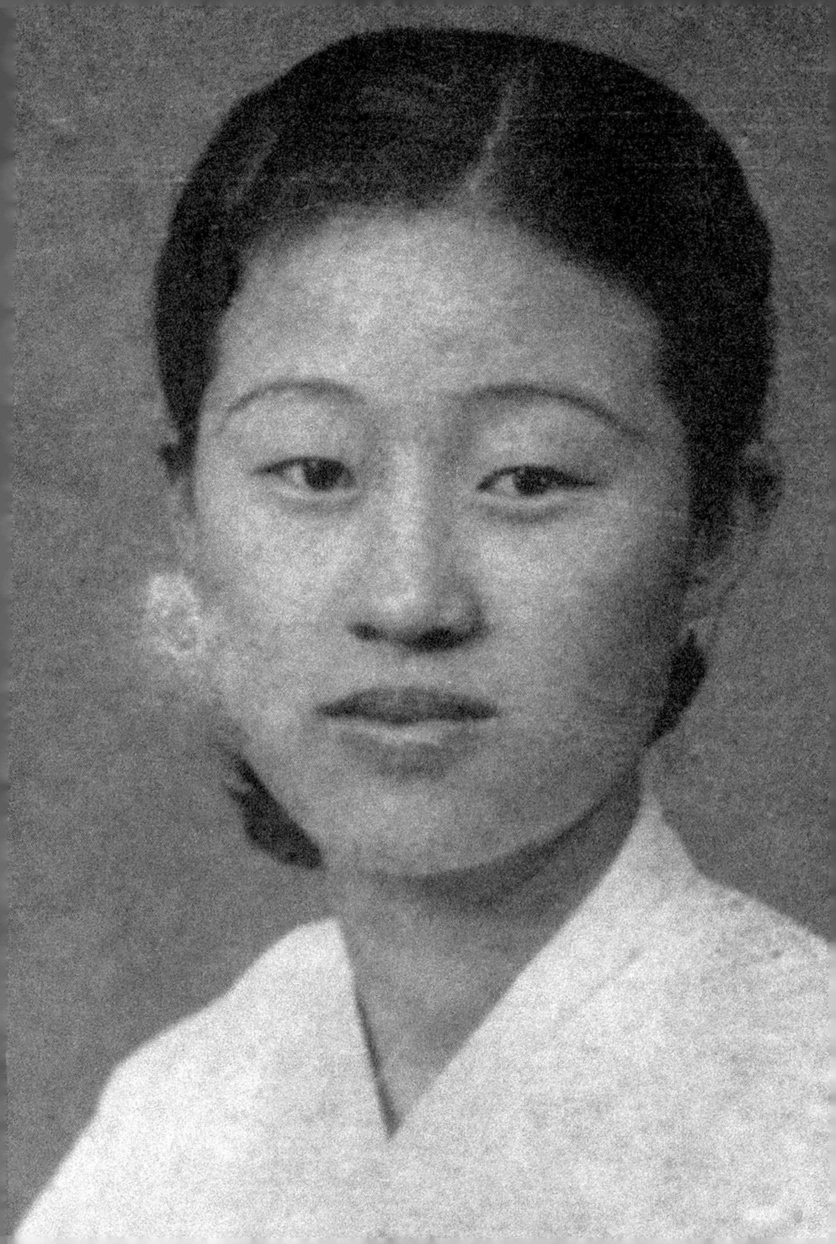

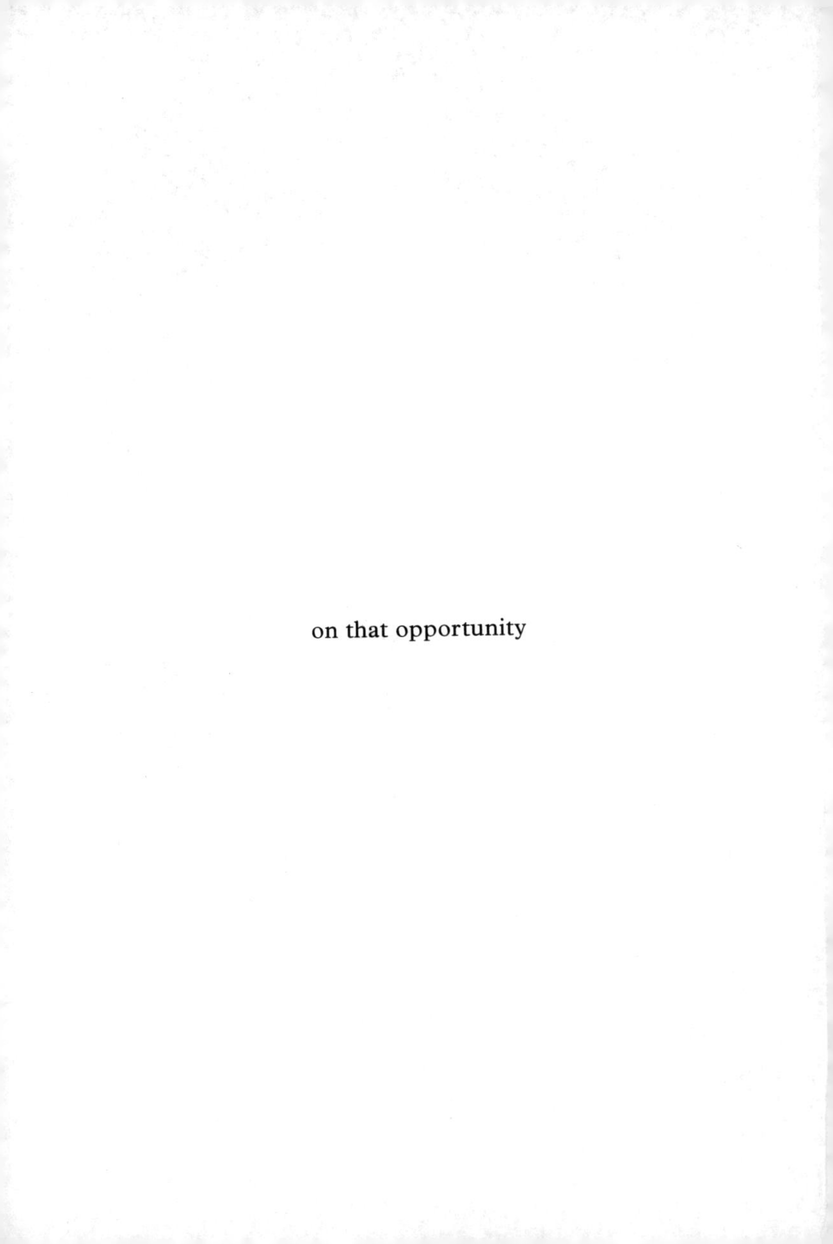

on that opportunity

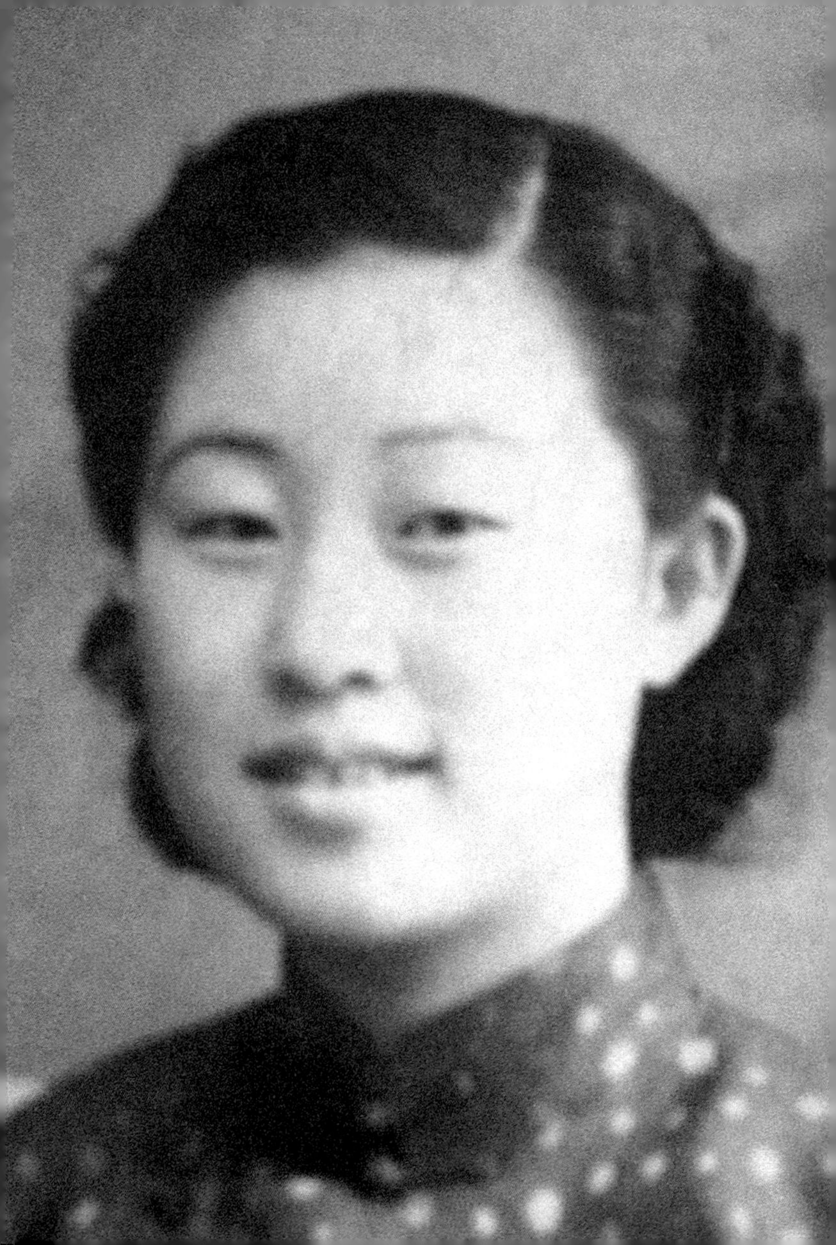

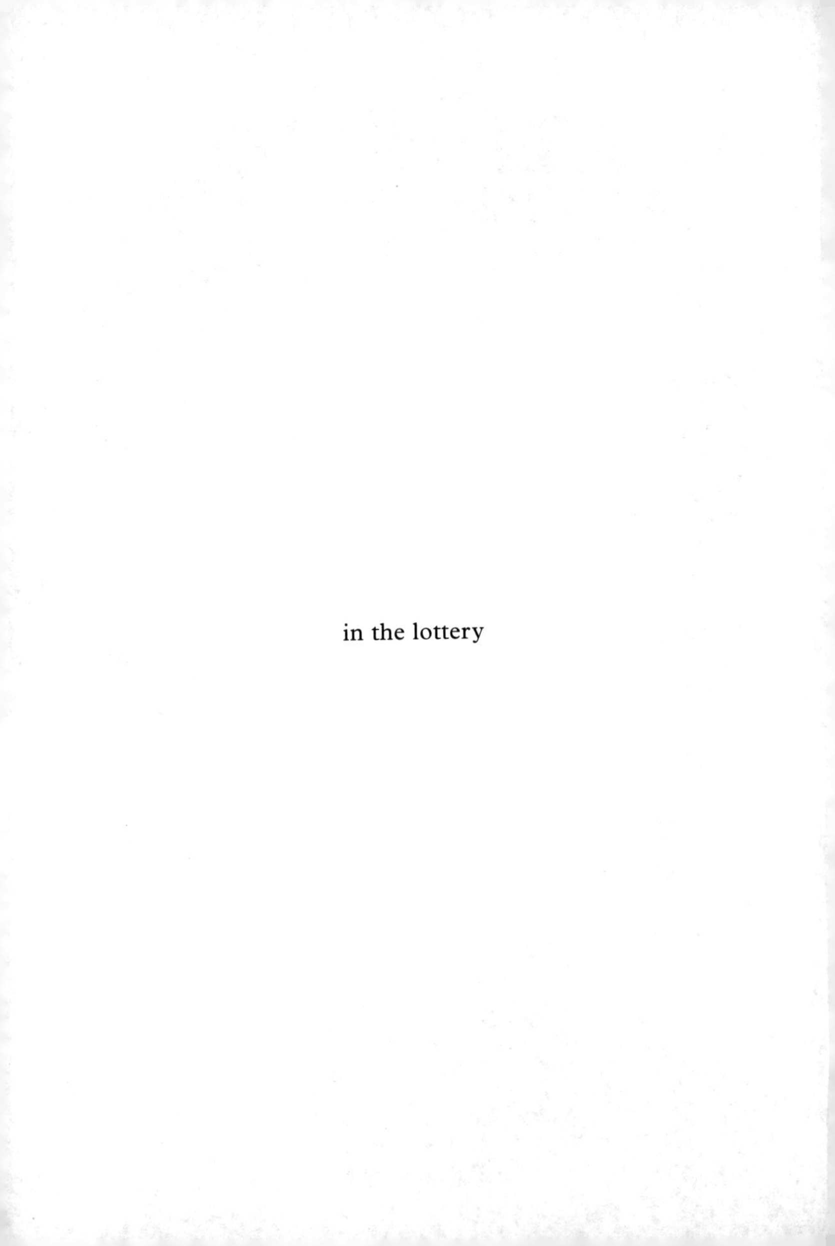

in the lottery

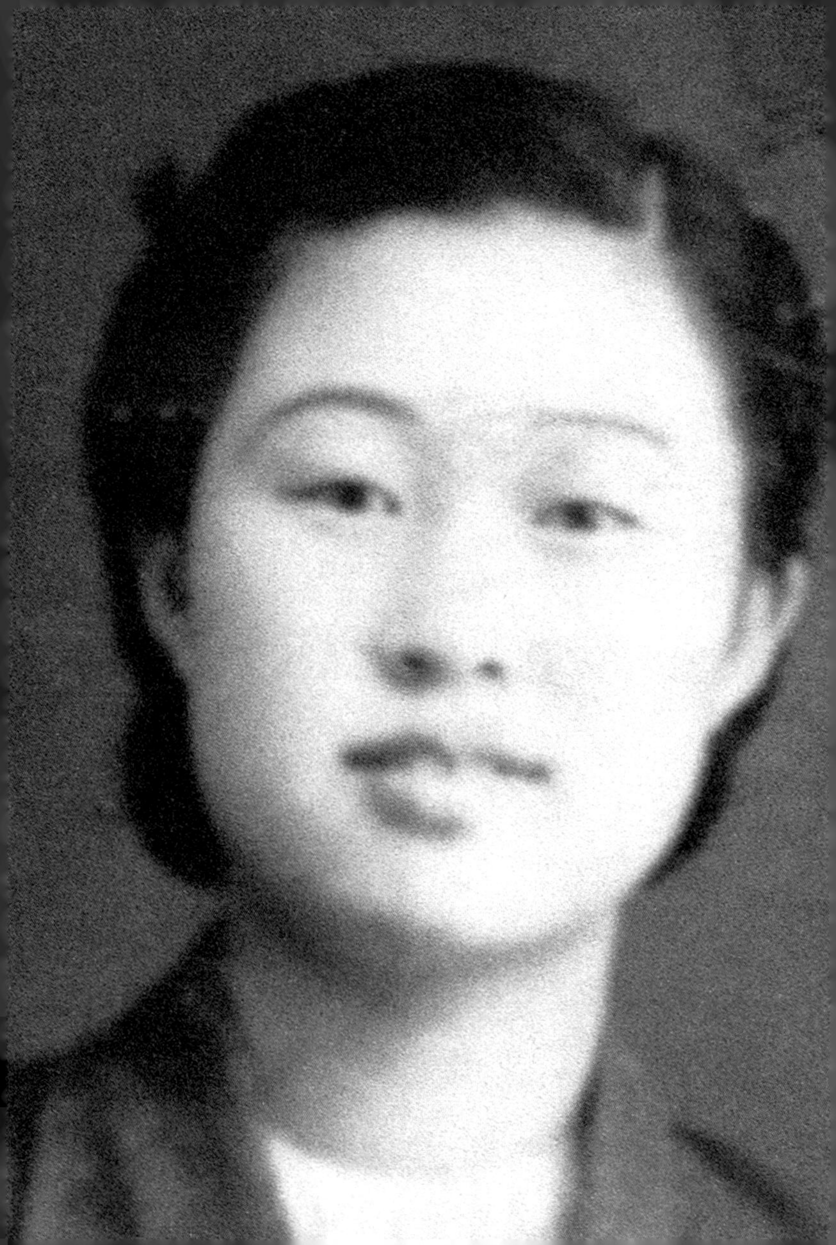

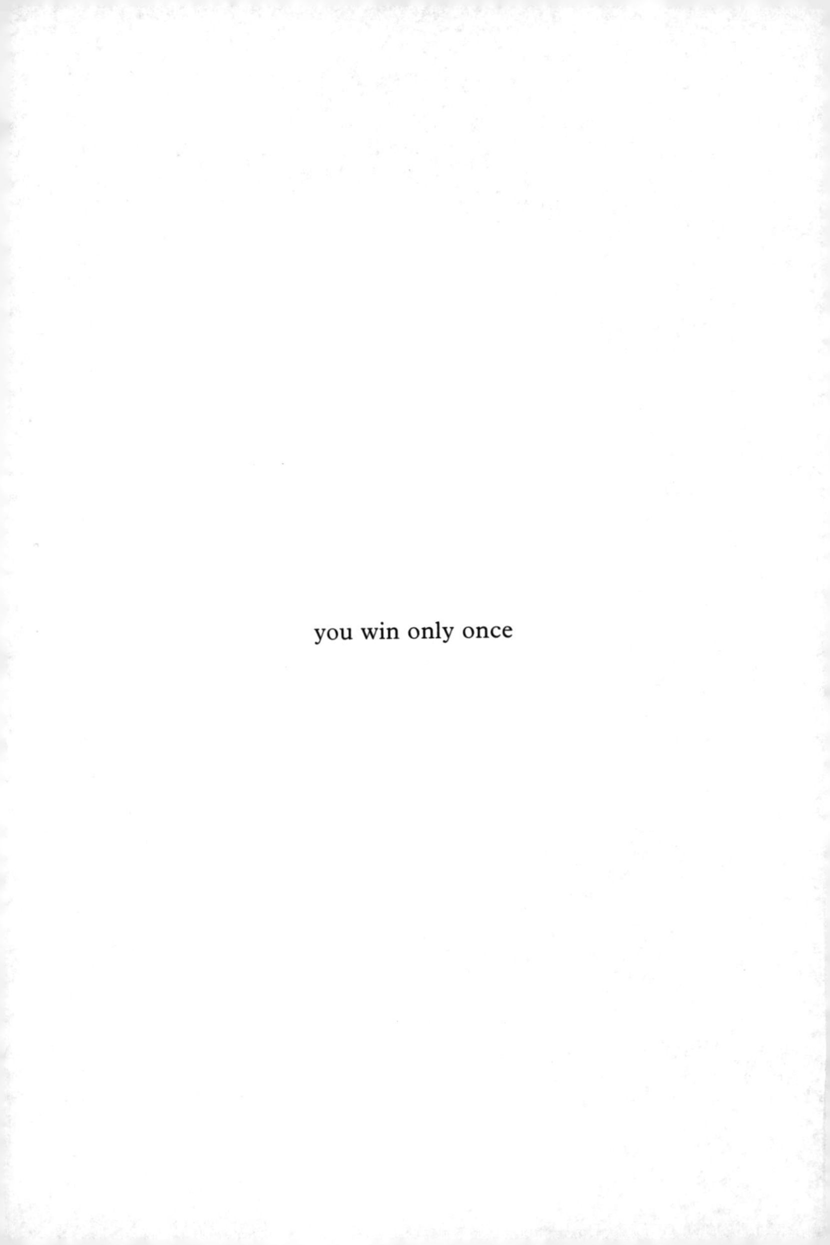

you win only once

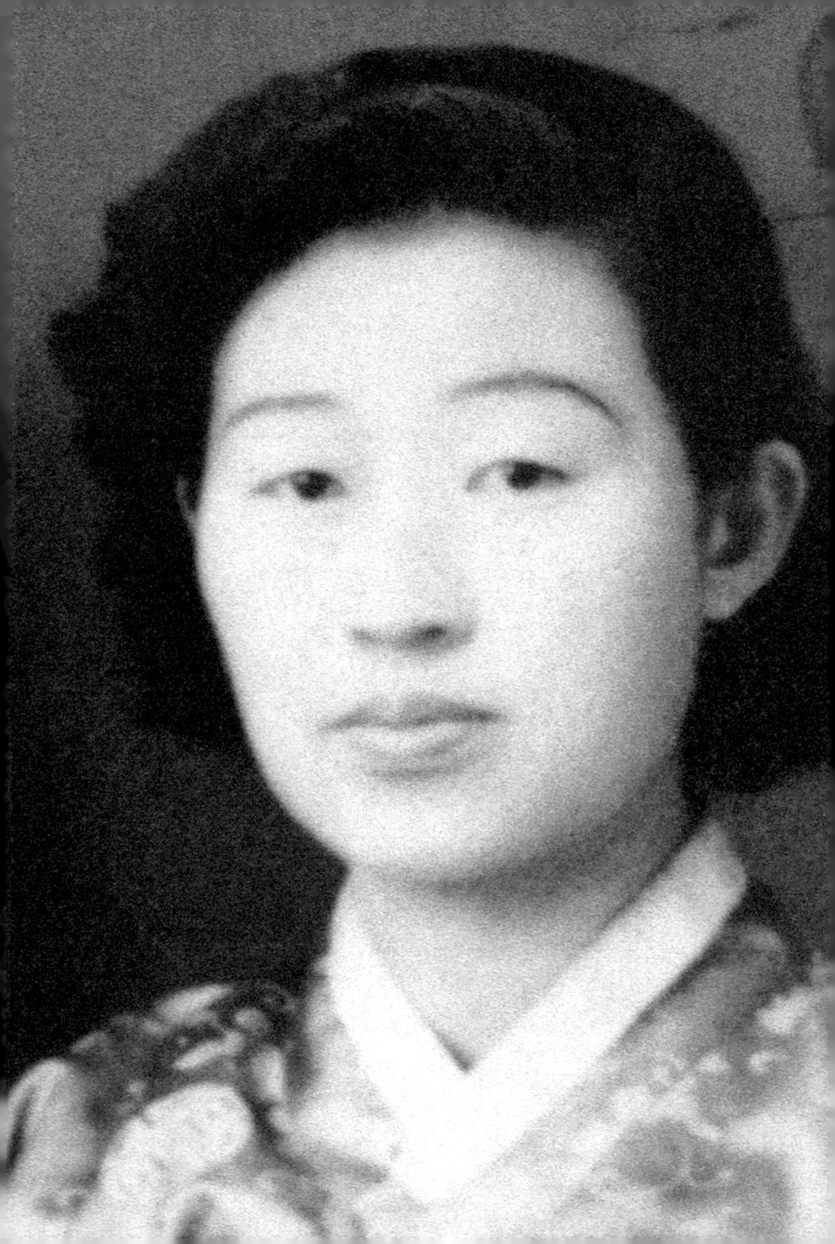

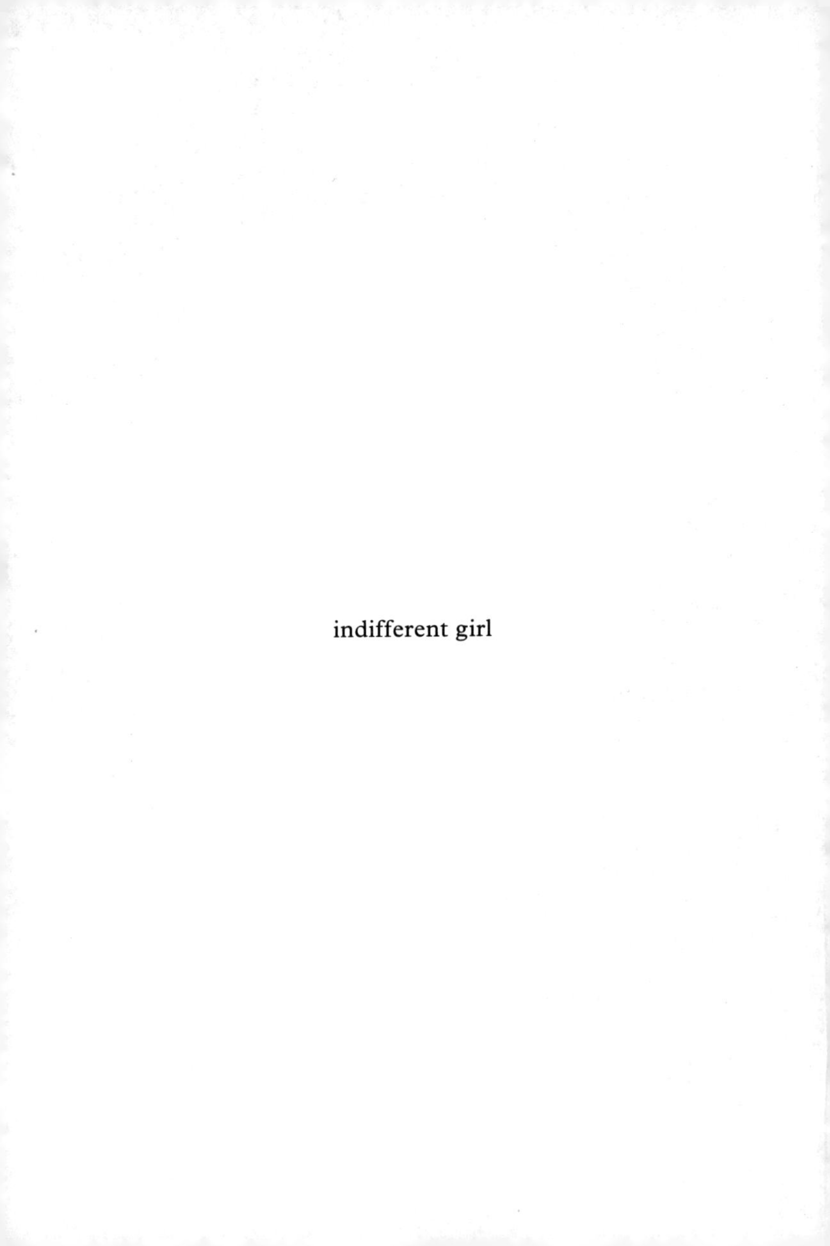

indifferent girl

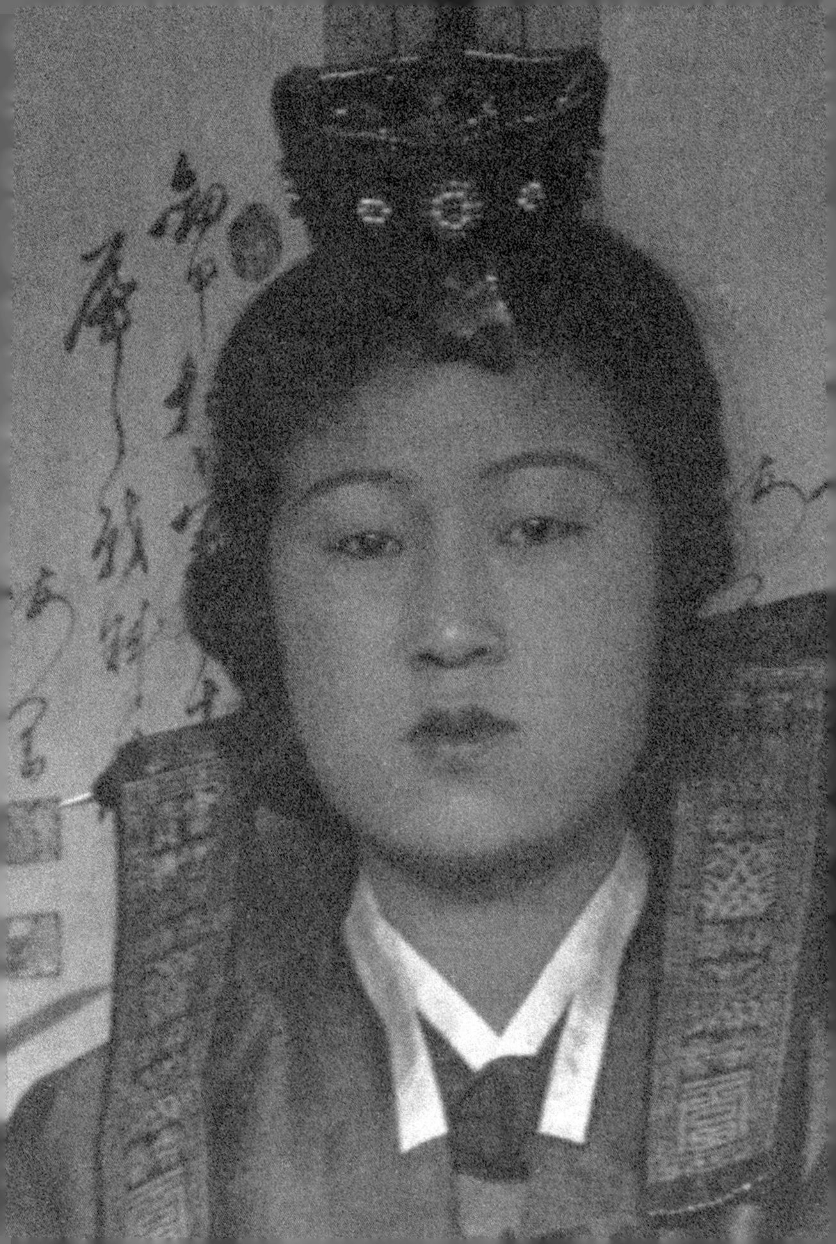

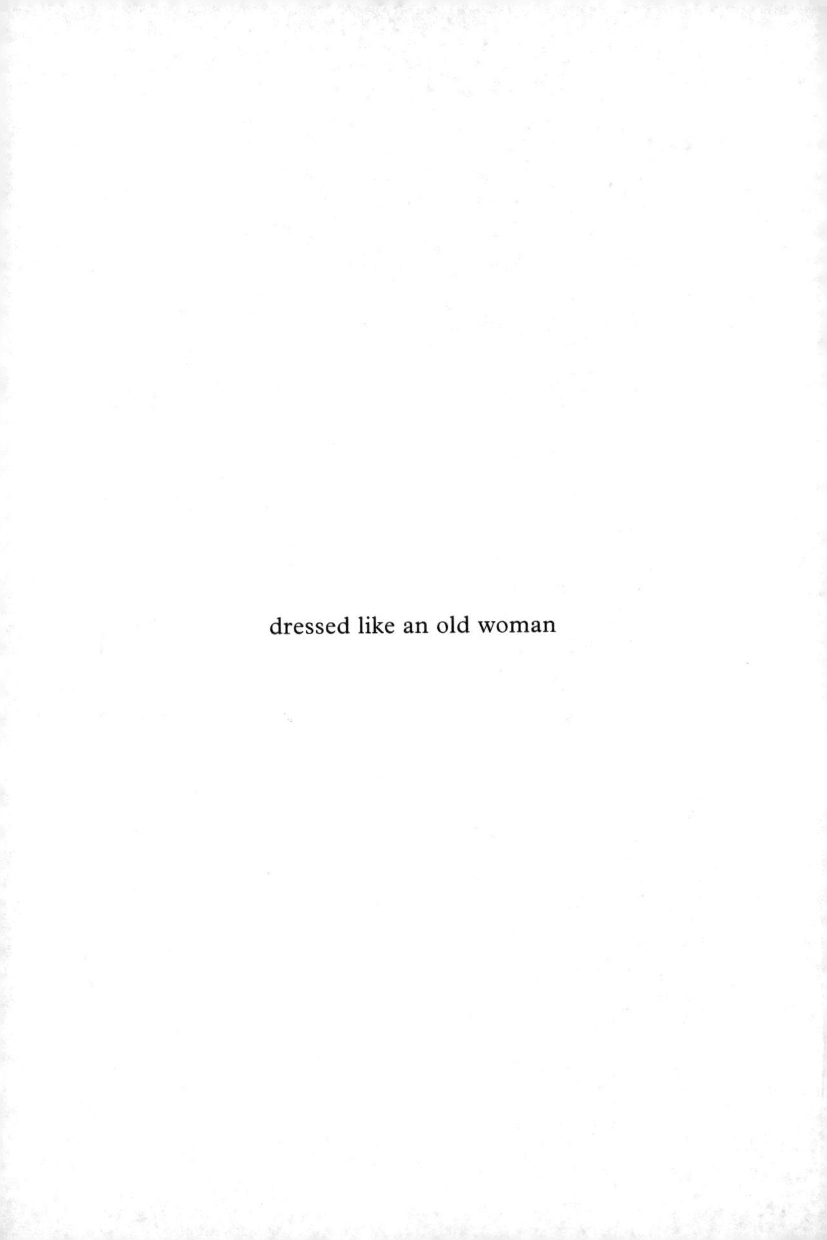

dressed like an old woman

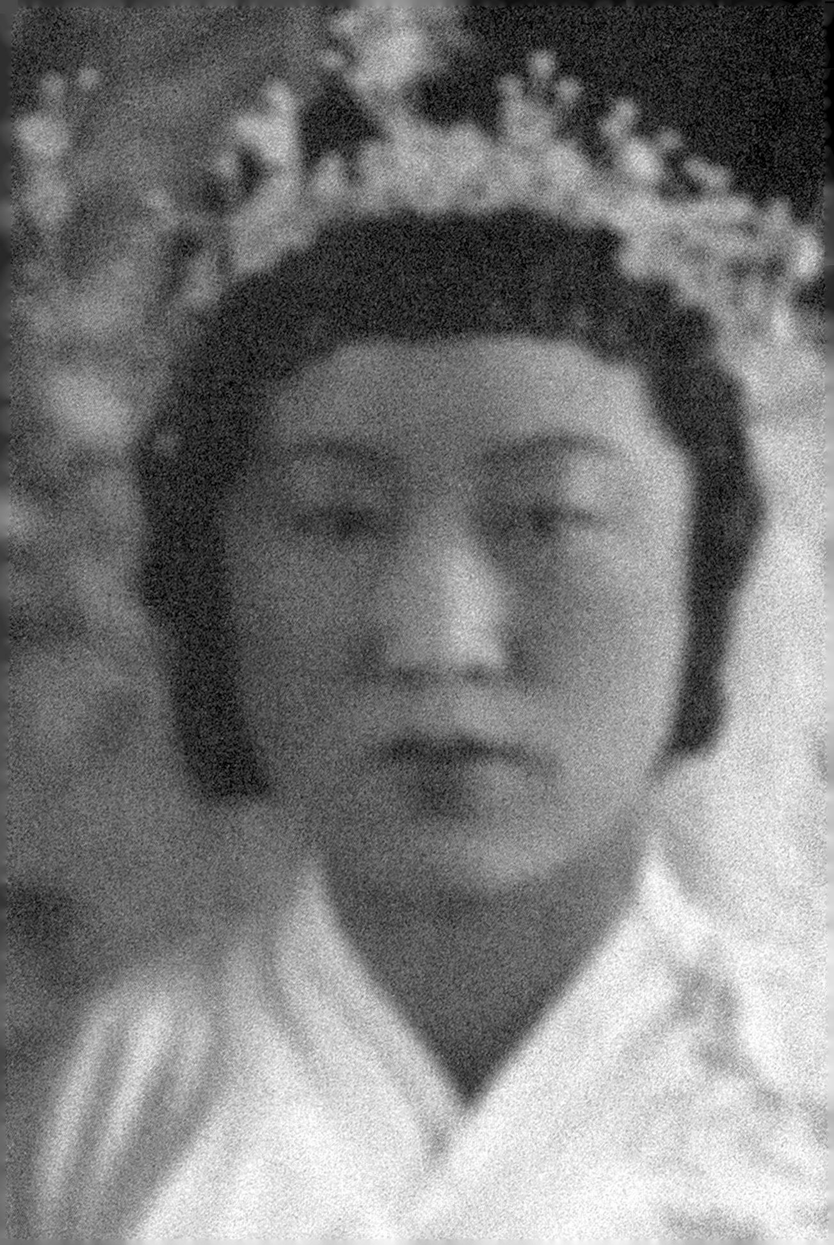

i reluctantly loved

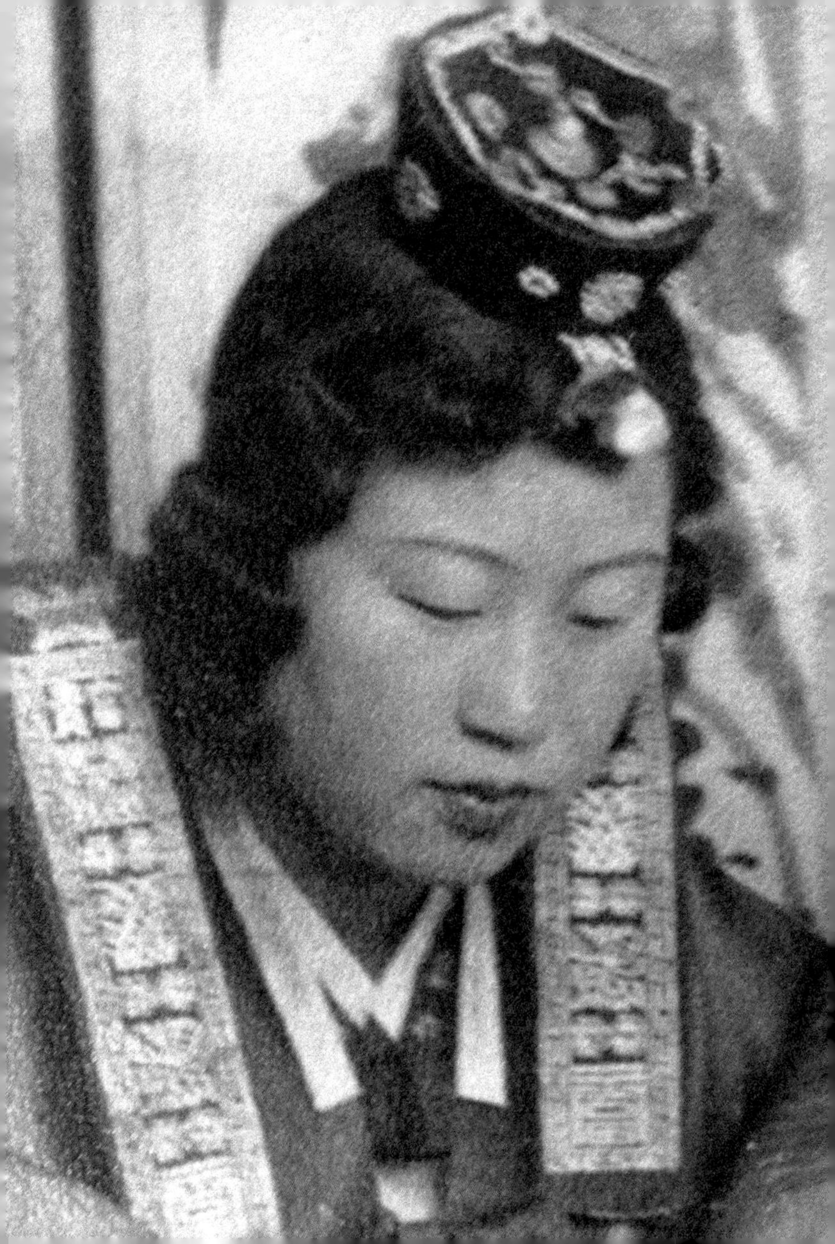

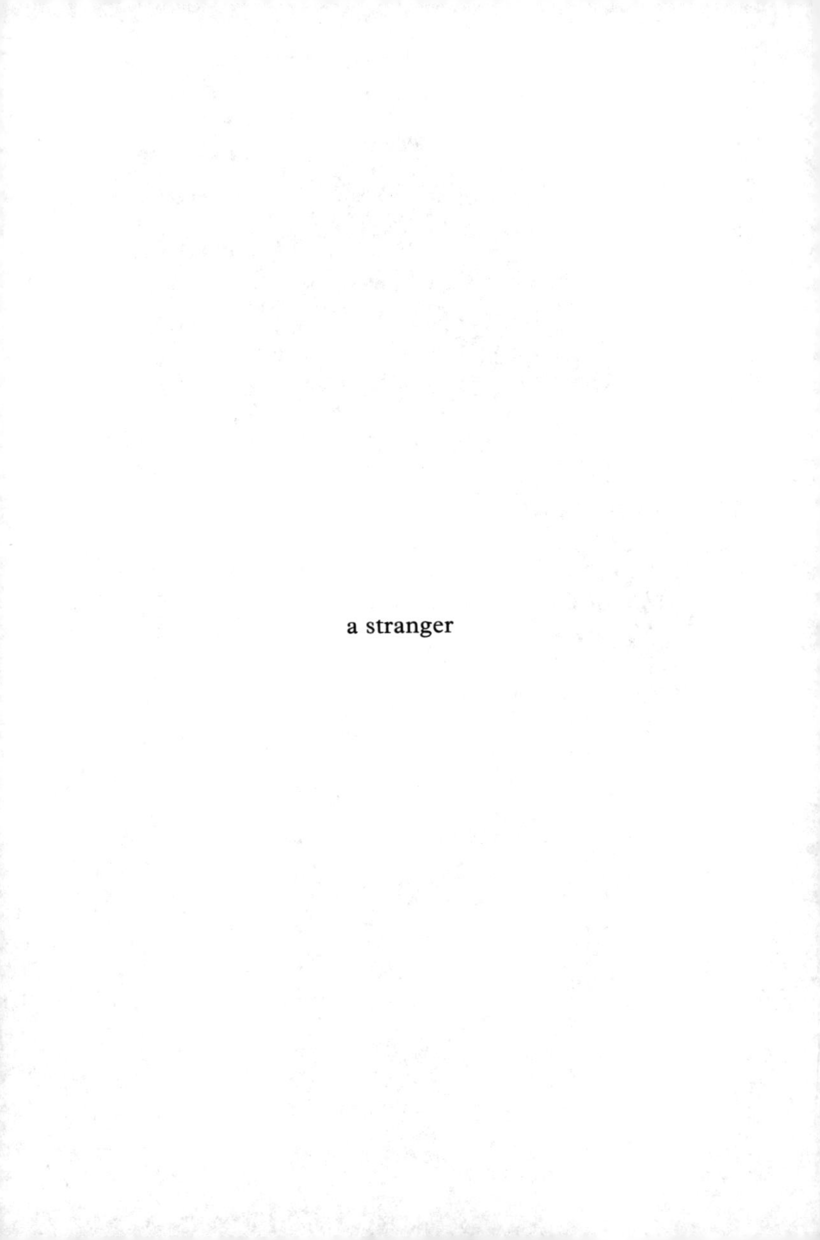

a stranger

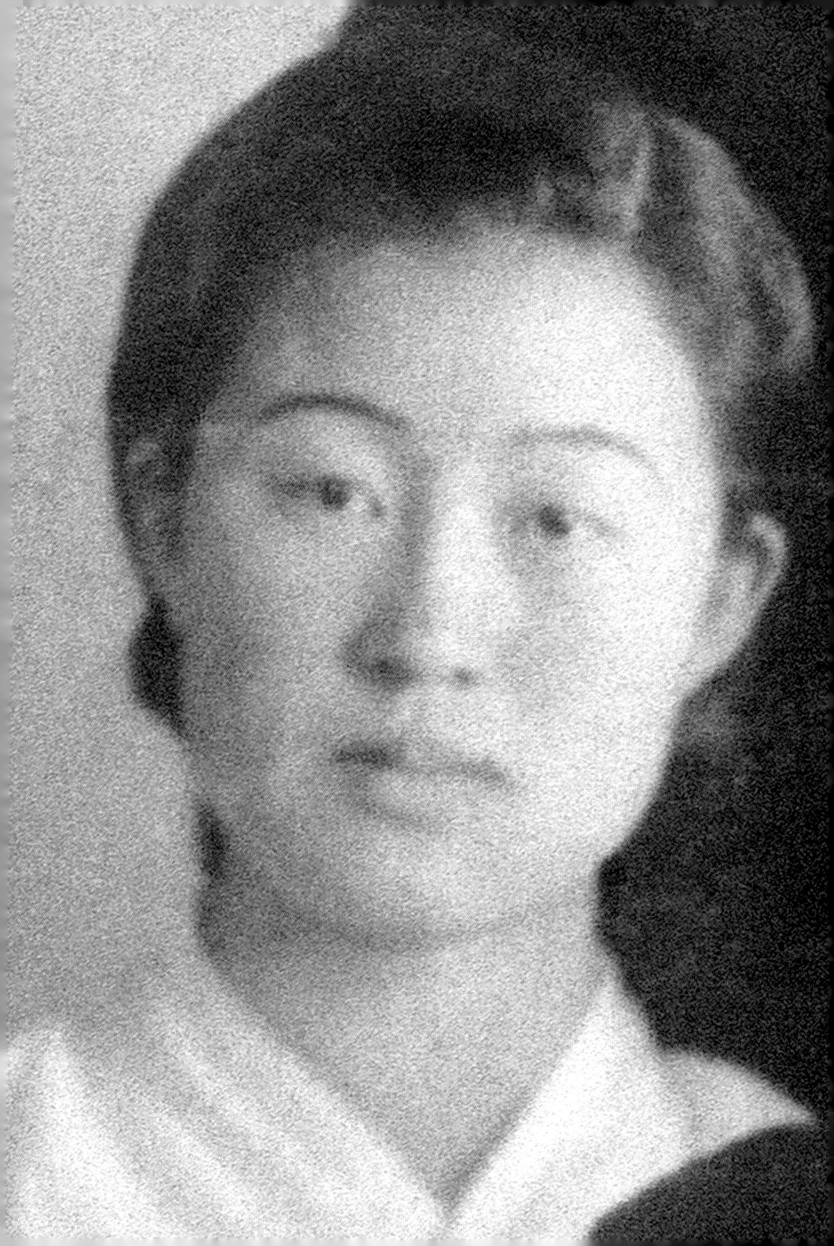

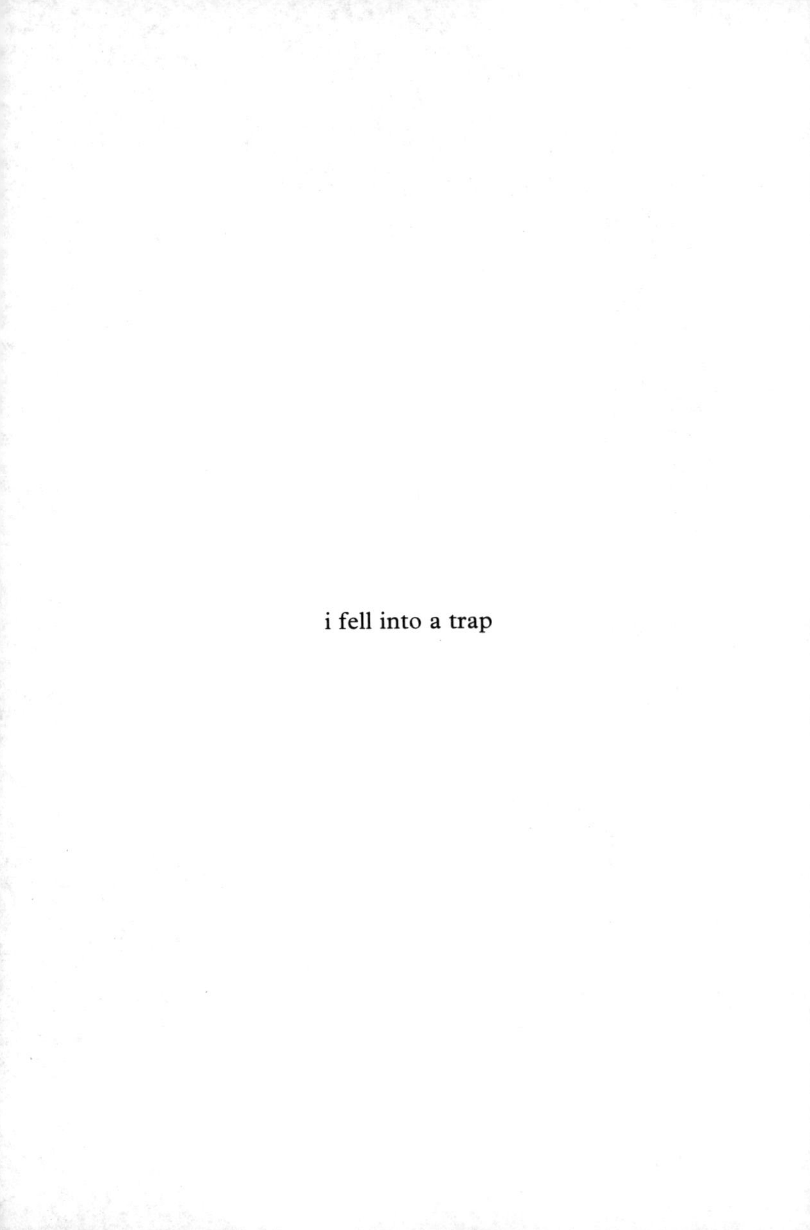

i fell into a trap

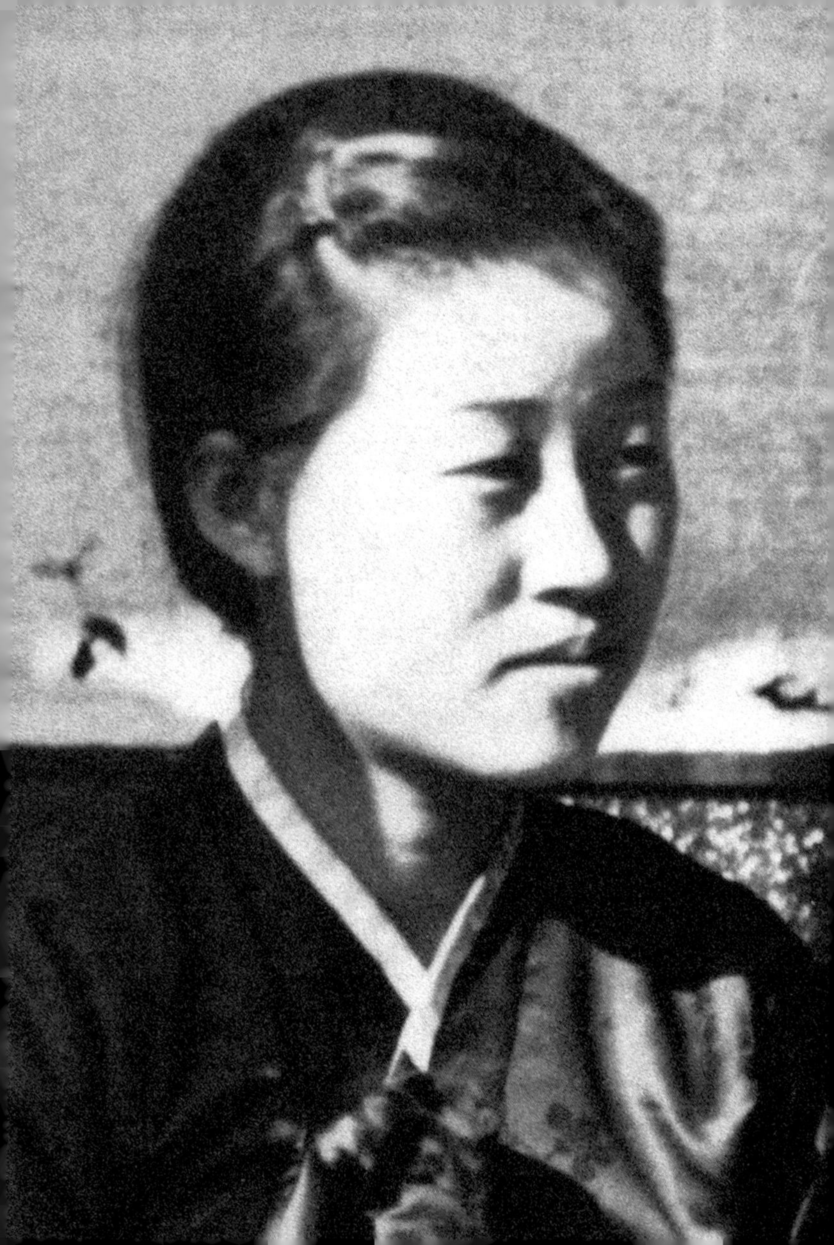

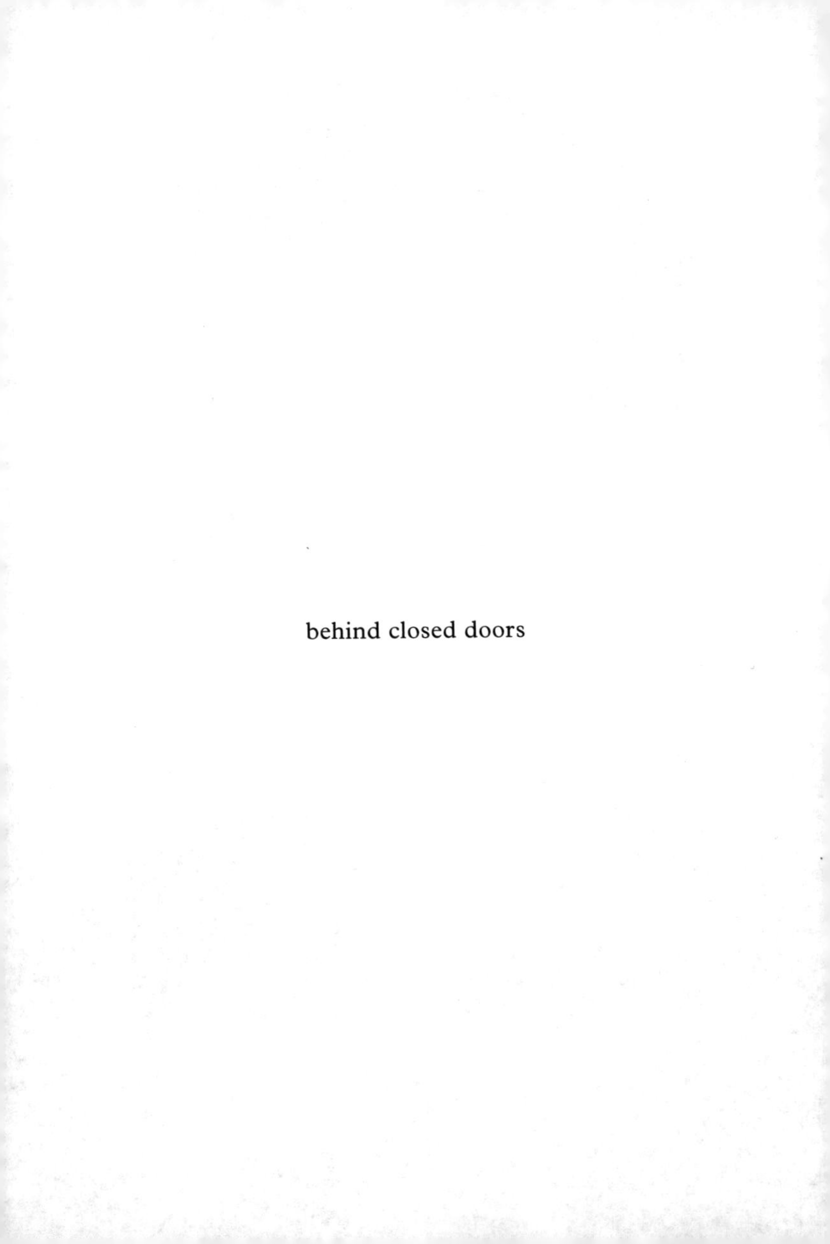

behind closed doors

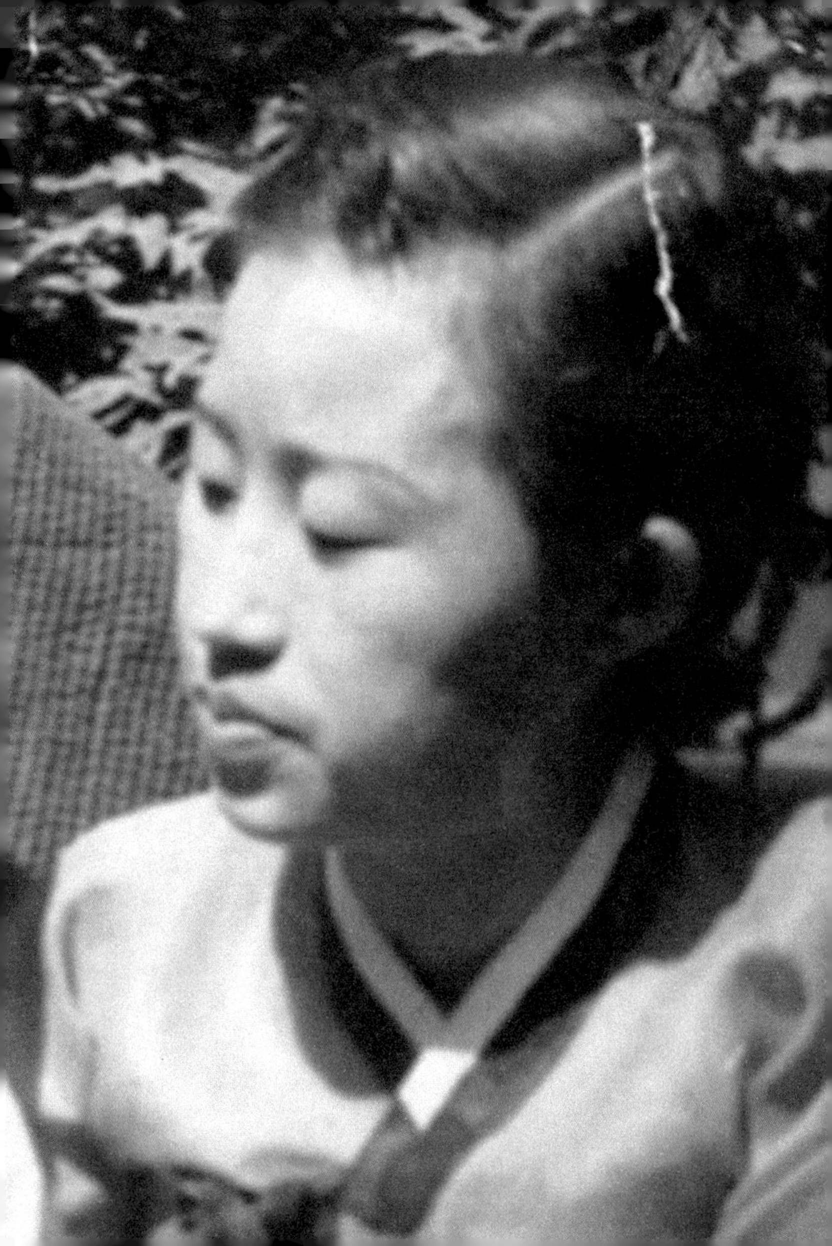

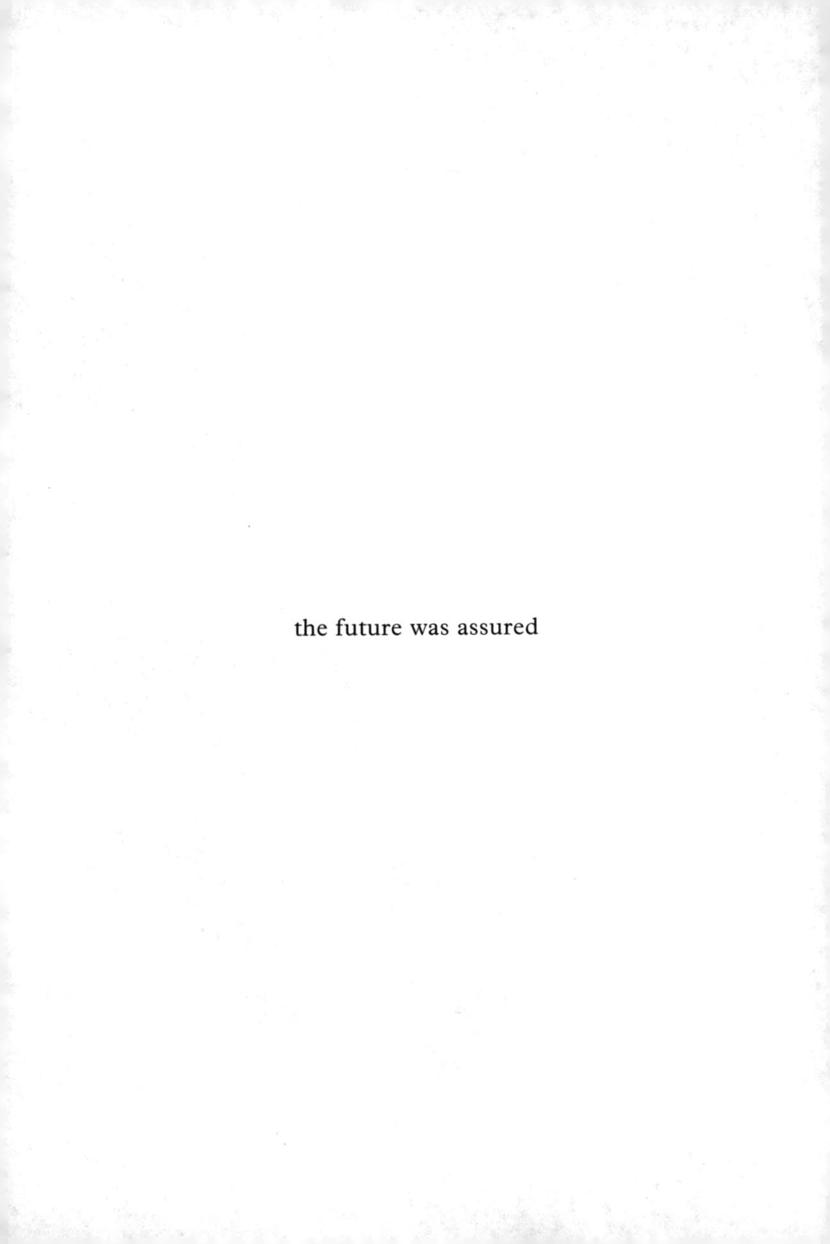

the future was assured

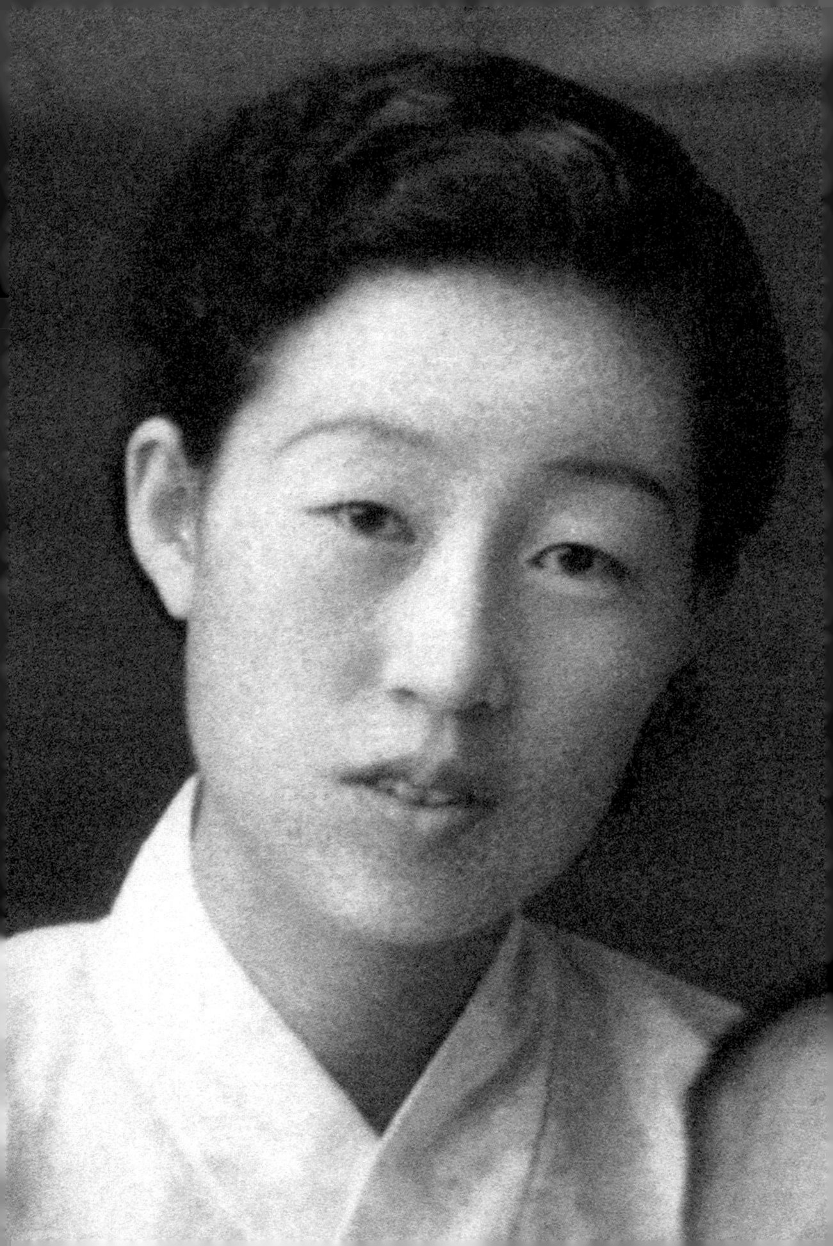

i was not curious

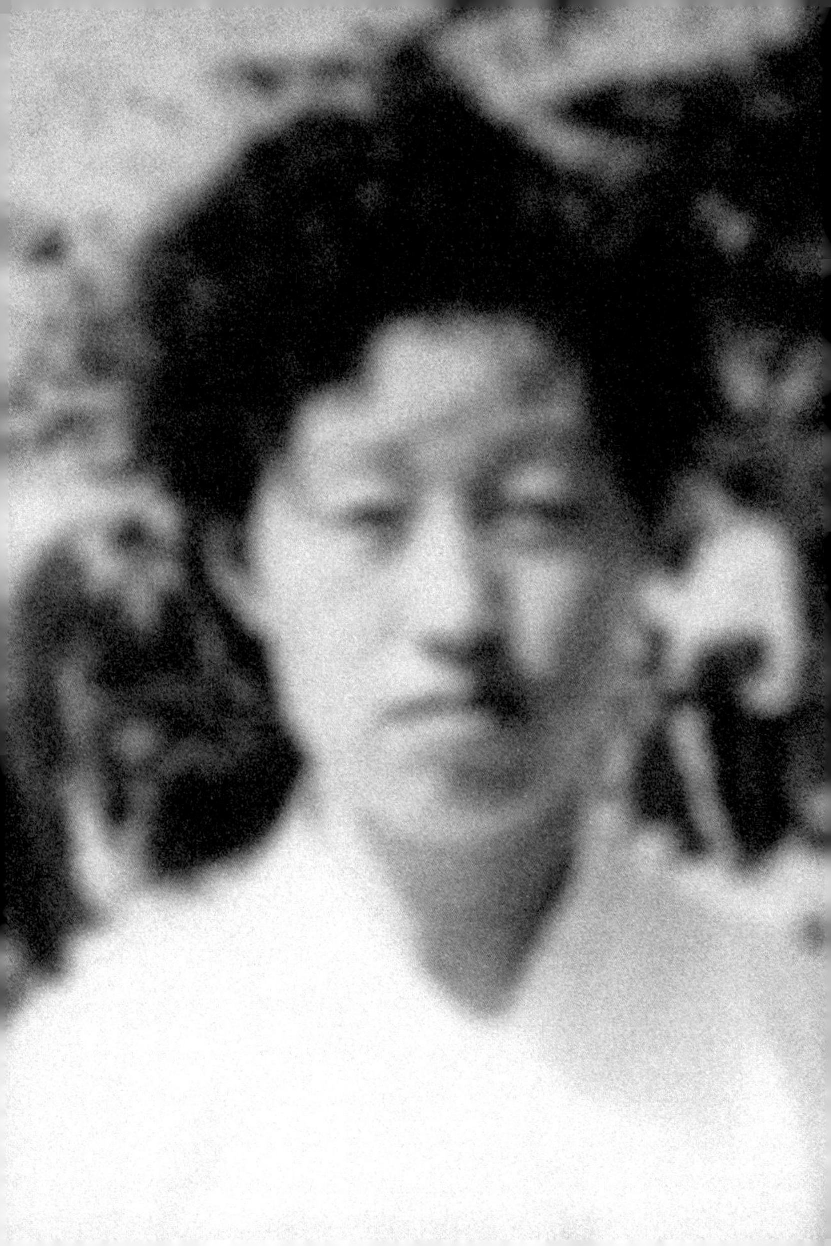

i was reasonable

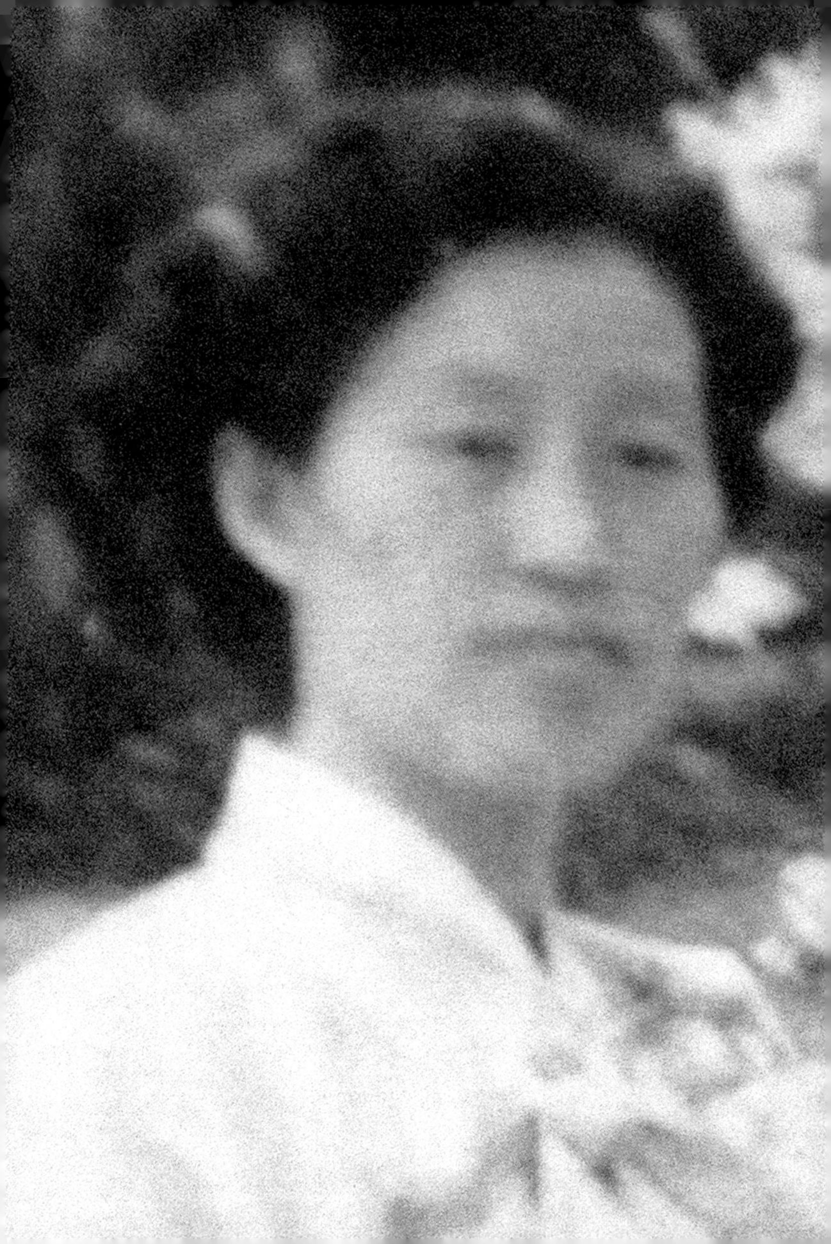

i looked straight ahead

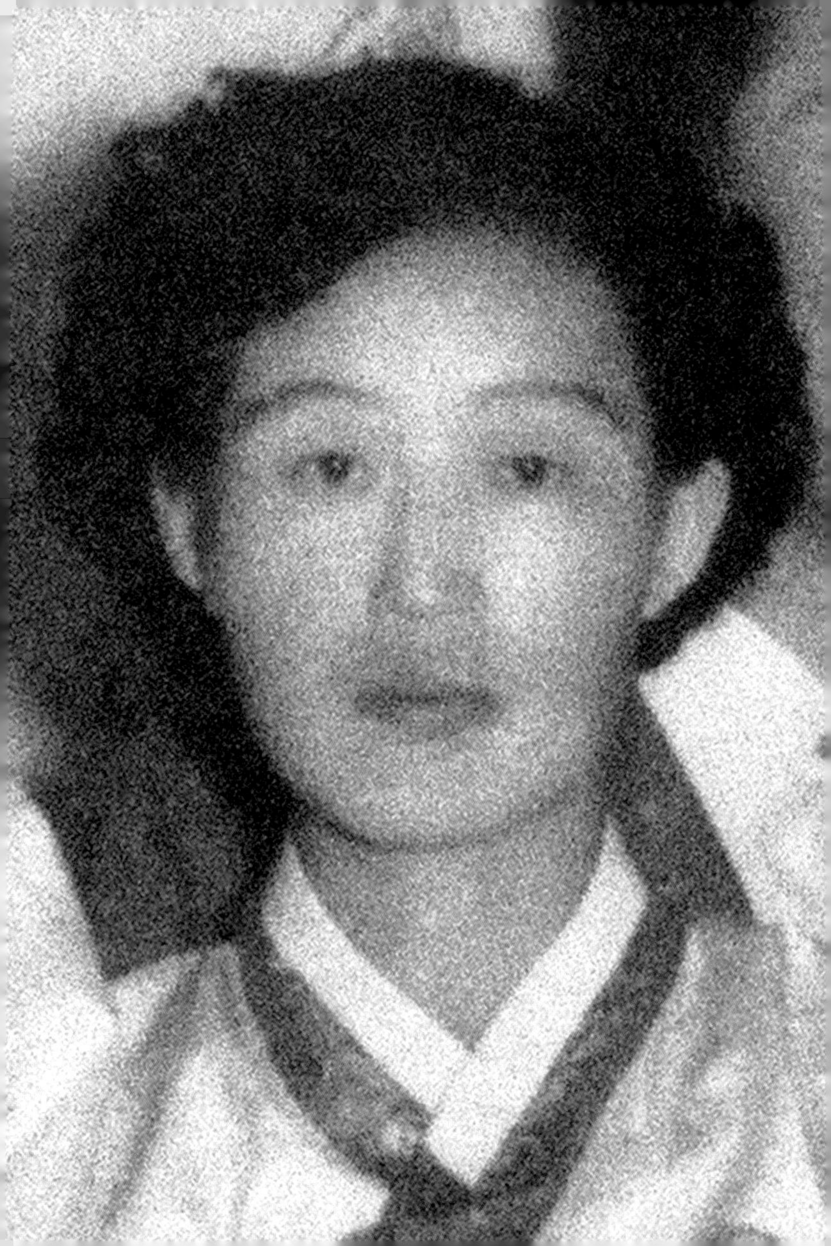

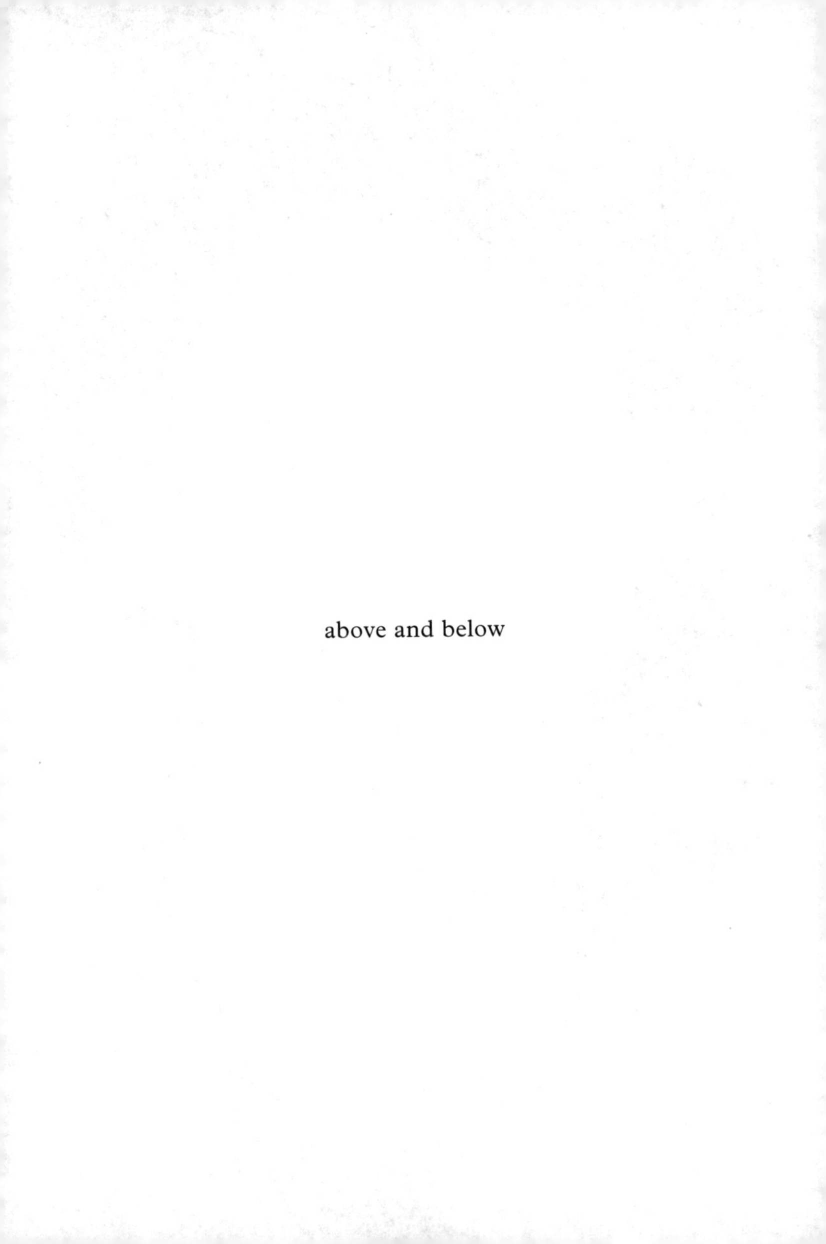

above and below

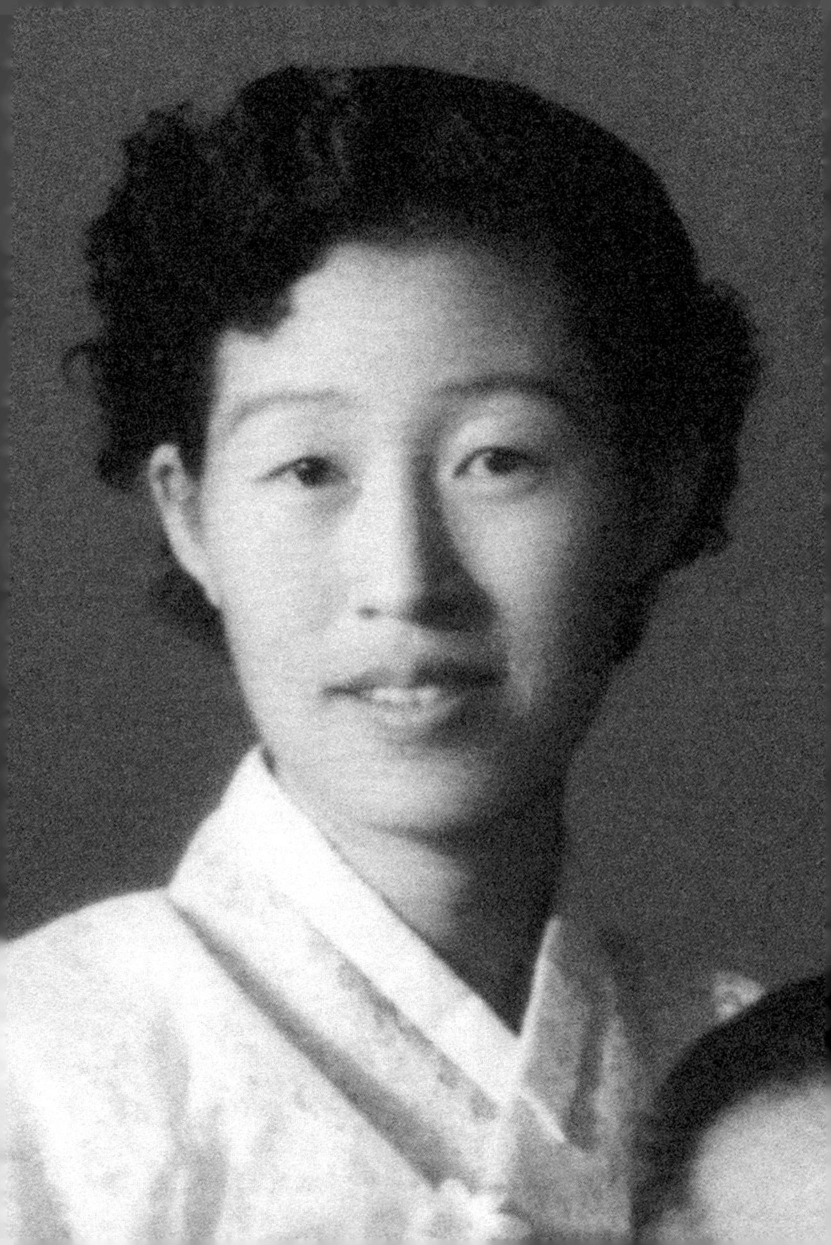

on a strict diet

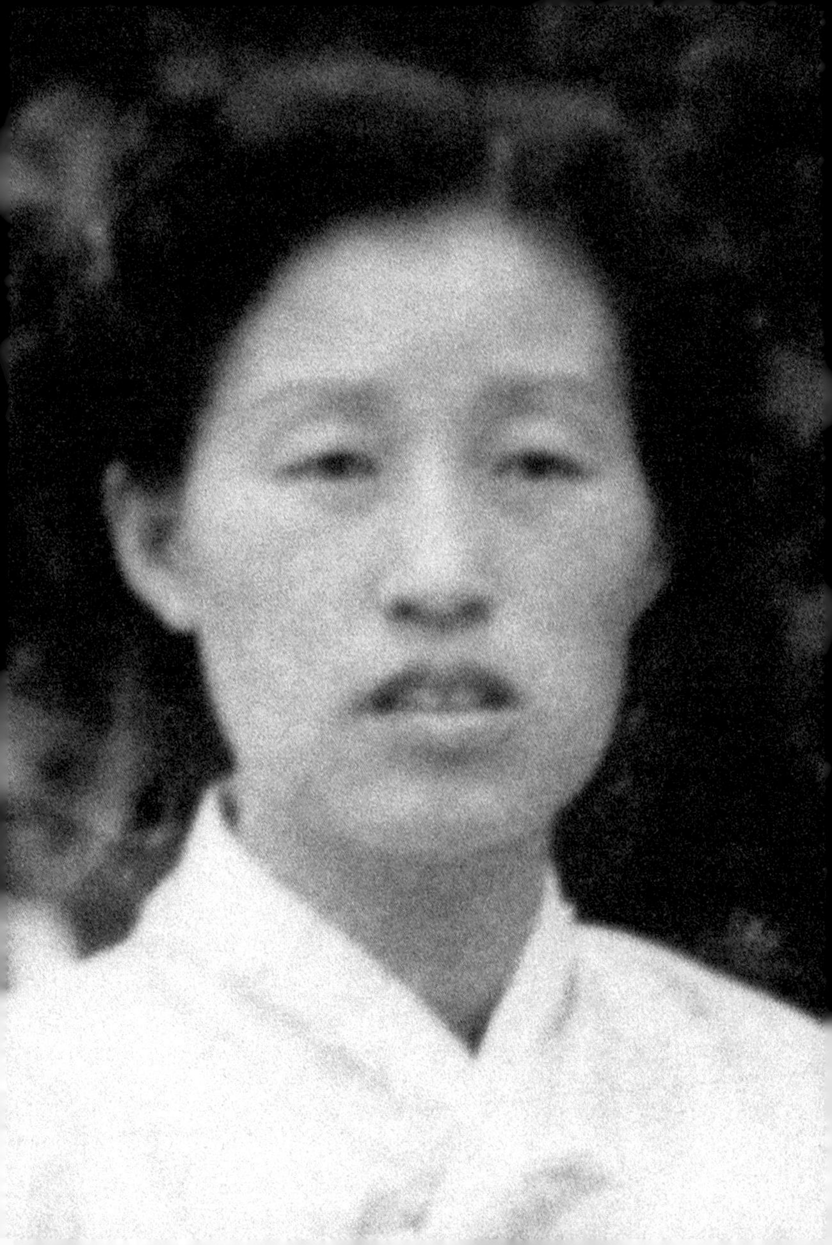

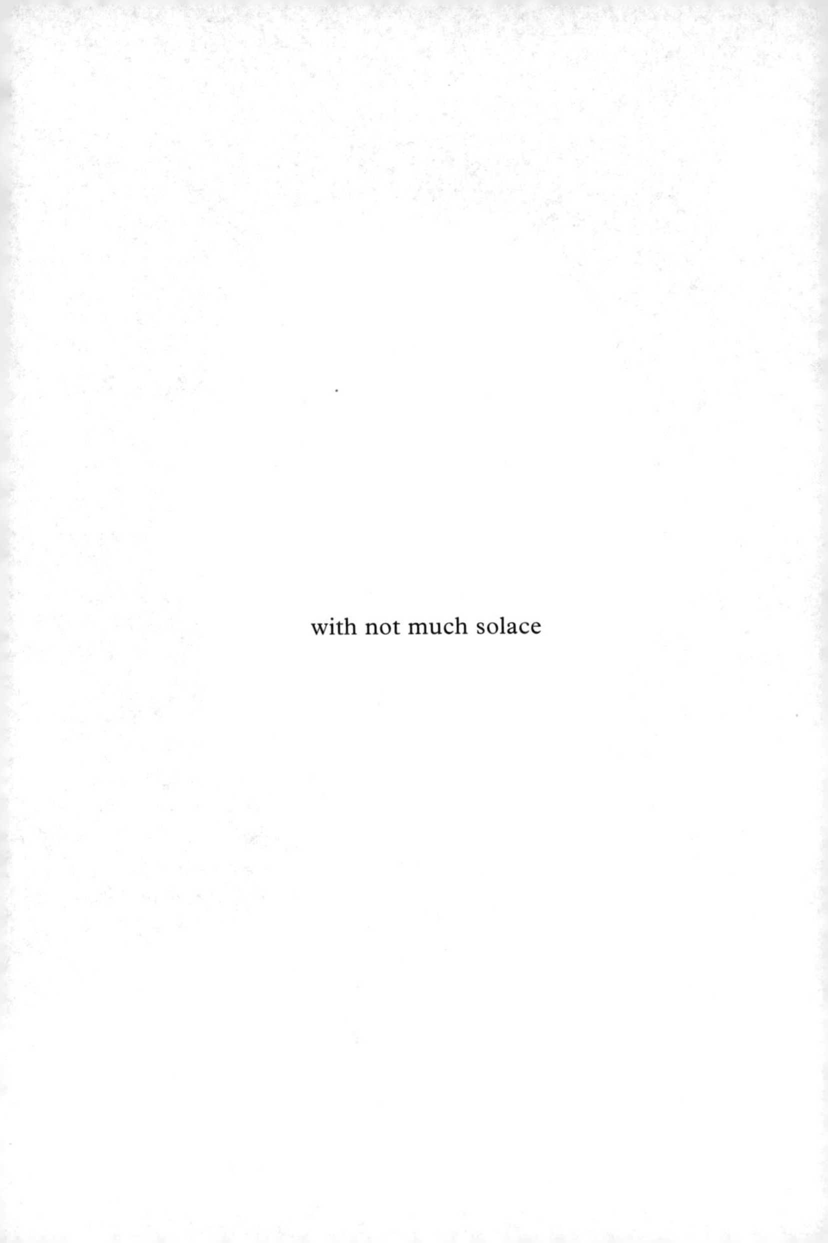

with not much solace

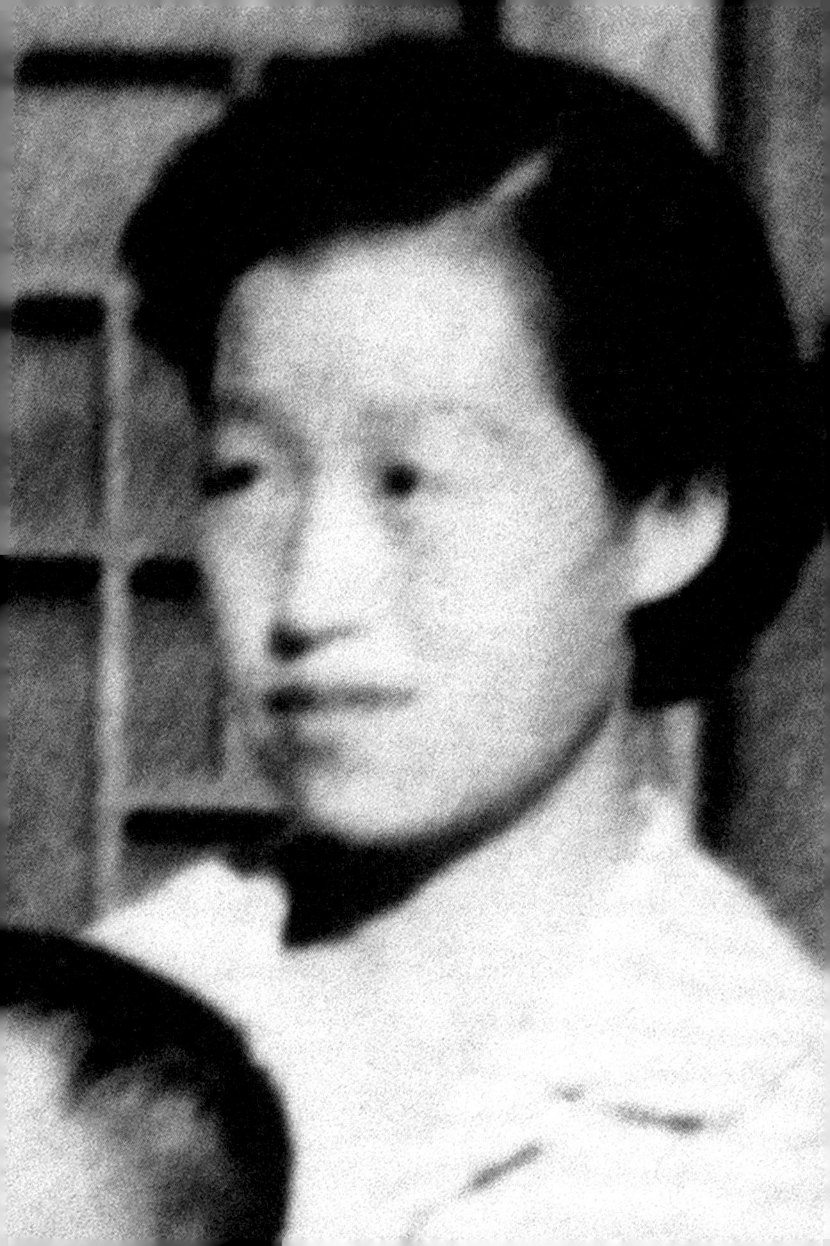

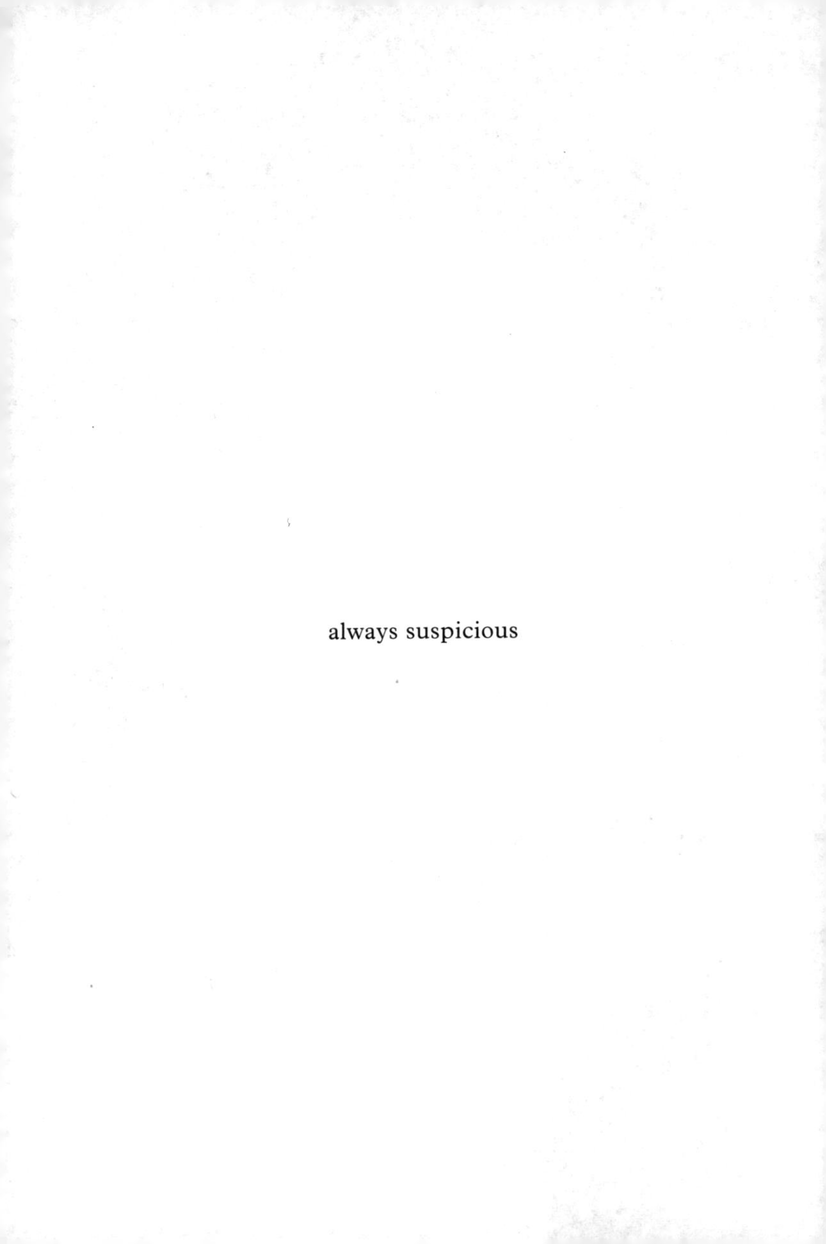

always suspicious

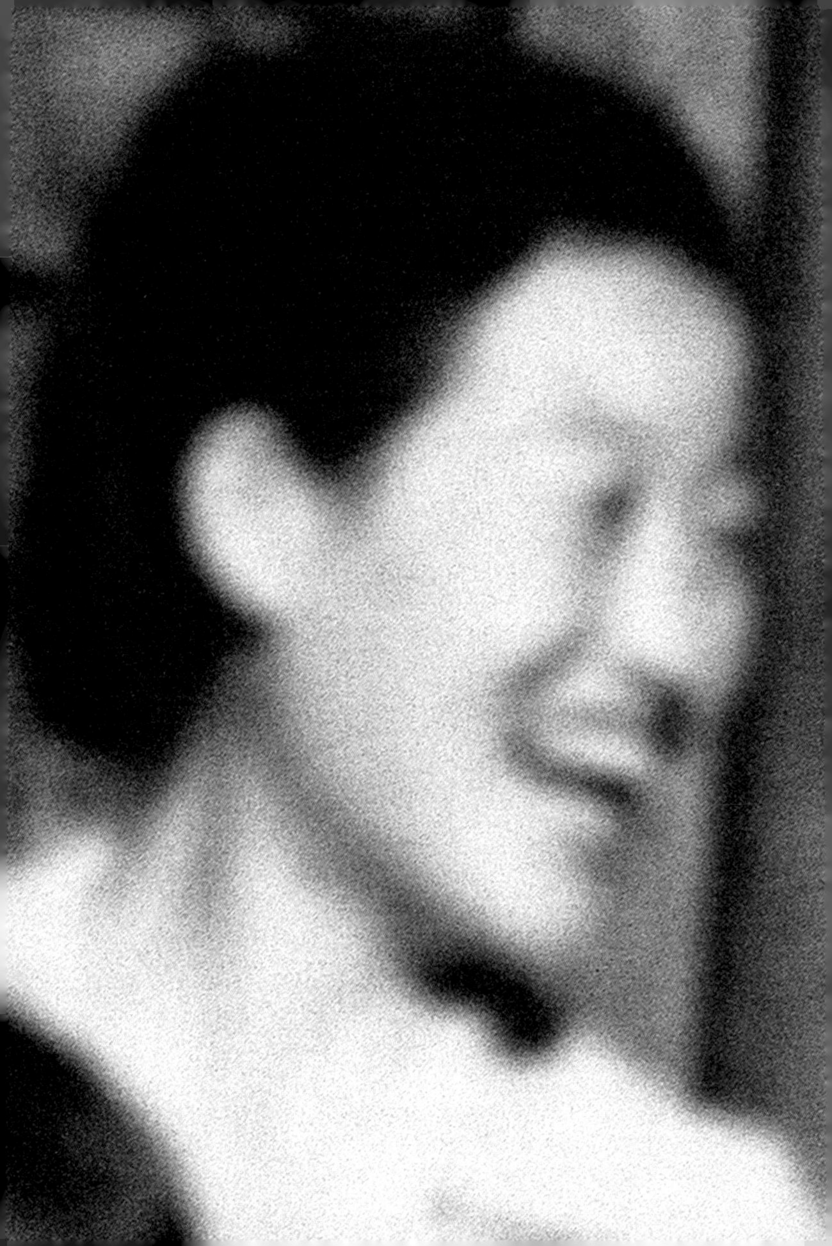

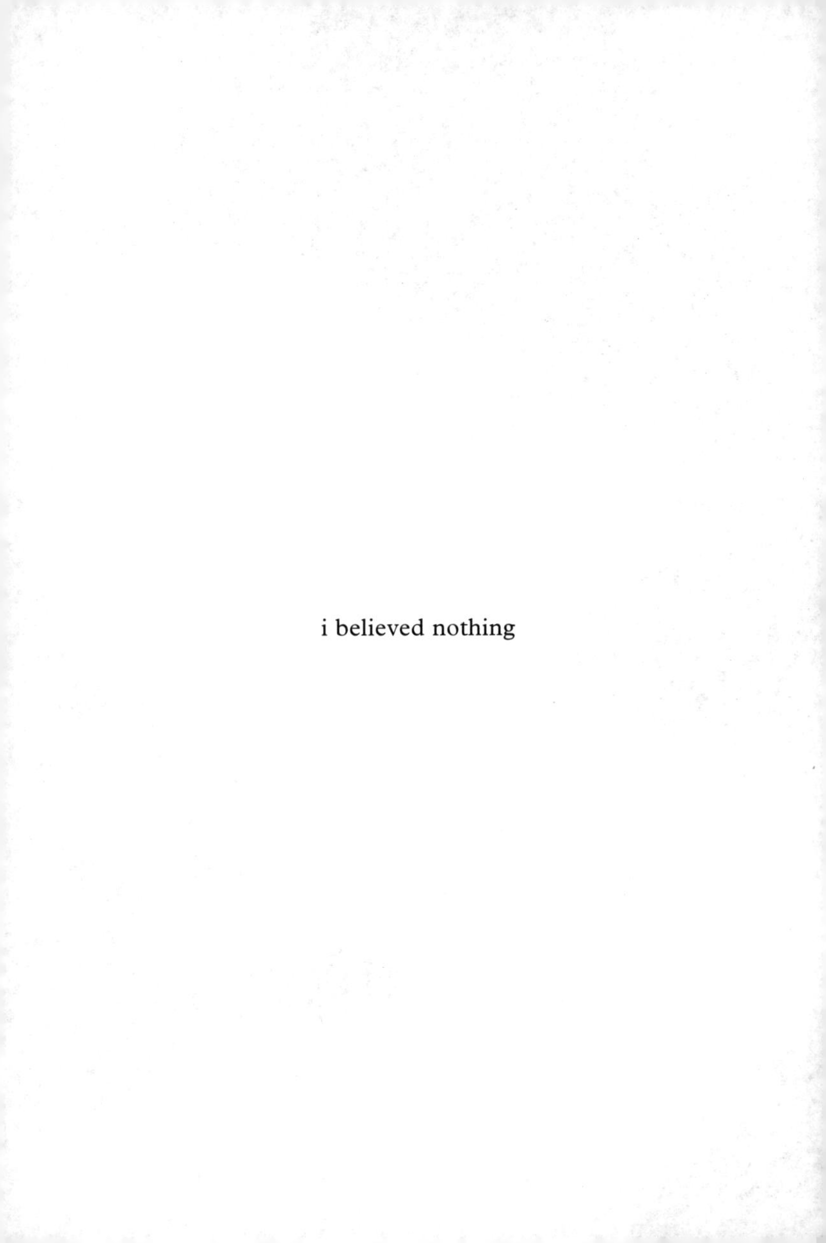

i believed nothing

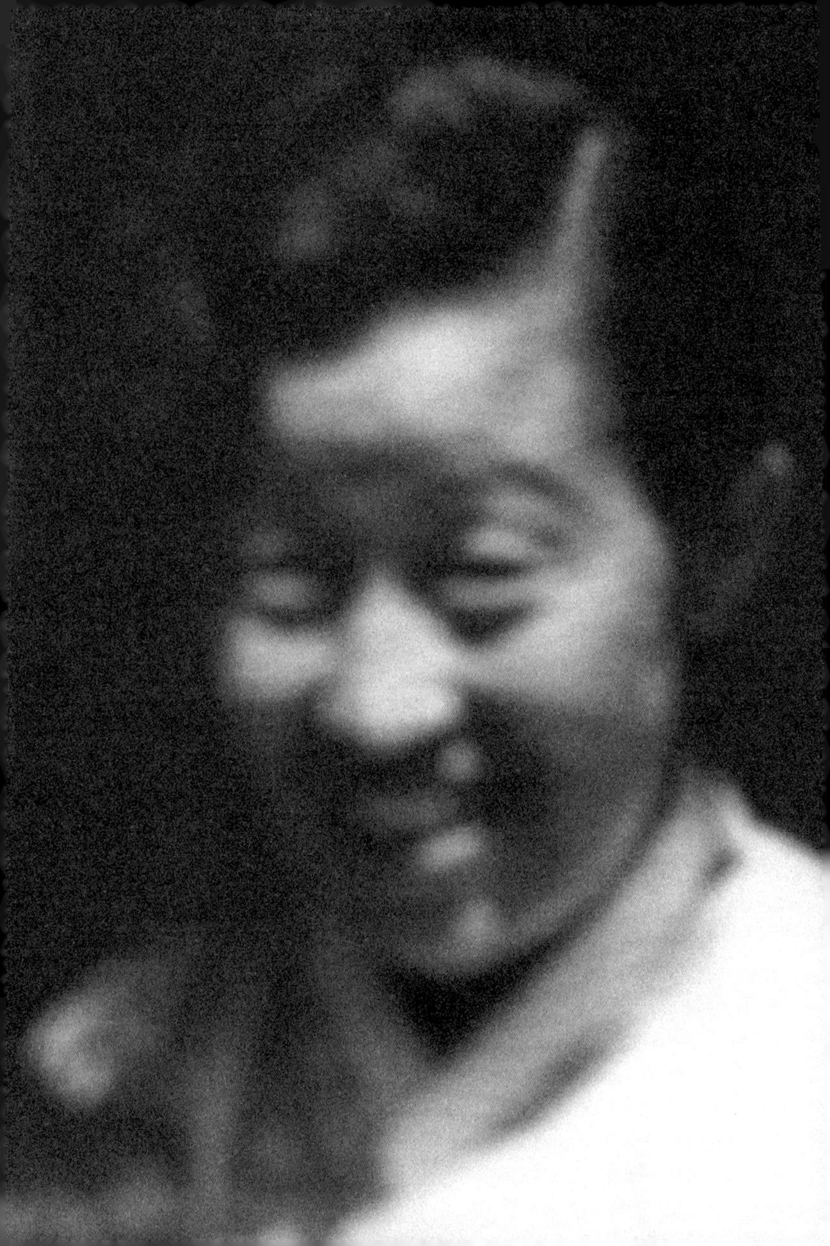

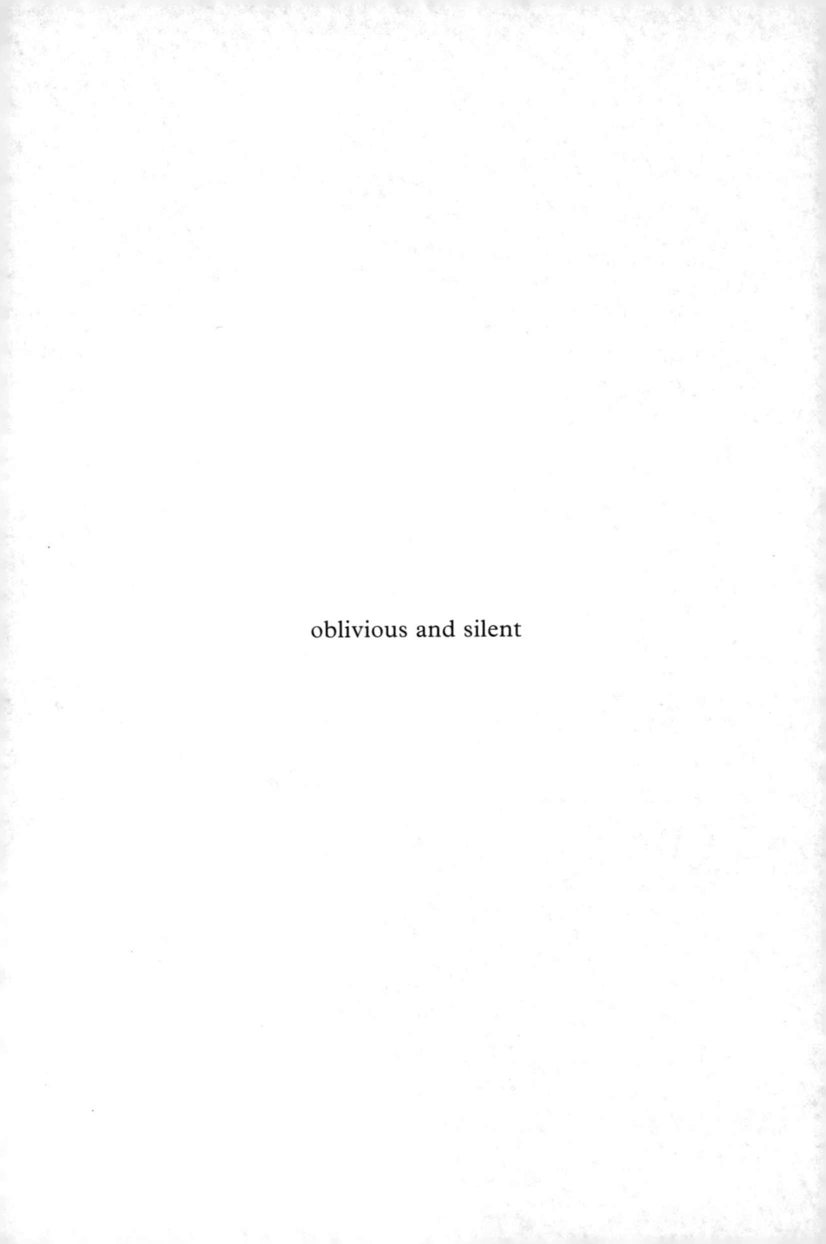

oblivious and silent

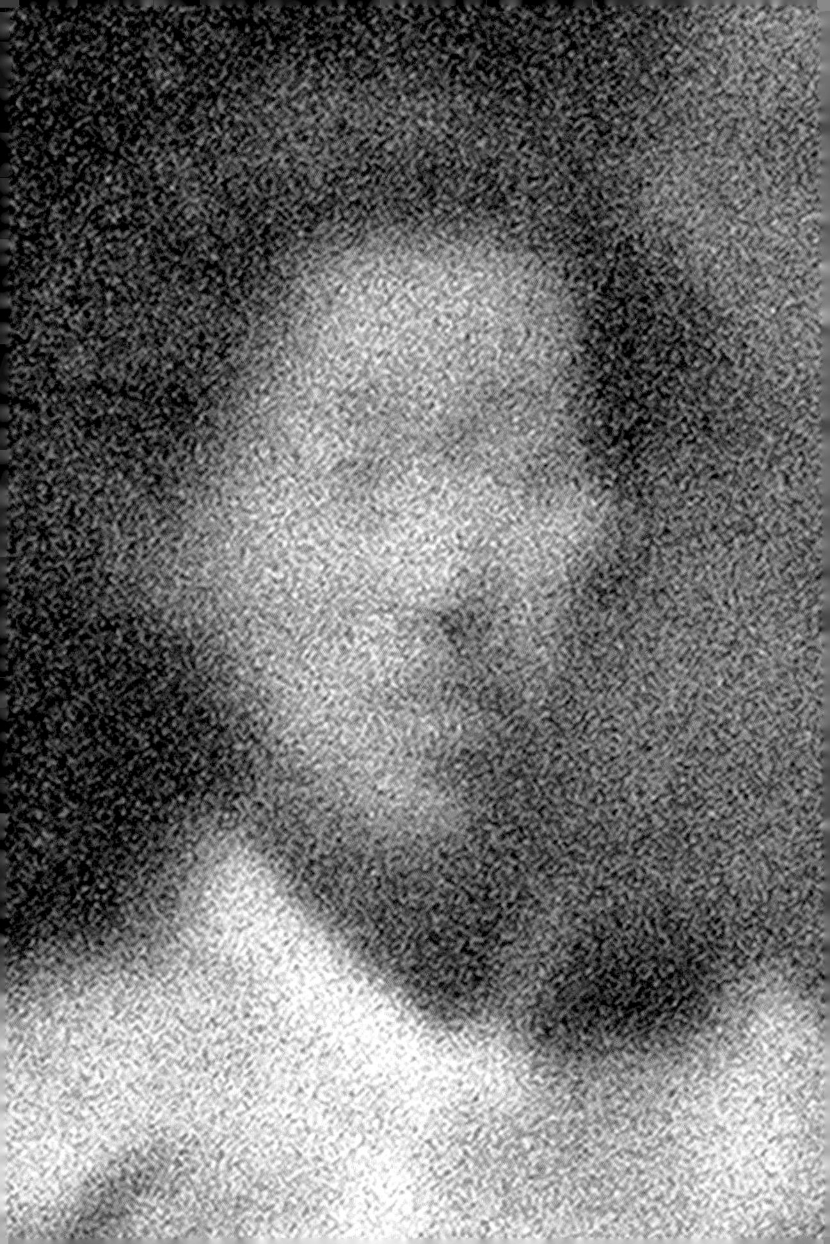

day after day

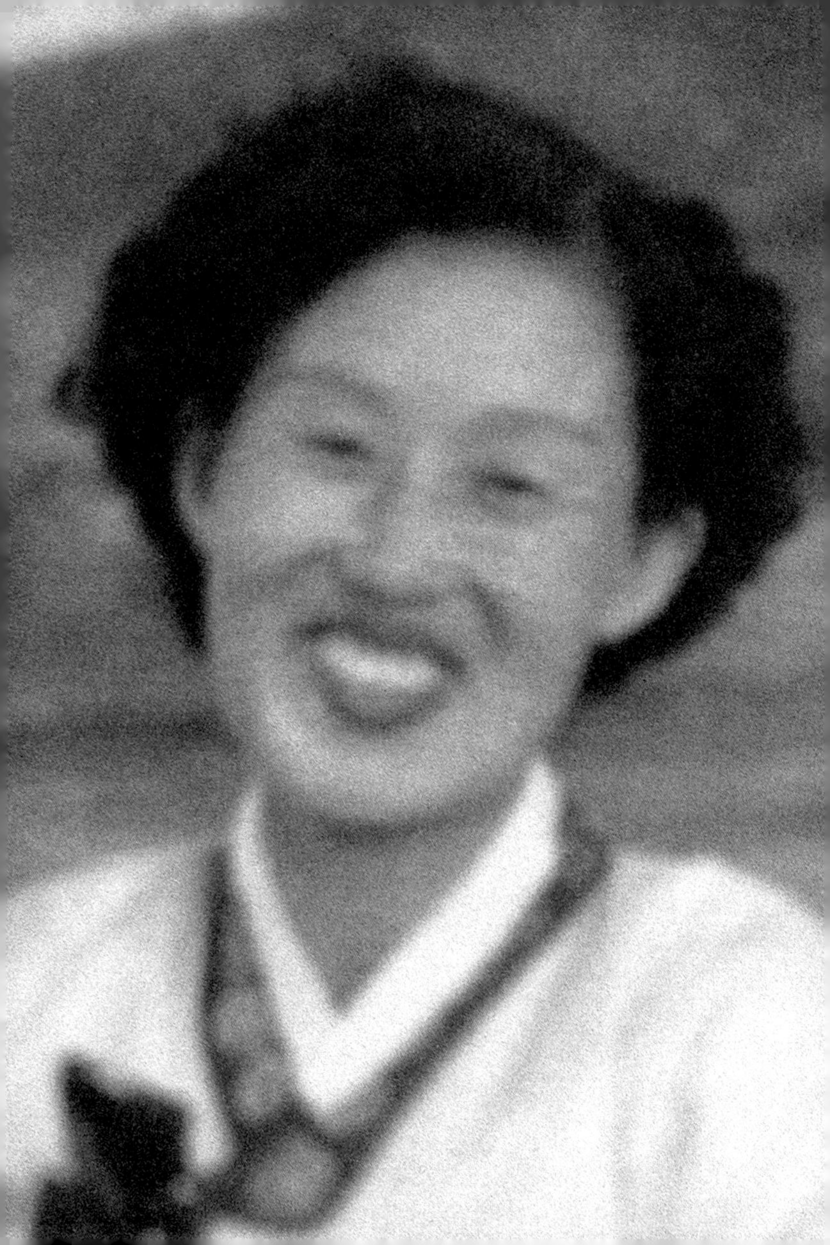

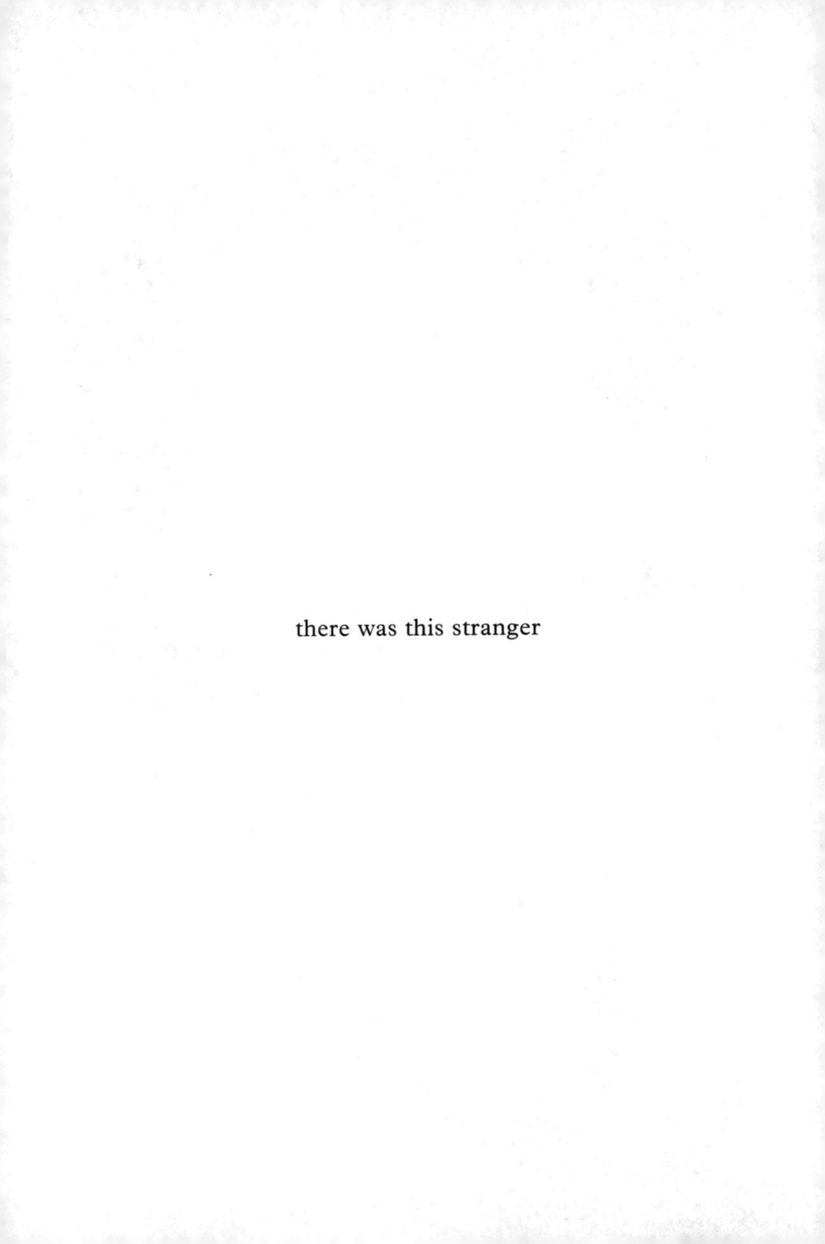

there was this stranger

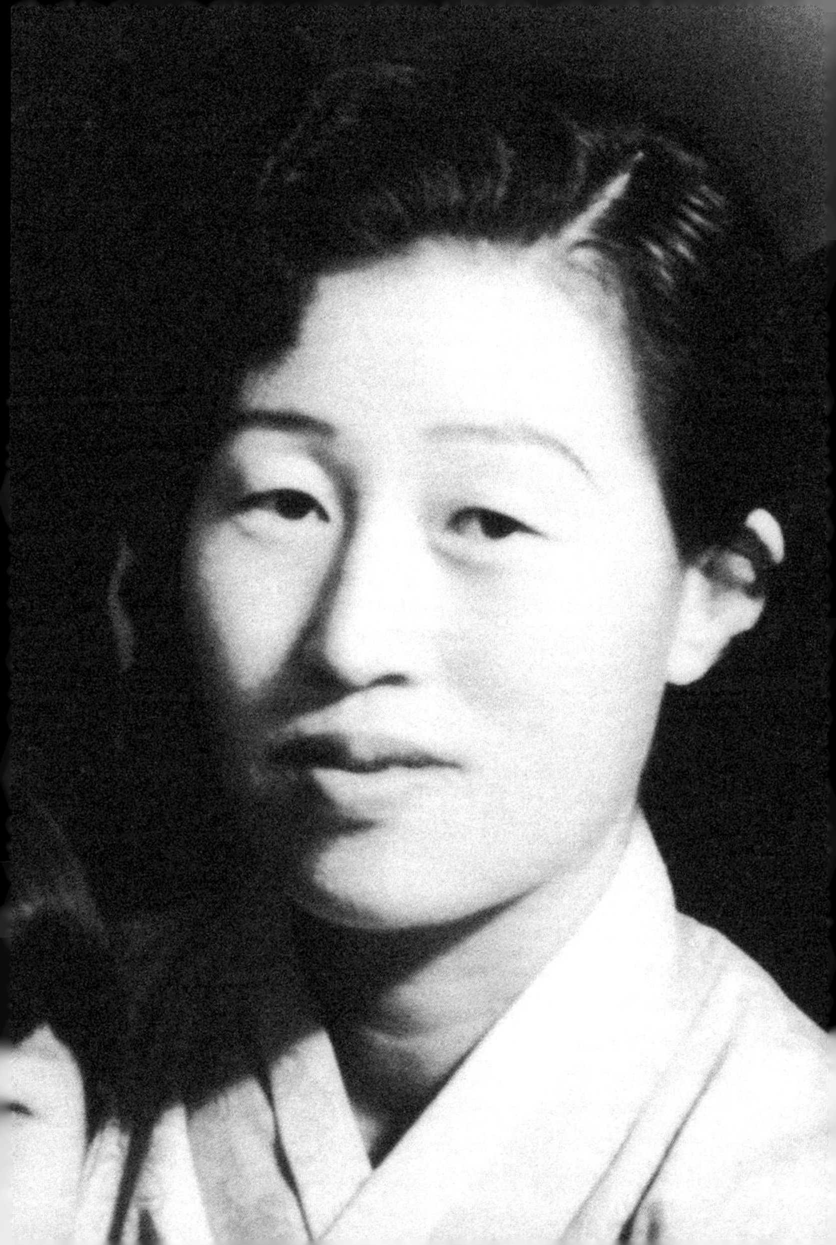

bitter mess

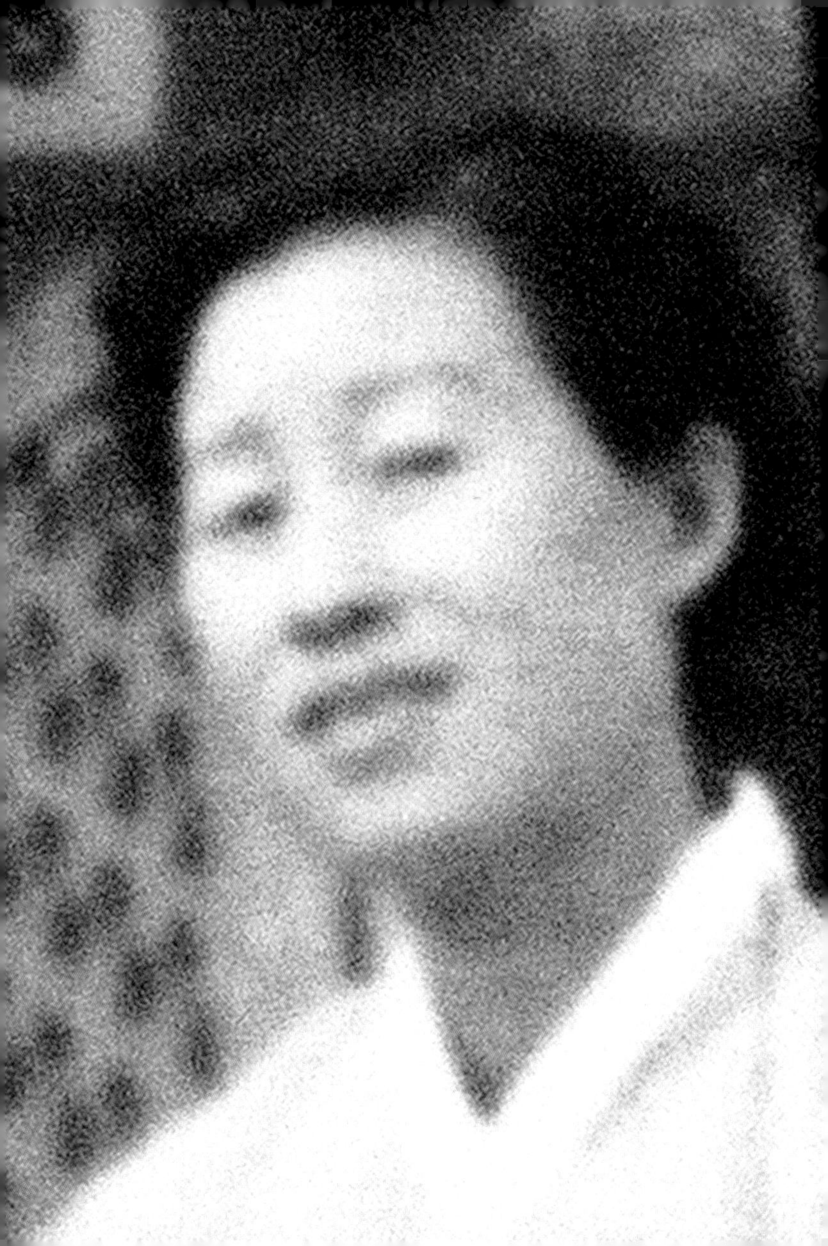

even so

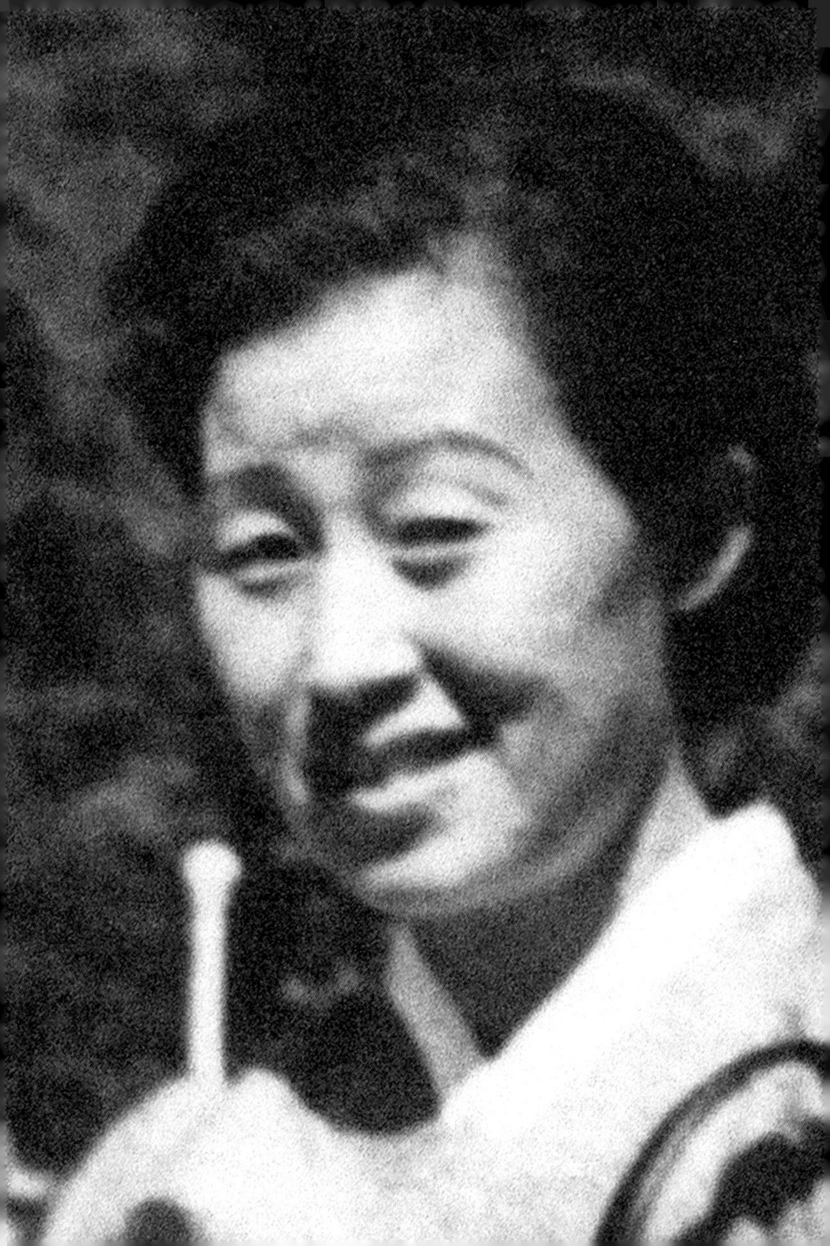

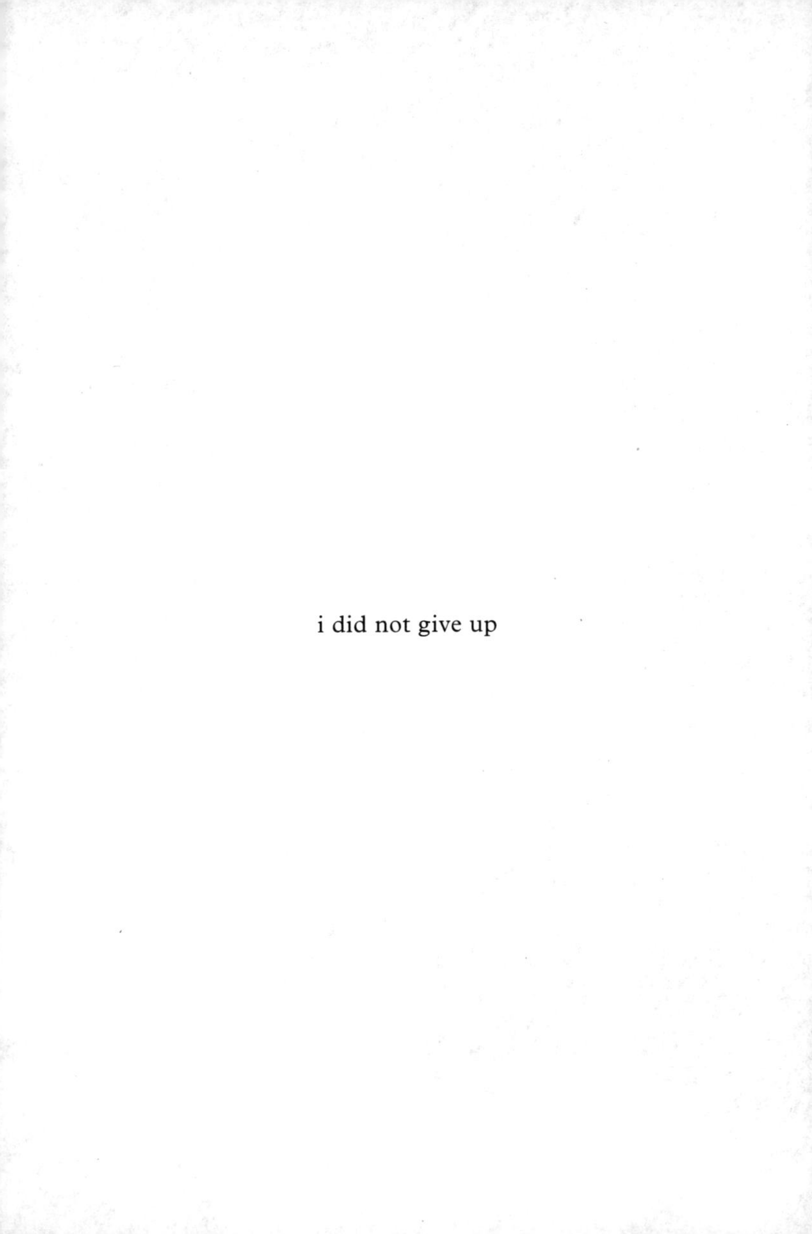

i did not give up

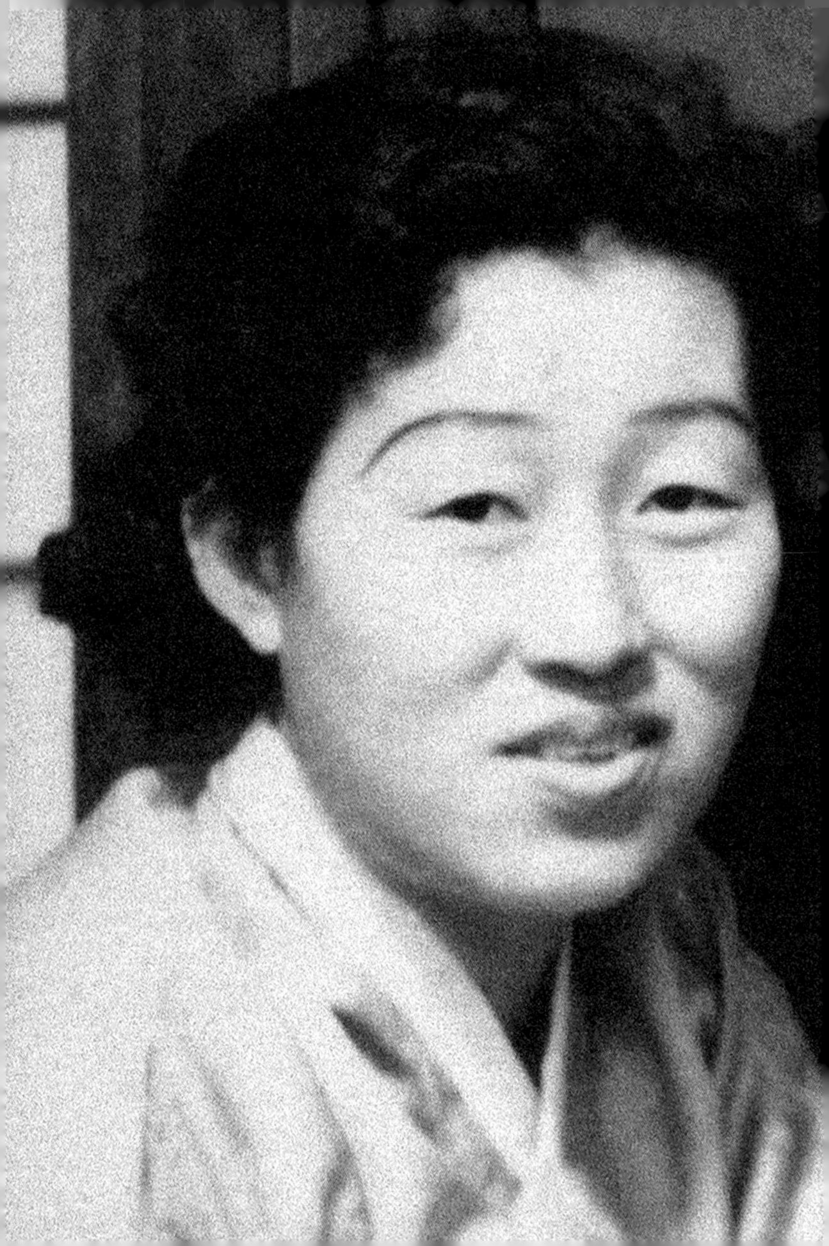

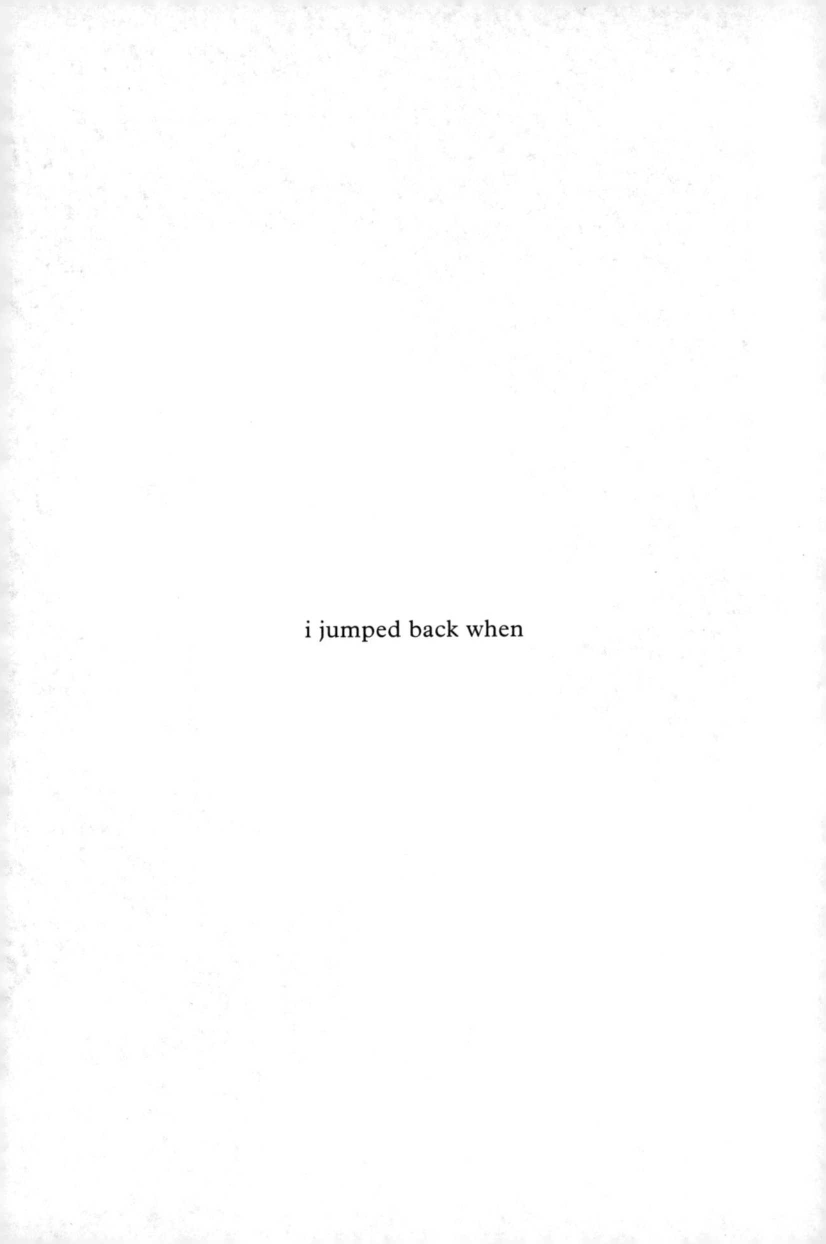

i jumped back when

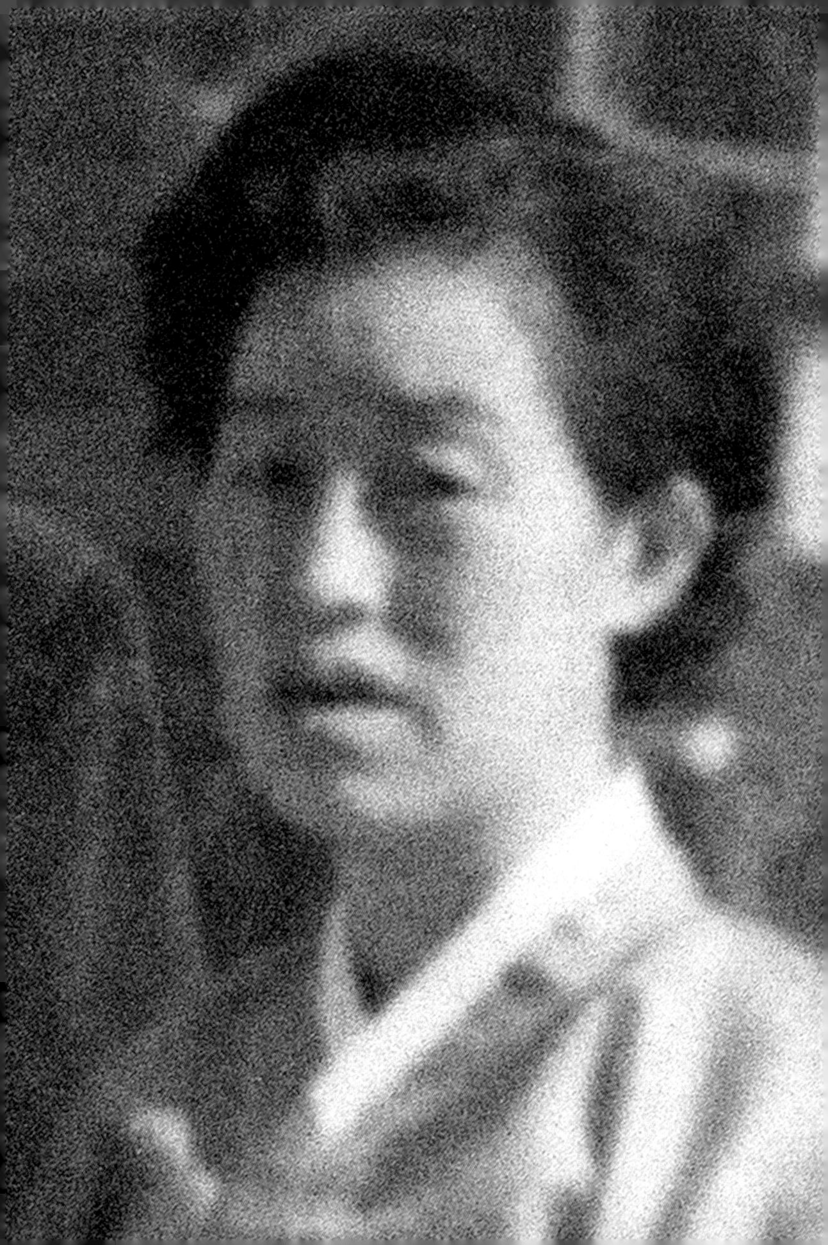

the knife fell

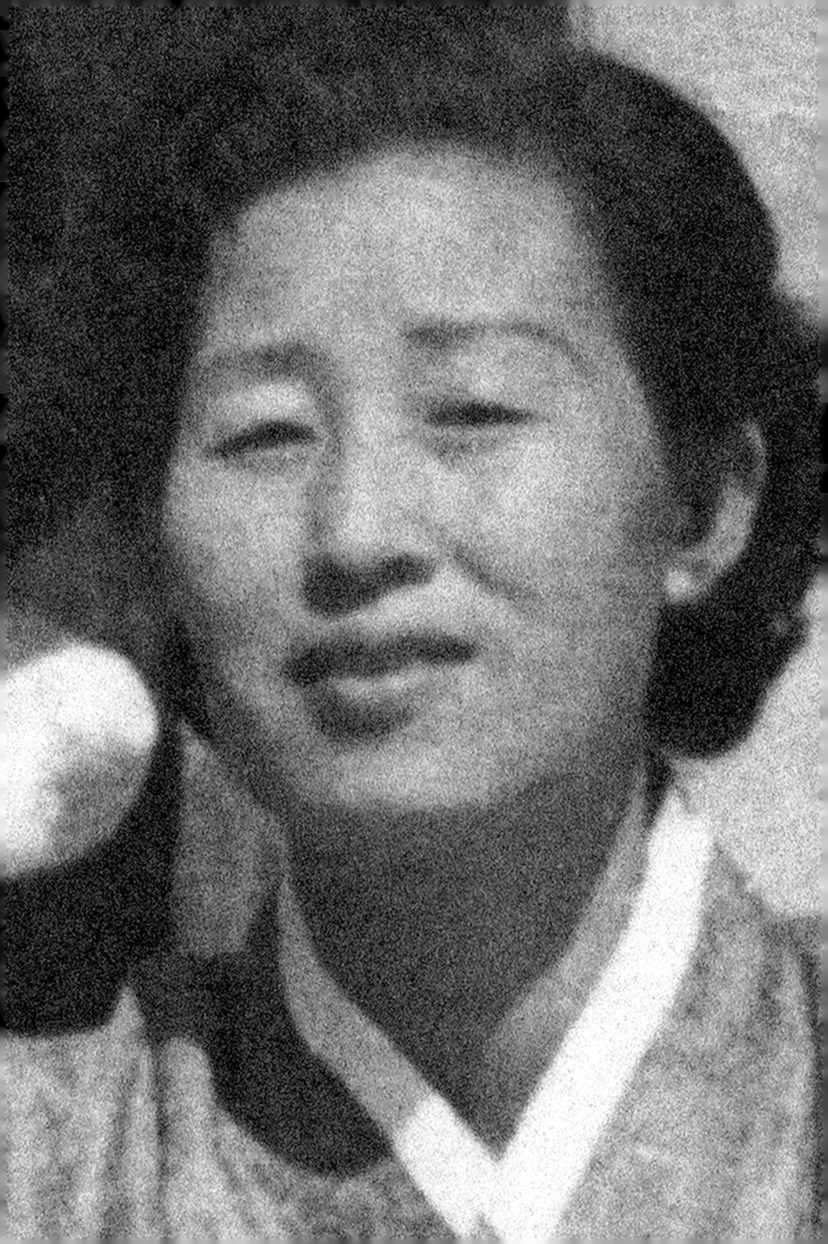

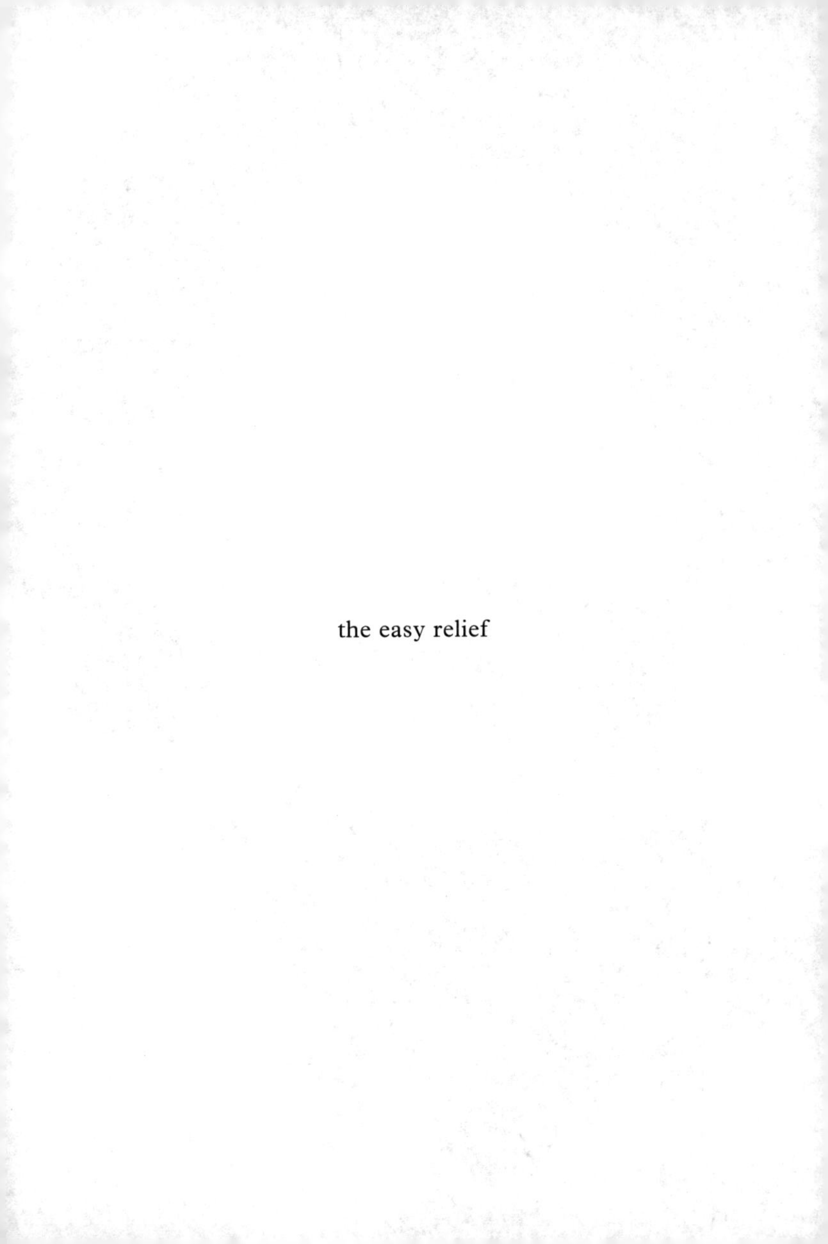

the easy relief

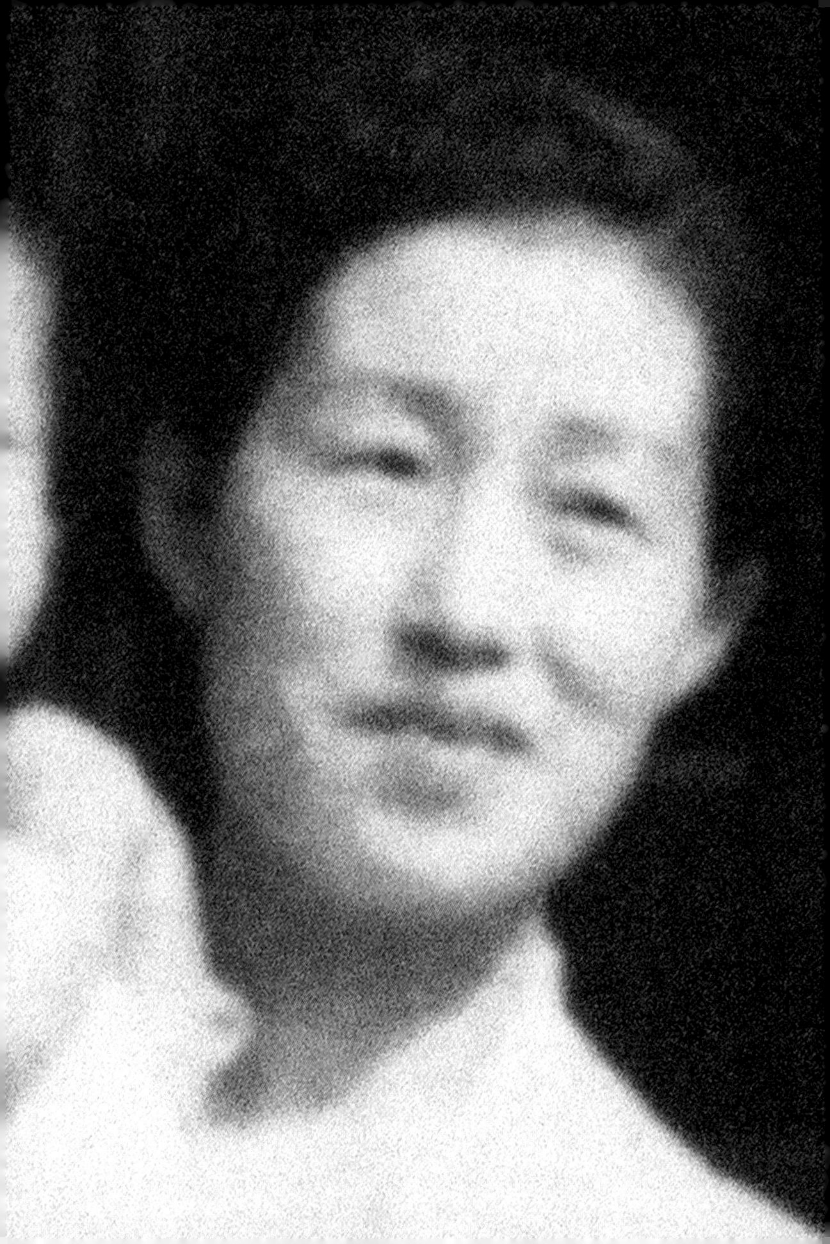

that i needed

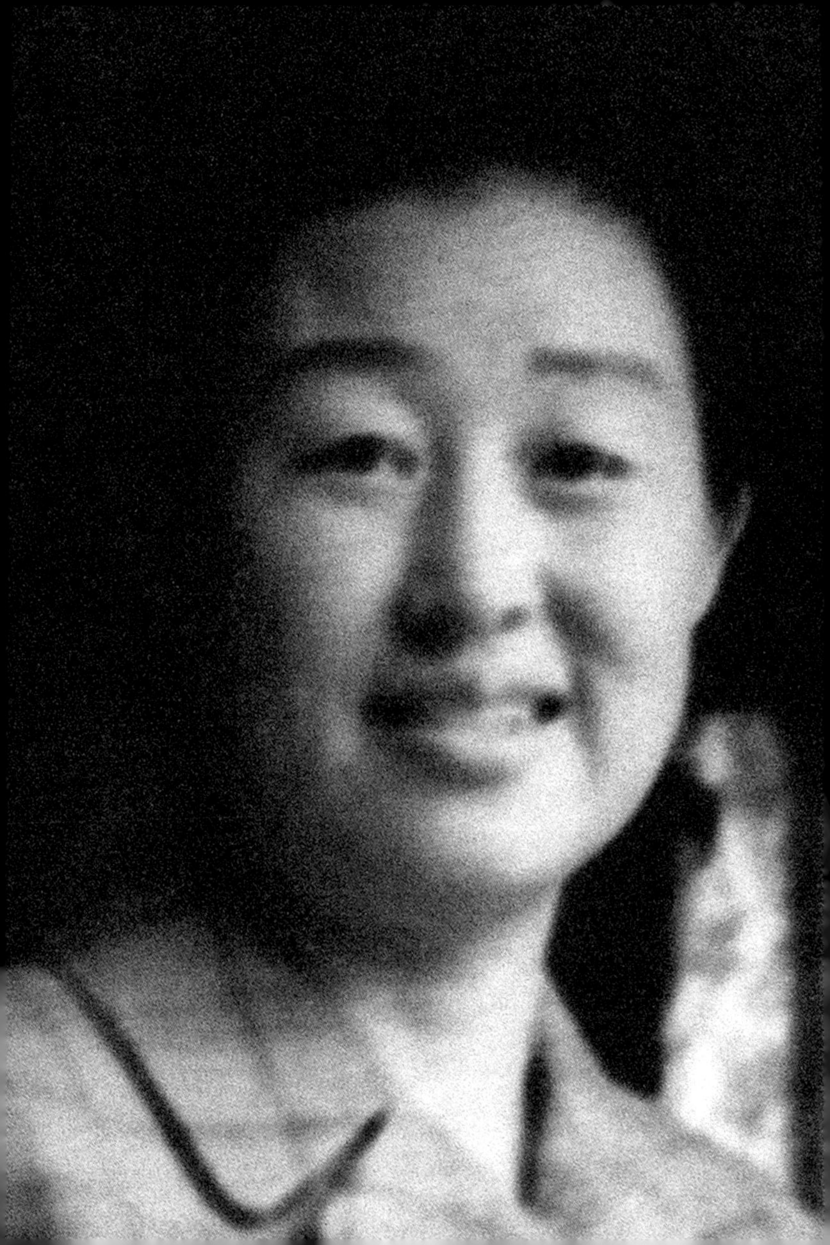

i did not know how to ask

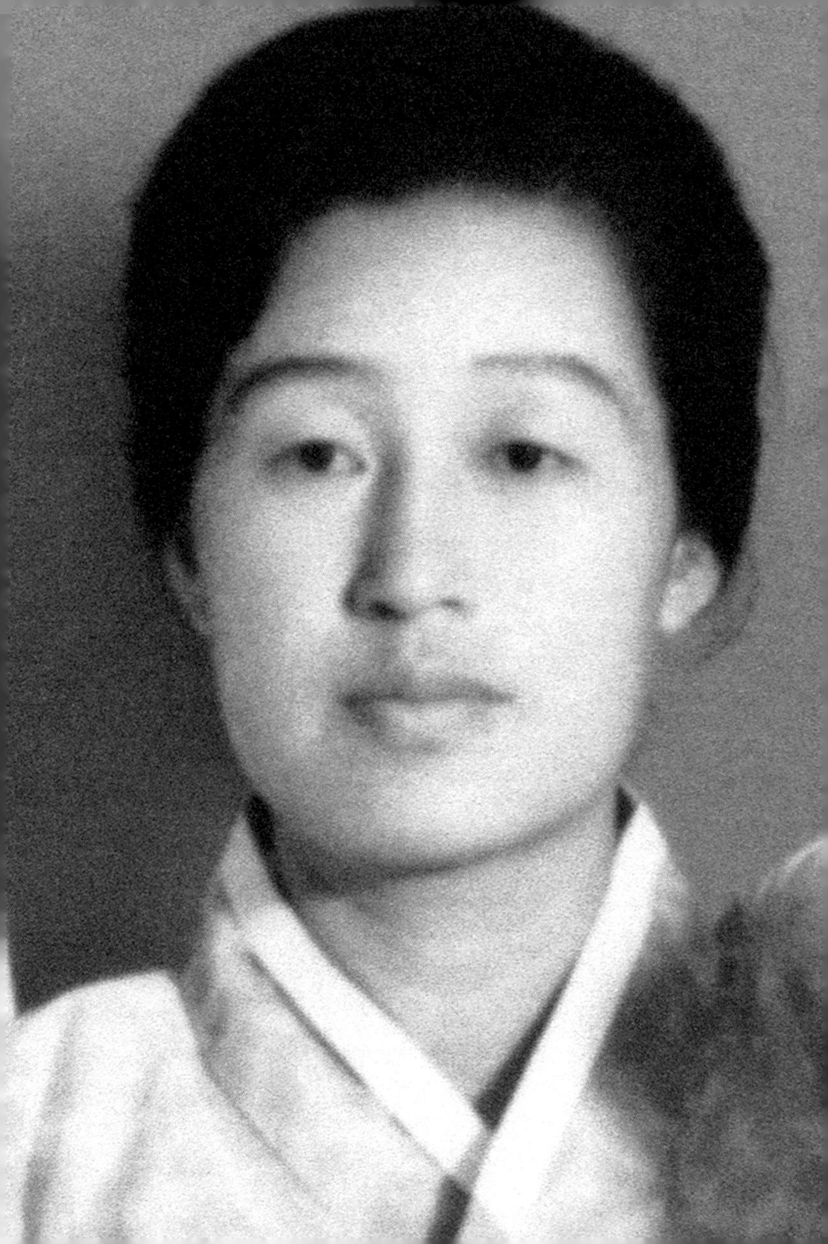

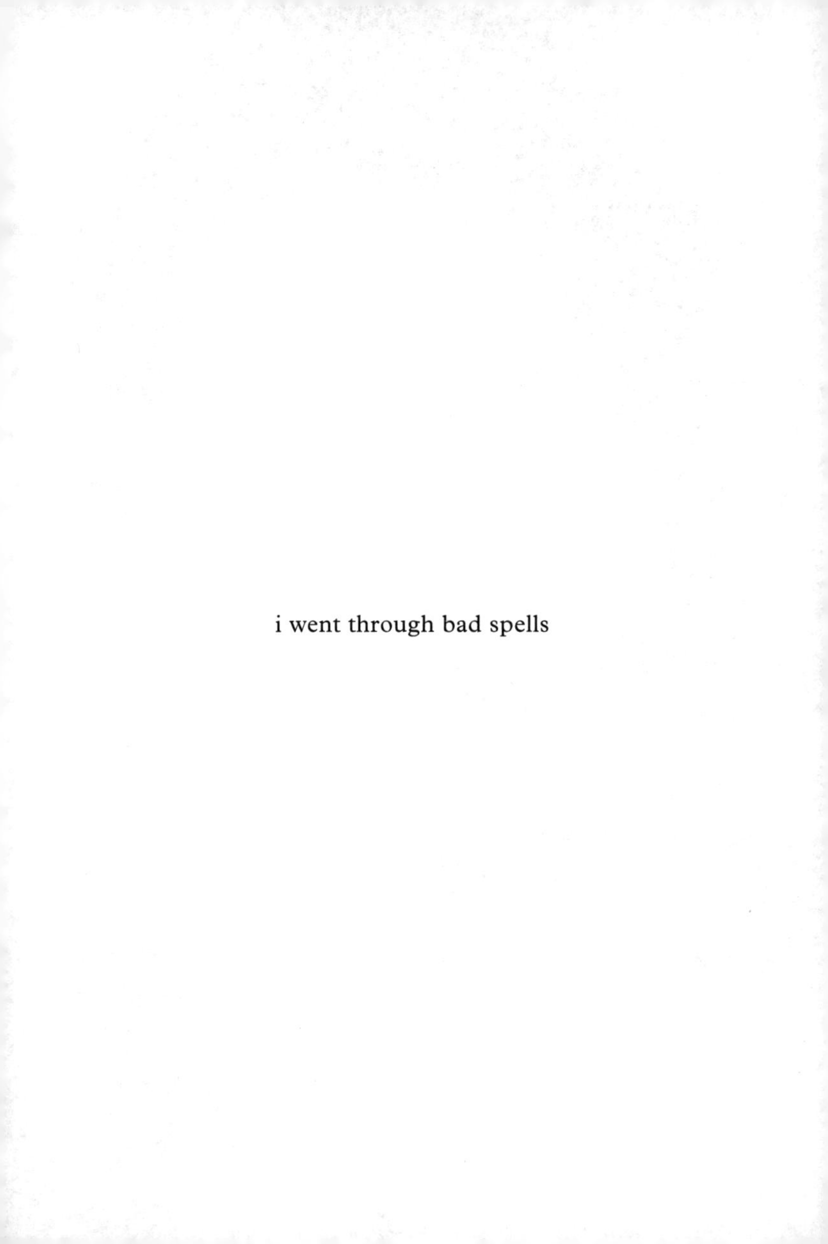

i went through bad spells

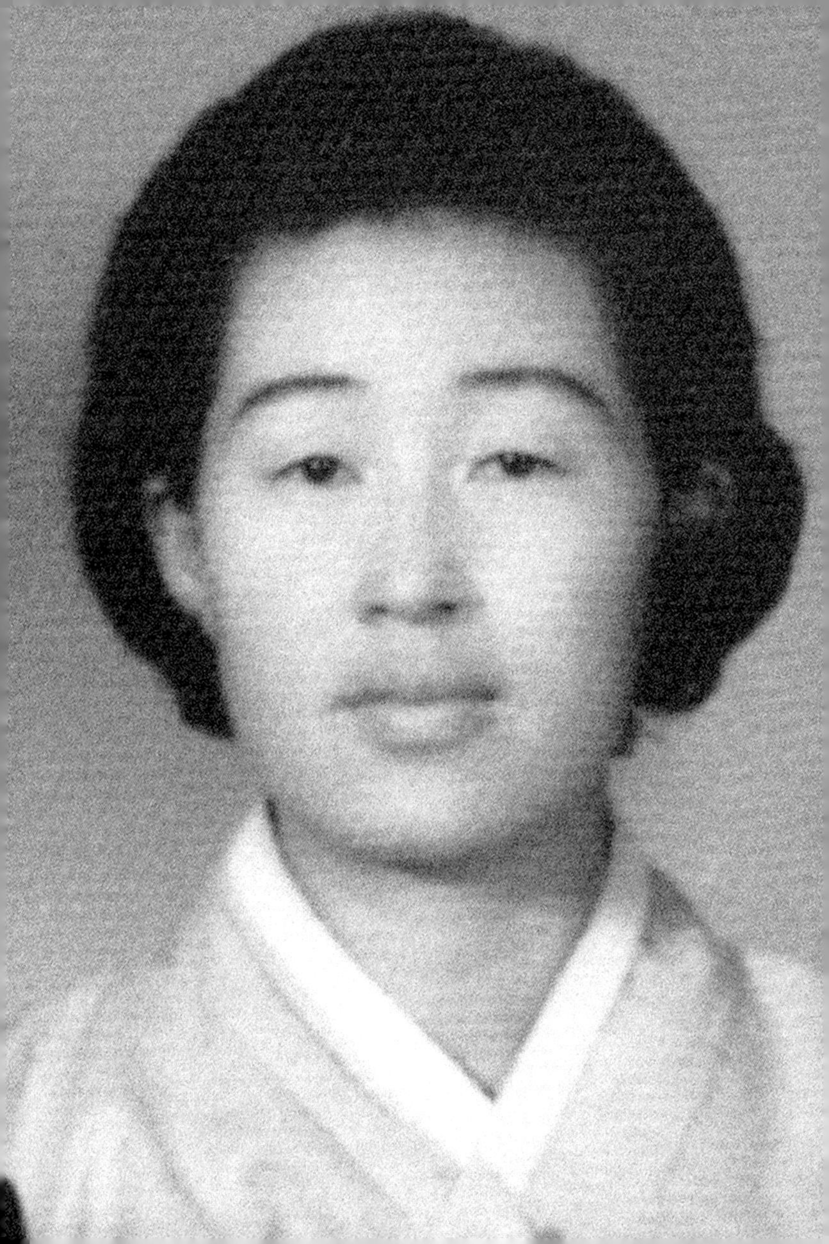

i spoke too much and was too silent

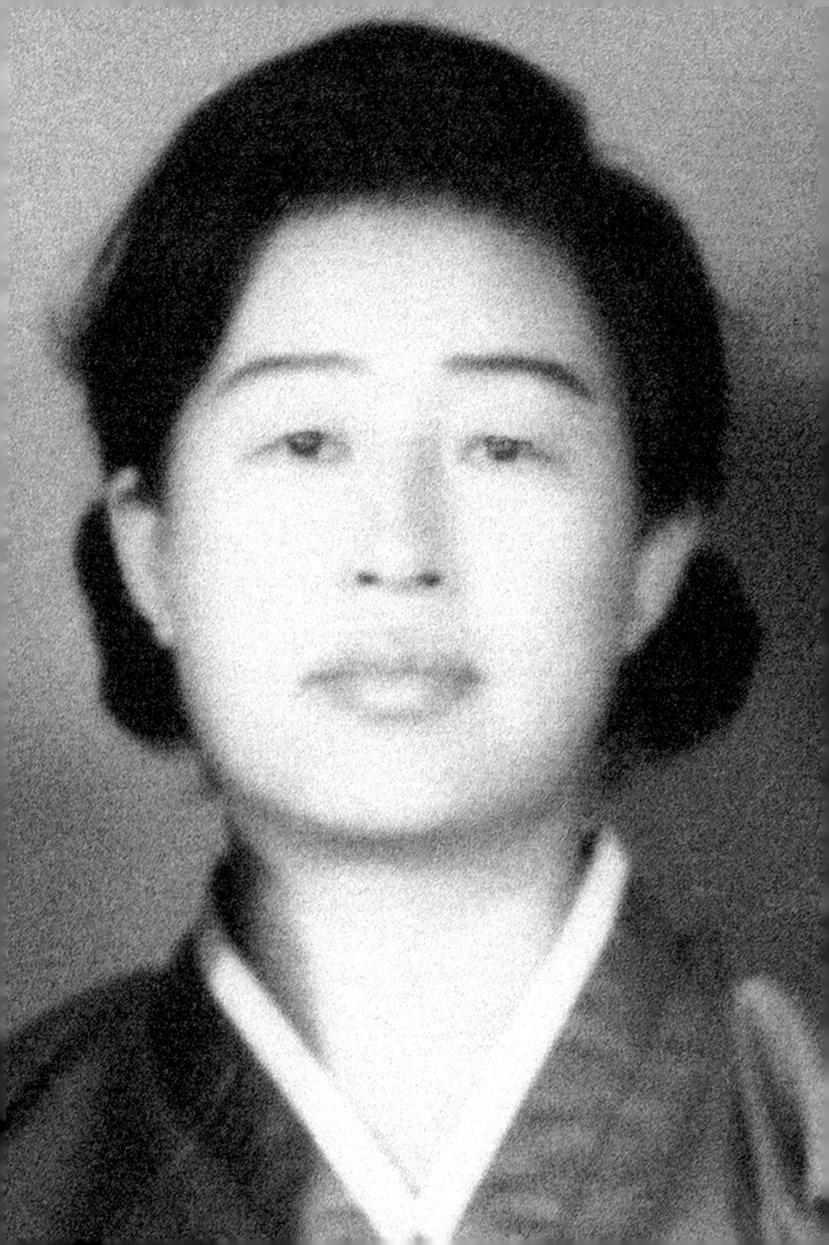

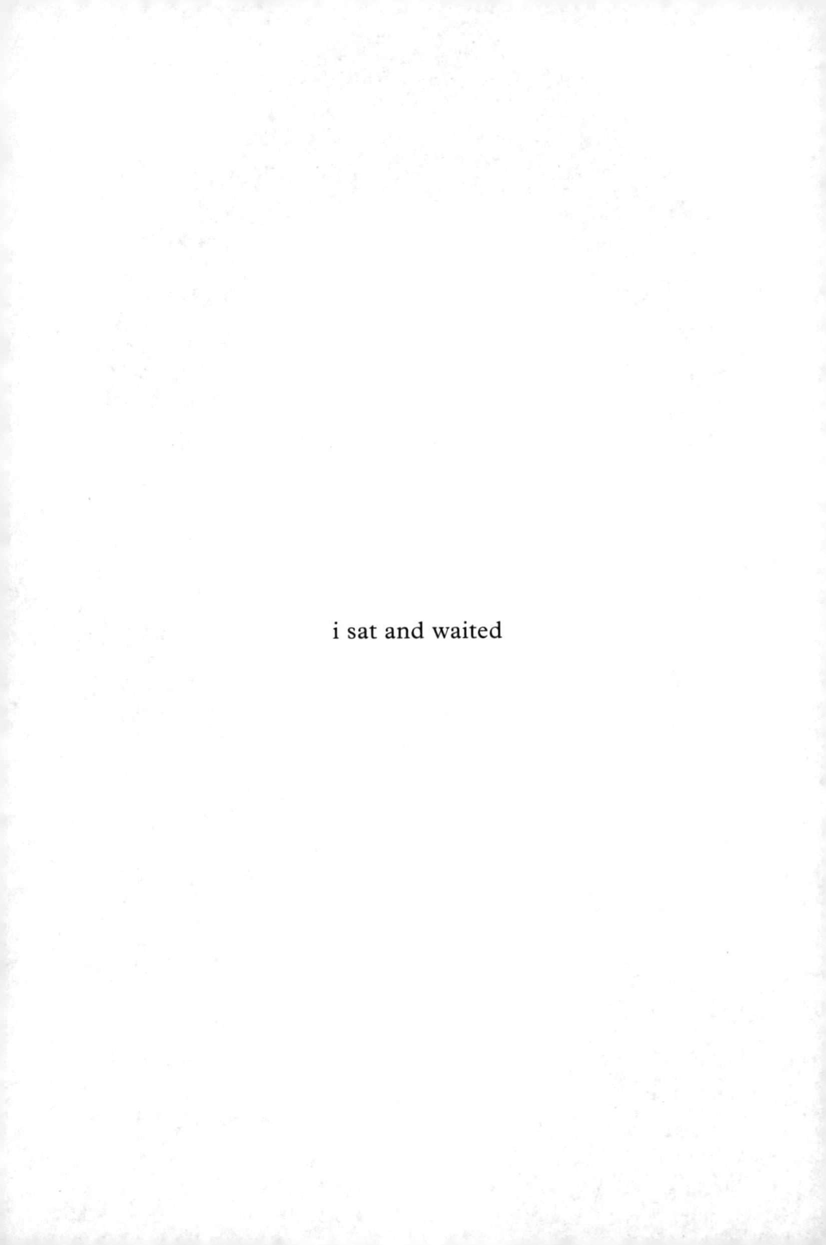

i sat and waited

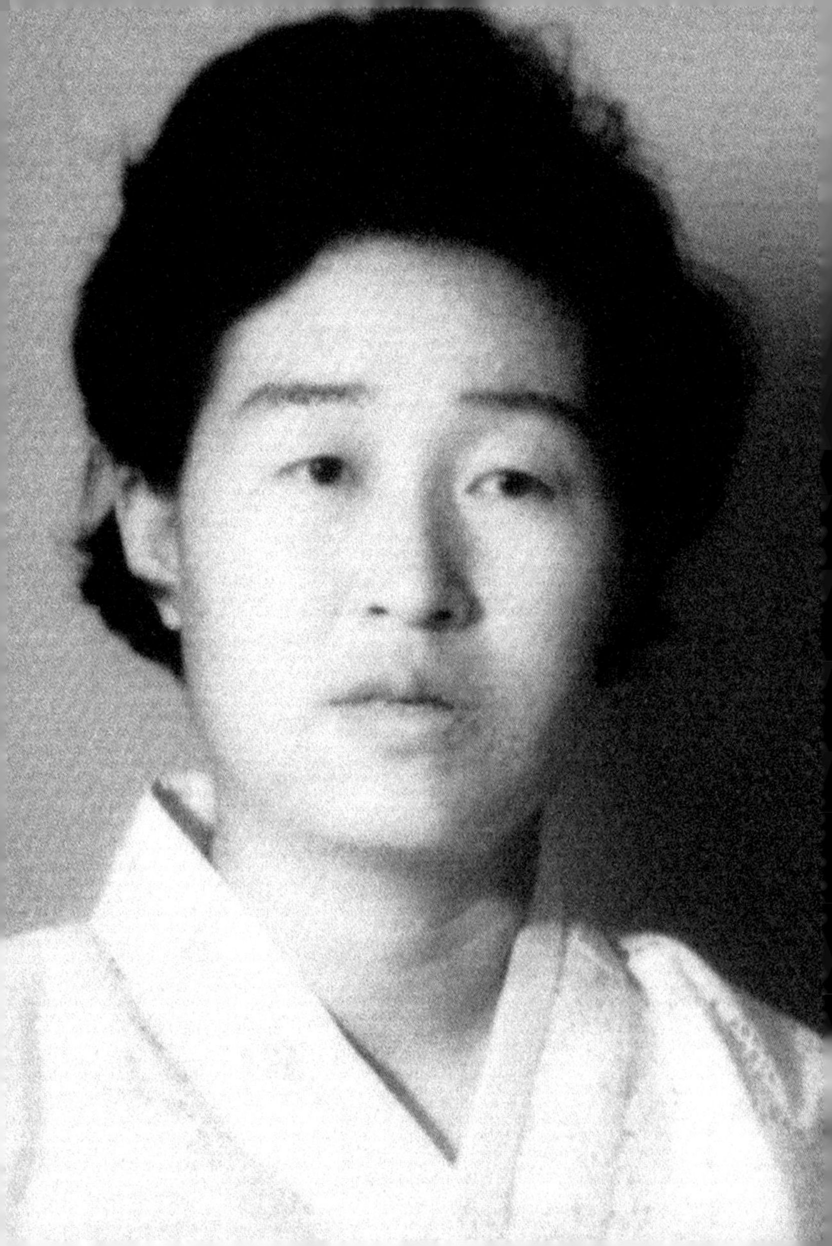

i bared my teeth

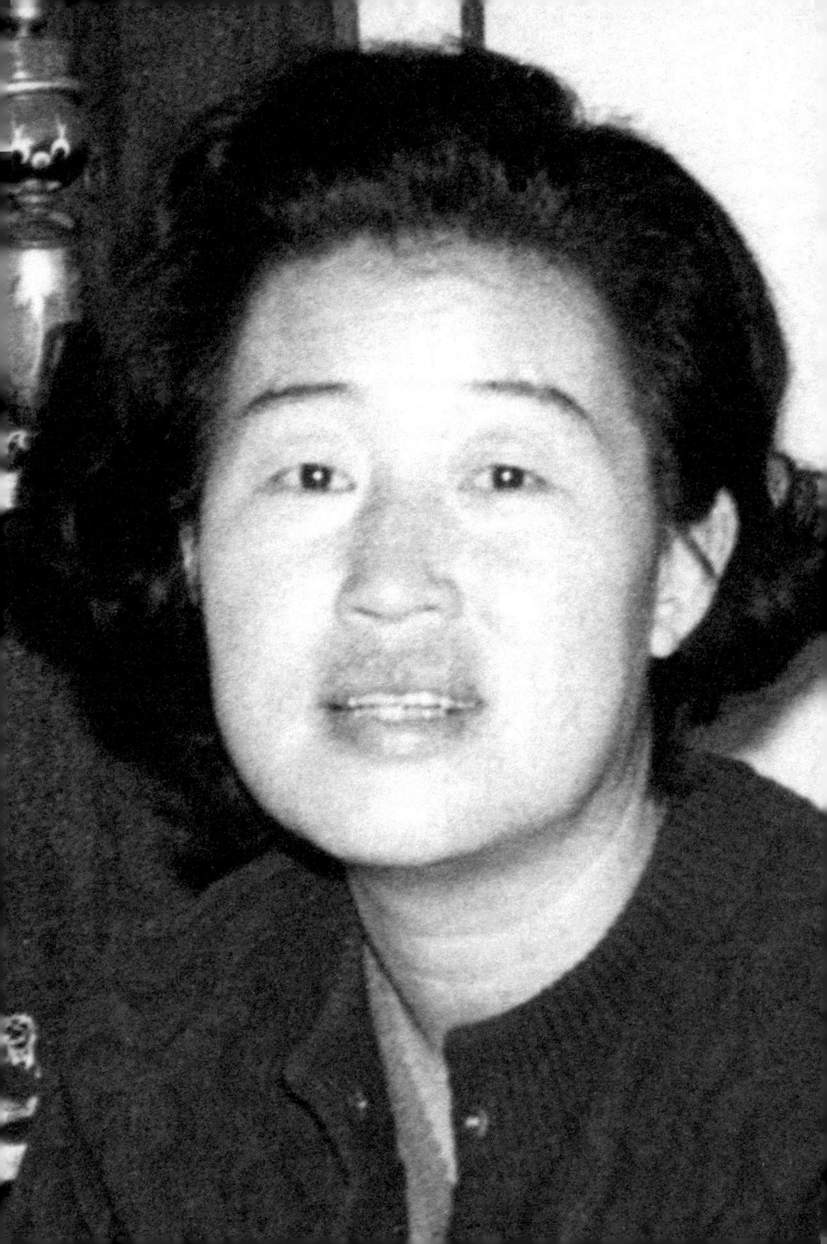

i was only alone

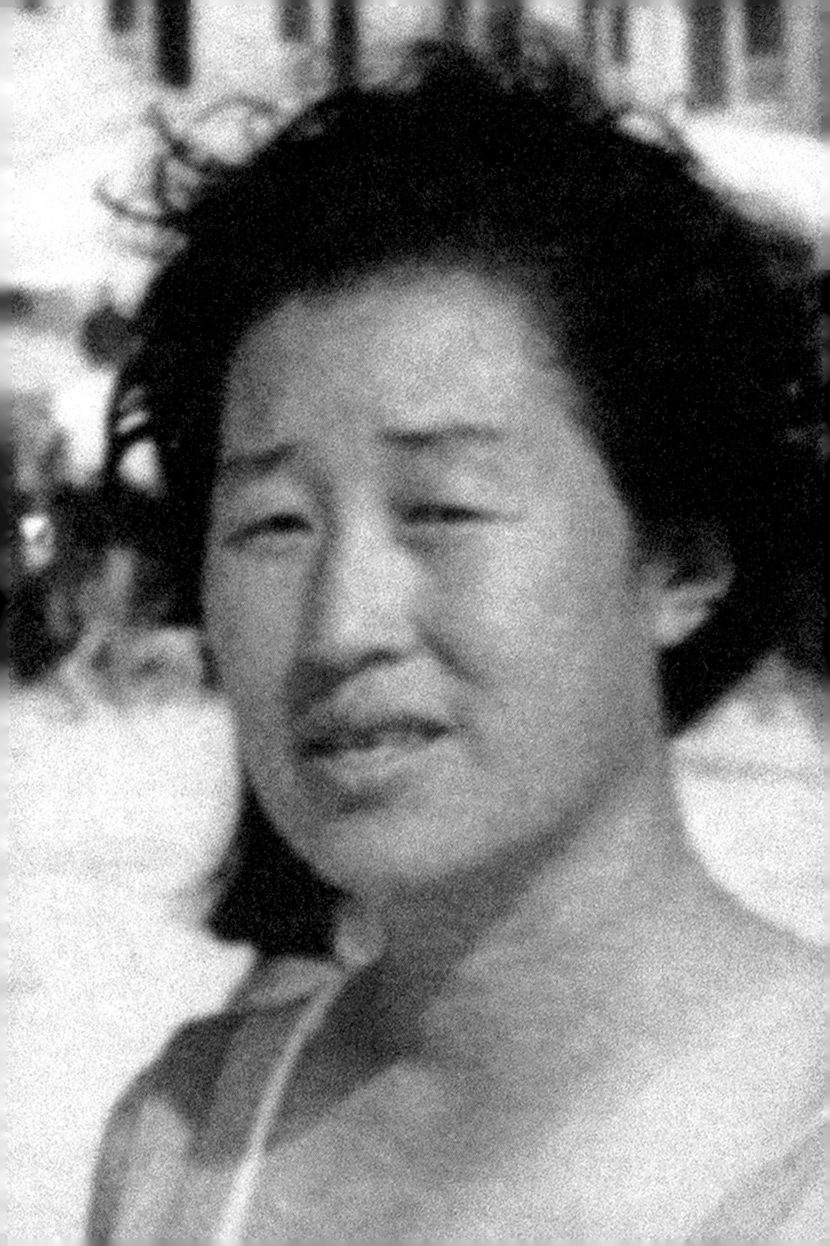

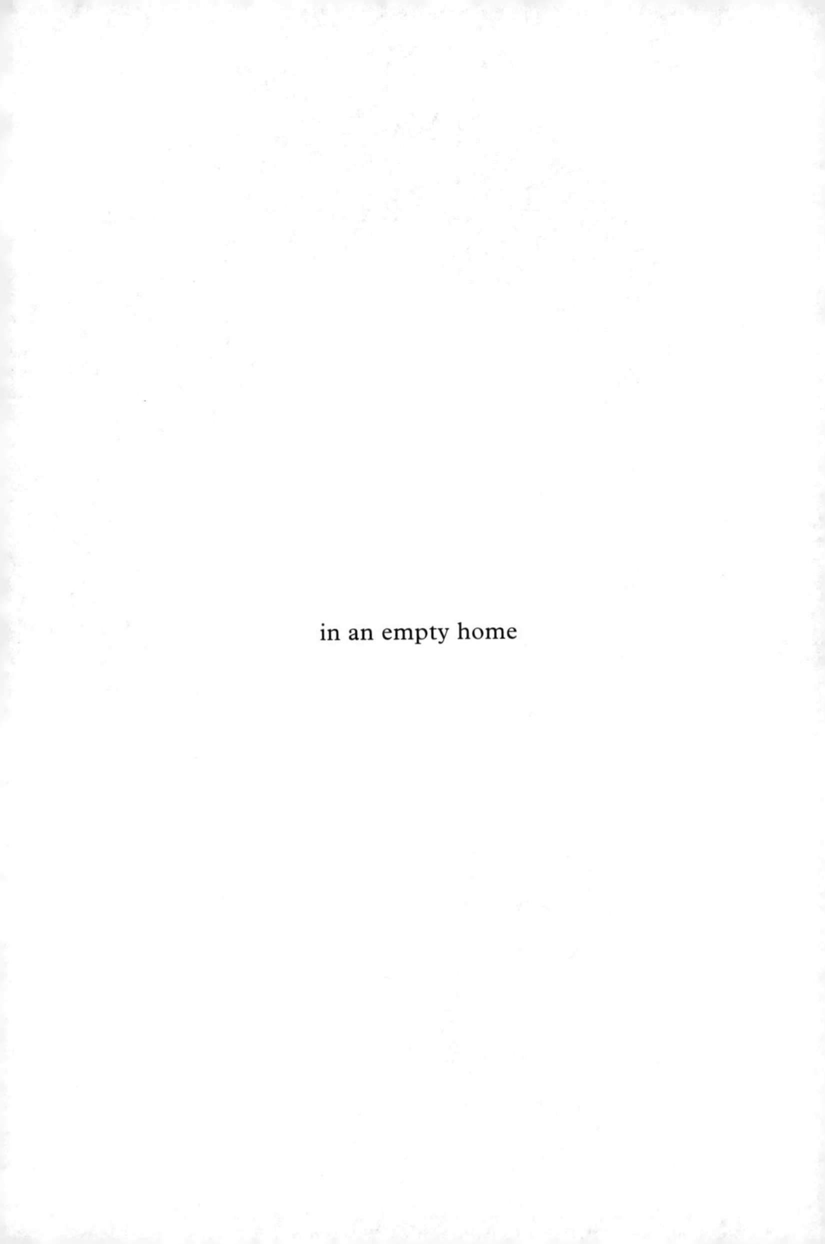

in an empty home

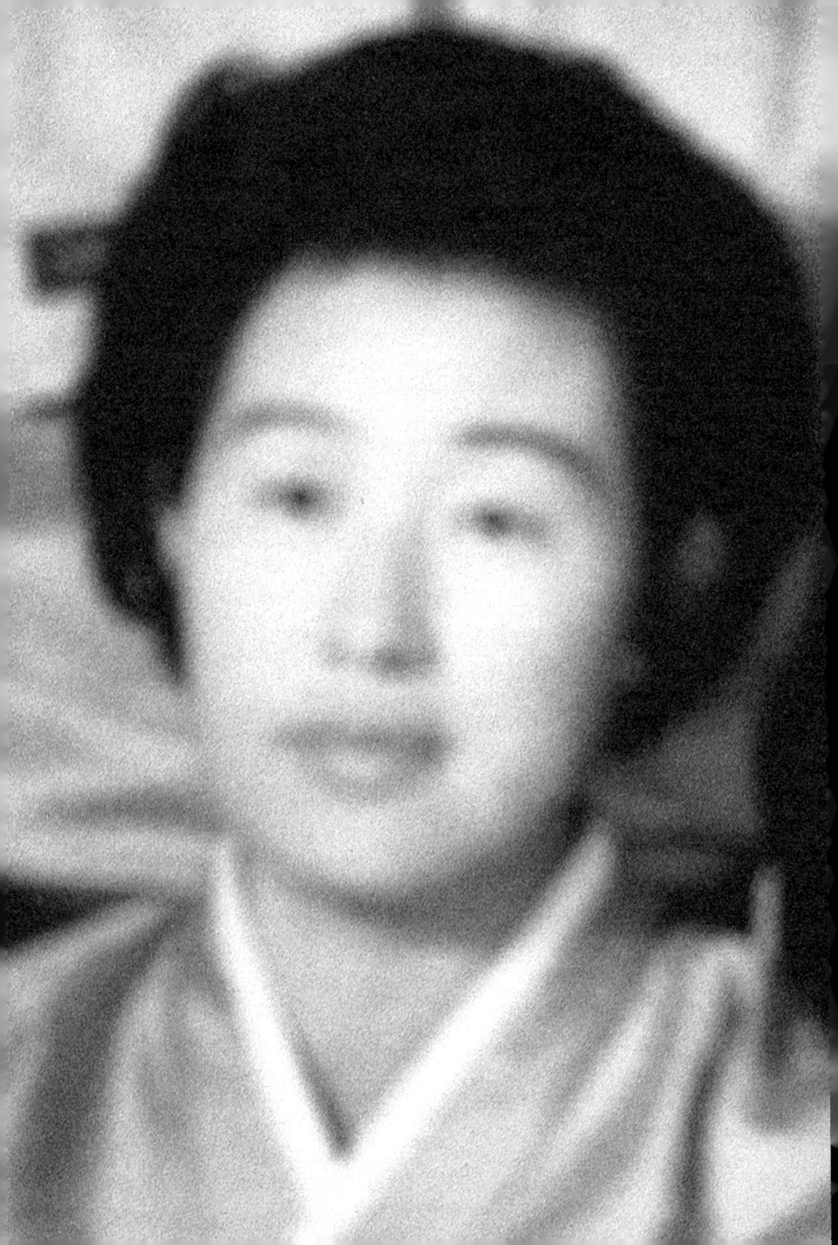

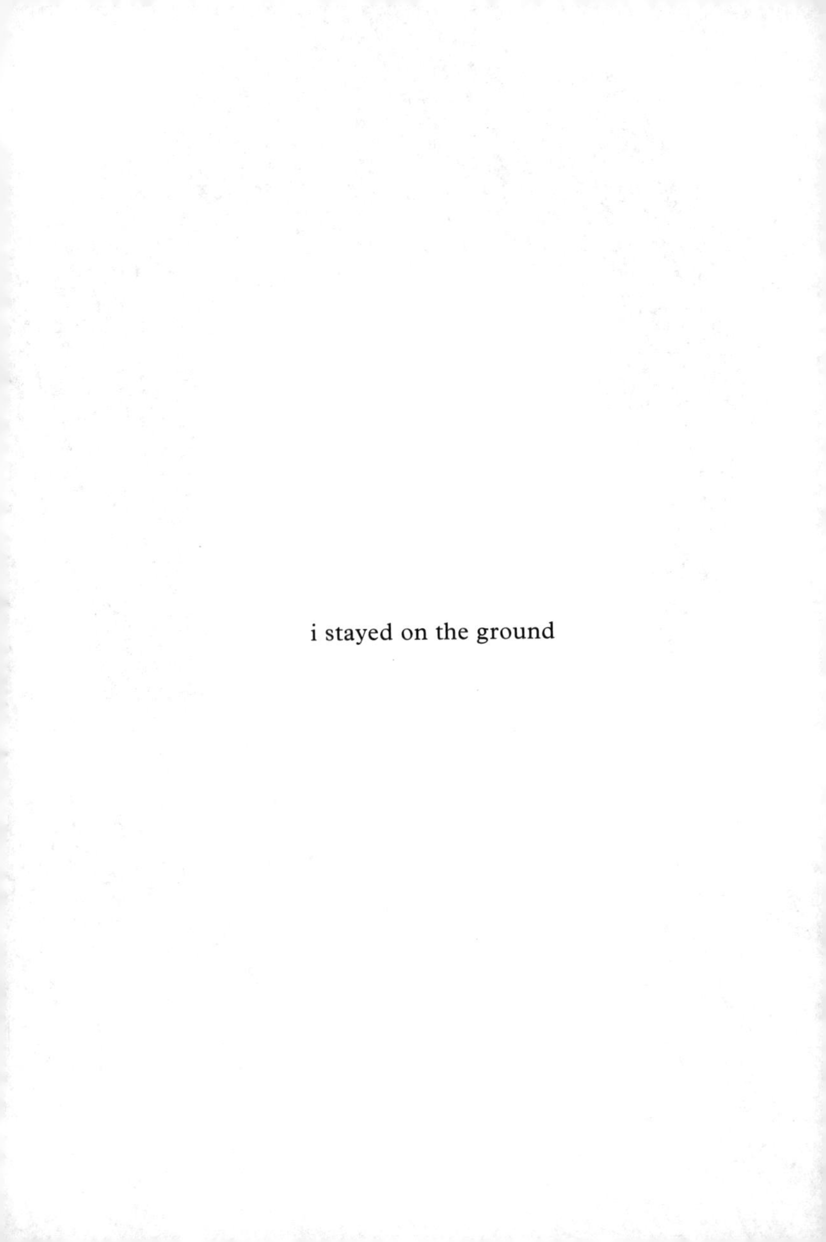

i stayed on the ground

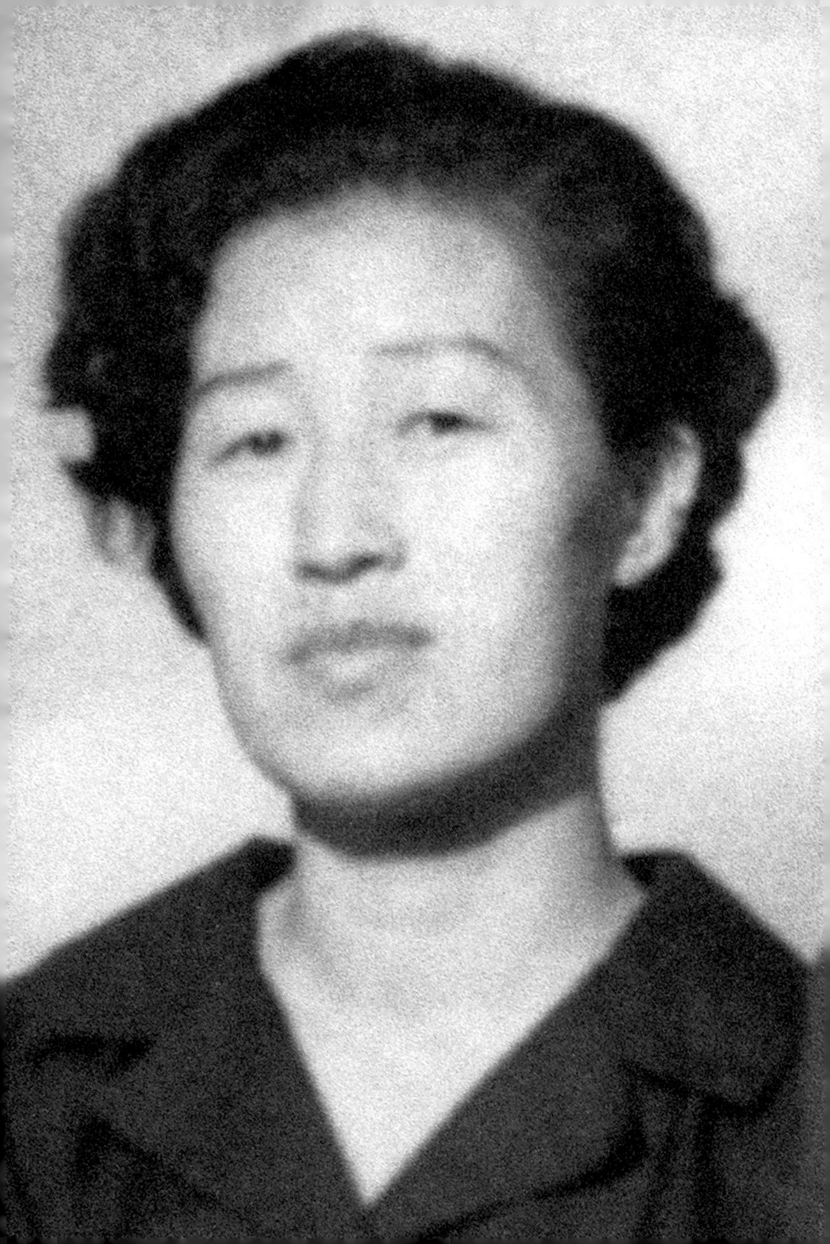

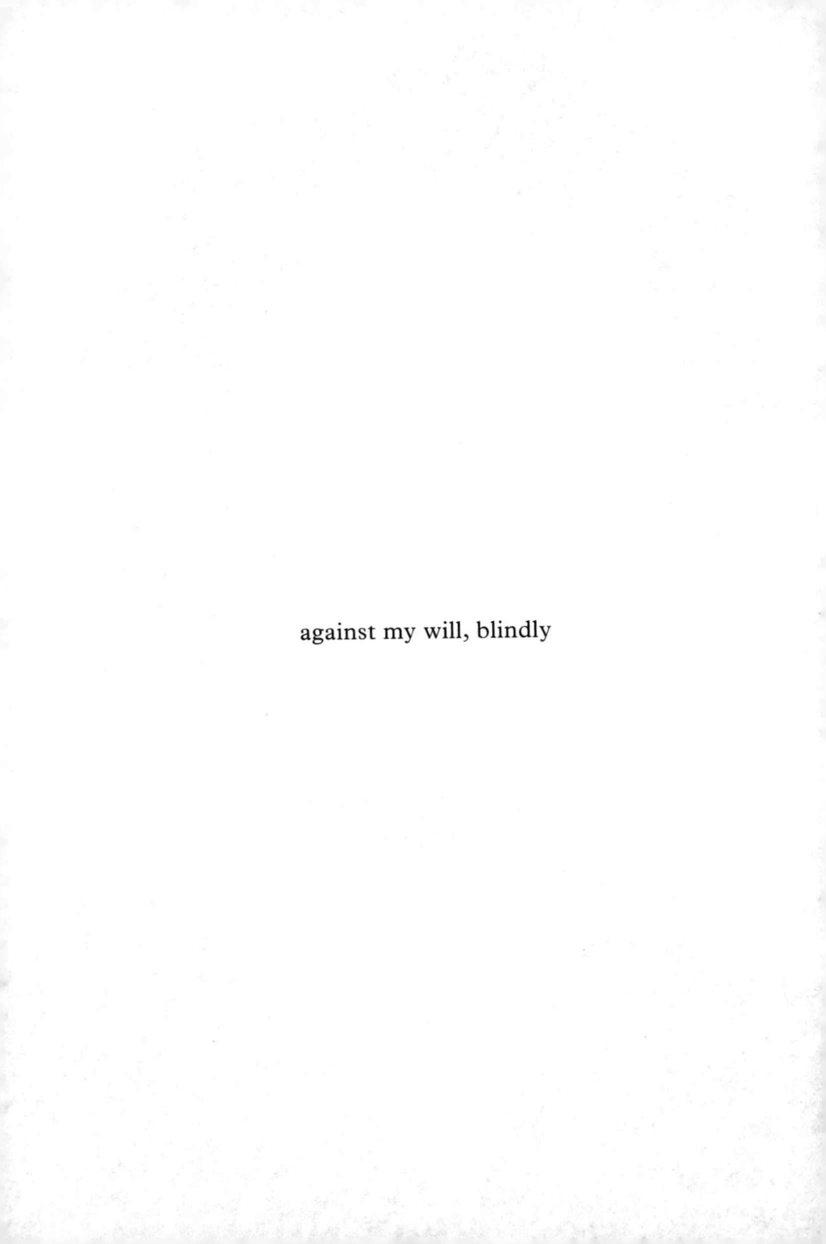

against my will, blindly

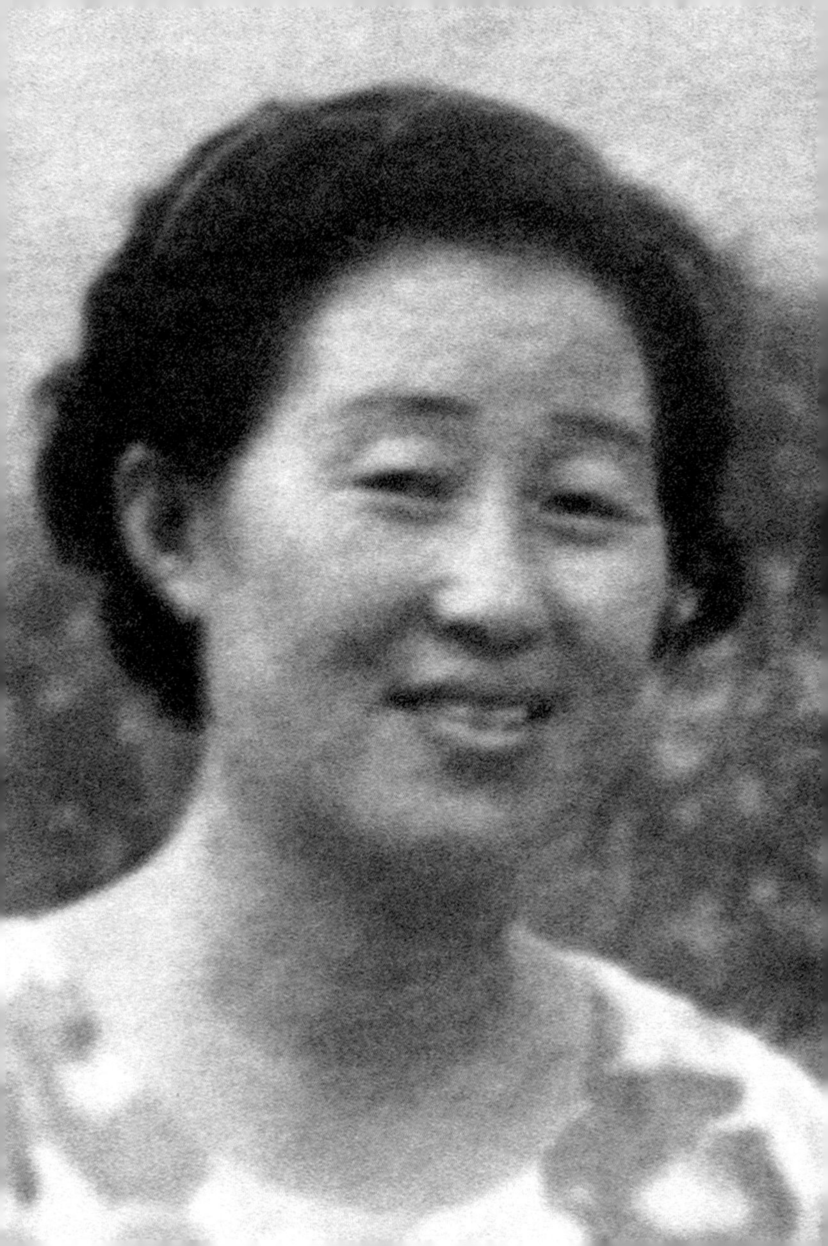

i tasted fear

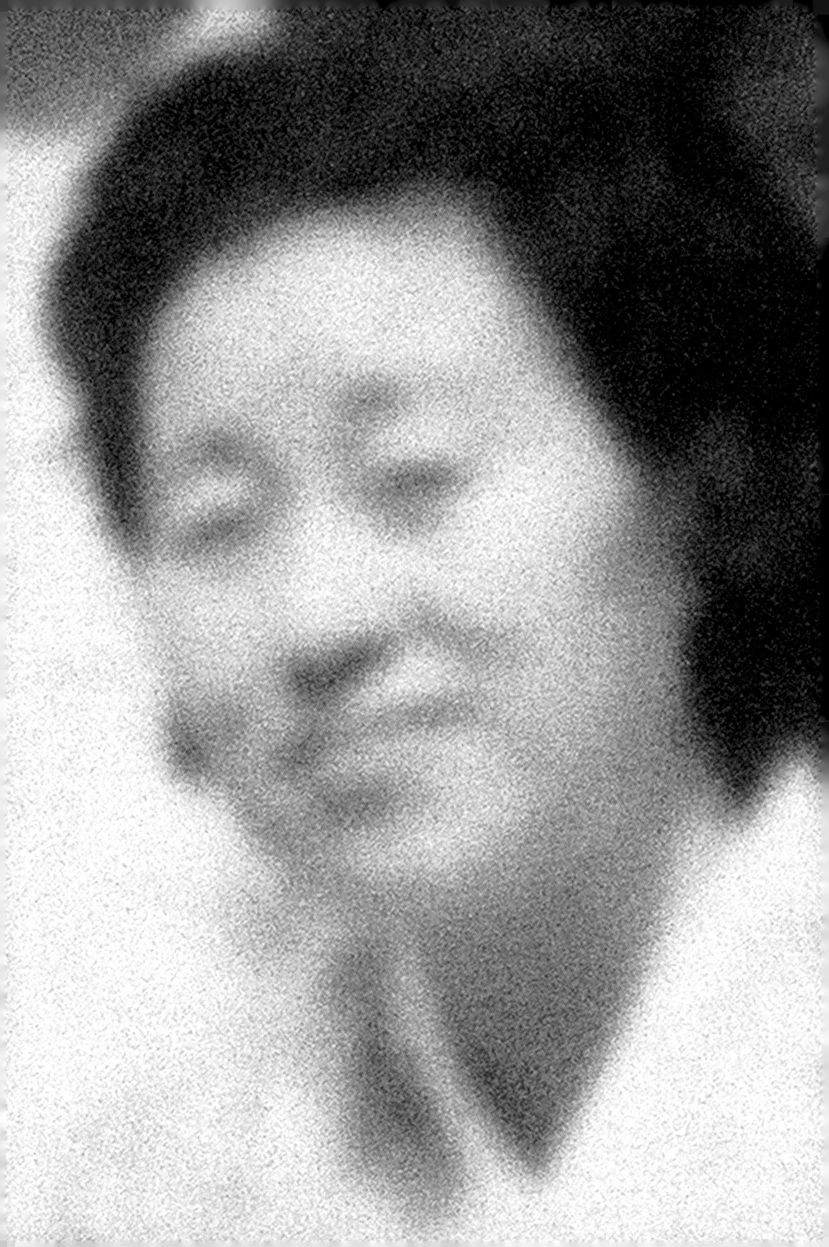

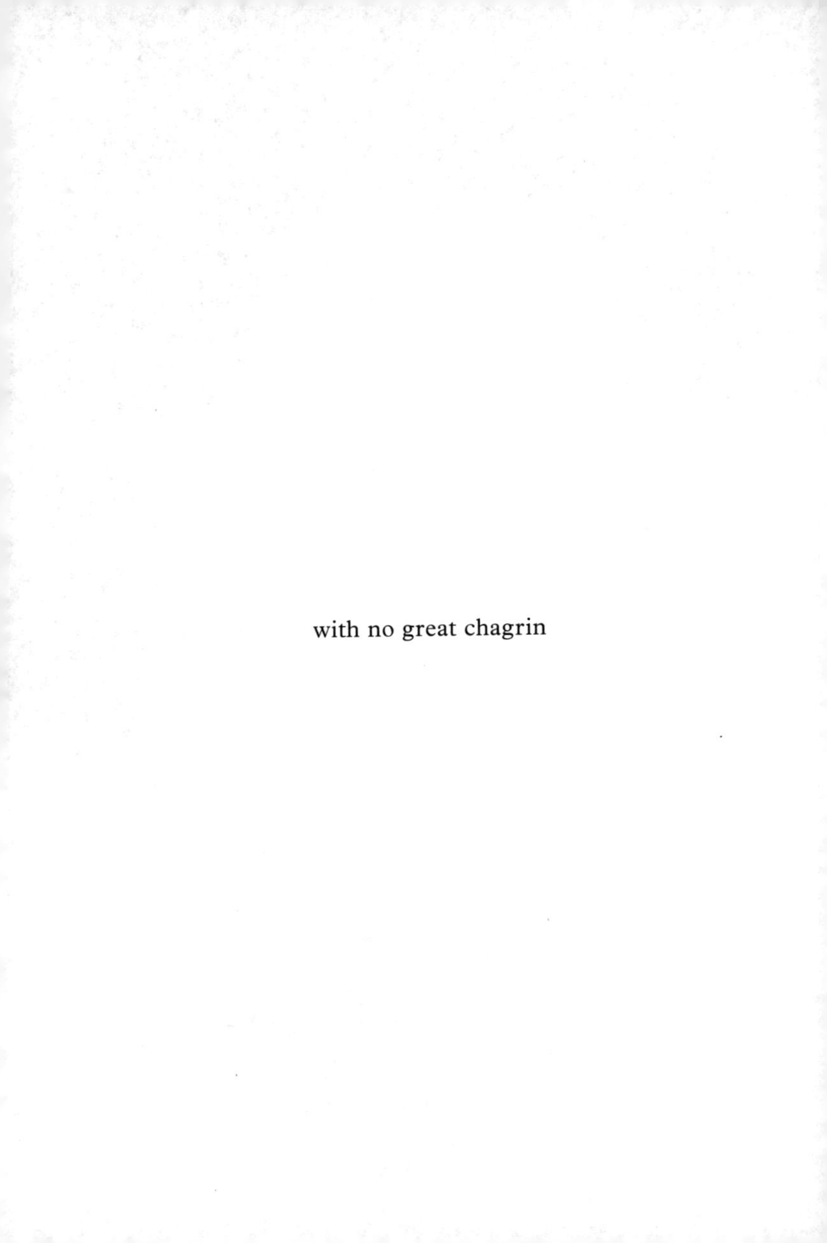

with no great chagrin

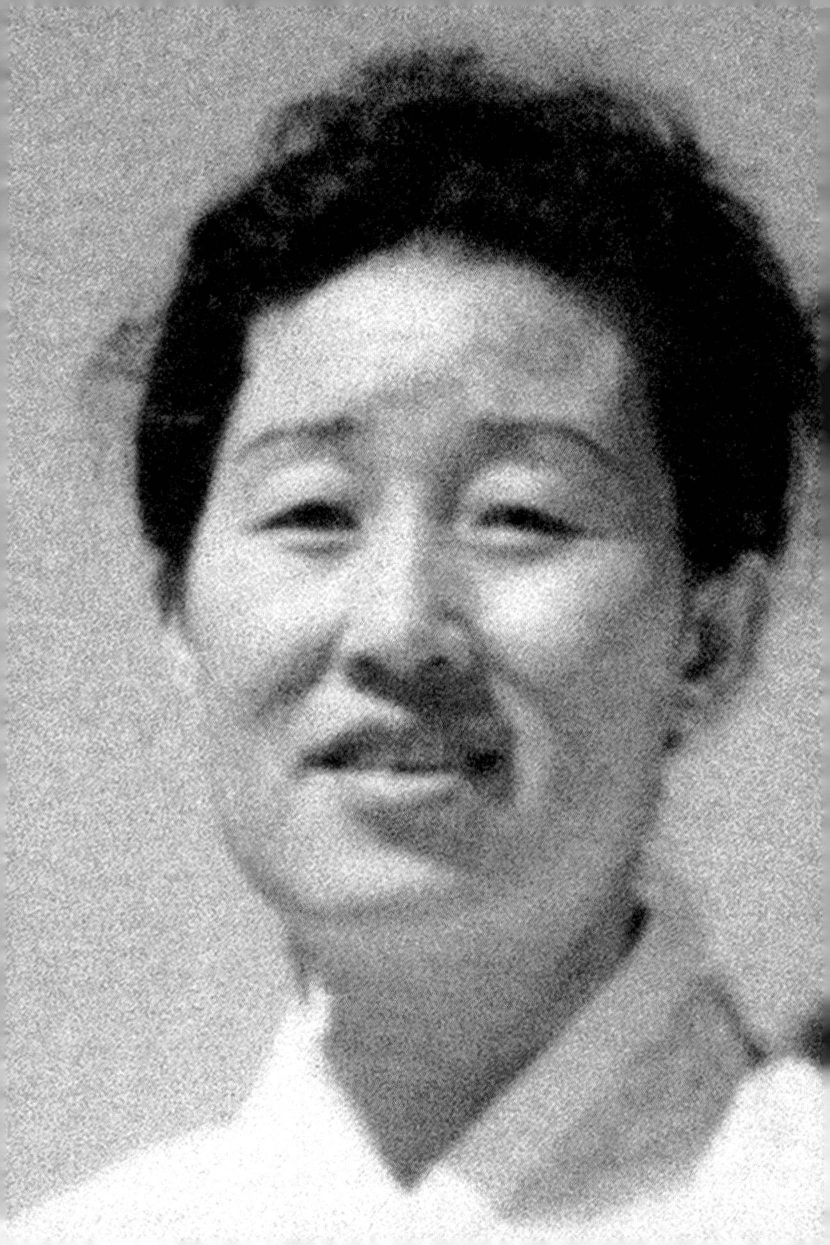

i did not surrender

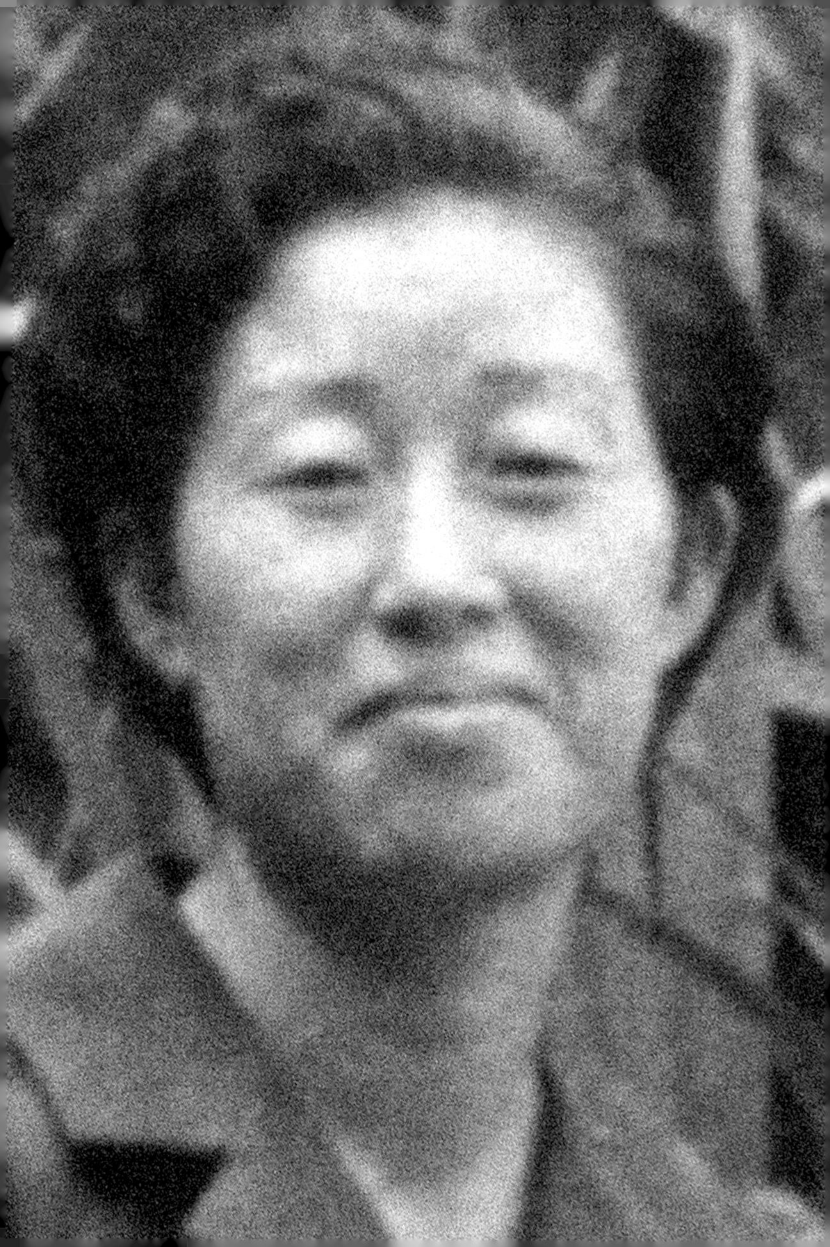

i feared not fear

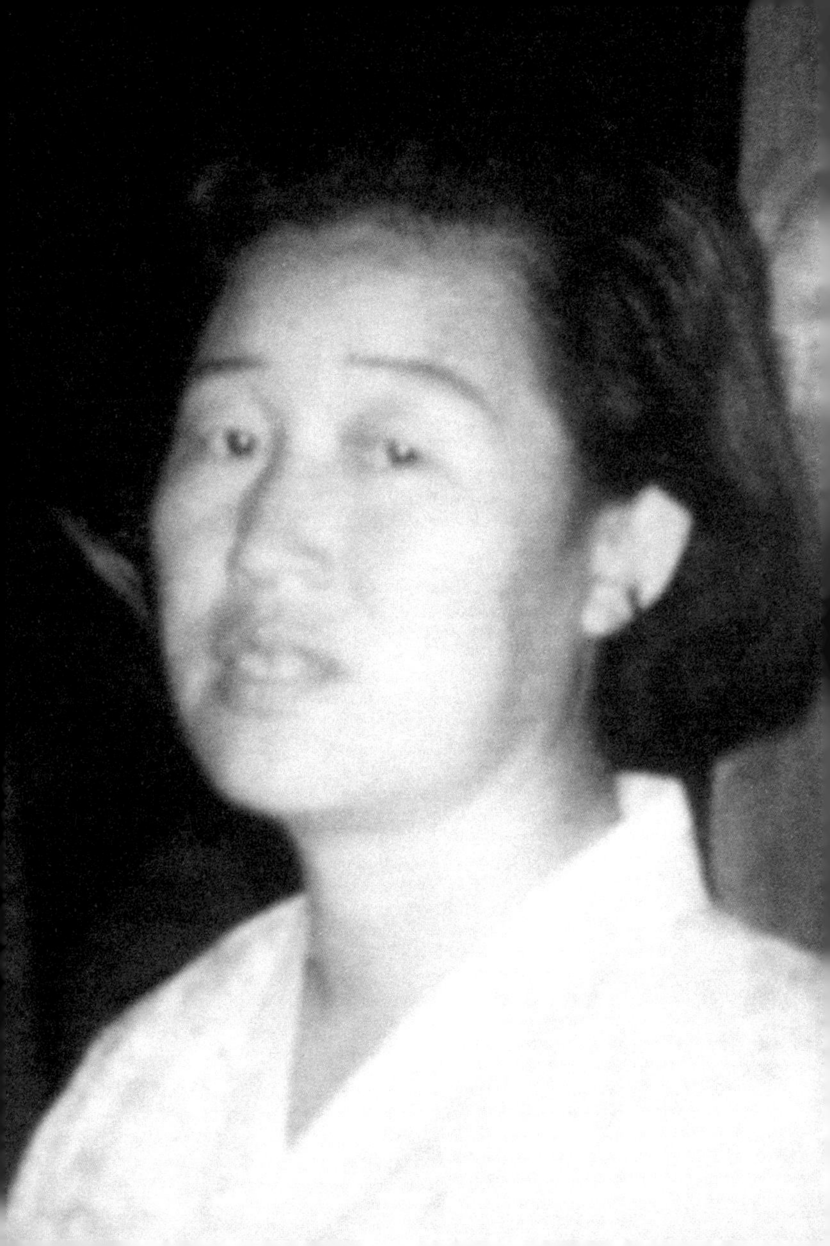

i was everyone

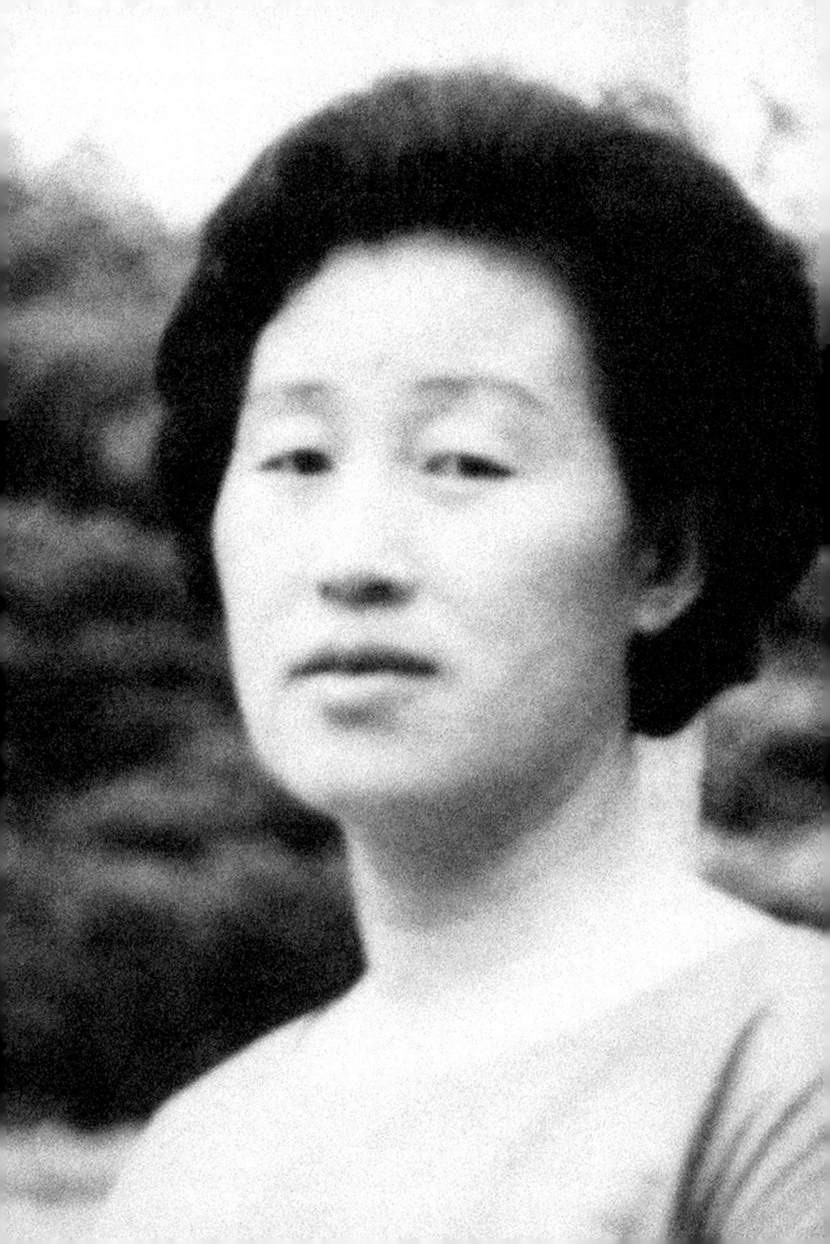

i often wanted

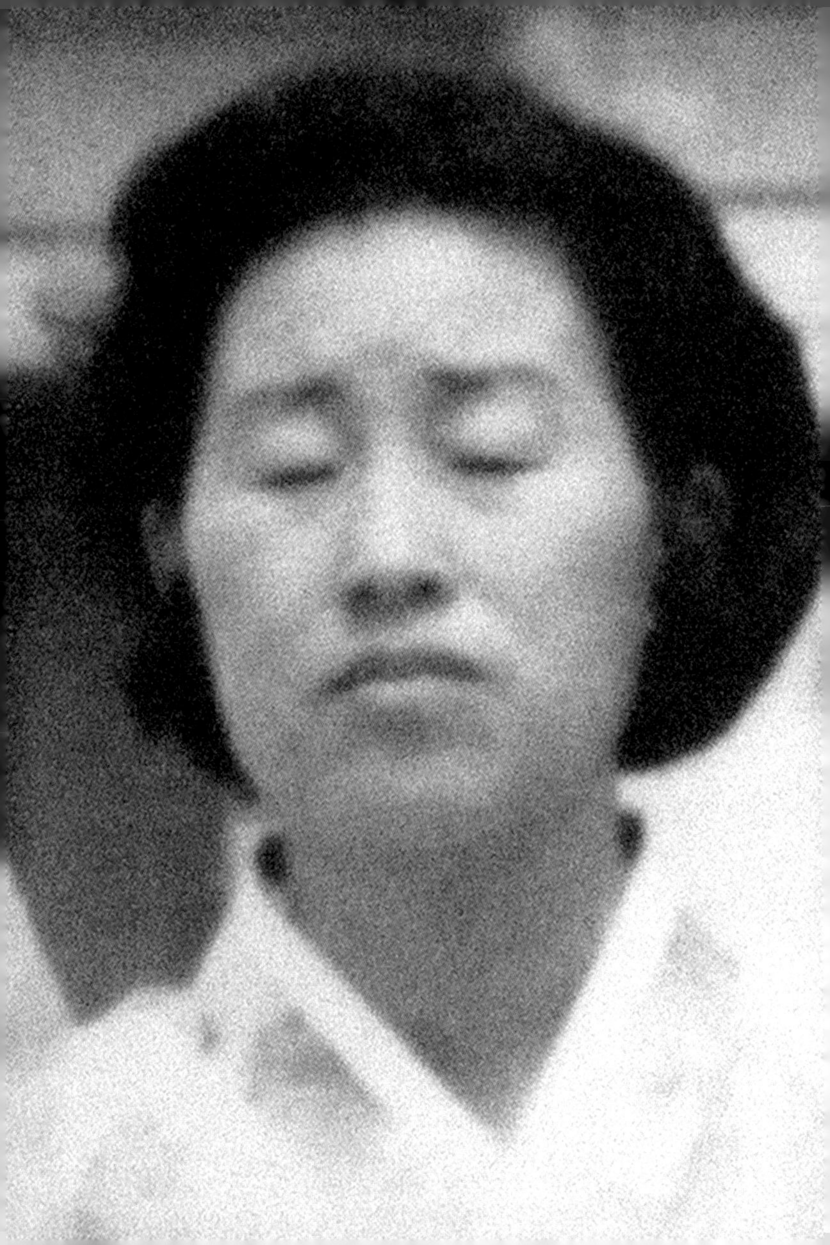

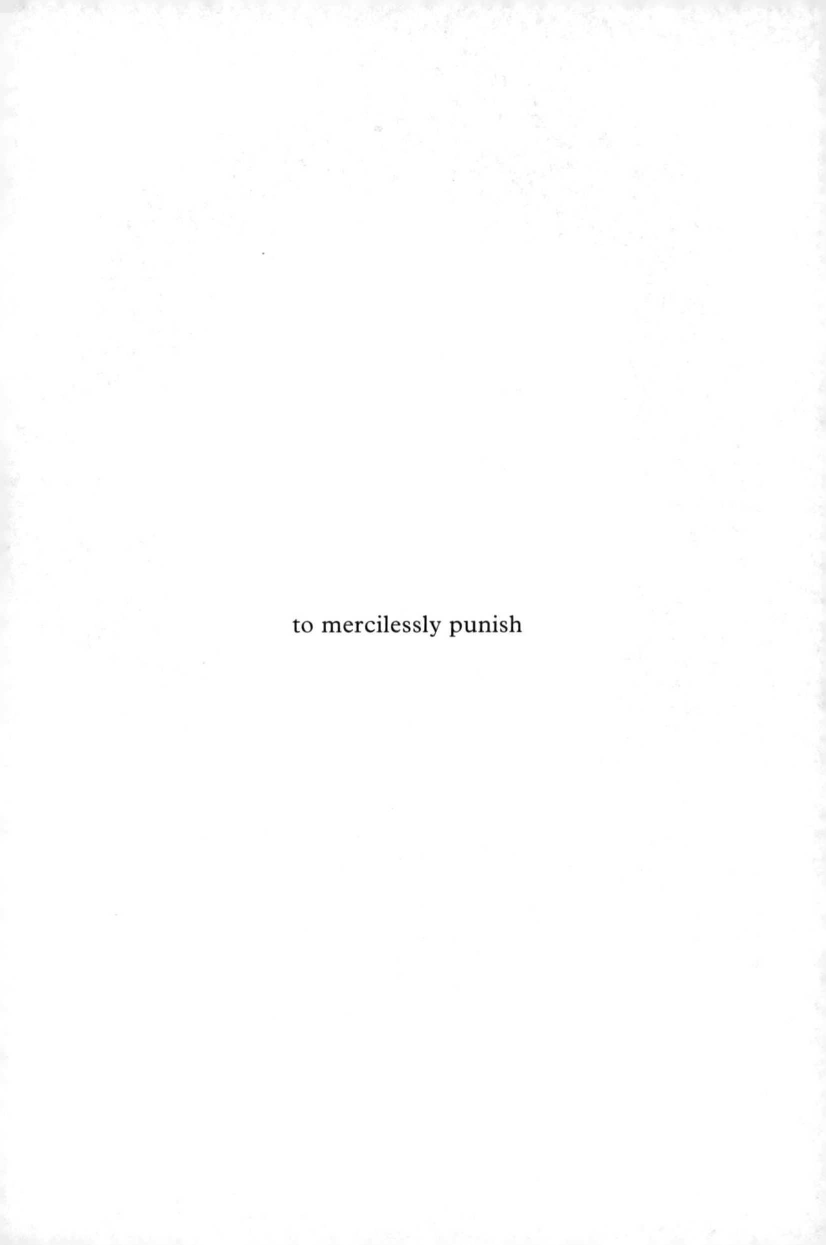

to mercilessly punish

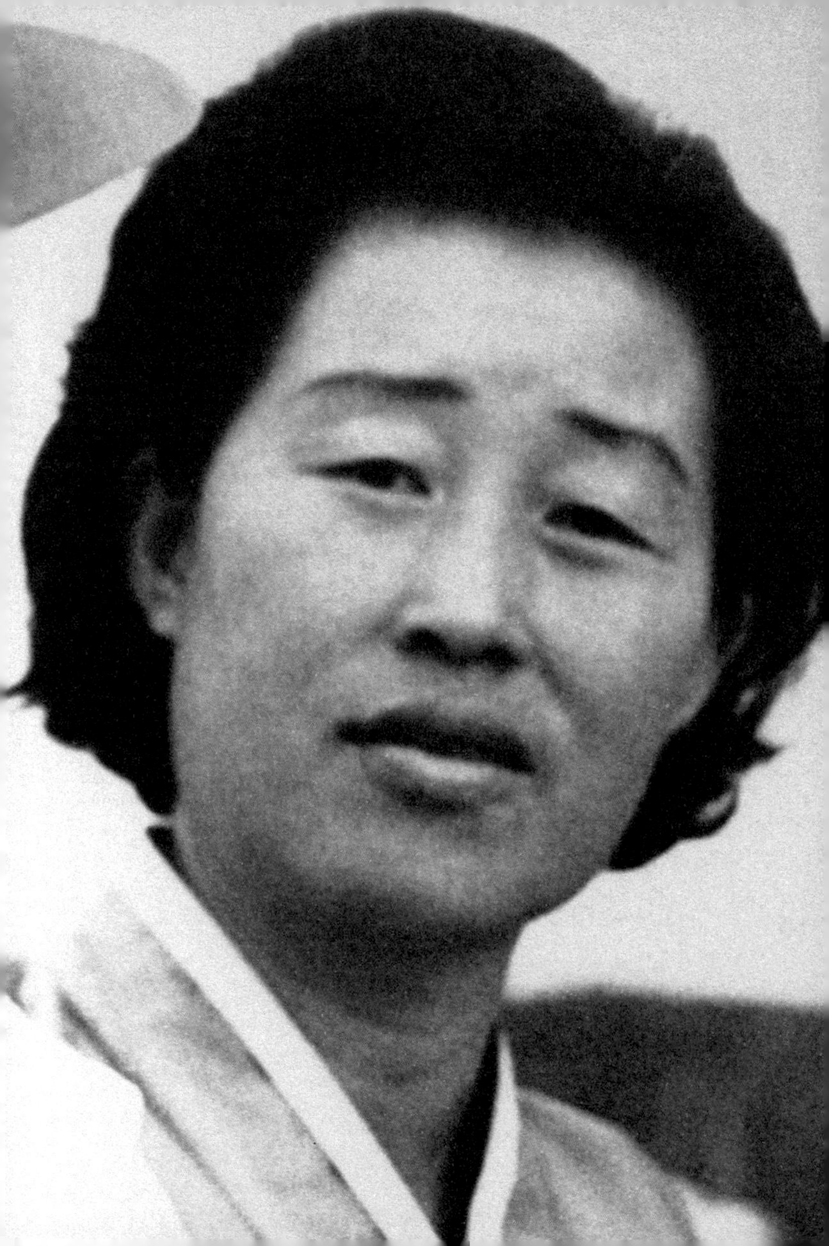

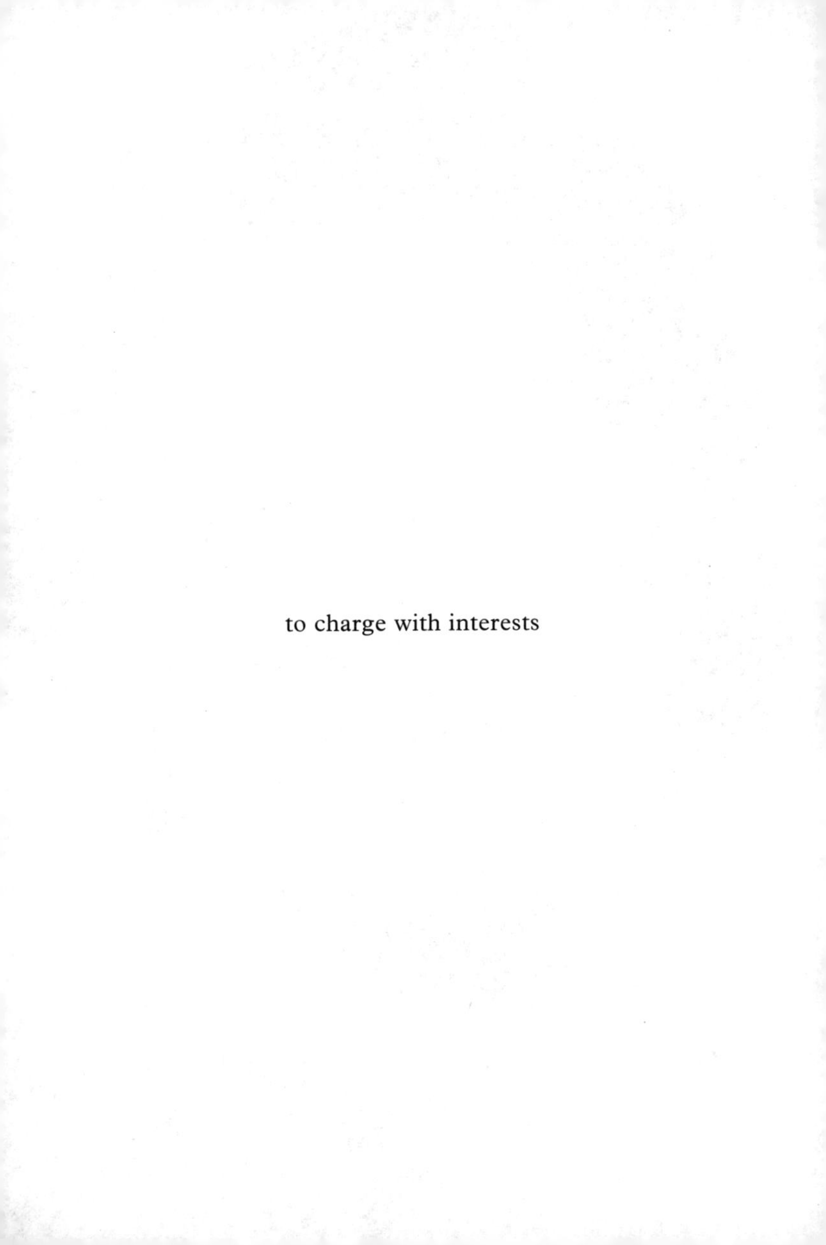

to charge with interests

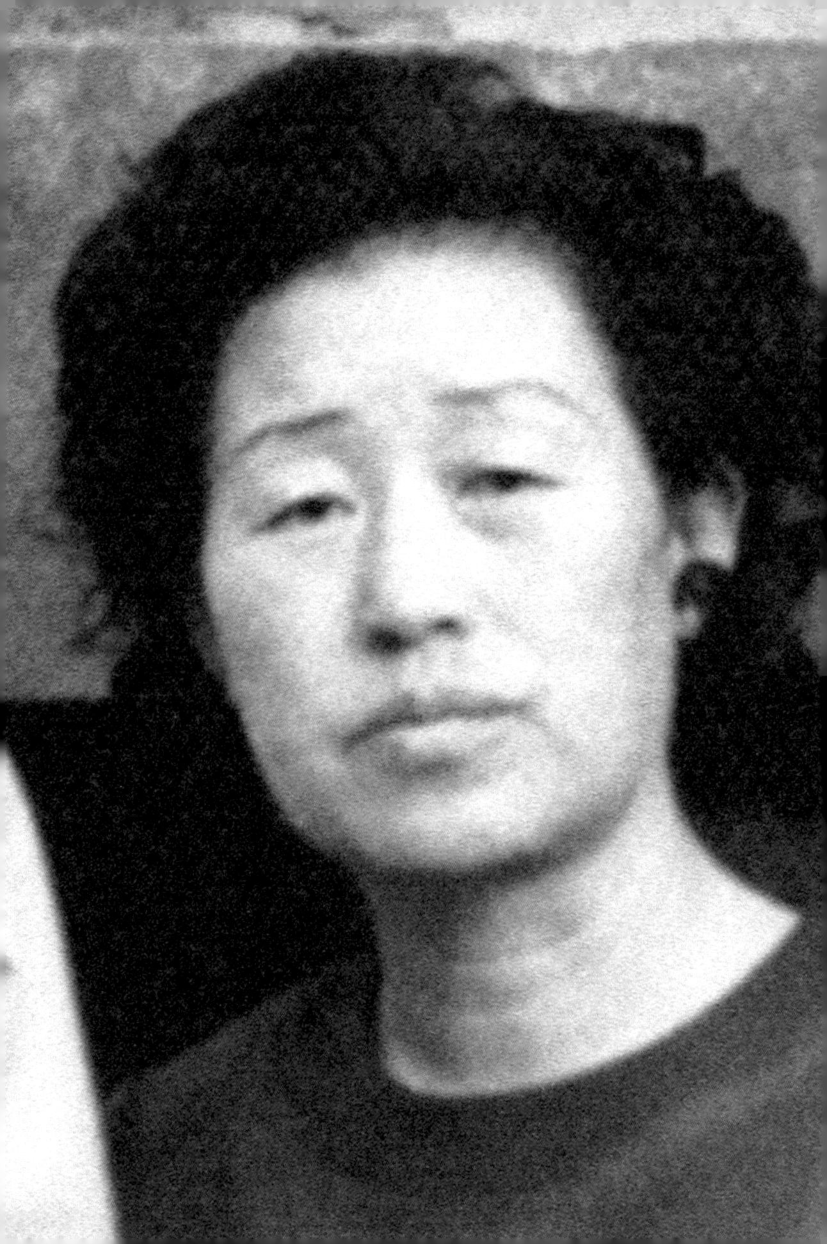

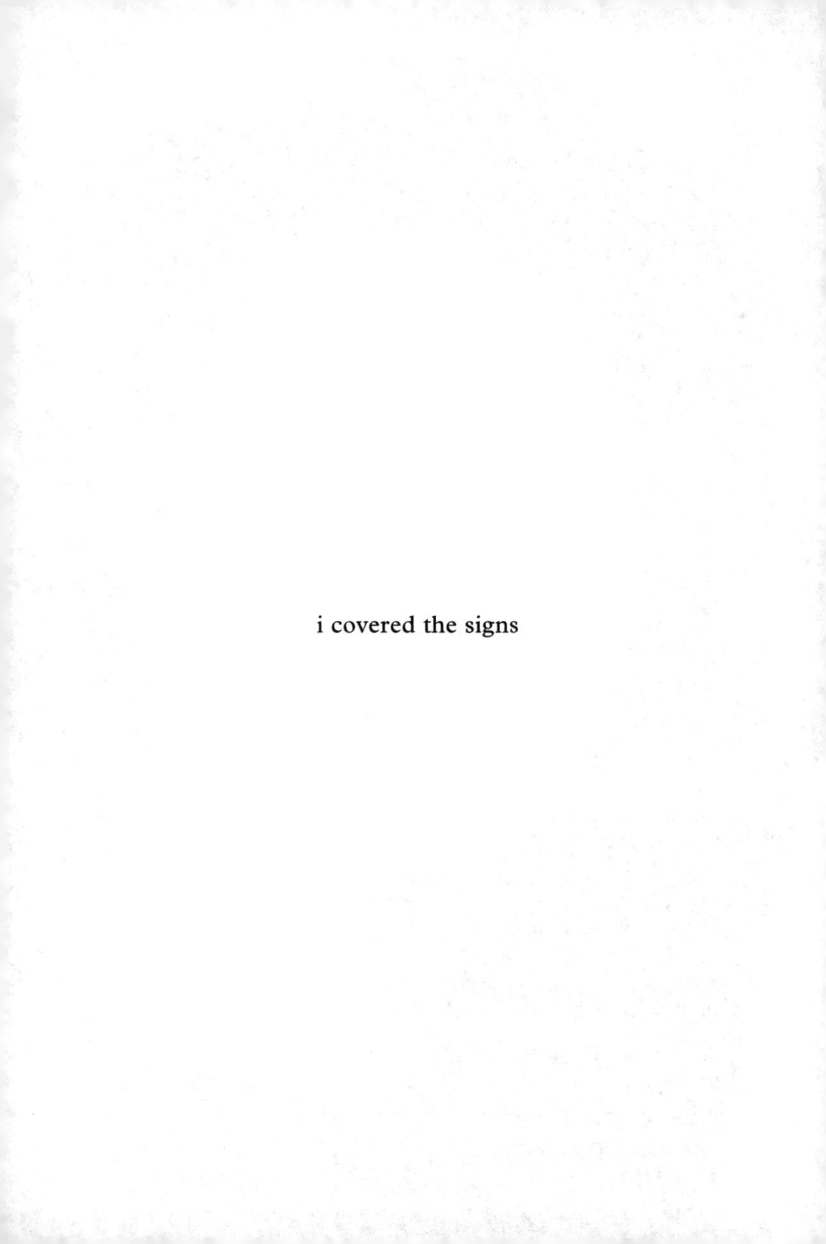

i covered the signs

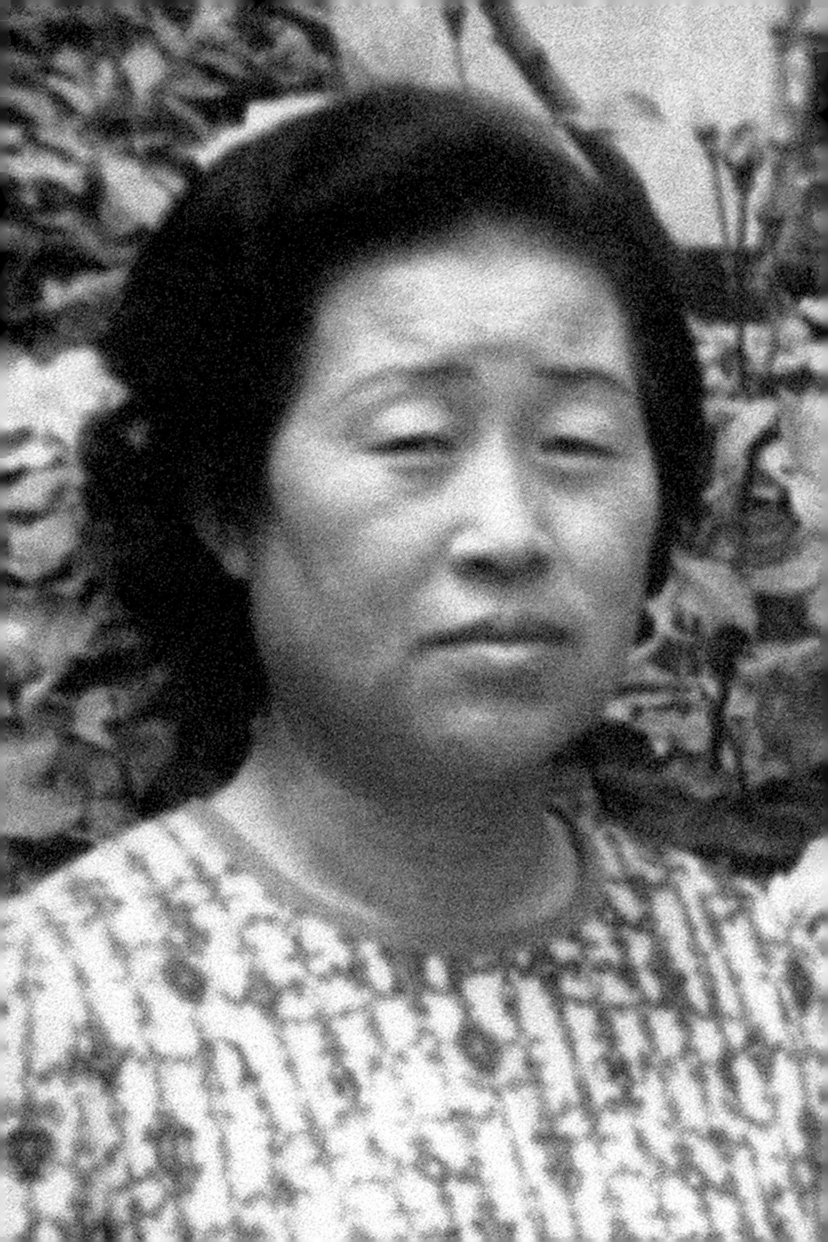

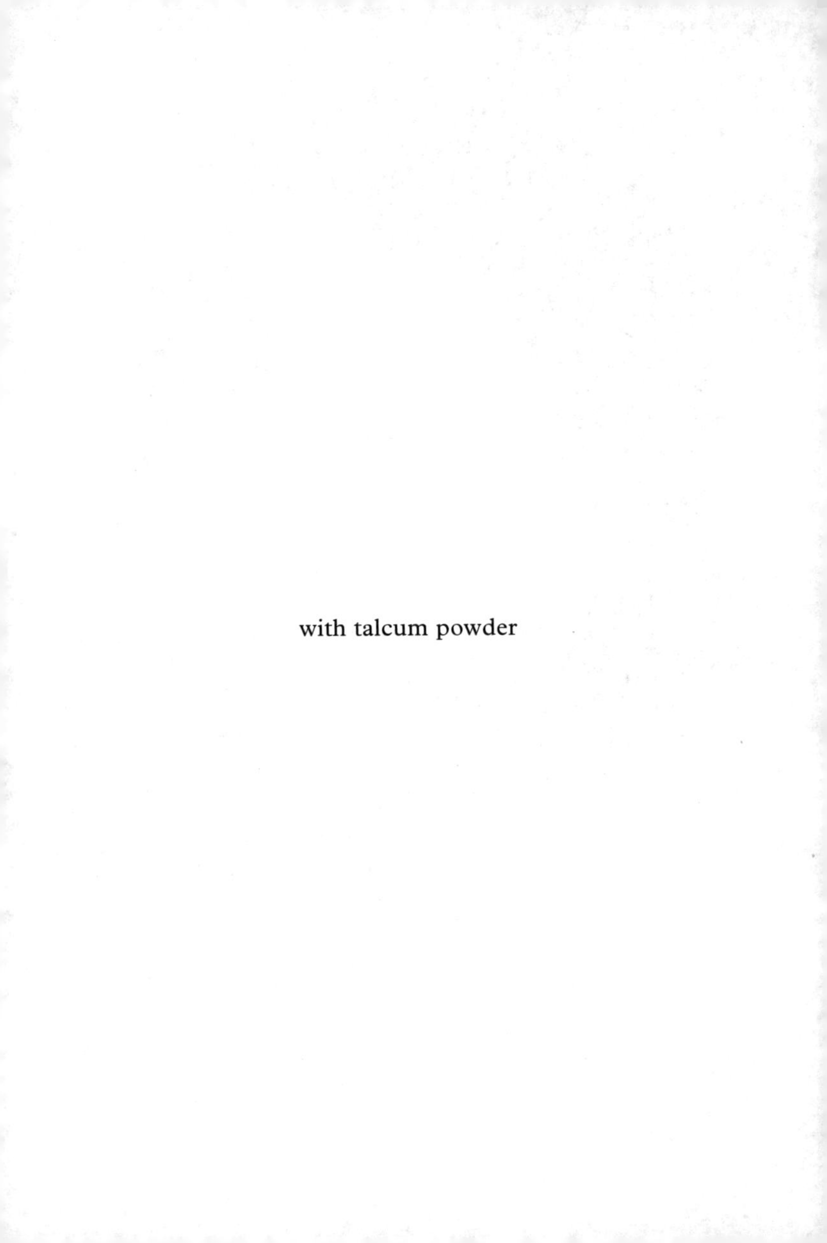

with talcum powder

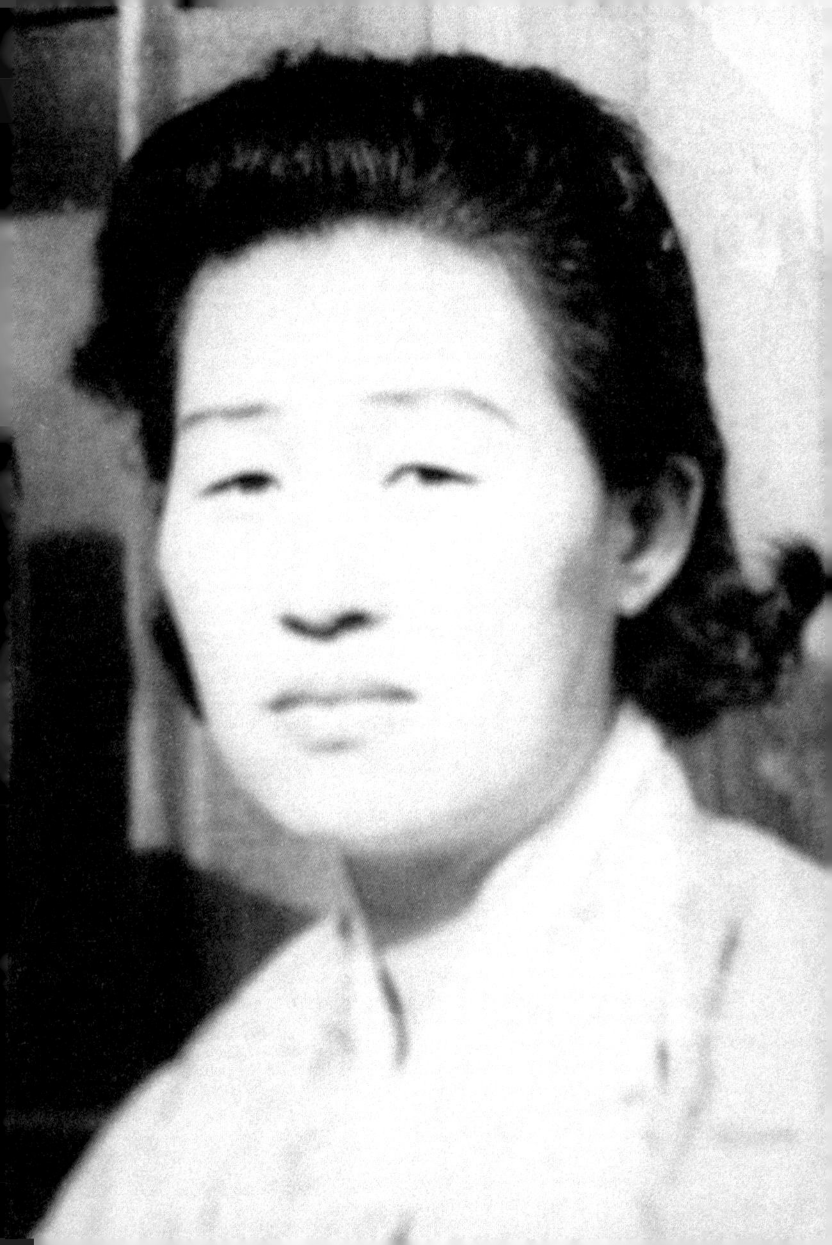

i fixed the drama

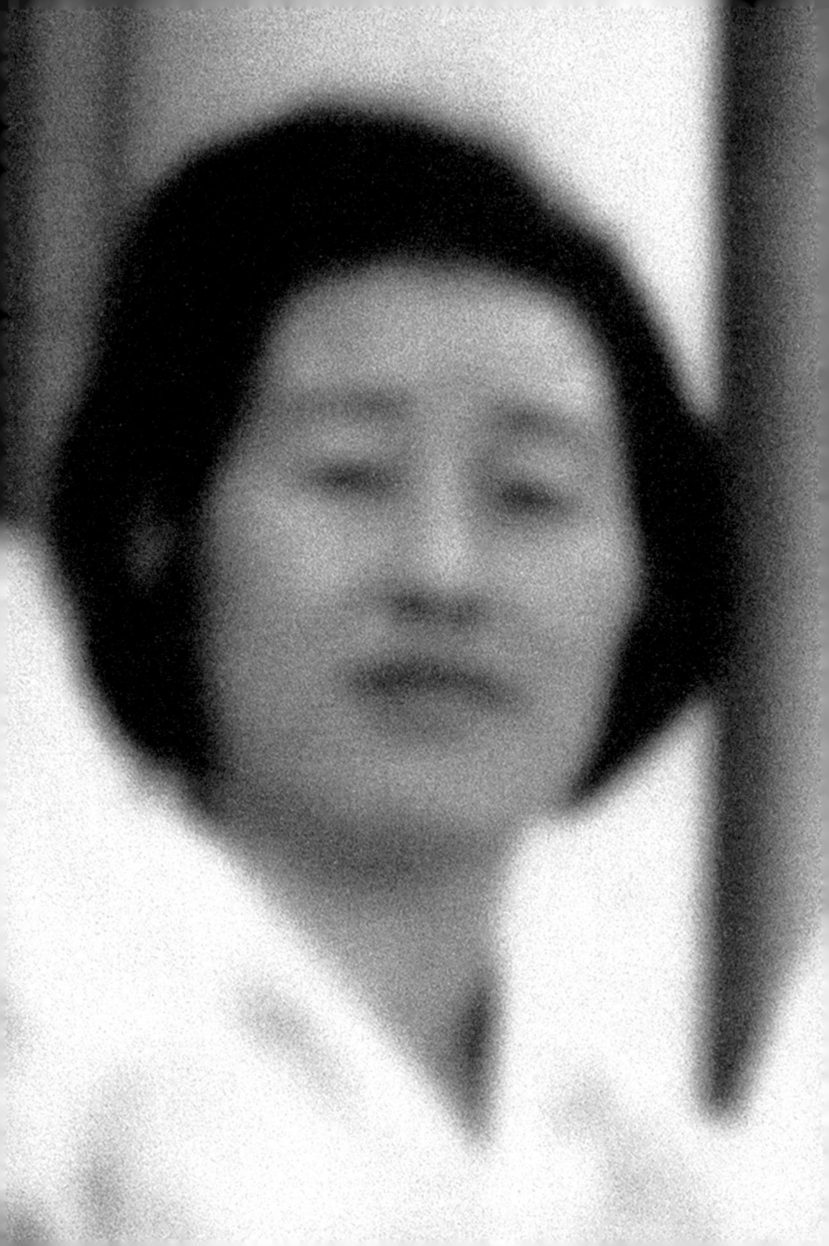

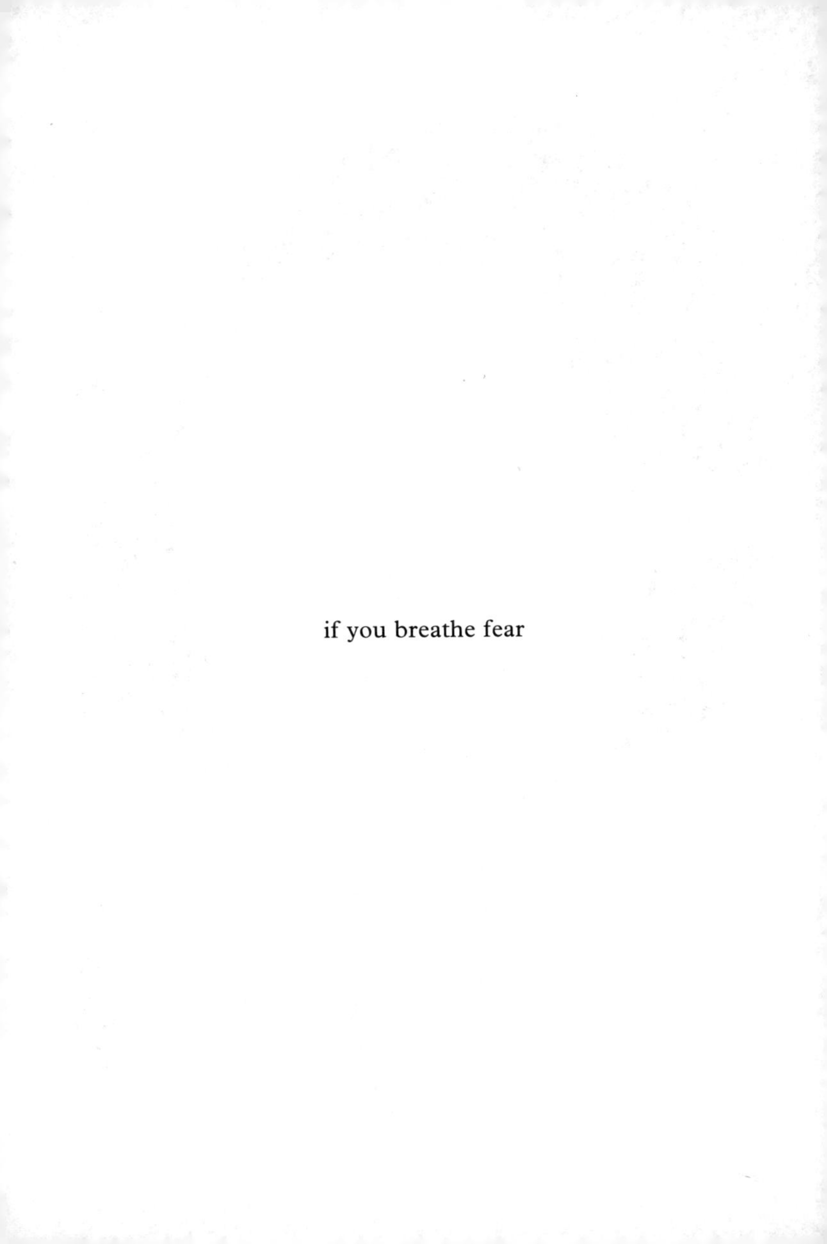

if you breathe fear

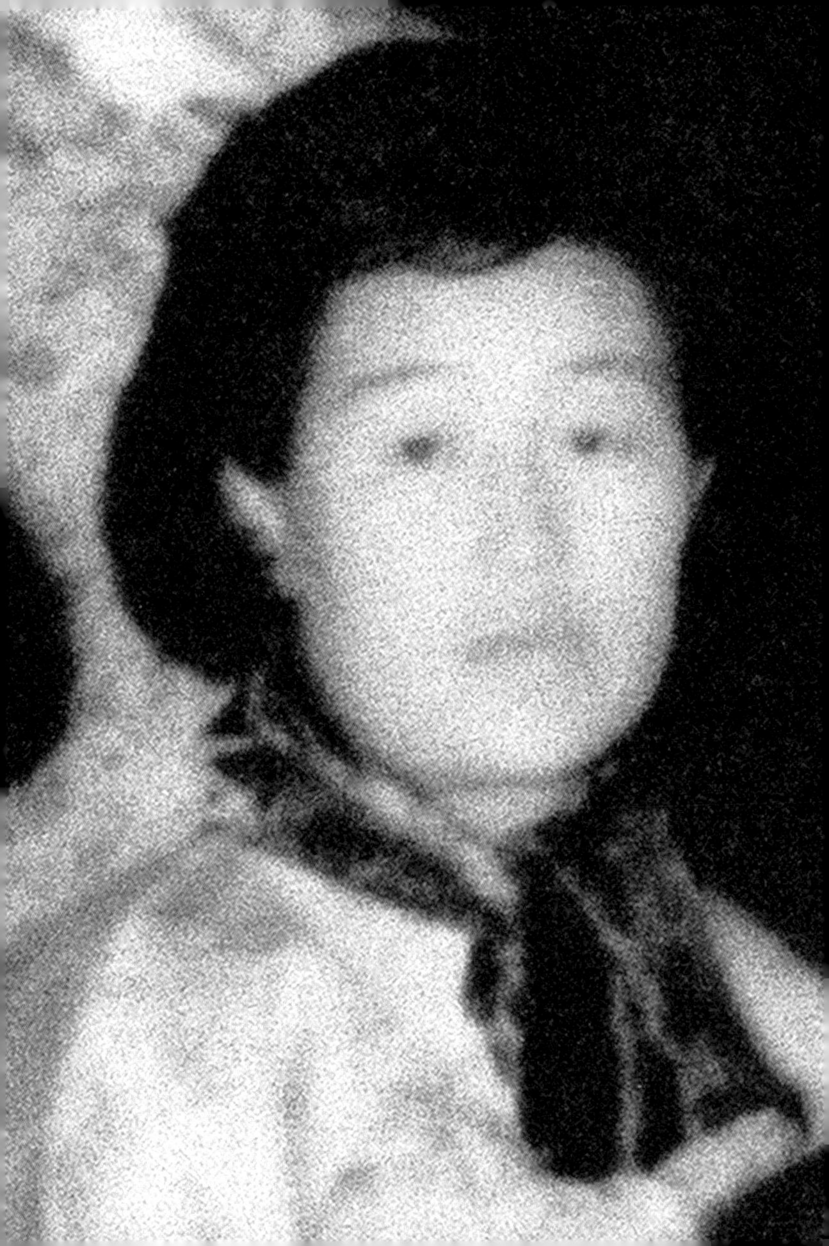

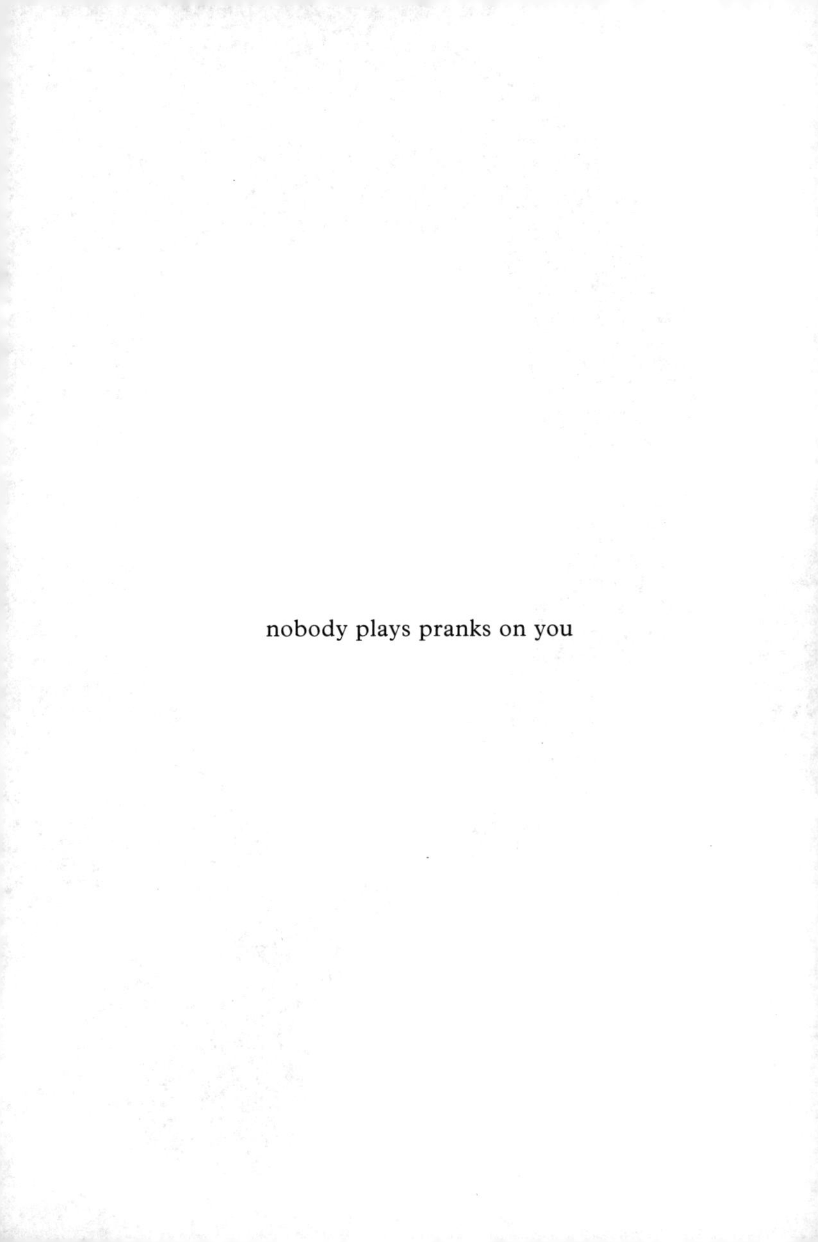

nobody plays pranks on you

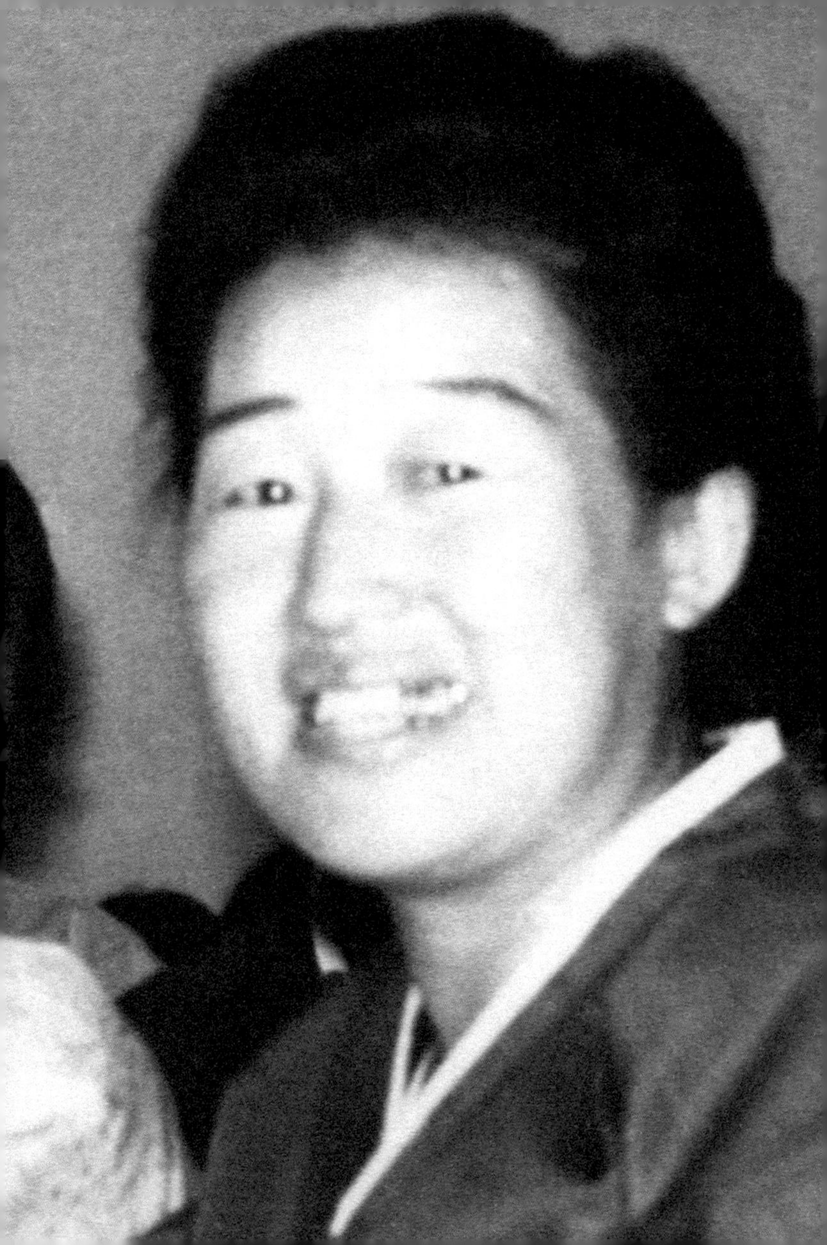

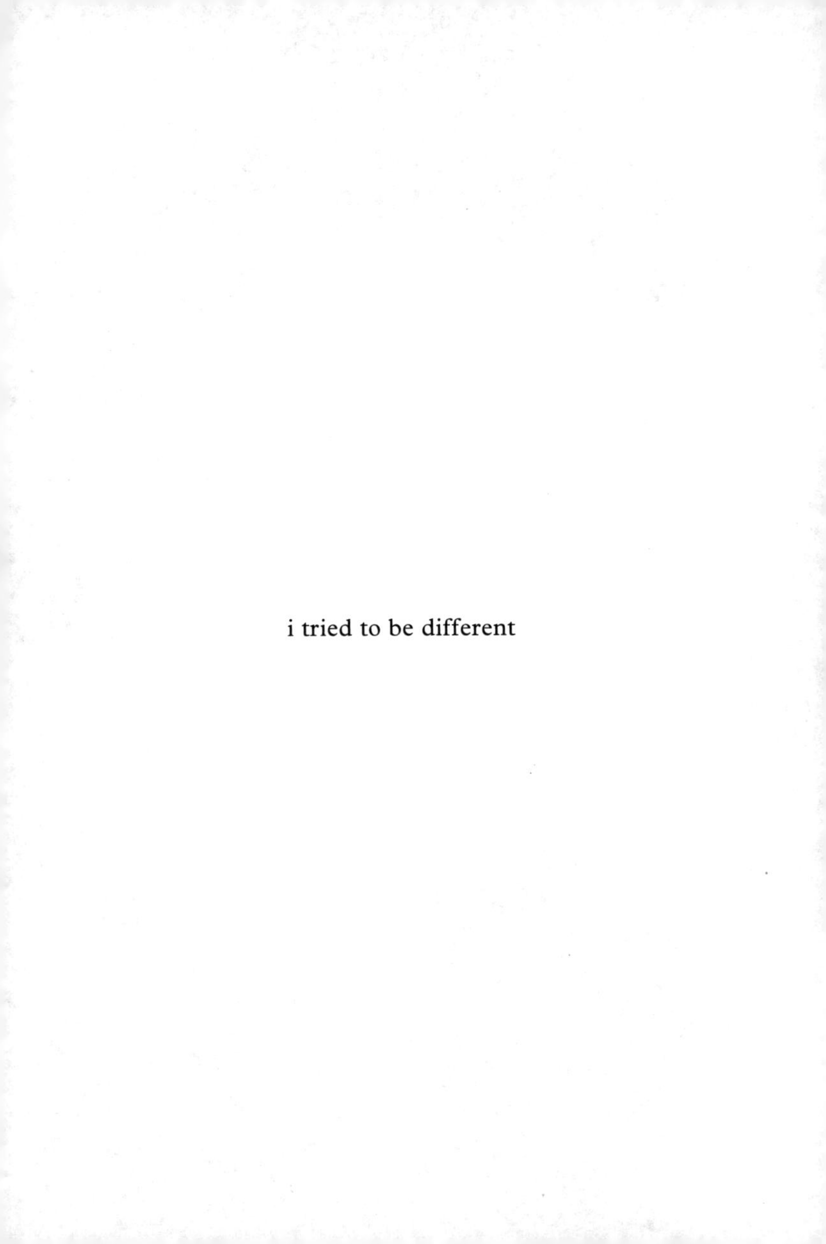

i tried to be different

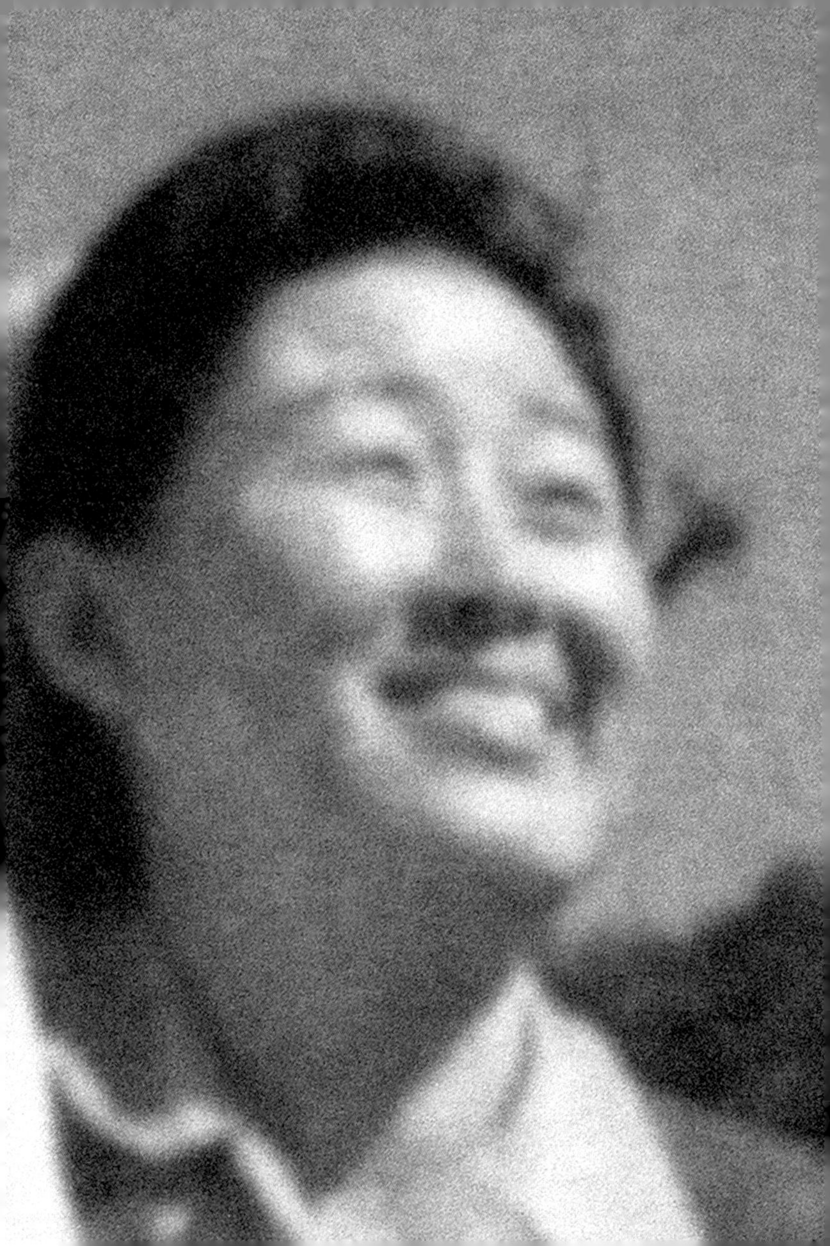

to be fully aware

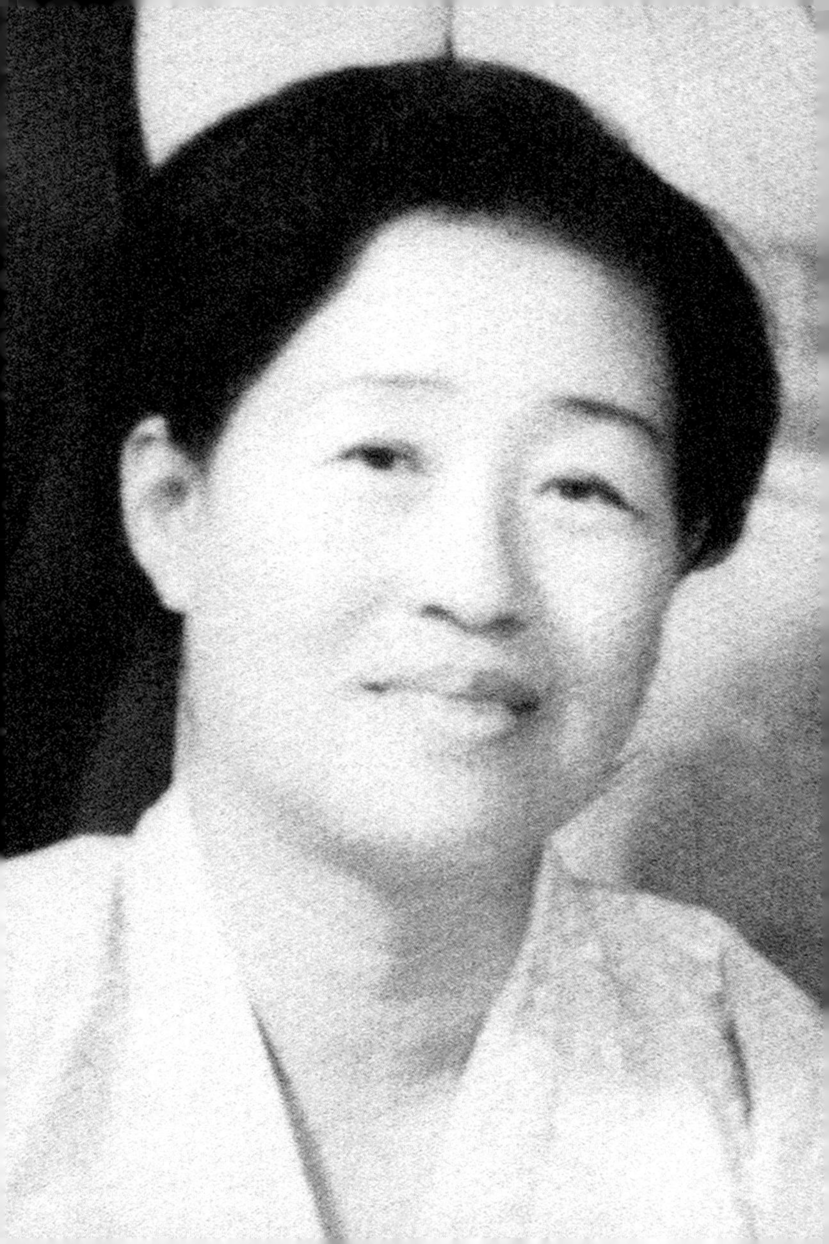

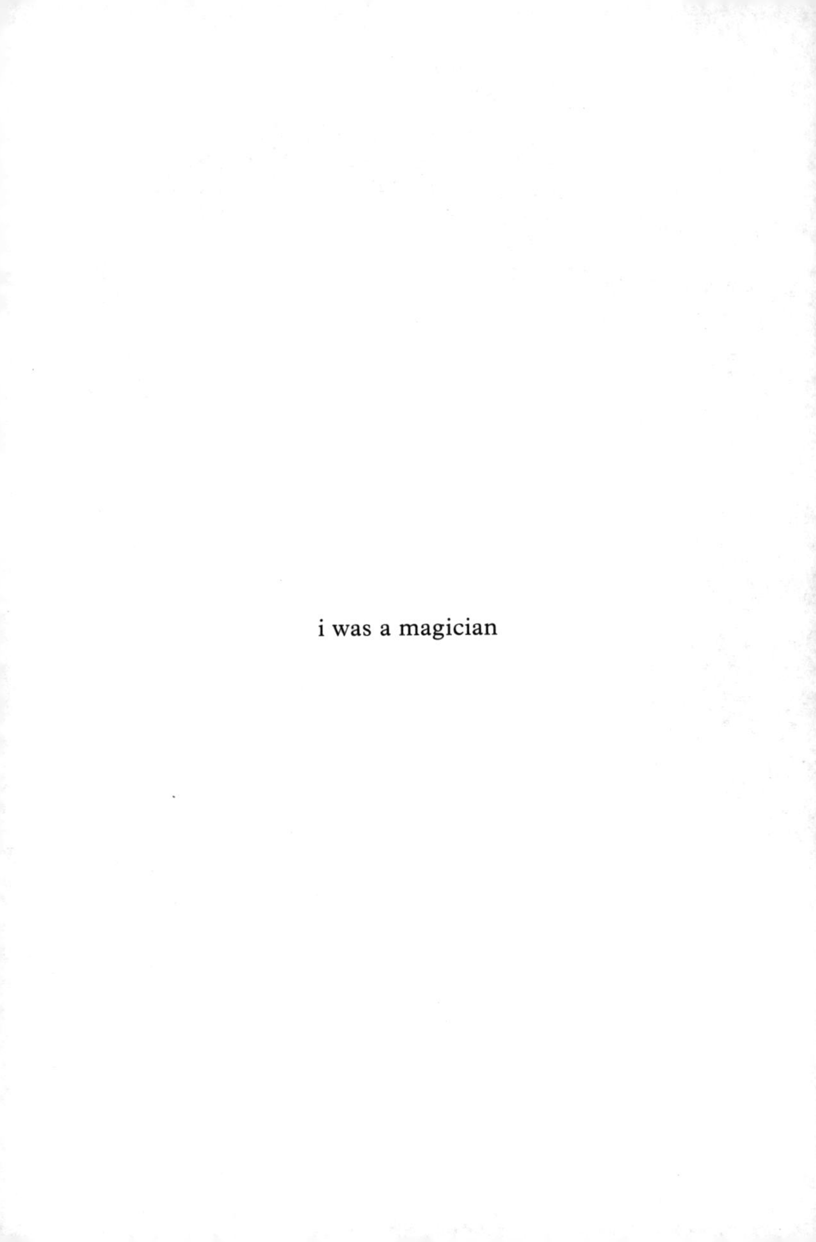

i was a magician

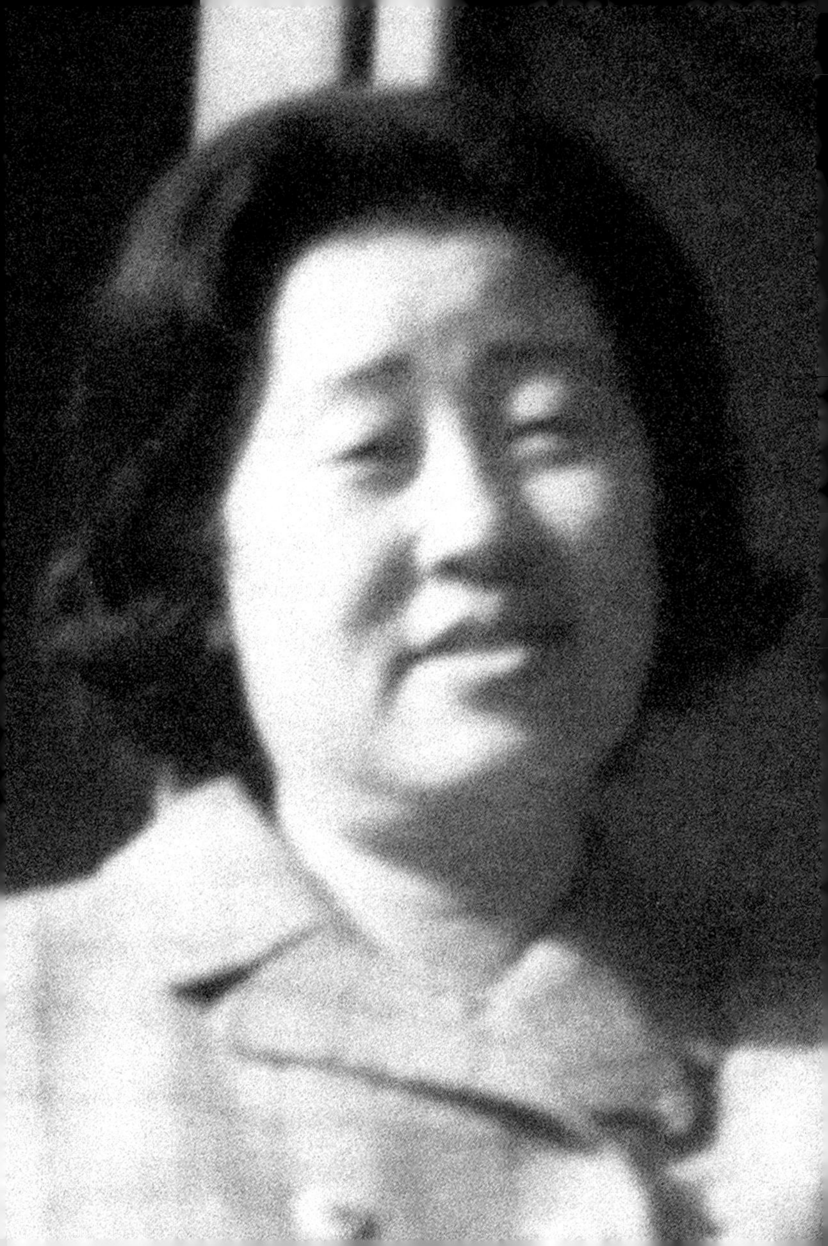

whose tricks did not work

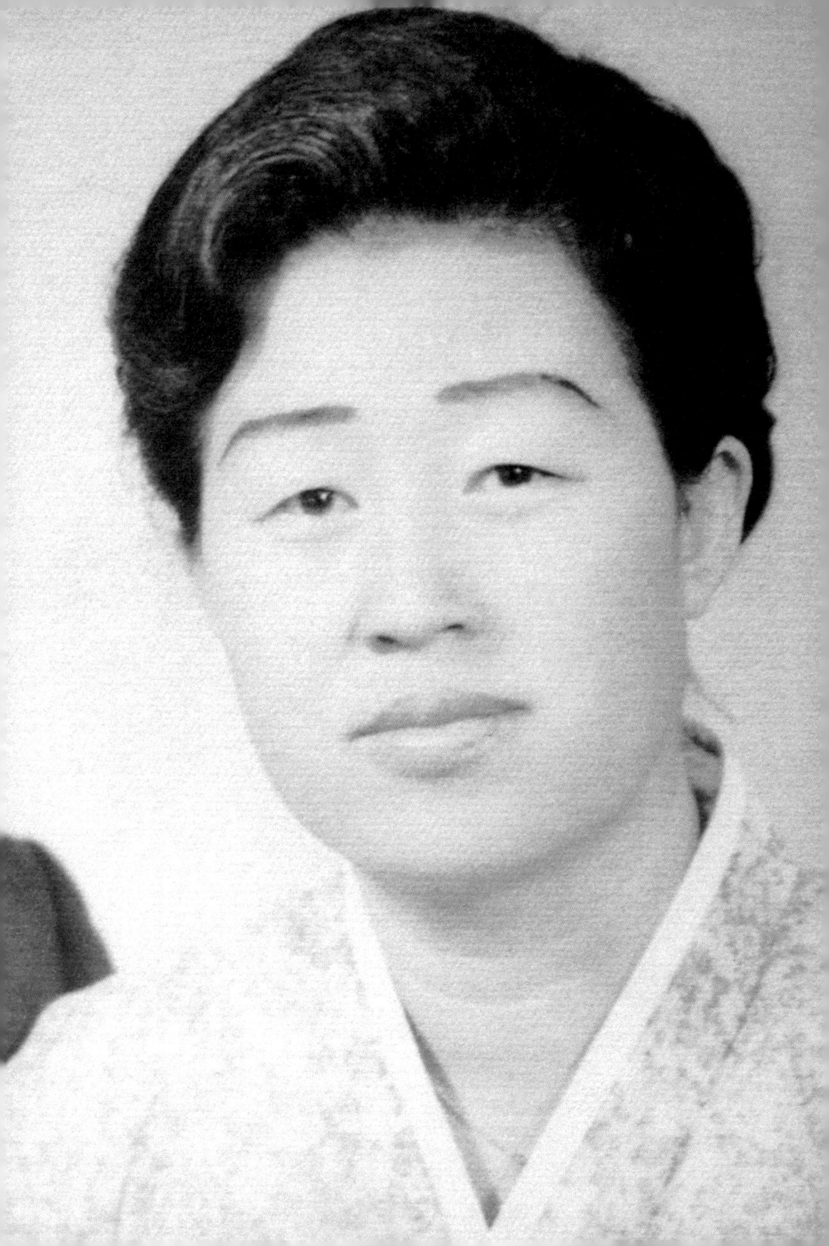

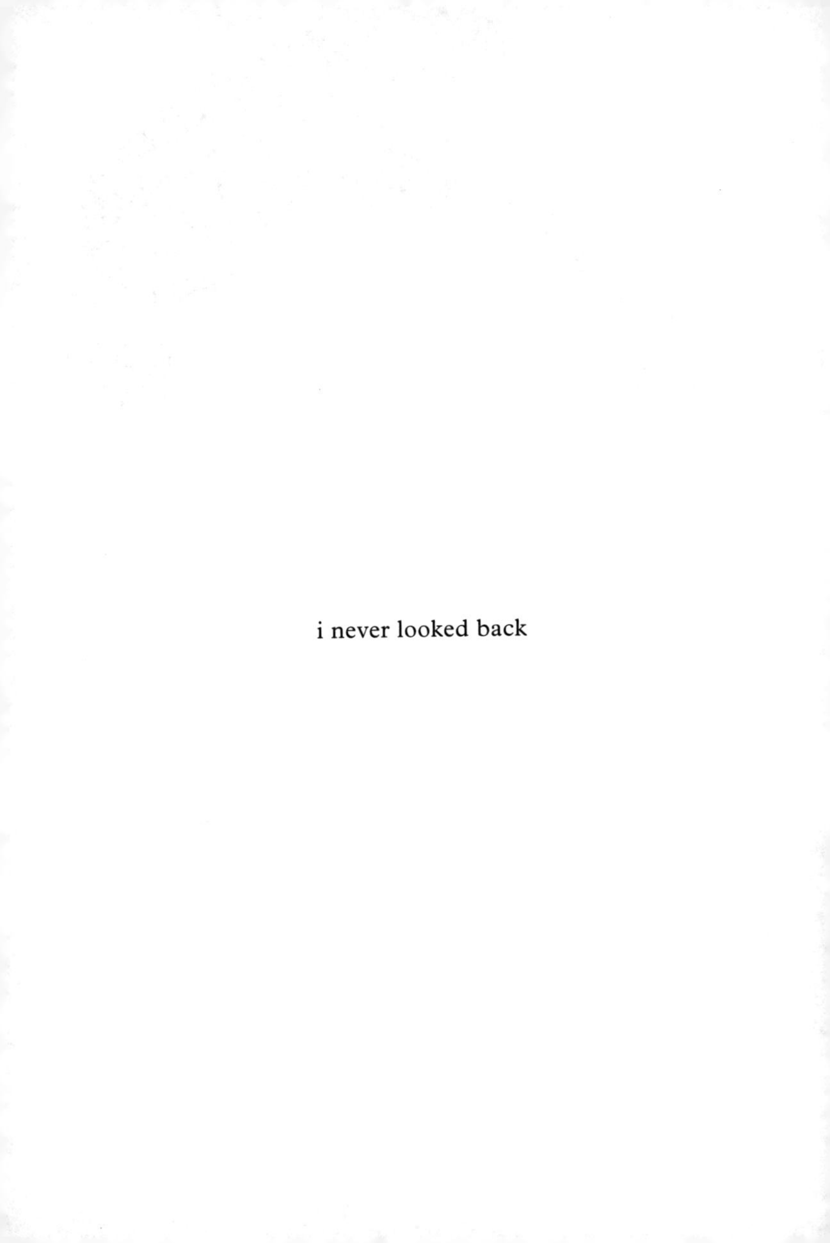

i never looked back

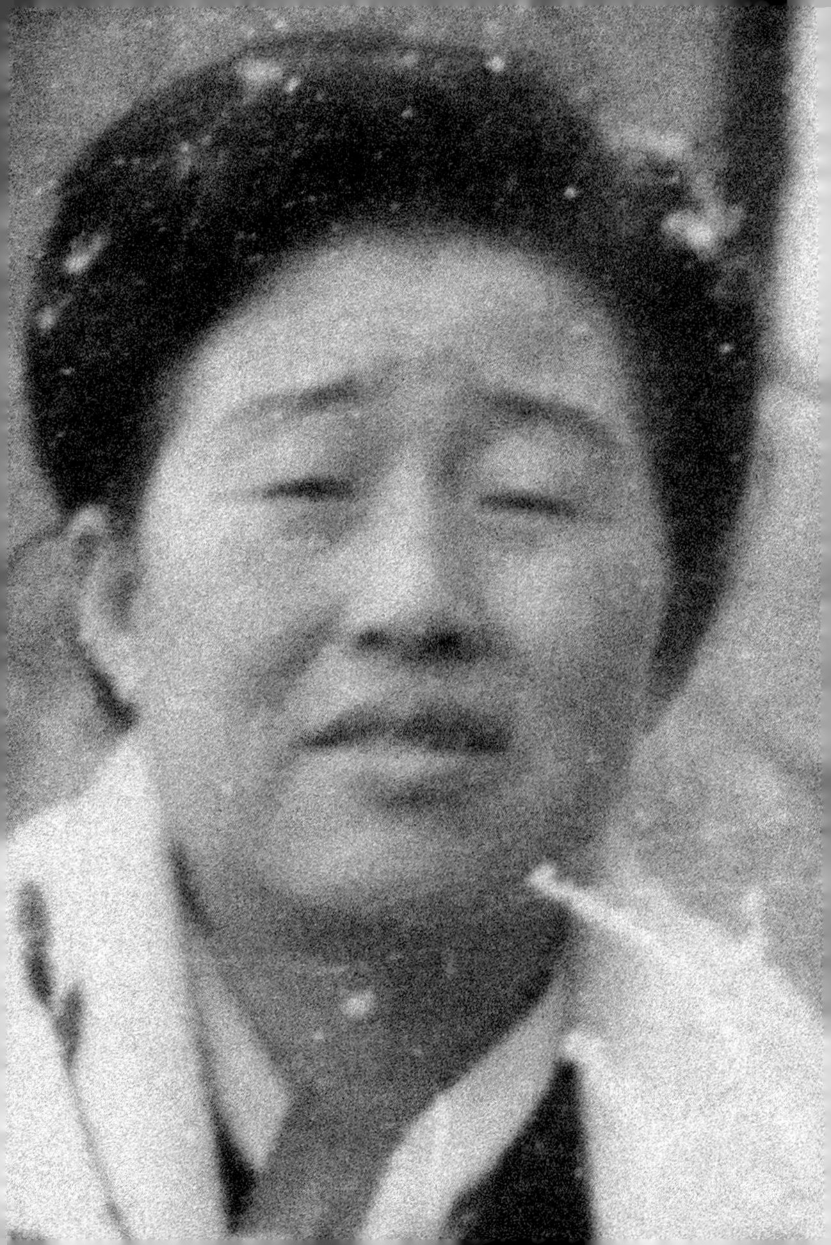

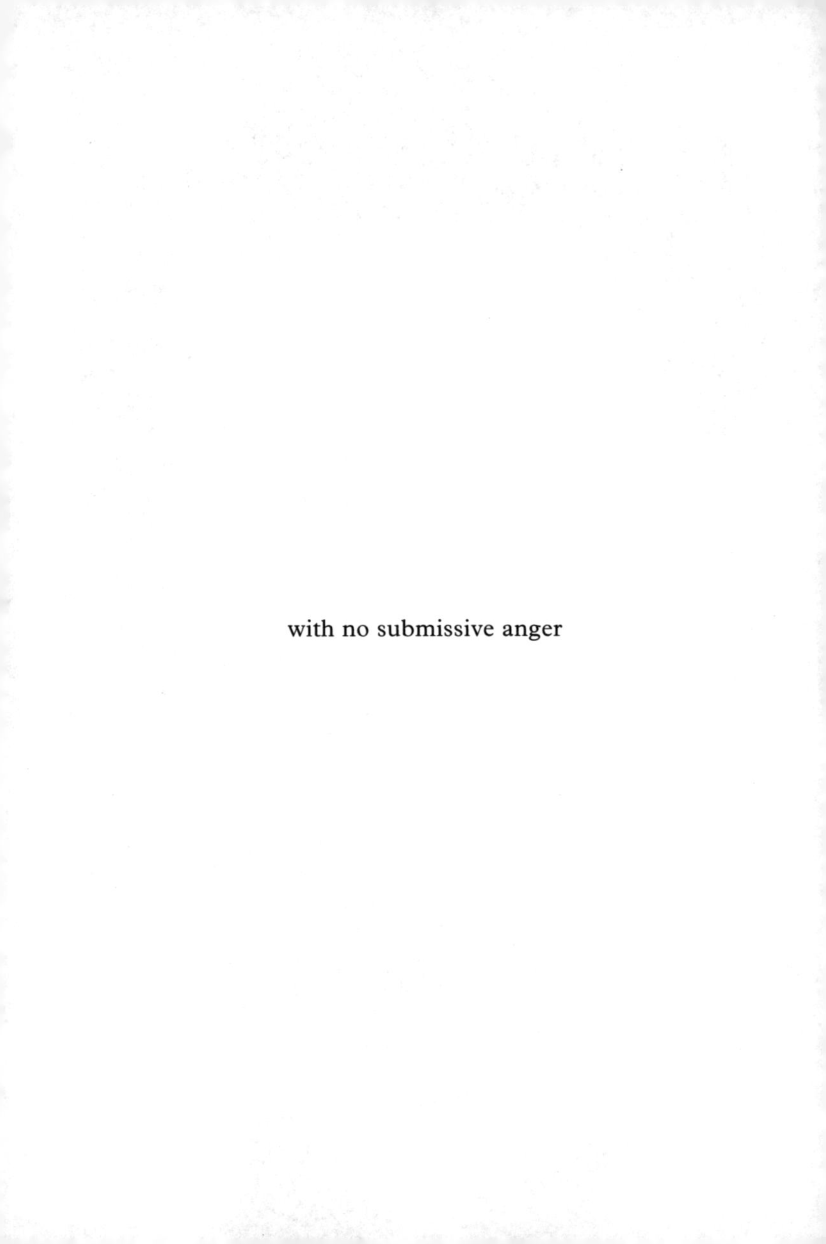

with no submissive anger

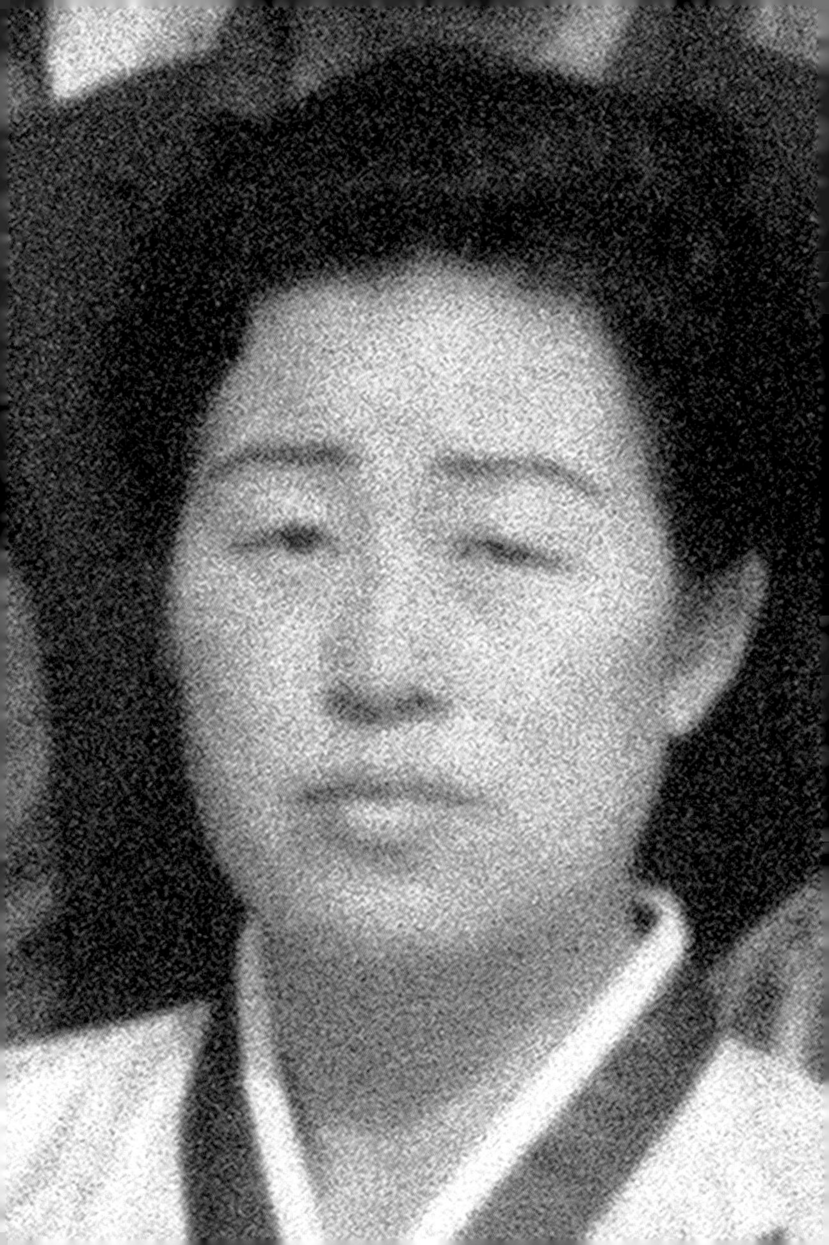

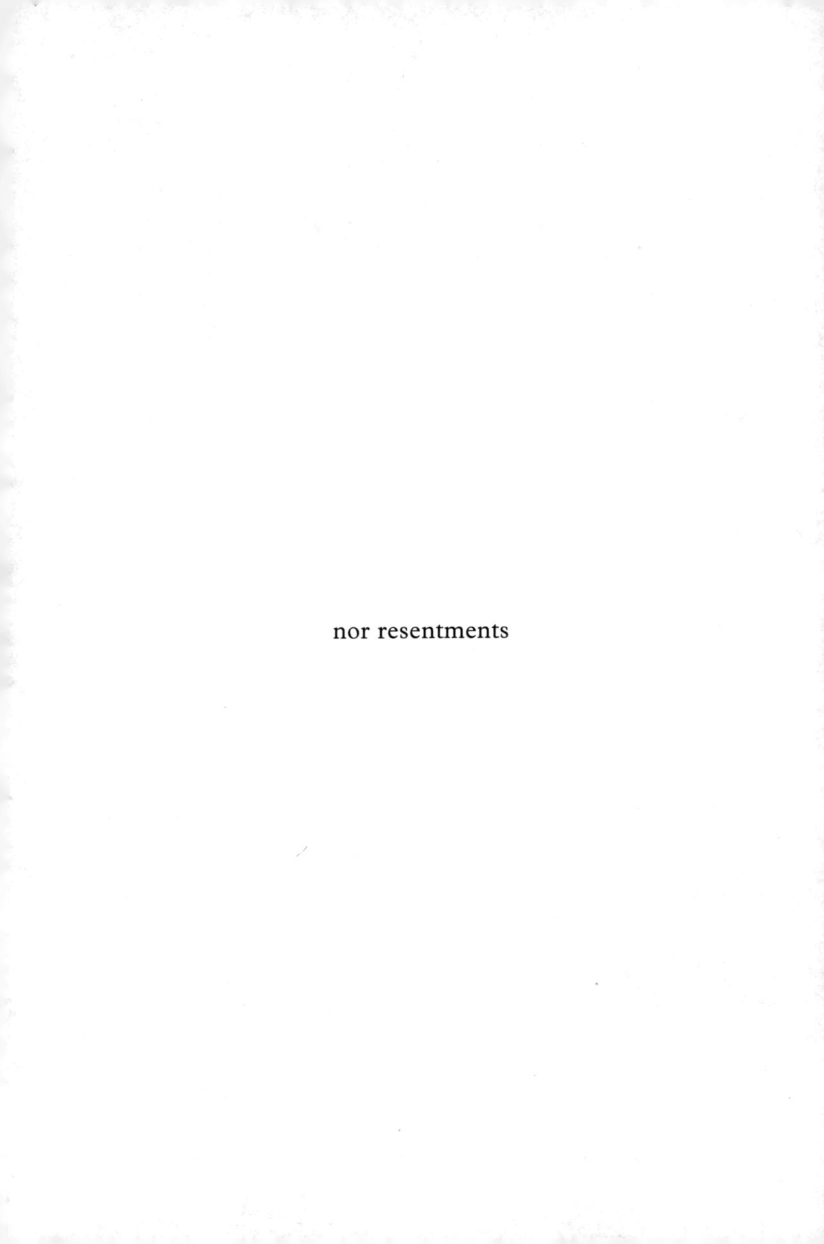

nor resentments

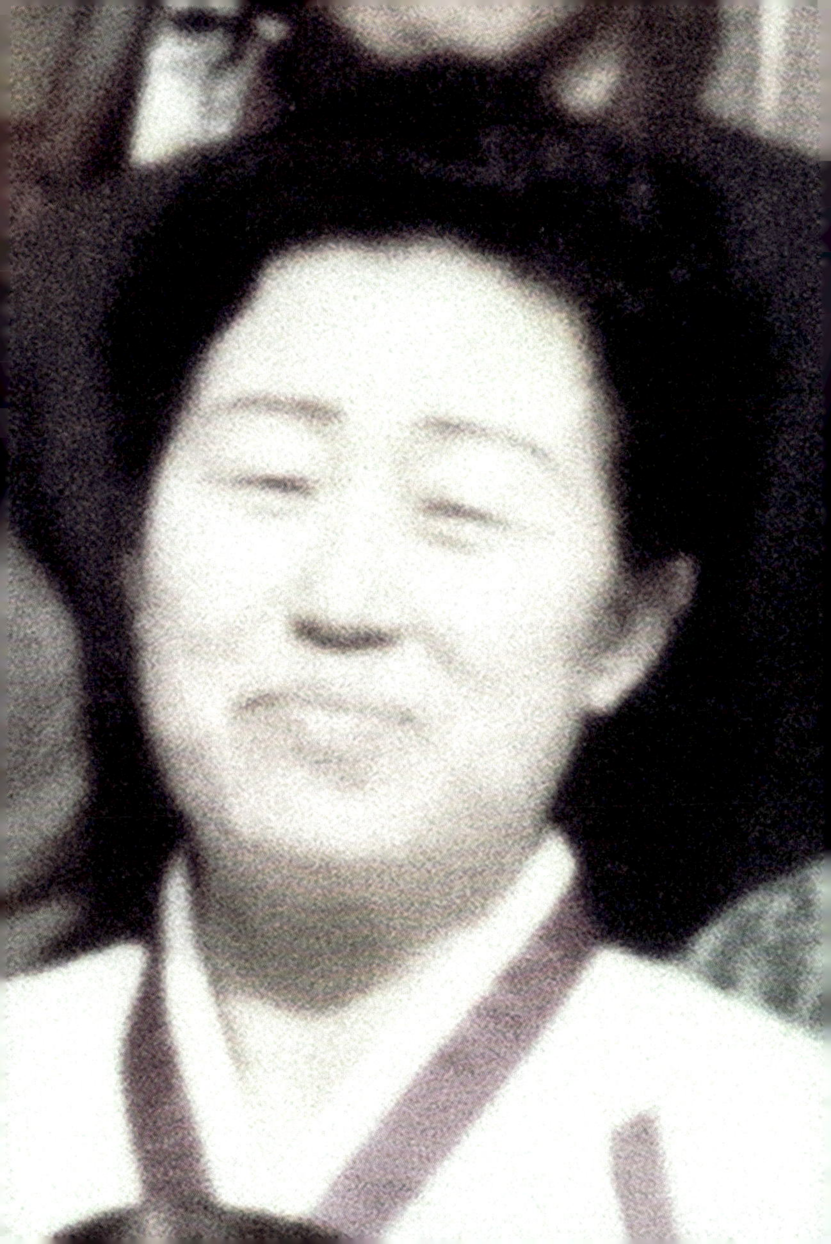

i owned up to my mistakes

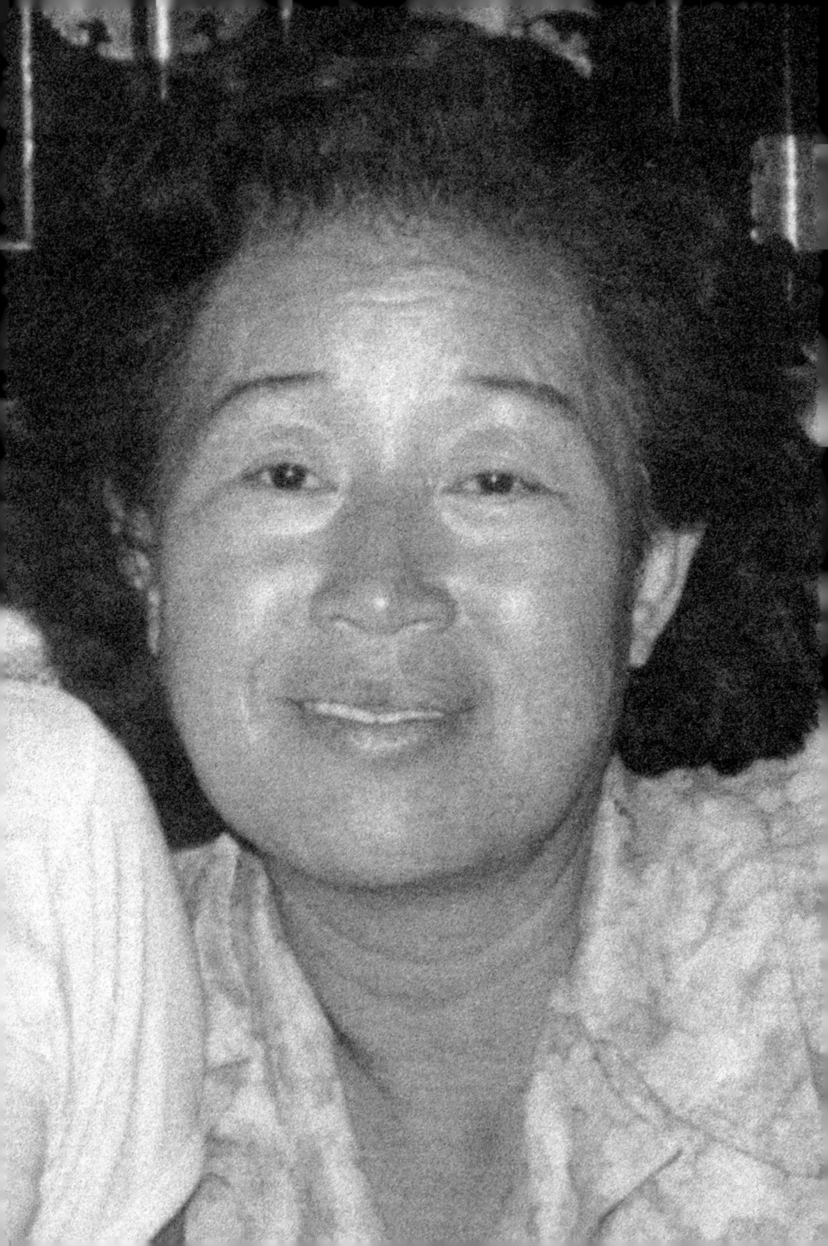

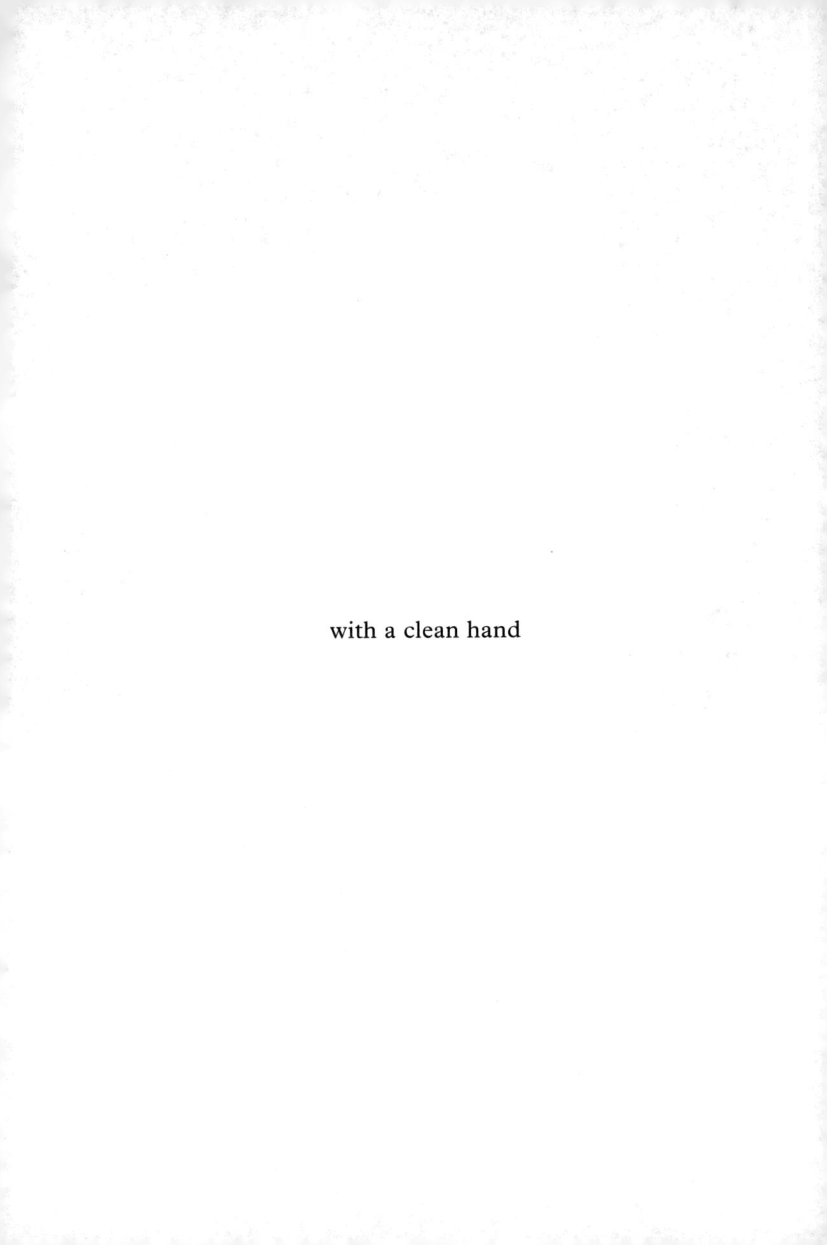

with a clean hand

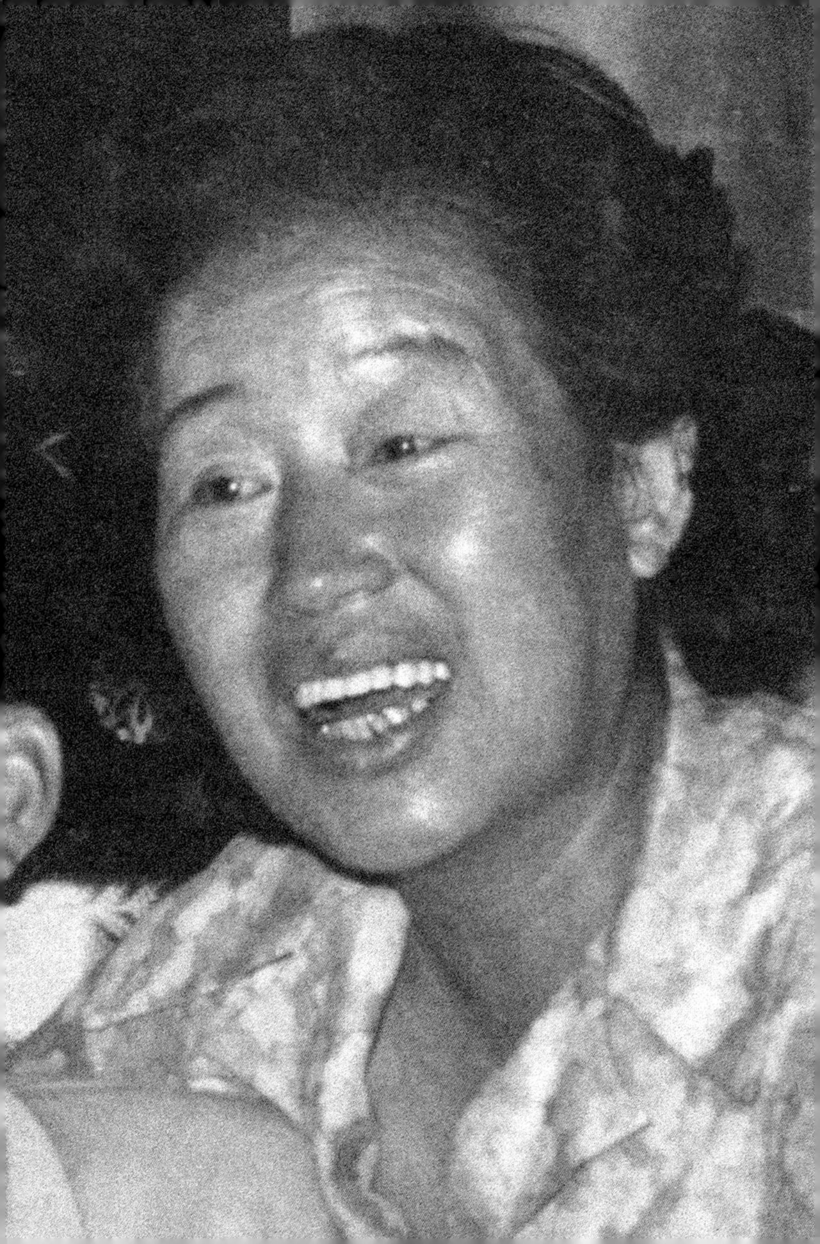

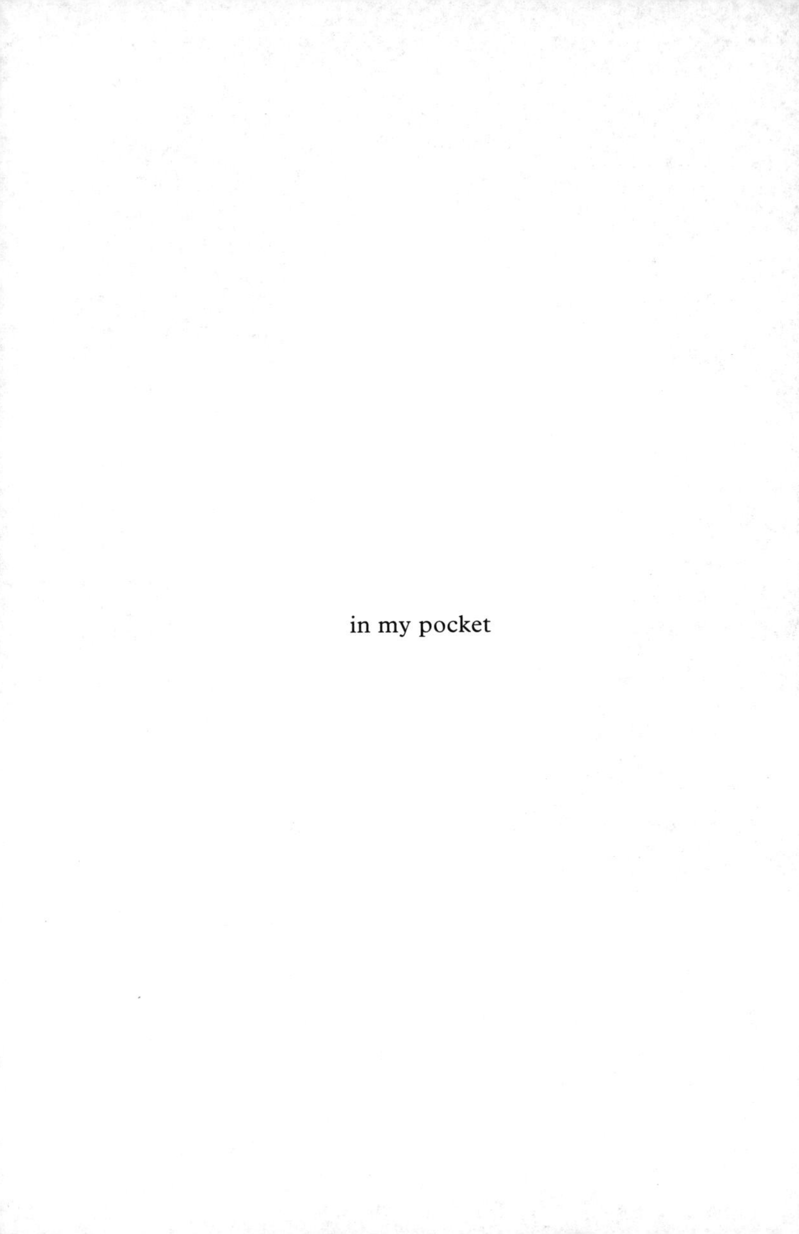

in my pocket

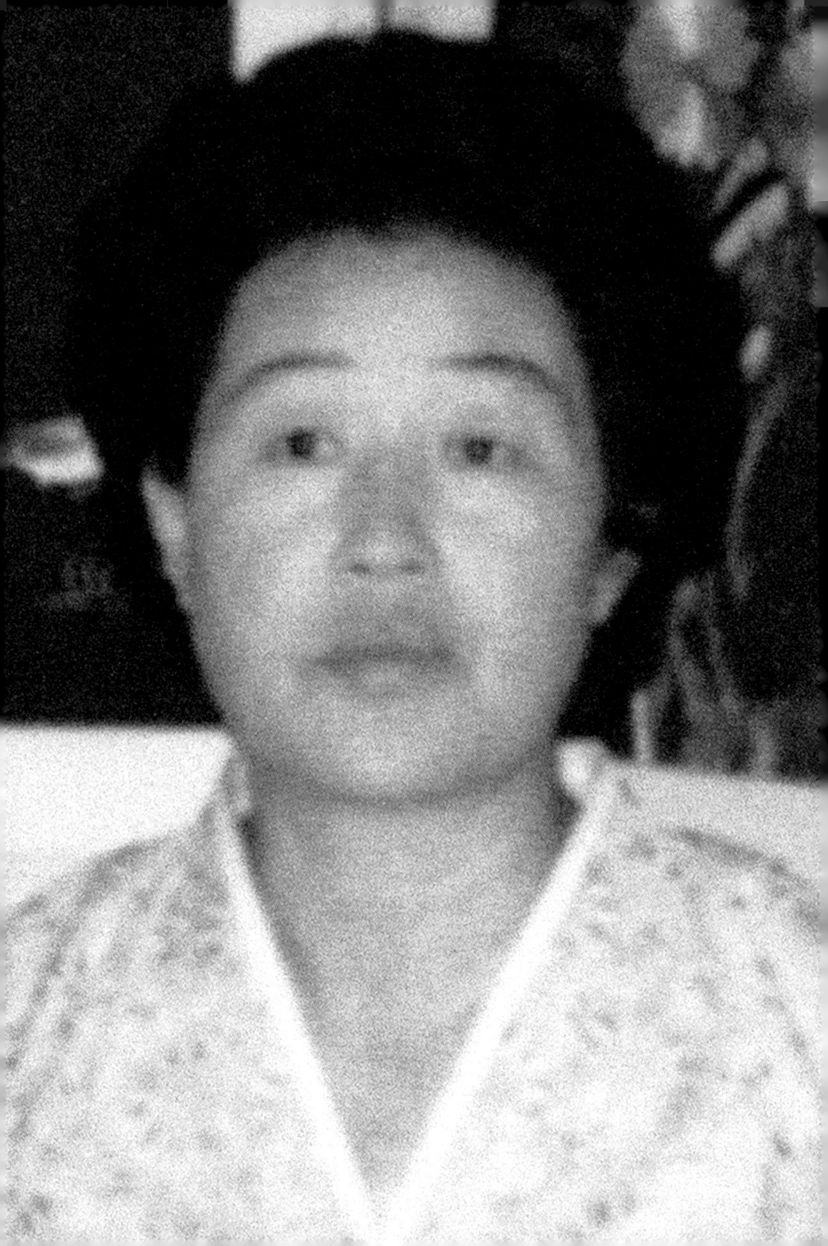

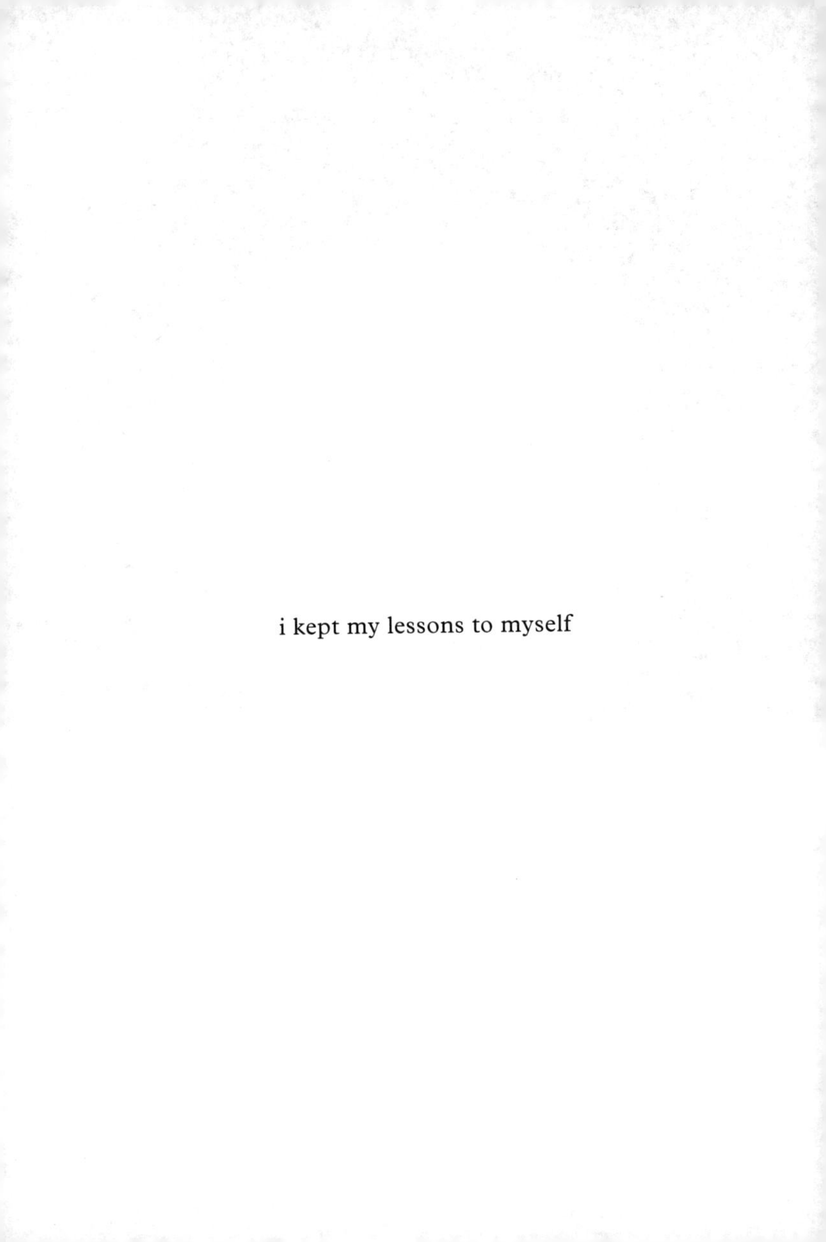

i kept my lessons to myself

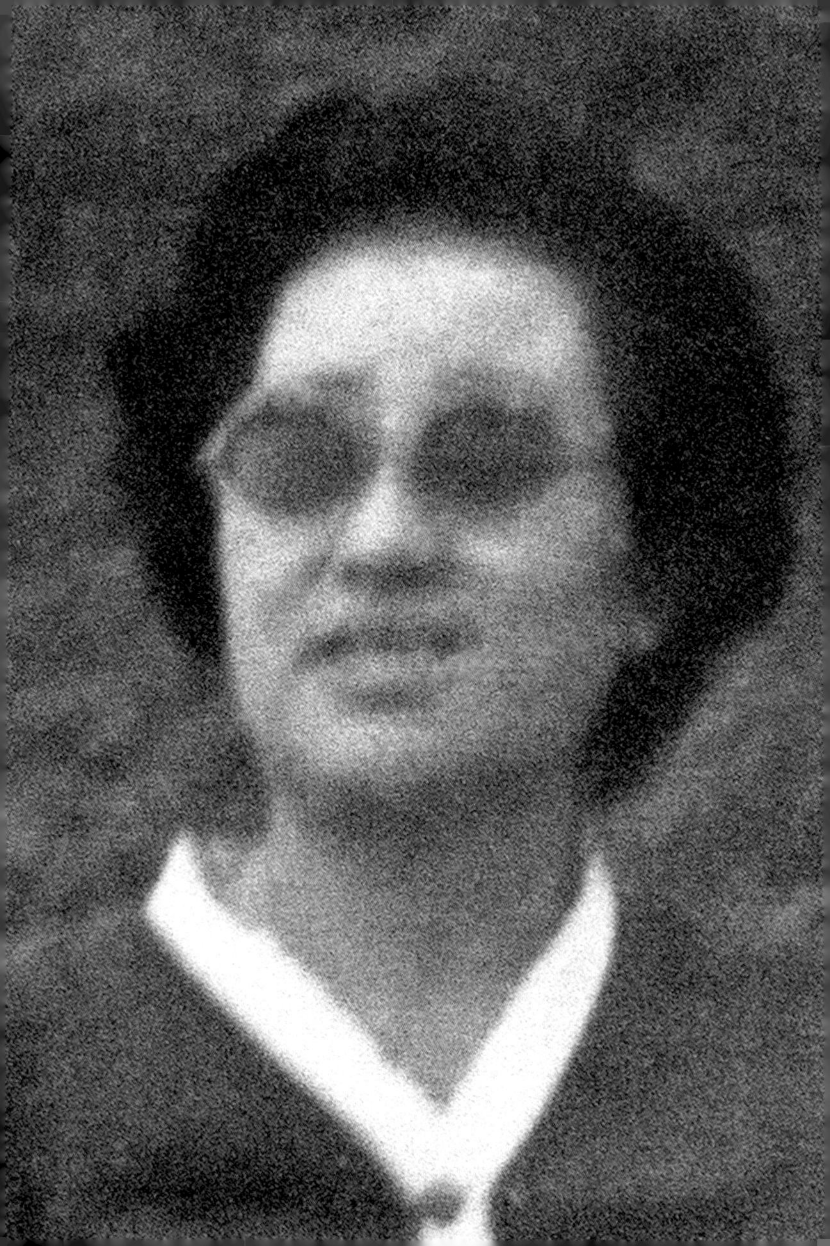

i was fading fast

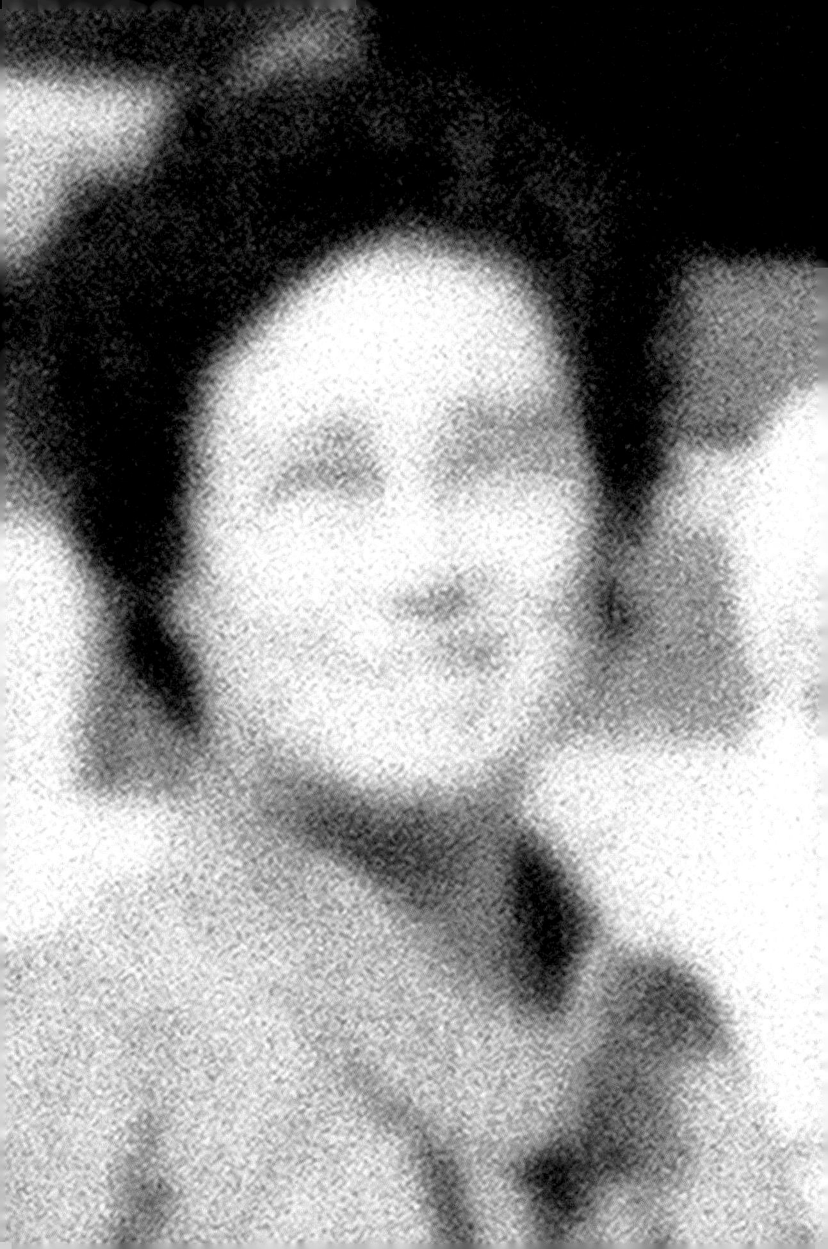

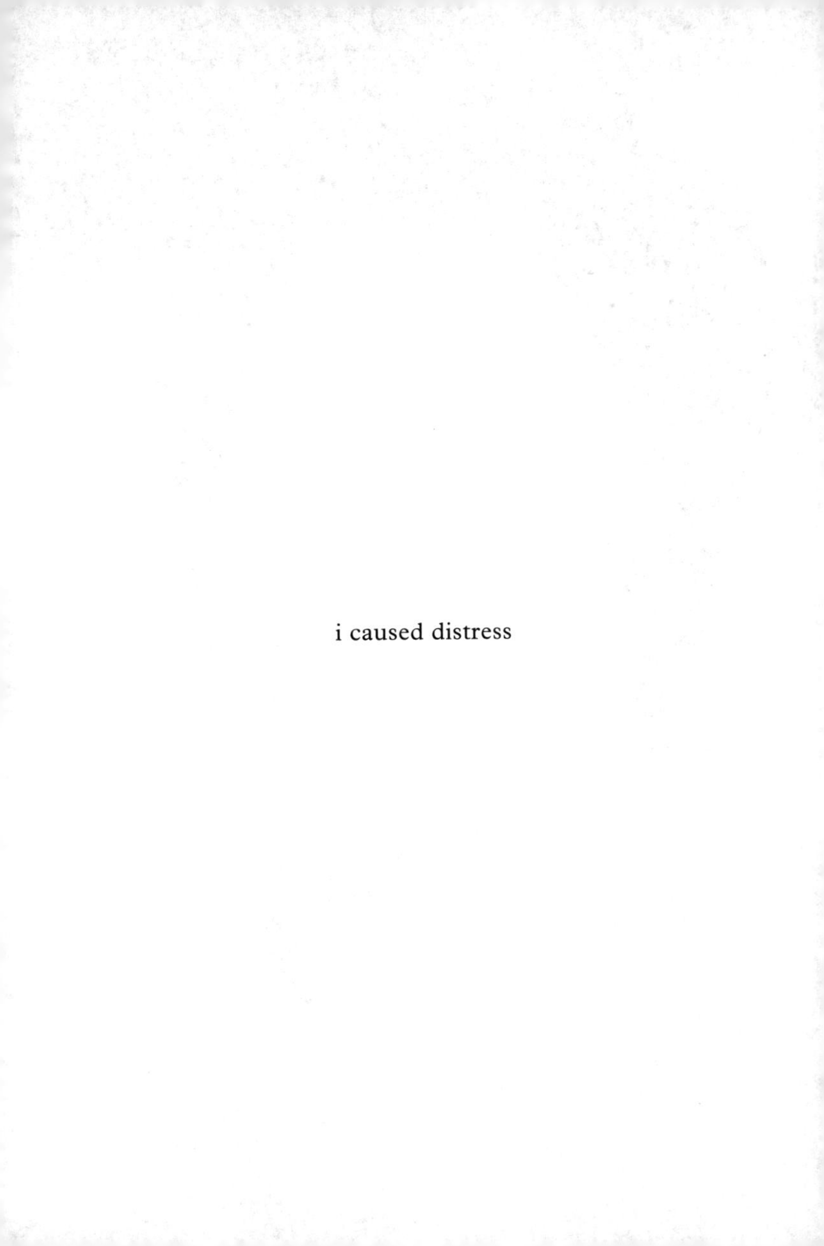

i caused distress

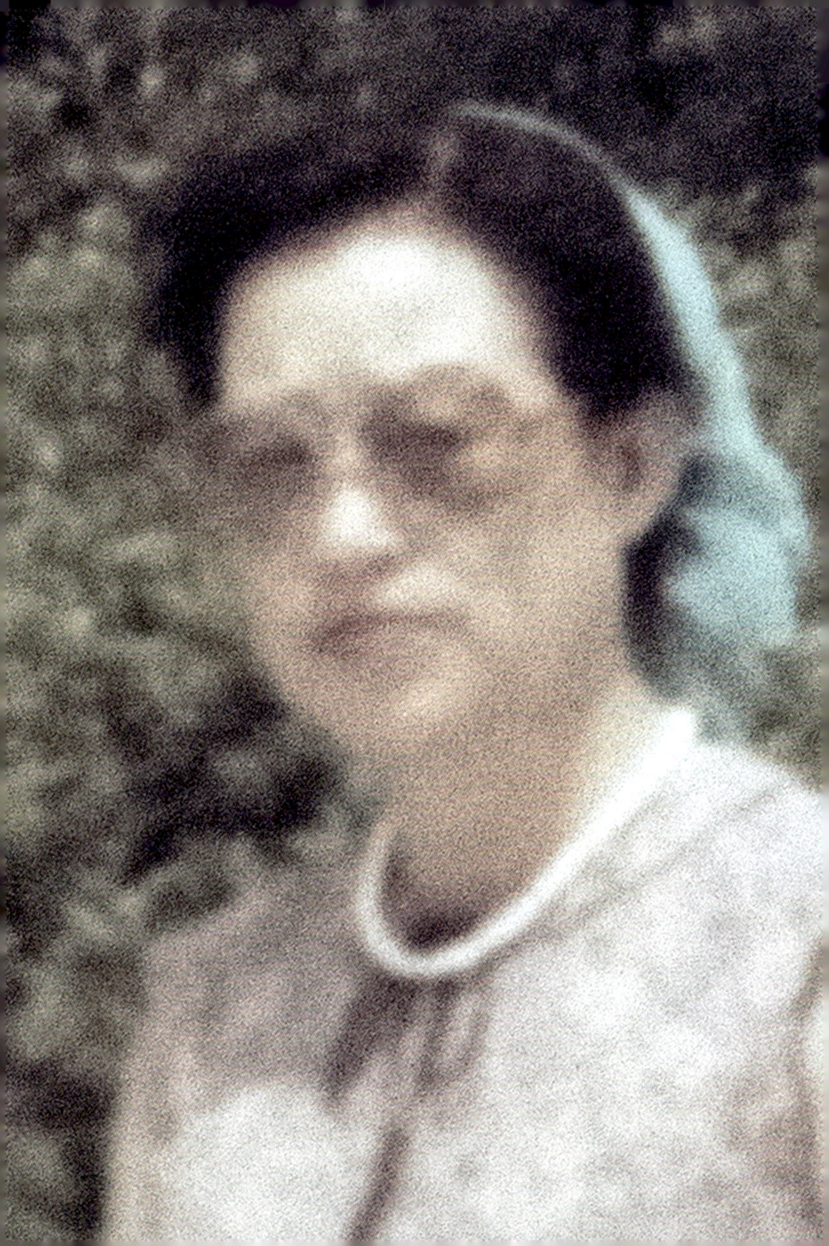

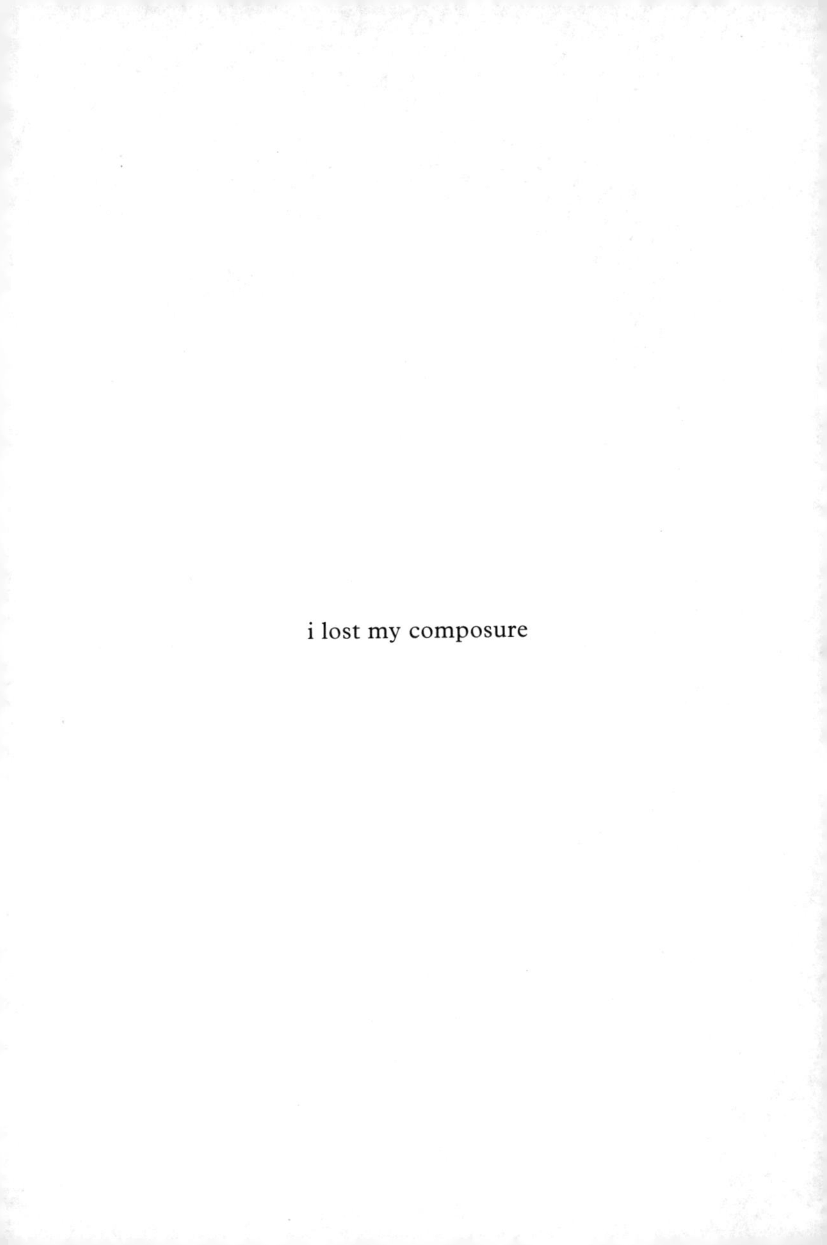

i lost my composure

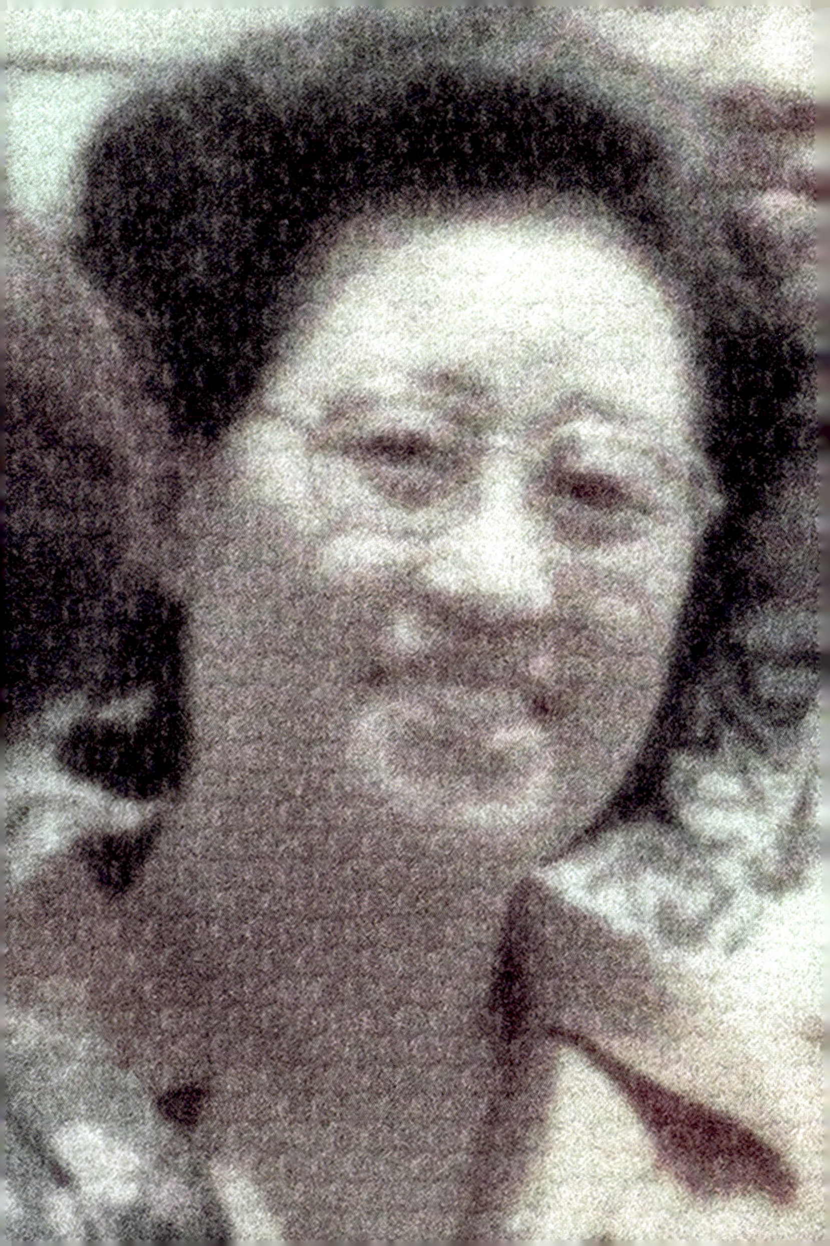

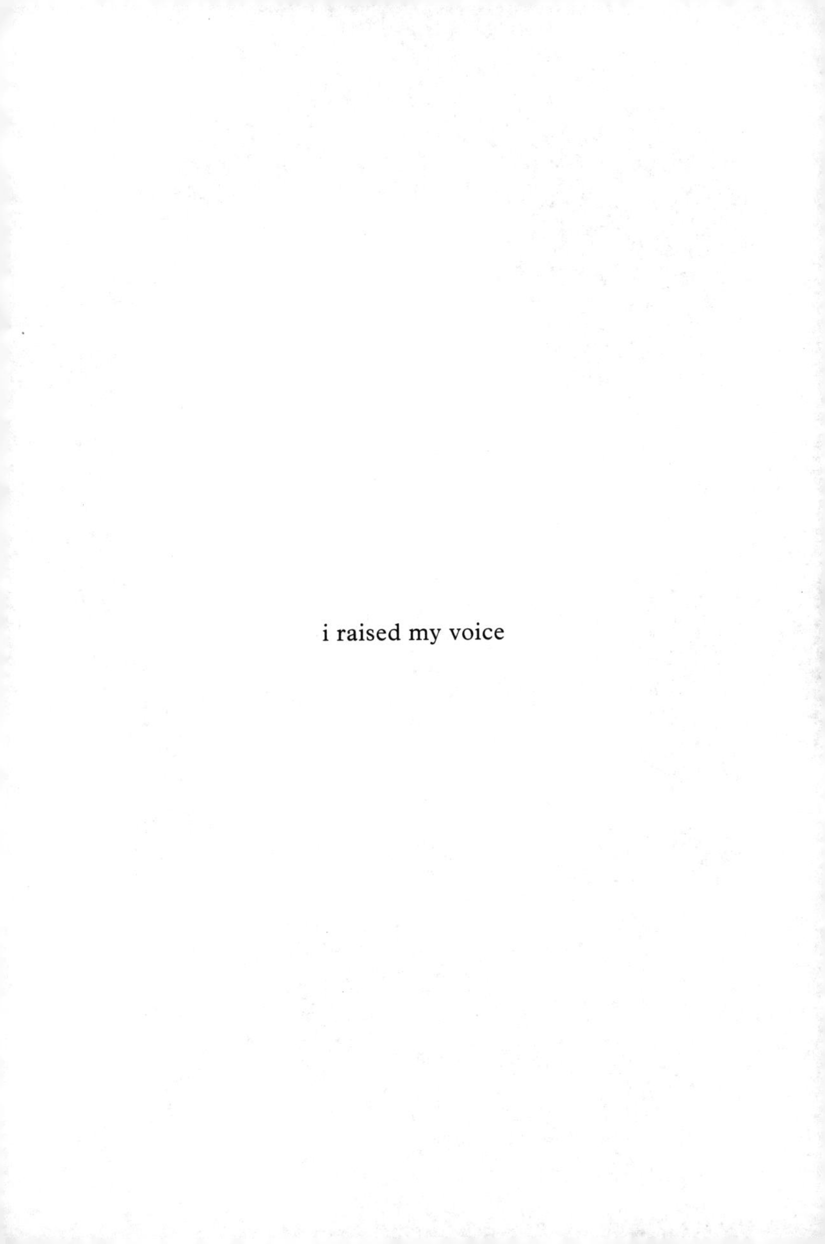

i raised my voice

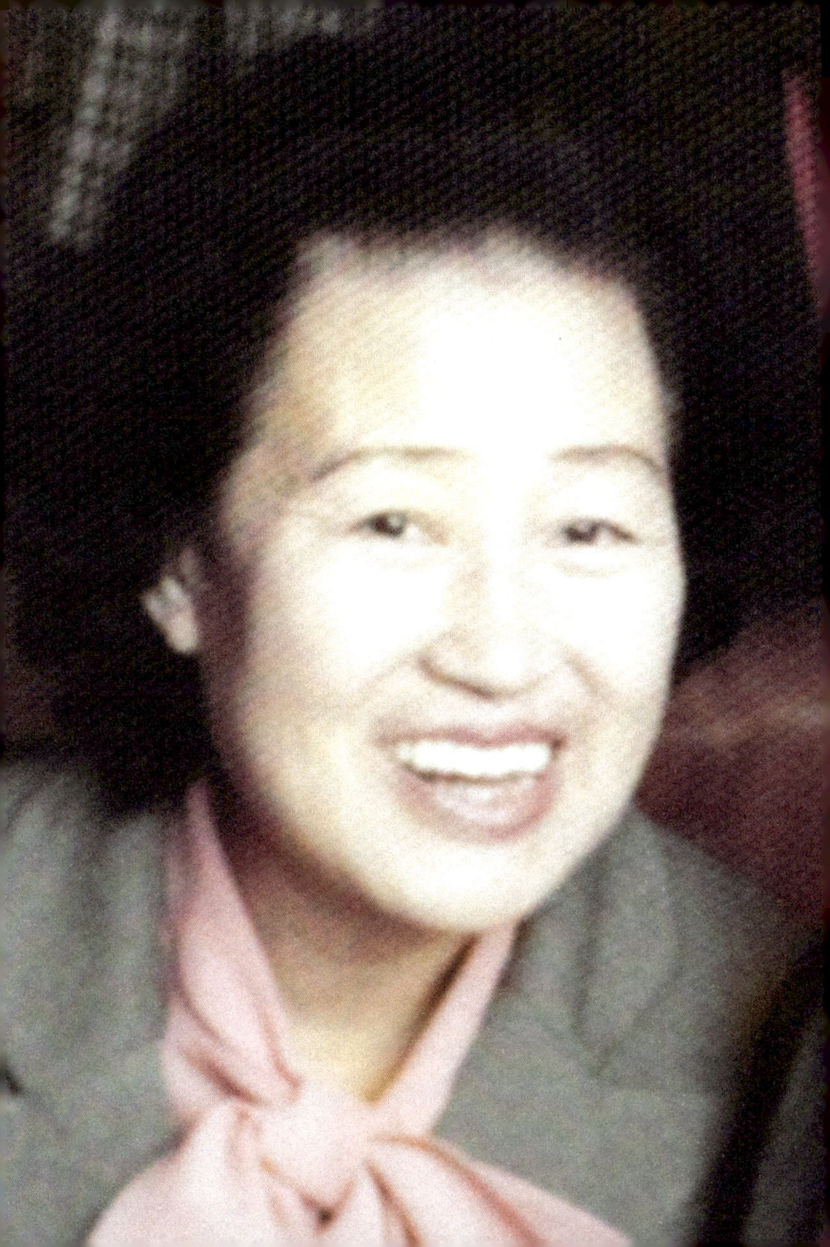

masks galore

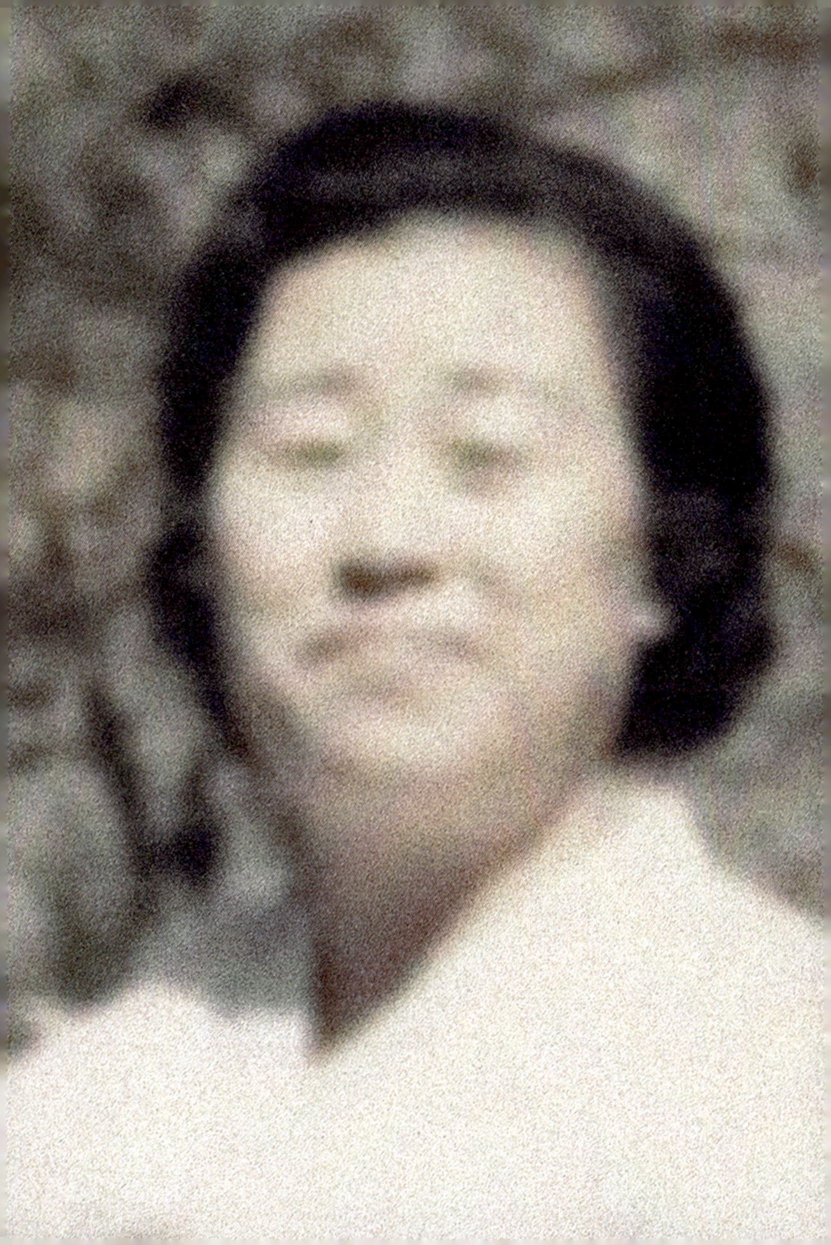

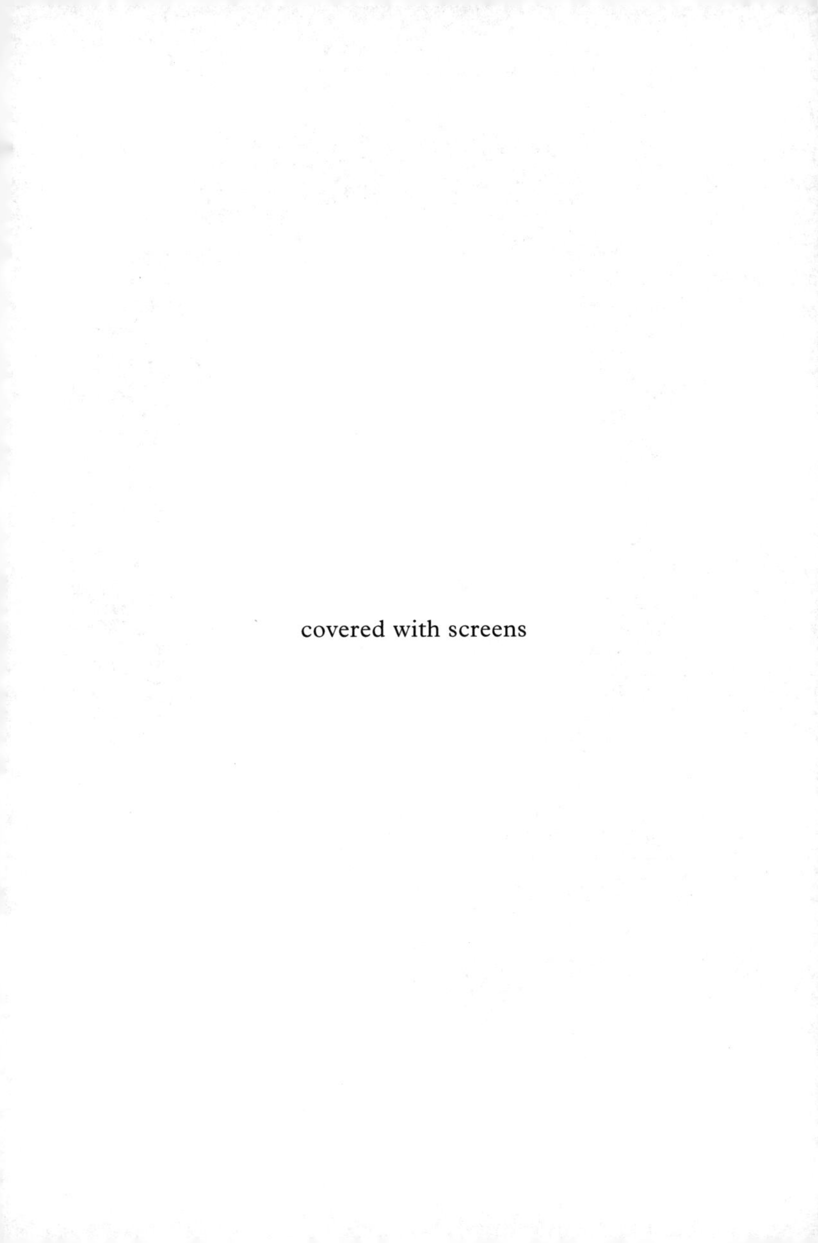

covered with screens

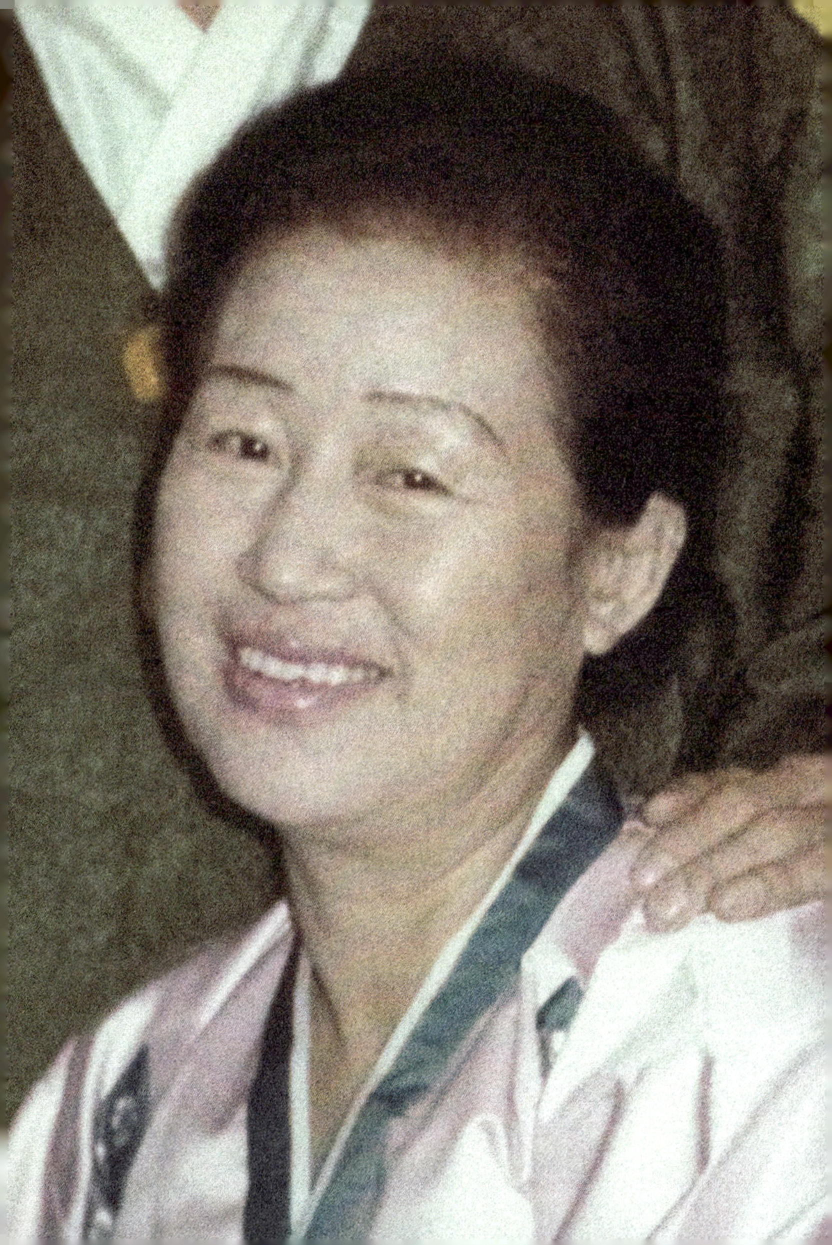

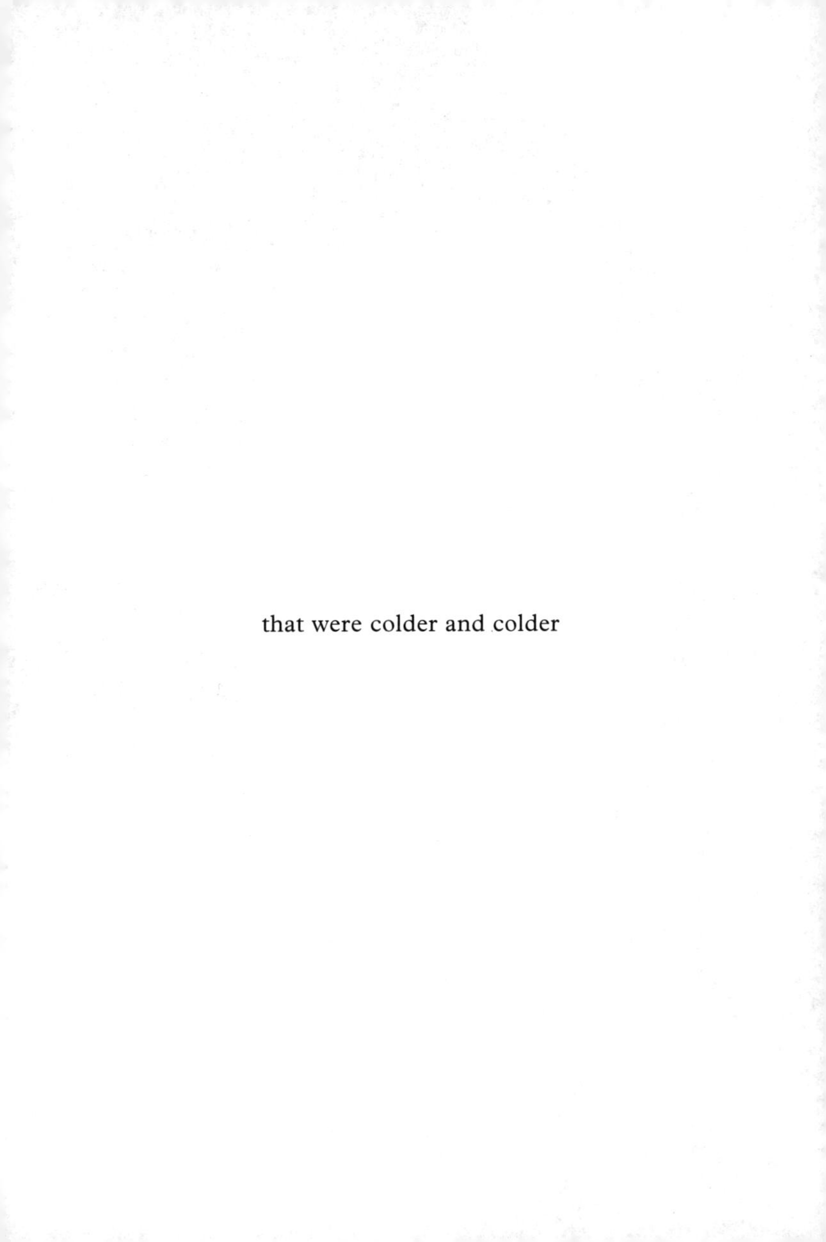

that were colder and colder

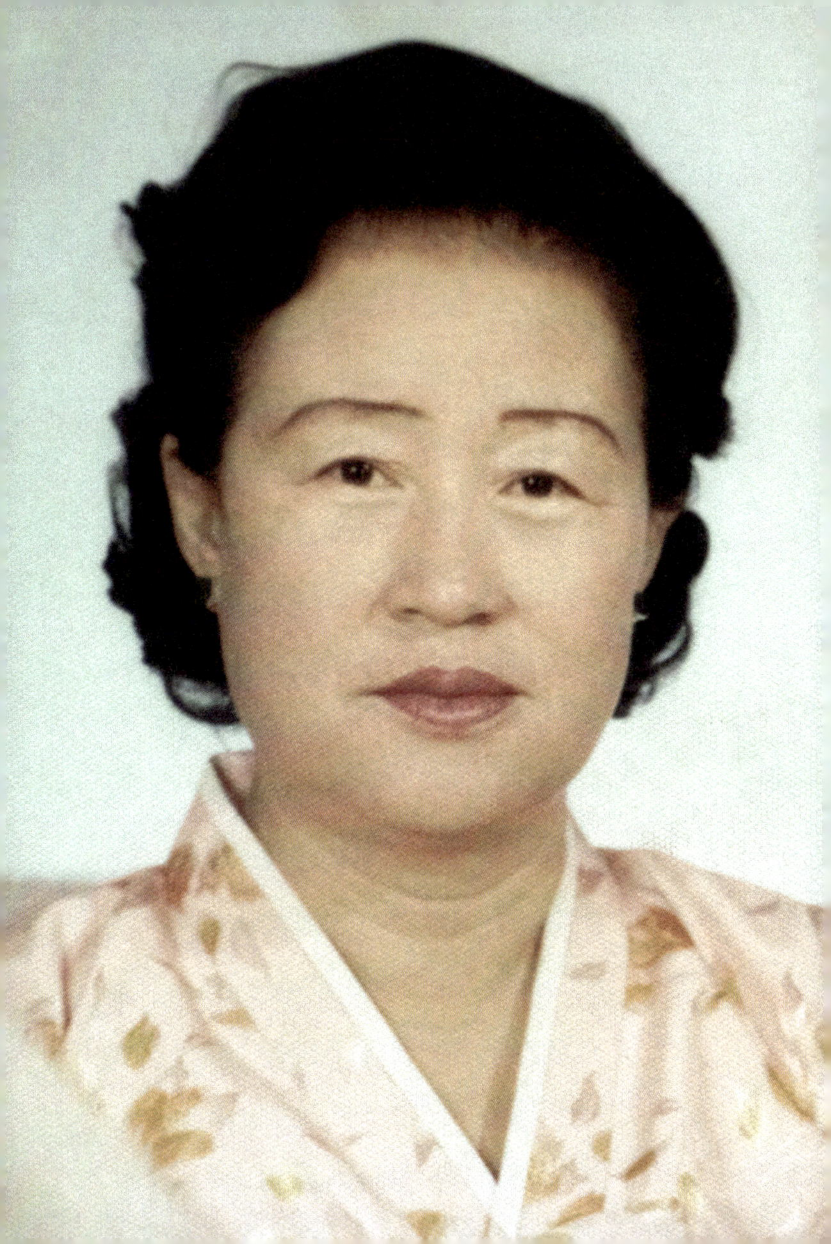

a tidy house

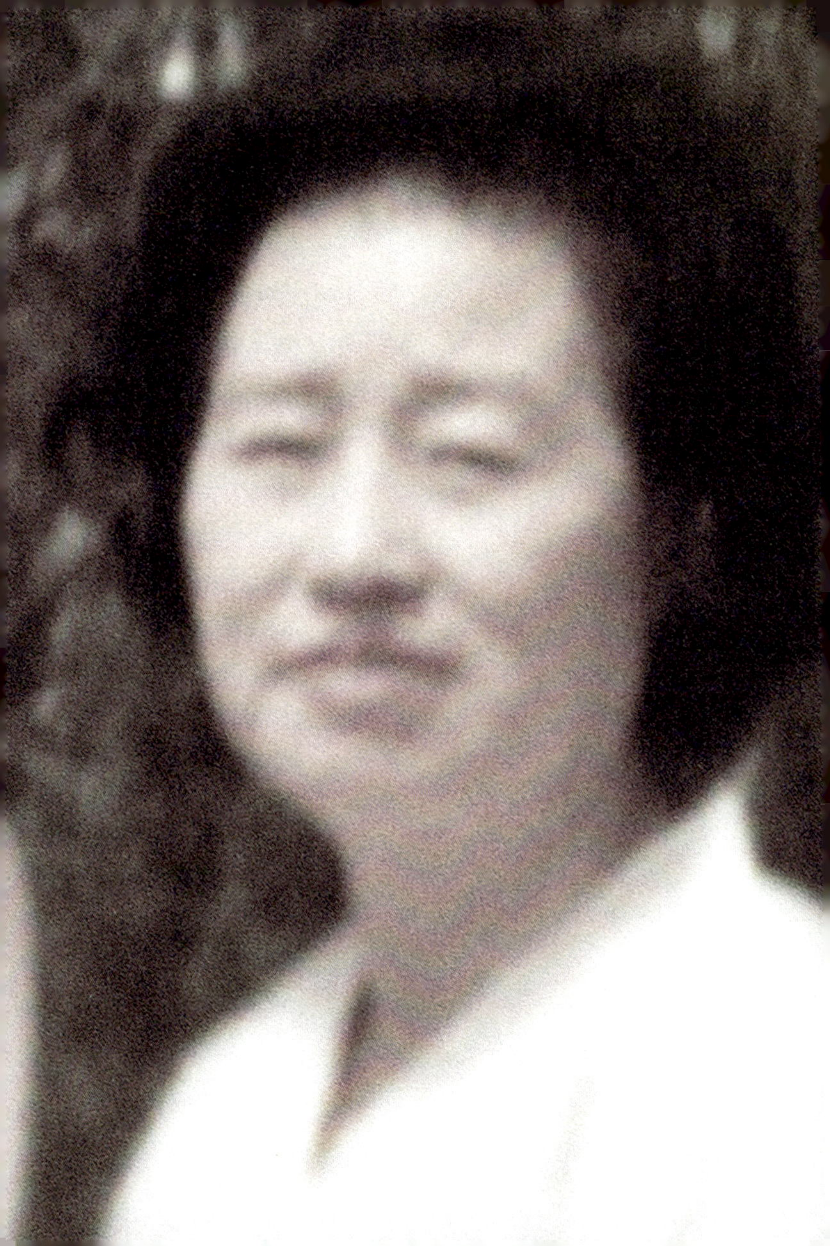

became my refuge

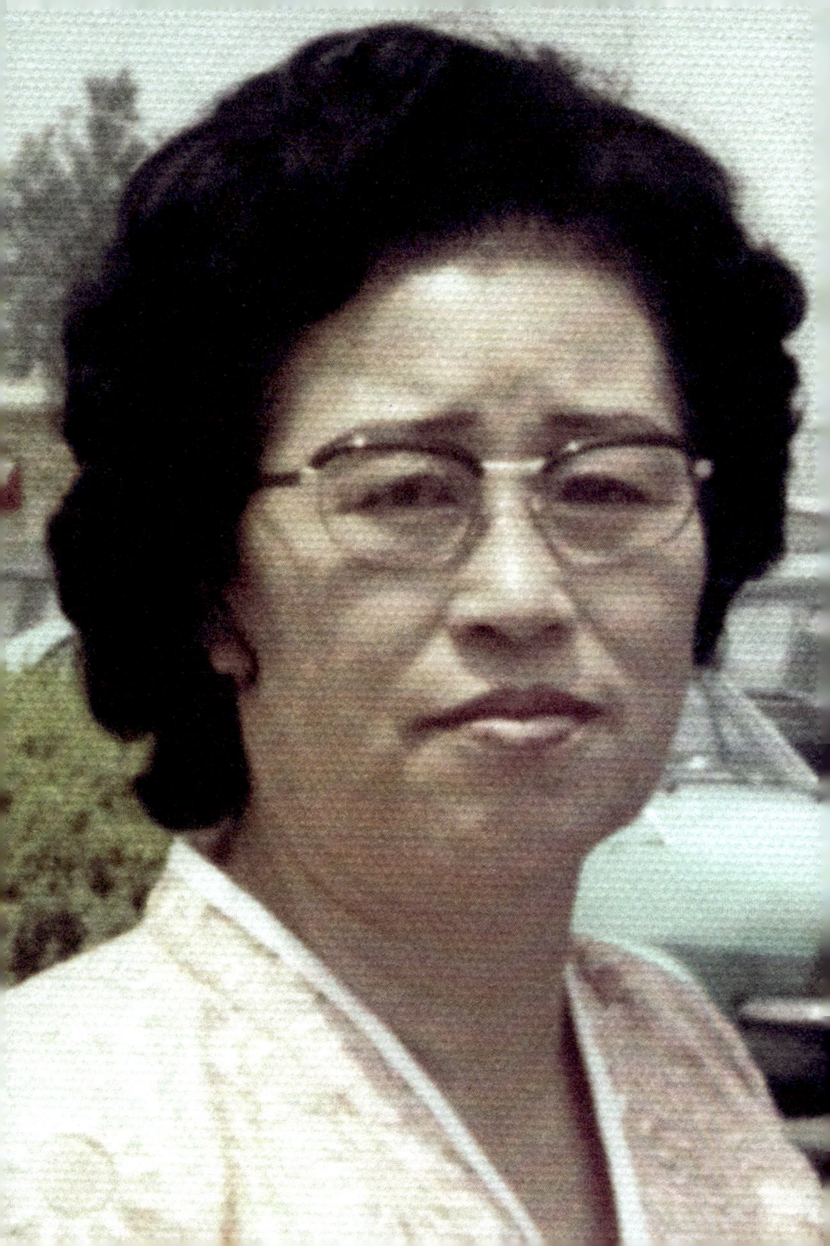

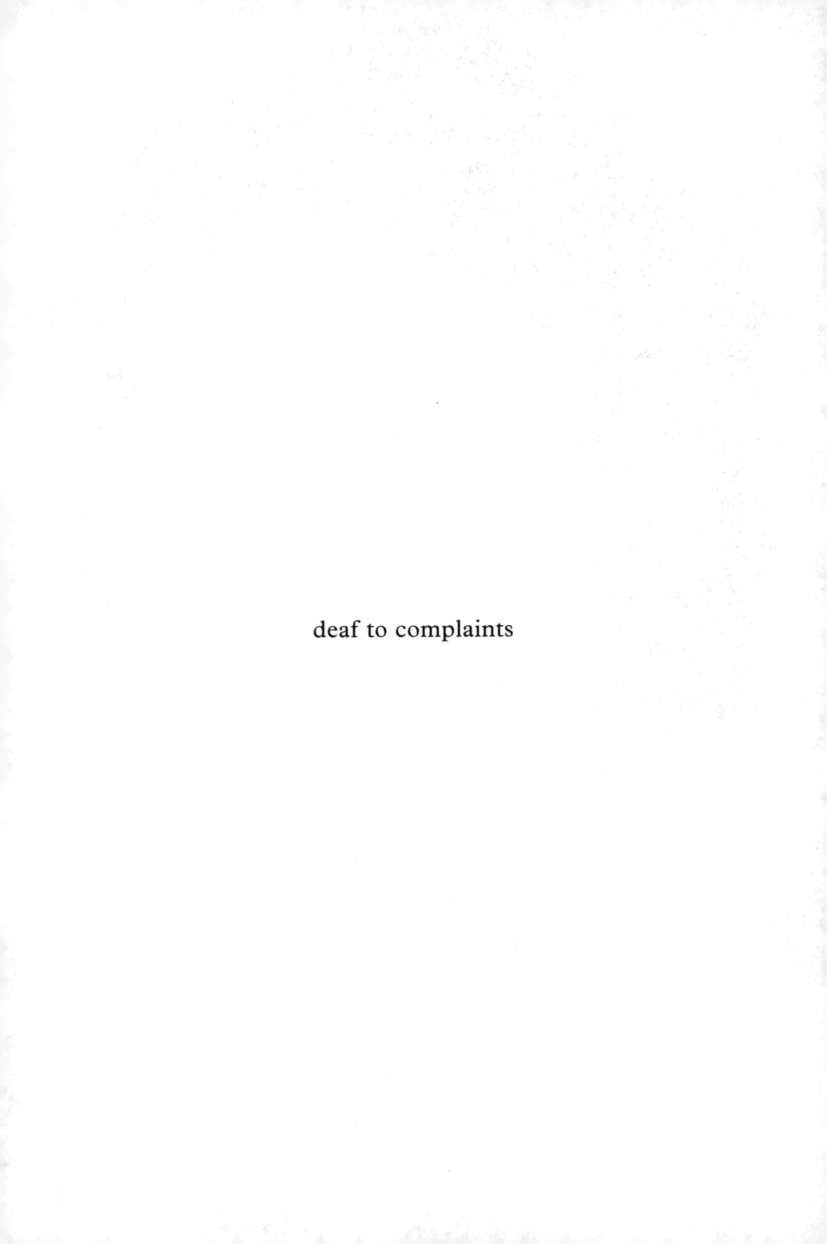

deaf to complaints

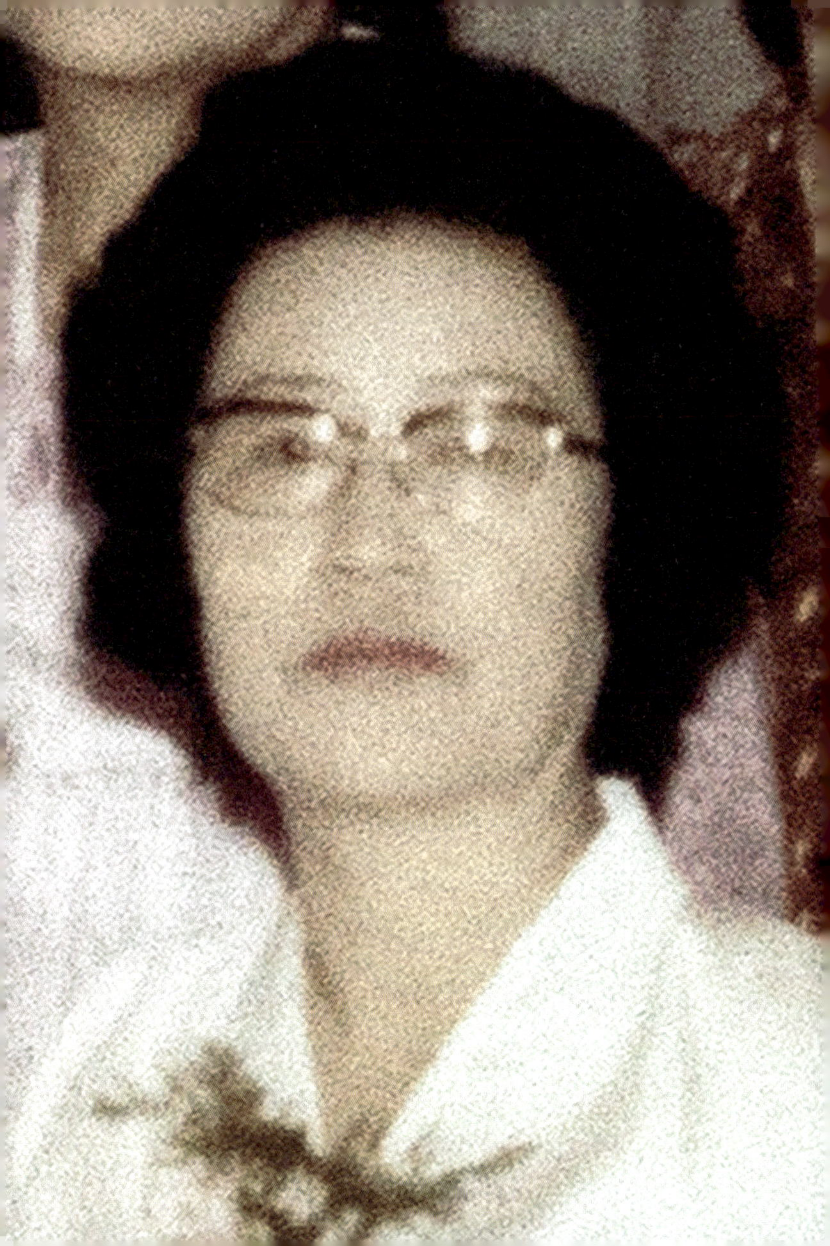

i was my own god

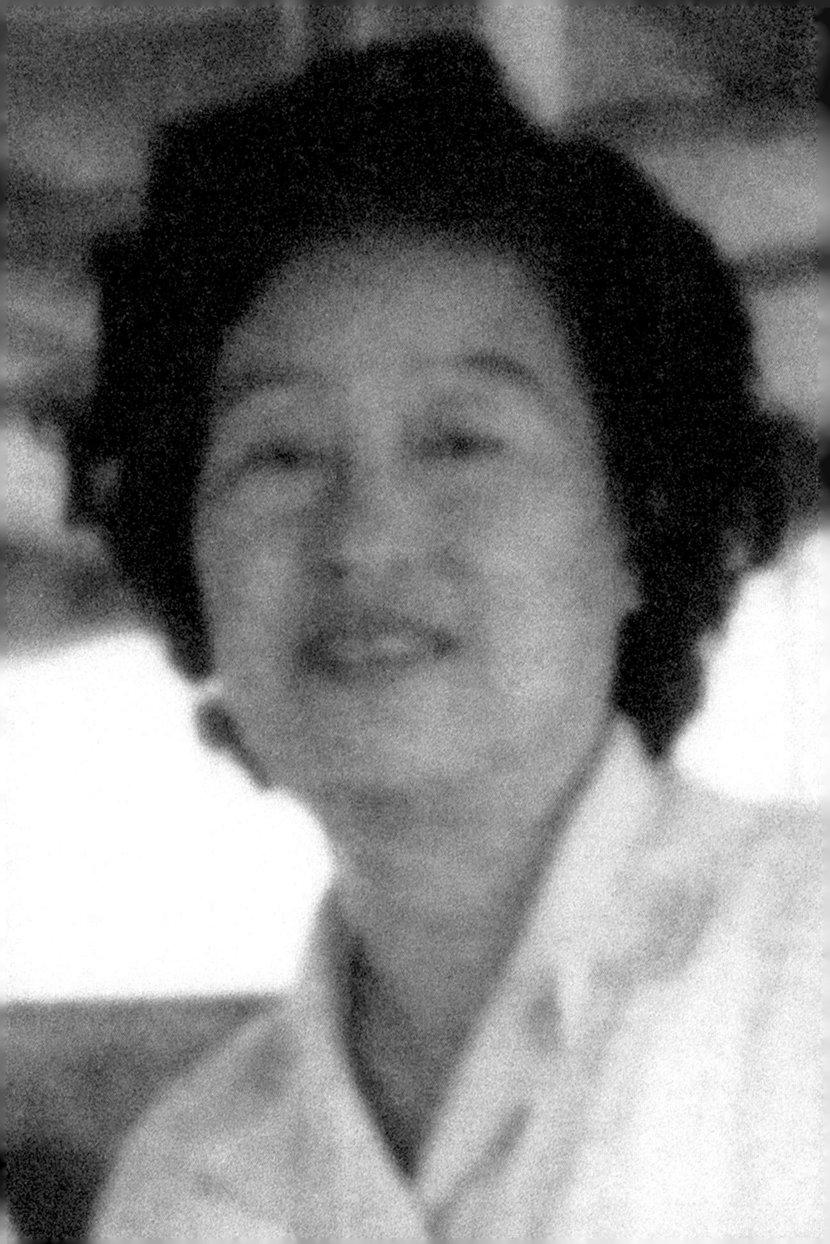

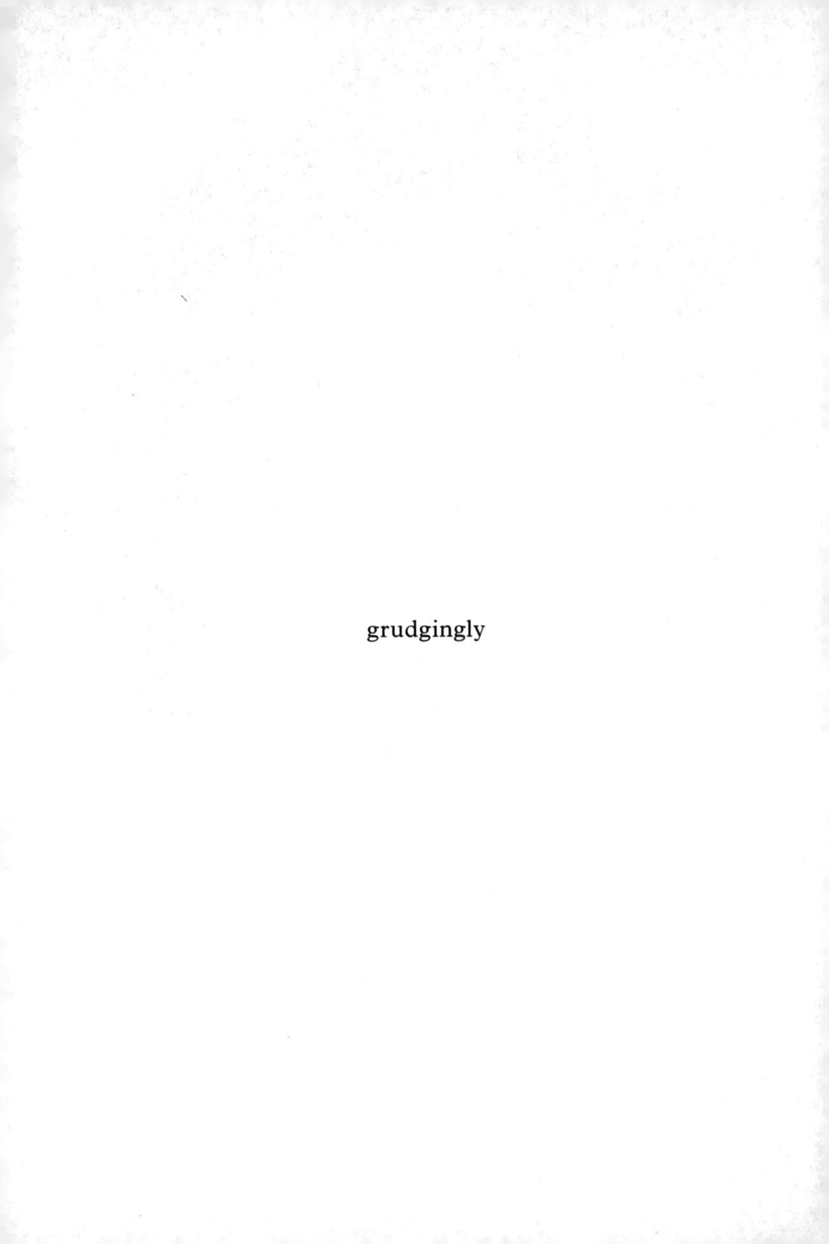

grudgingly

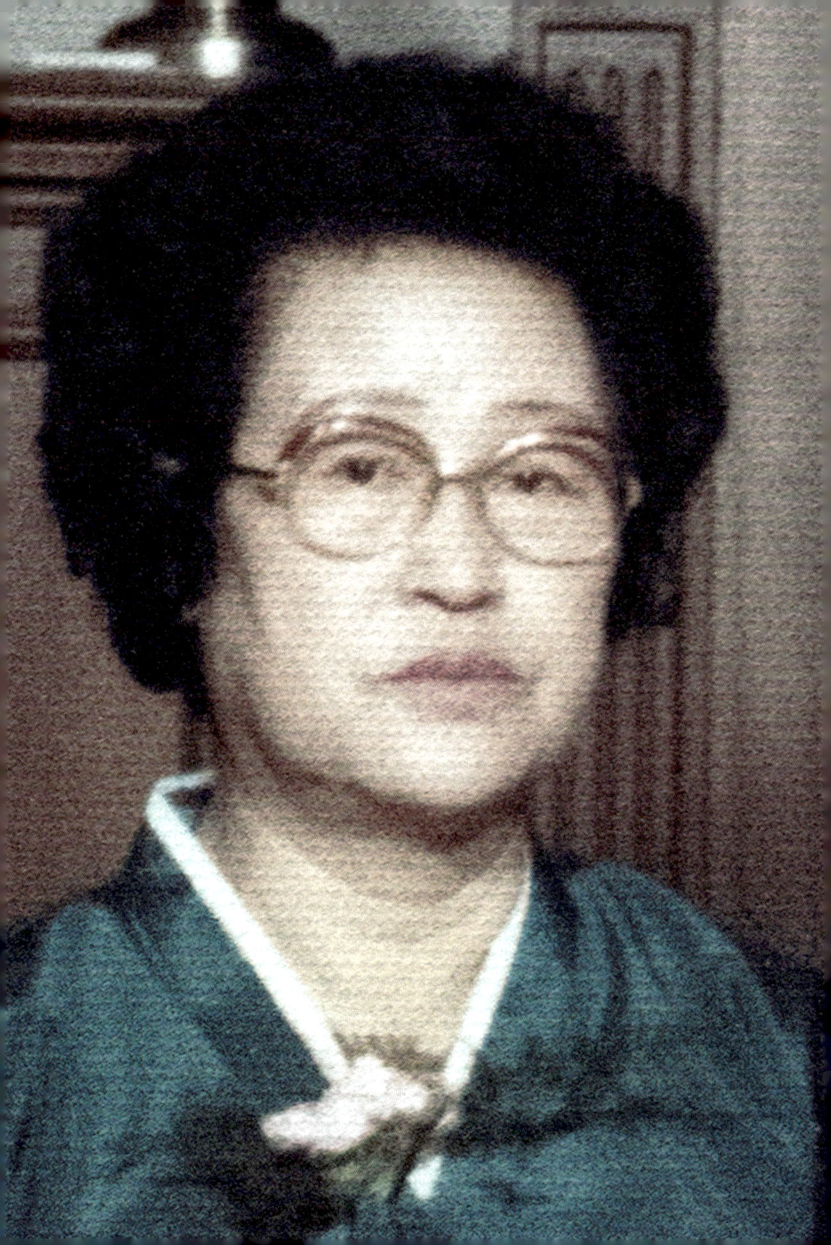

i swallowed black snow

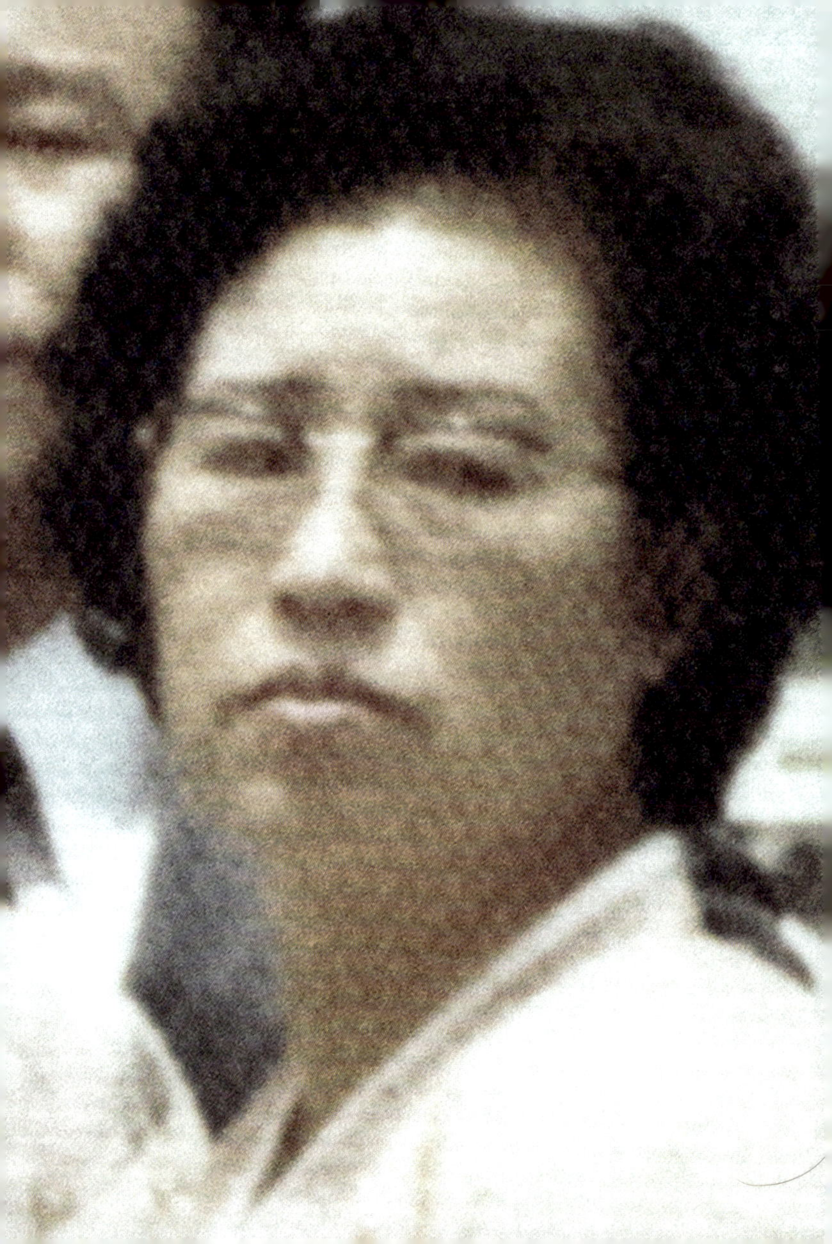

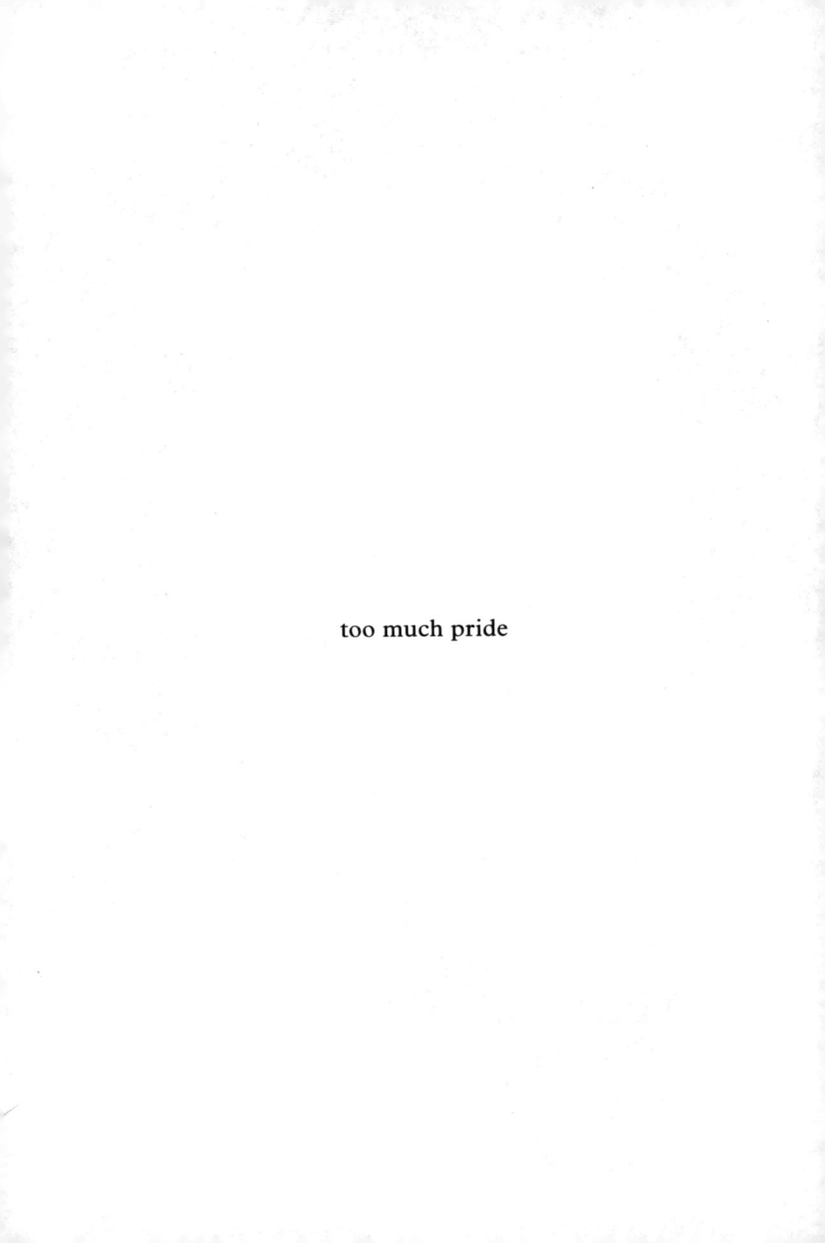

too much pride

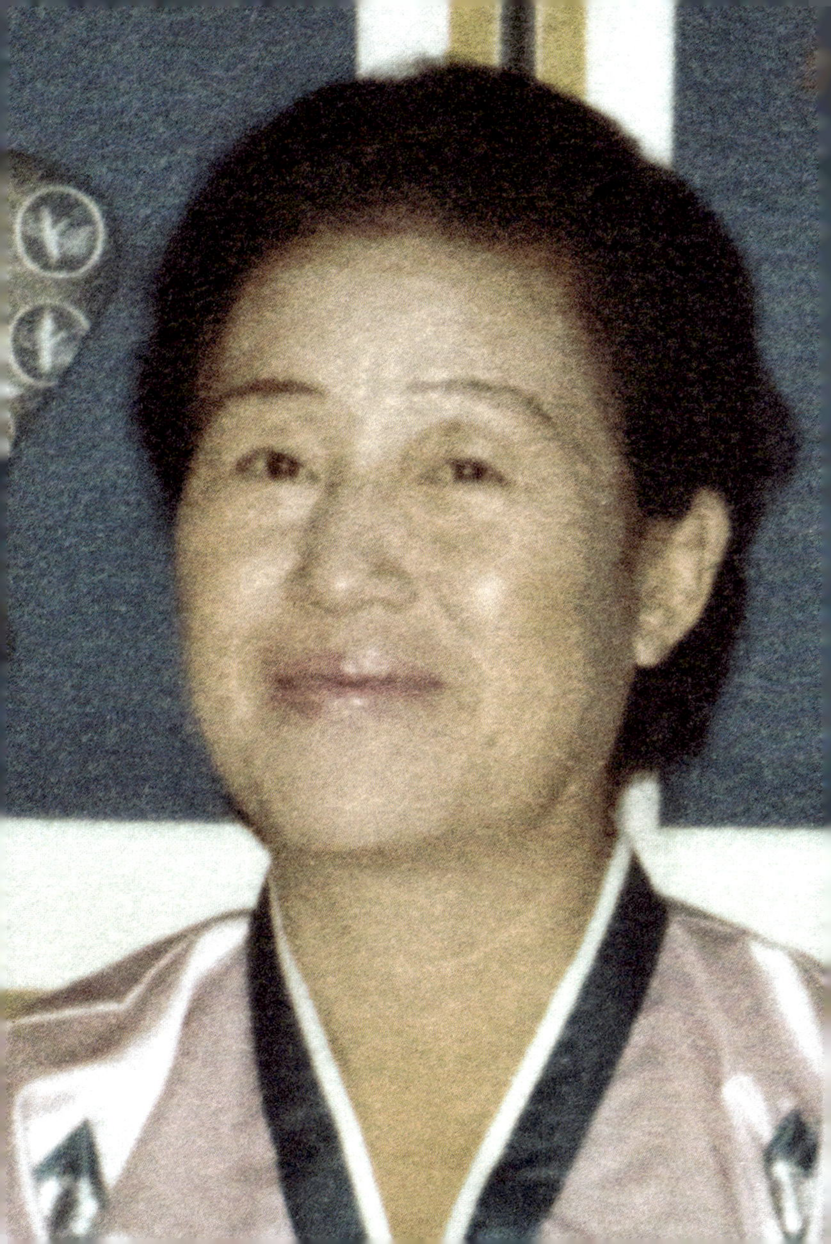

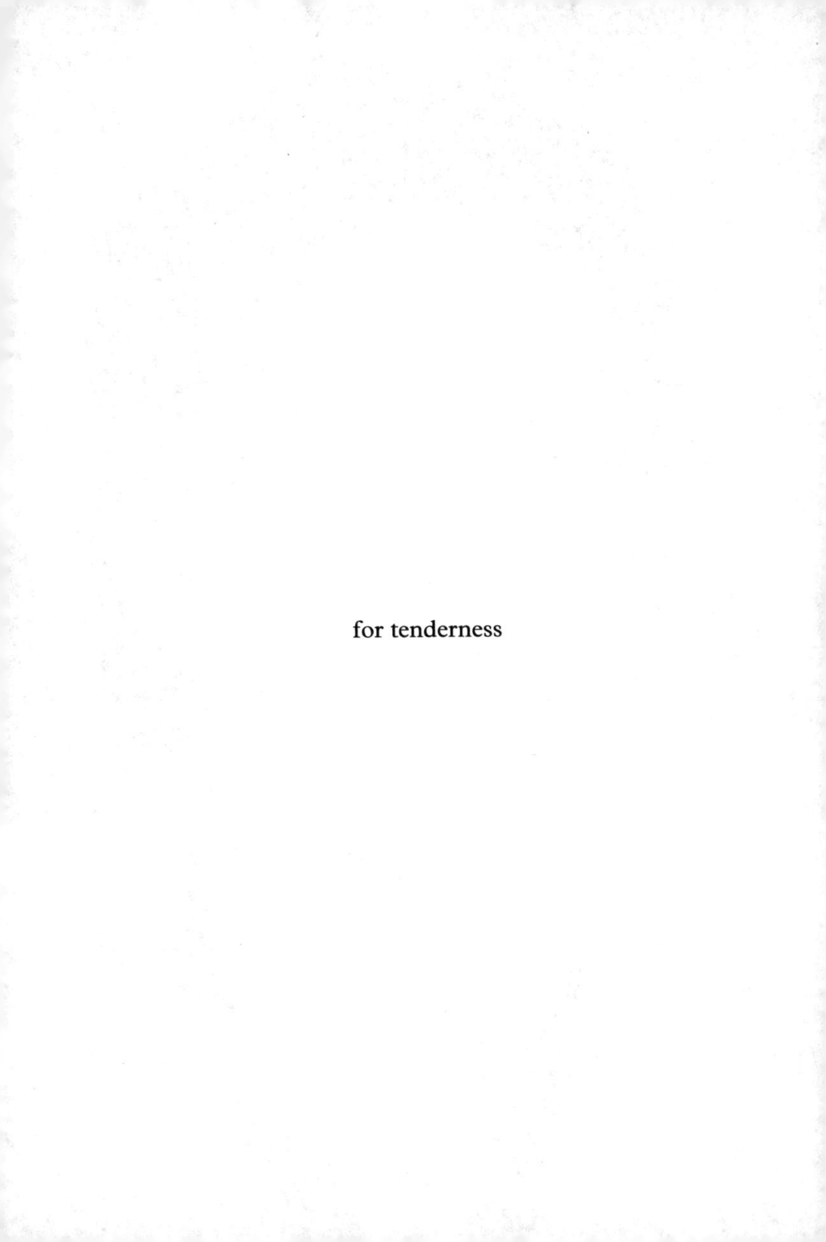

for tenderness

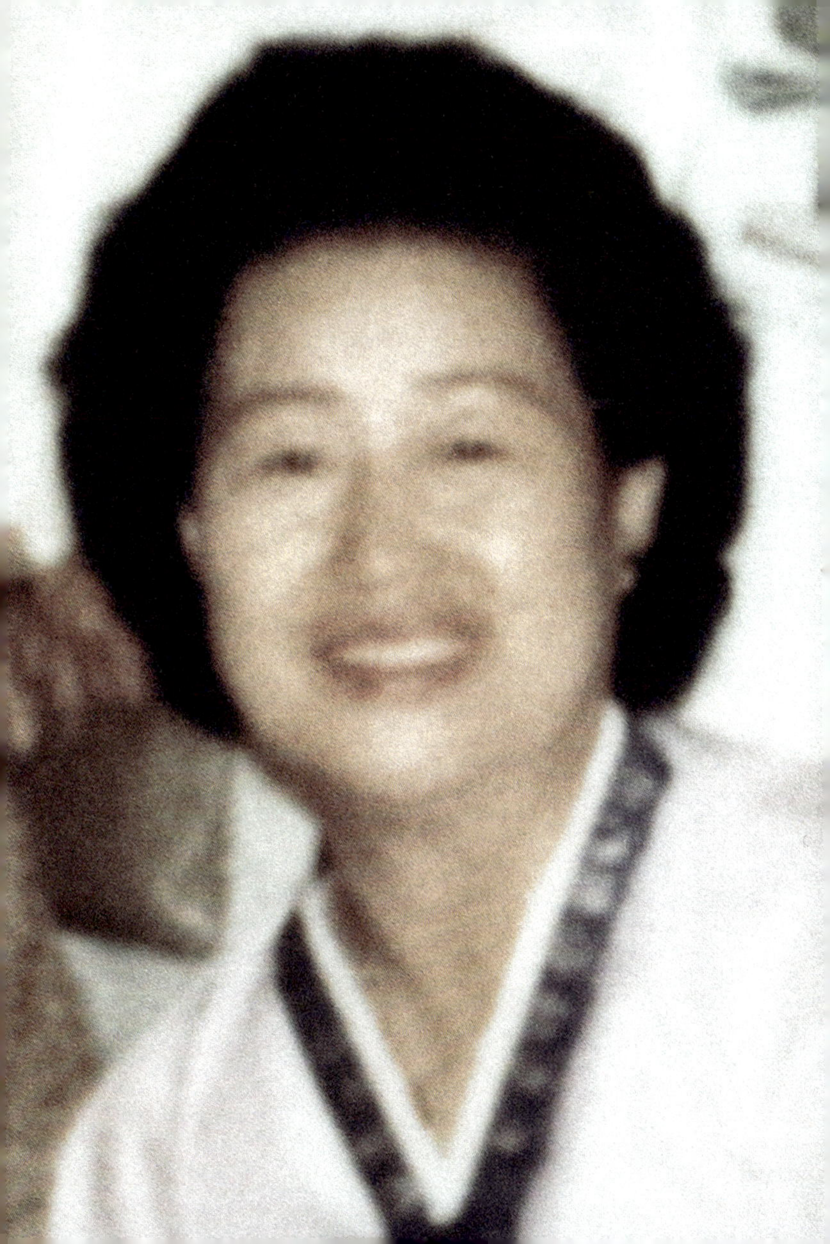

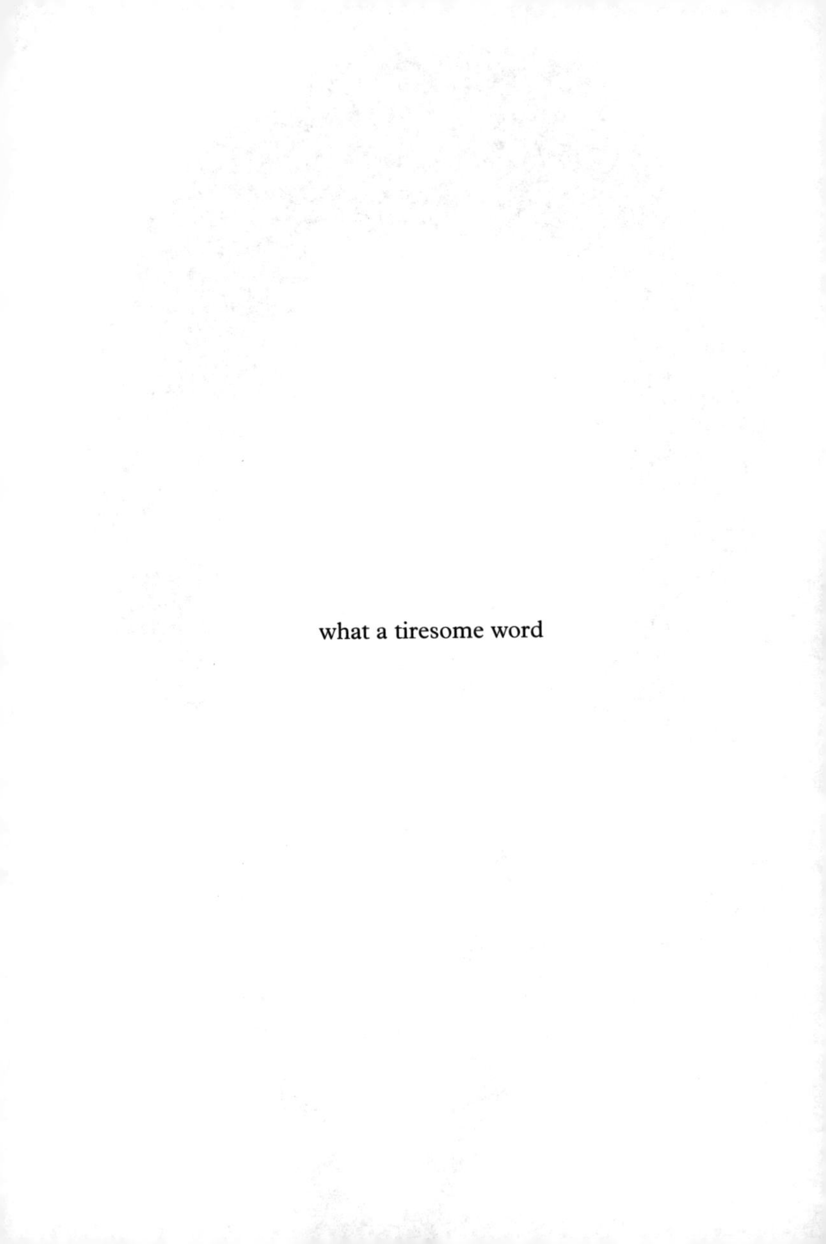

what a tiresome word

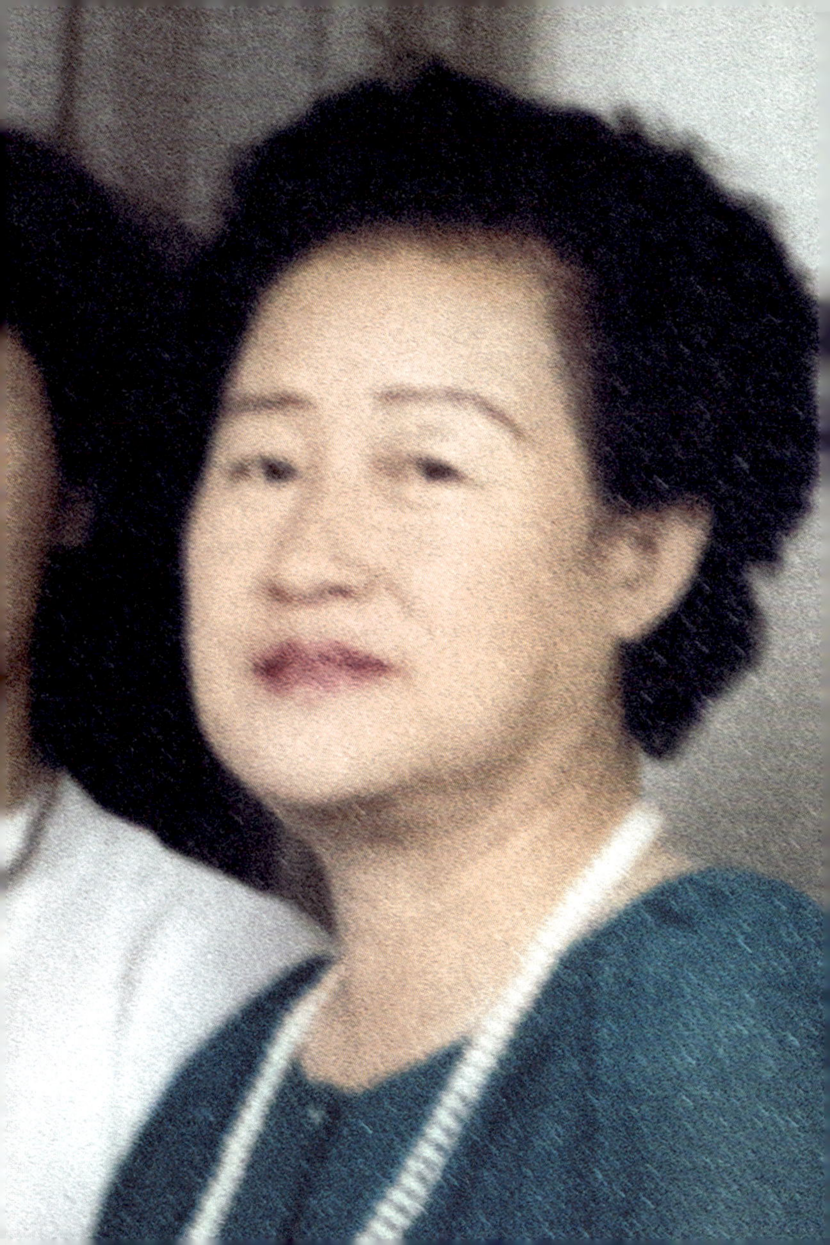

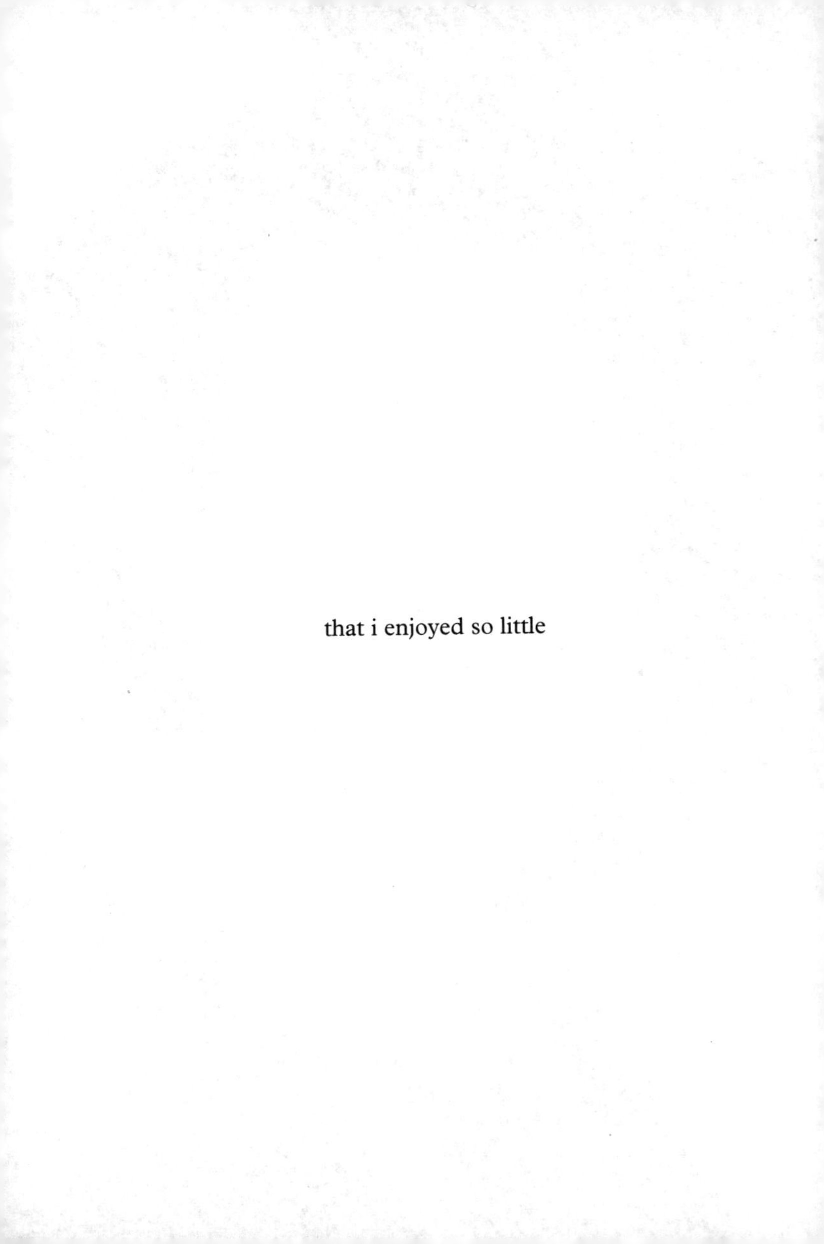

that i enjoyed so little

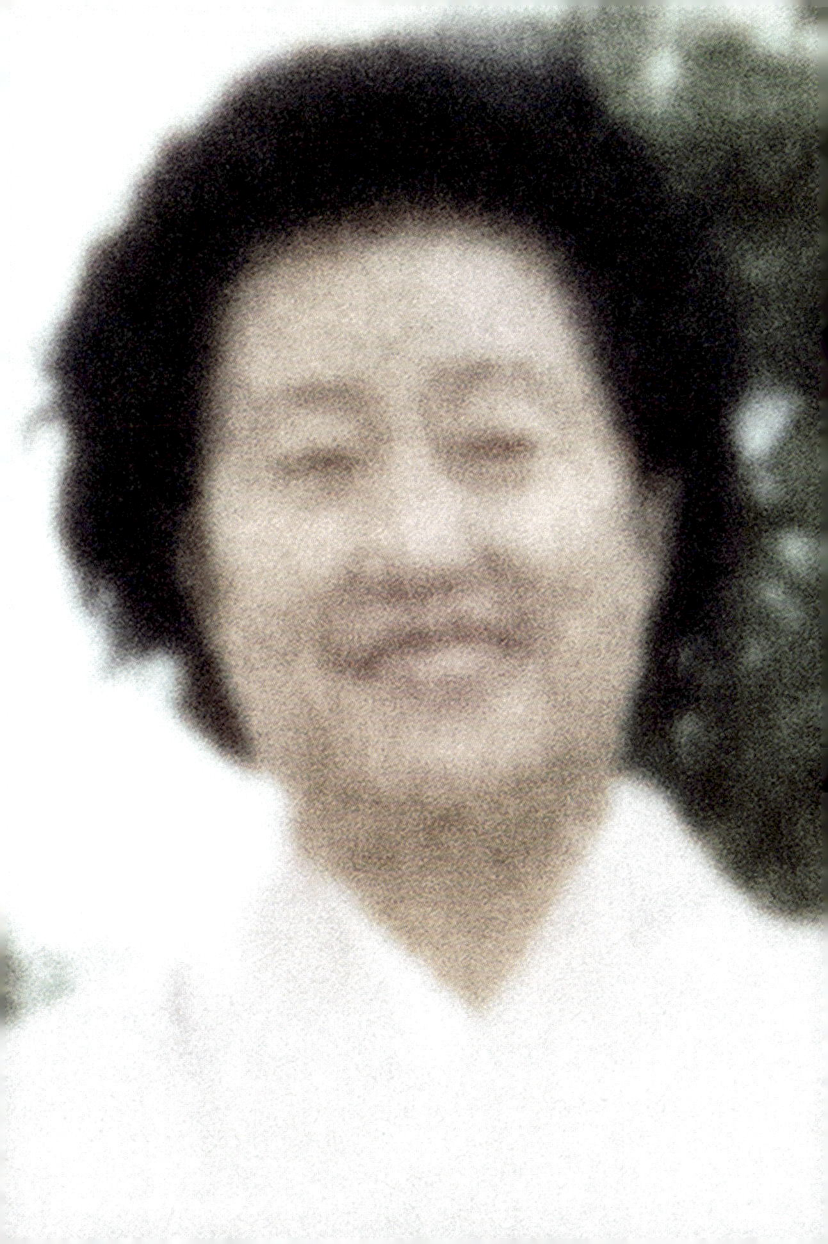

like a mirror

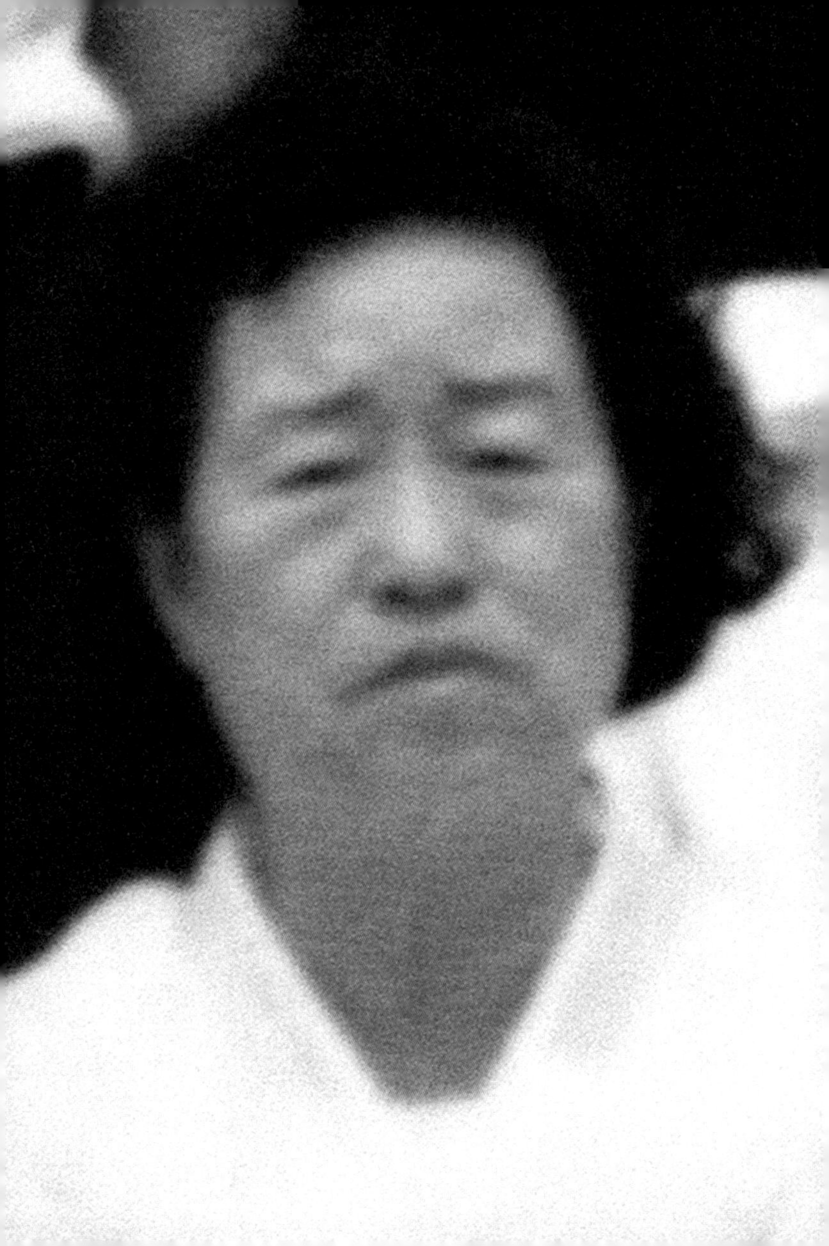

i did not show much affection

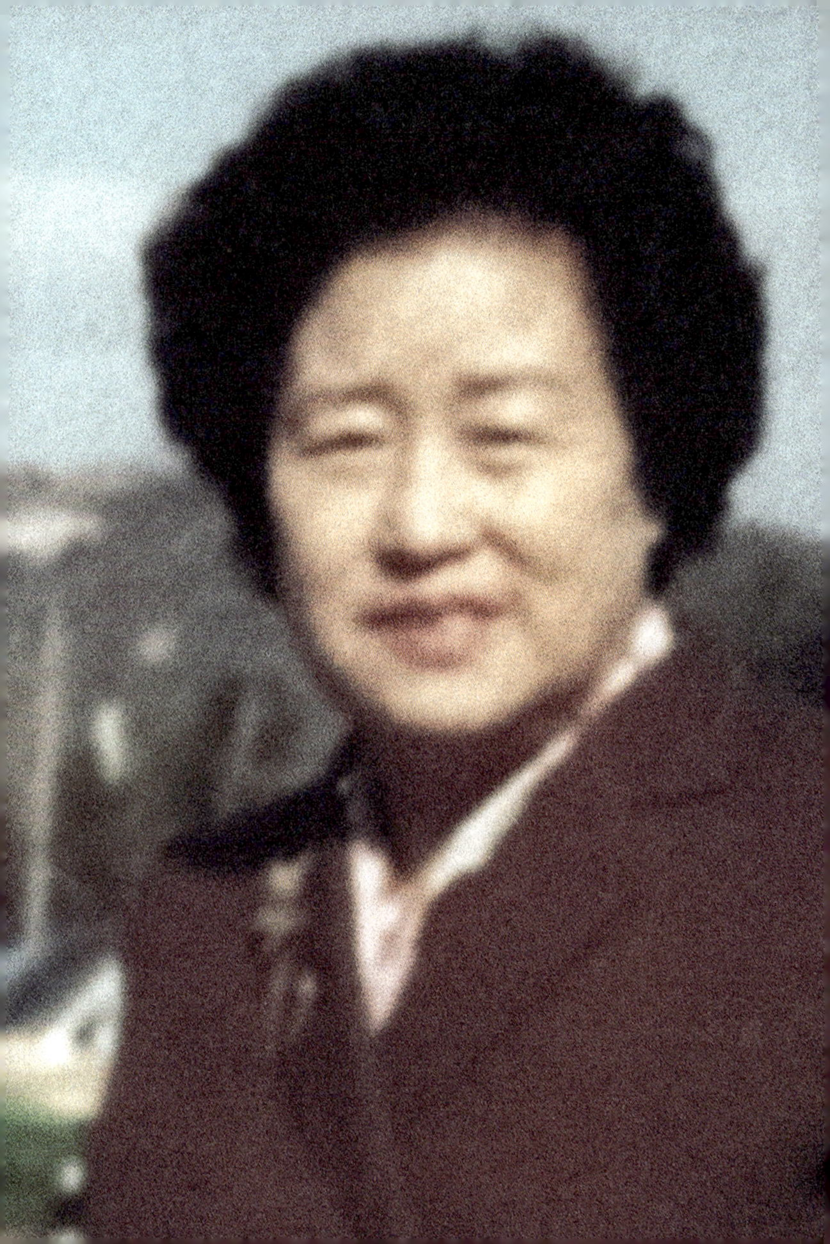

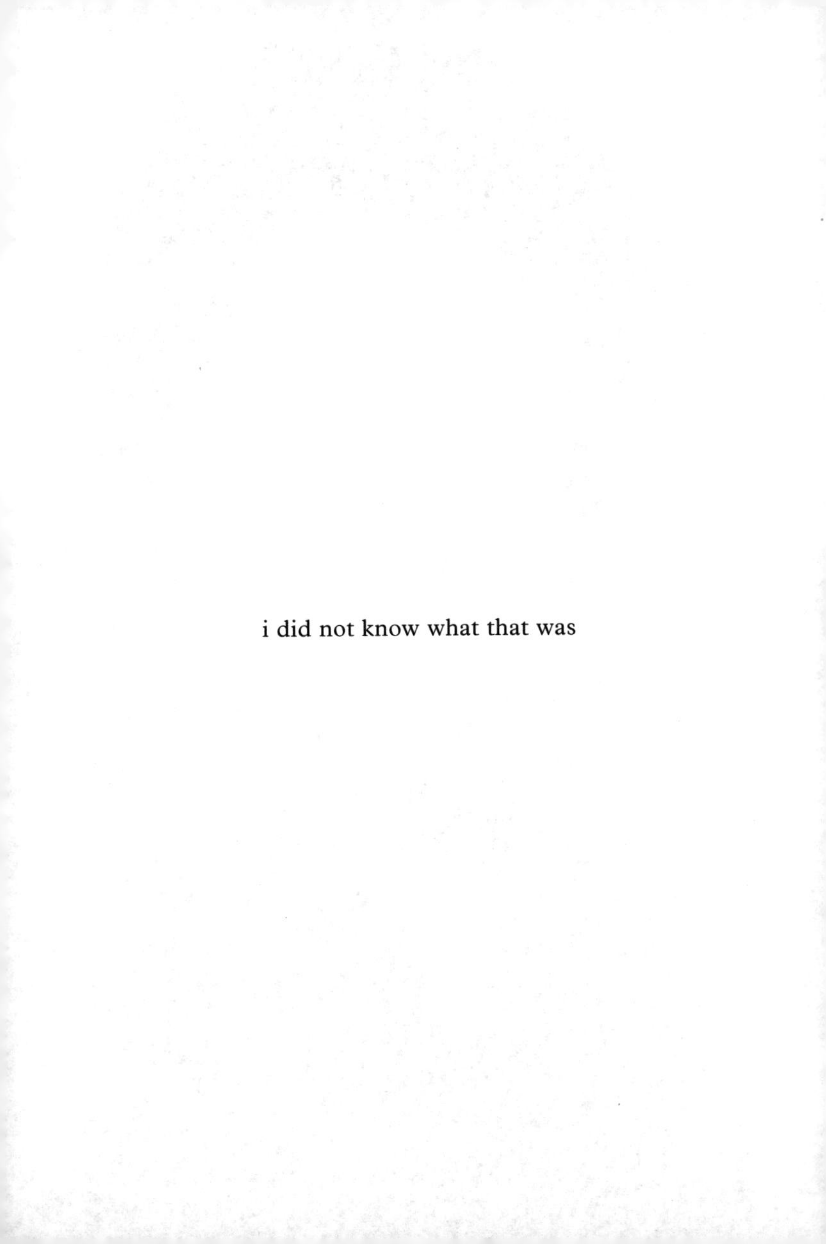

i did not know what that was

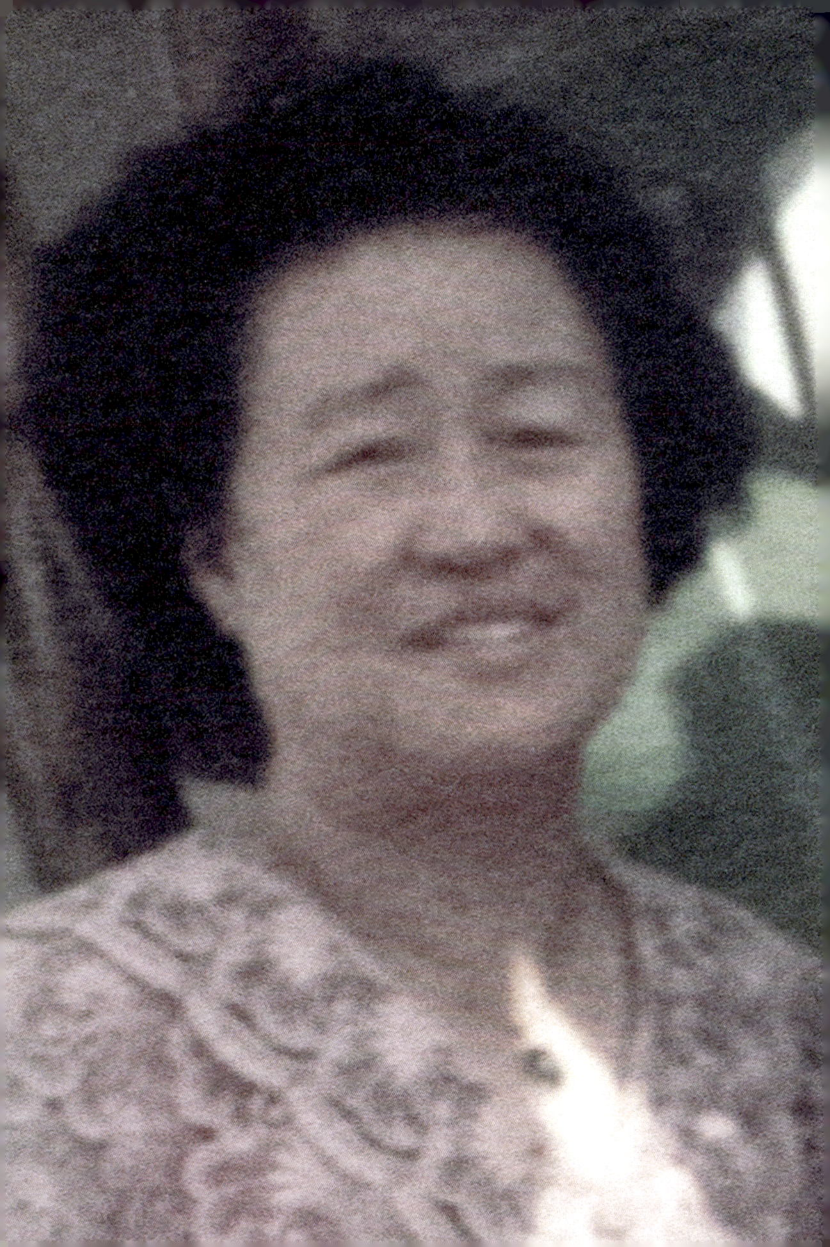

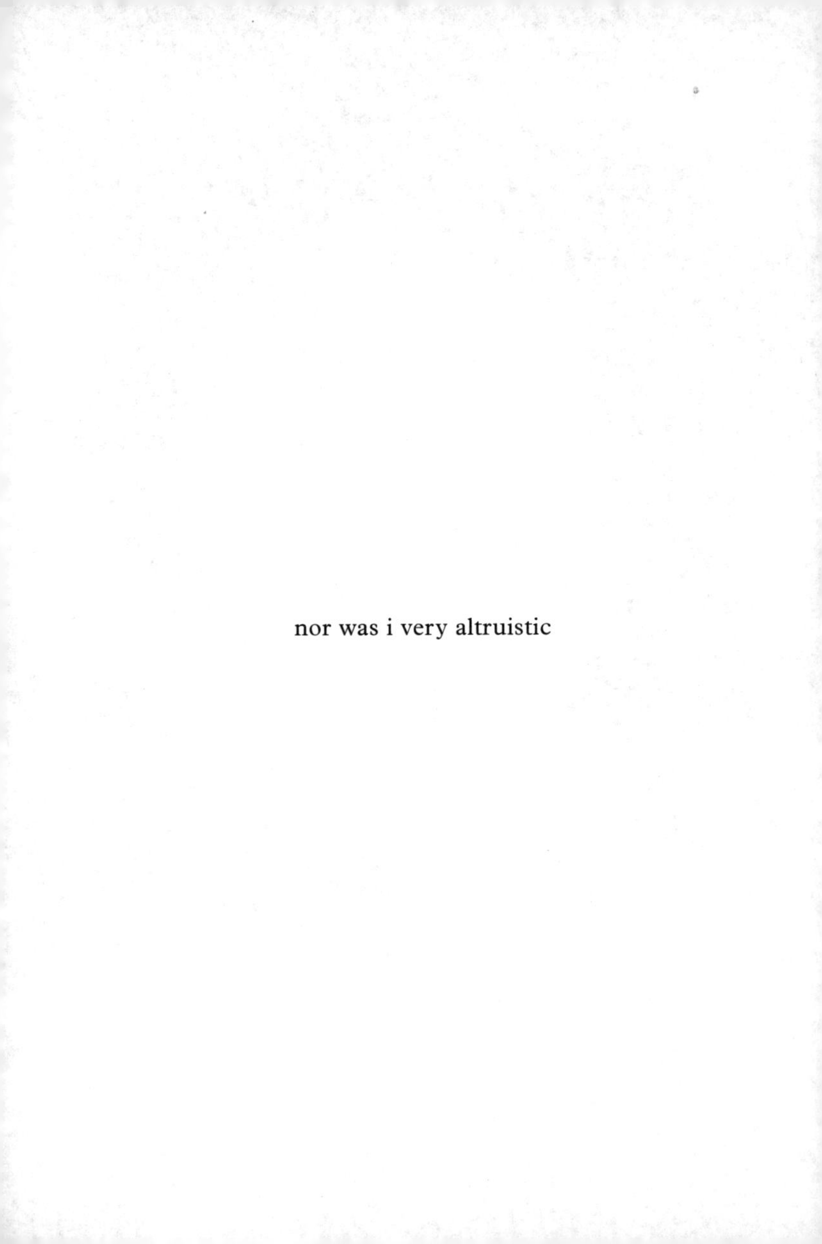
nor was i very altruistic

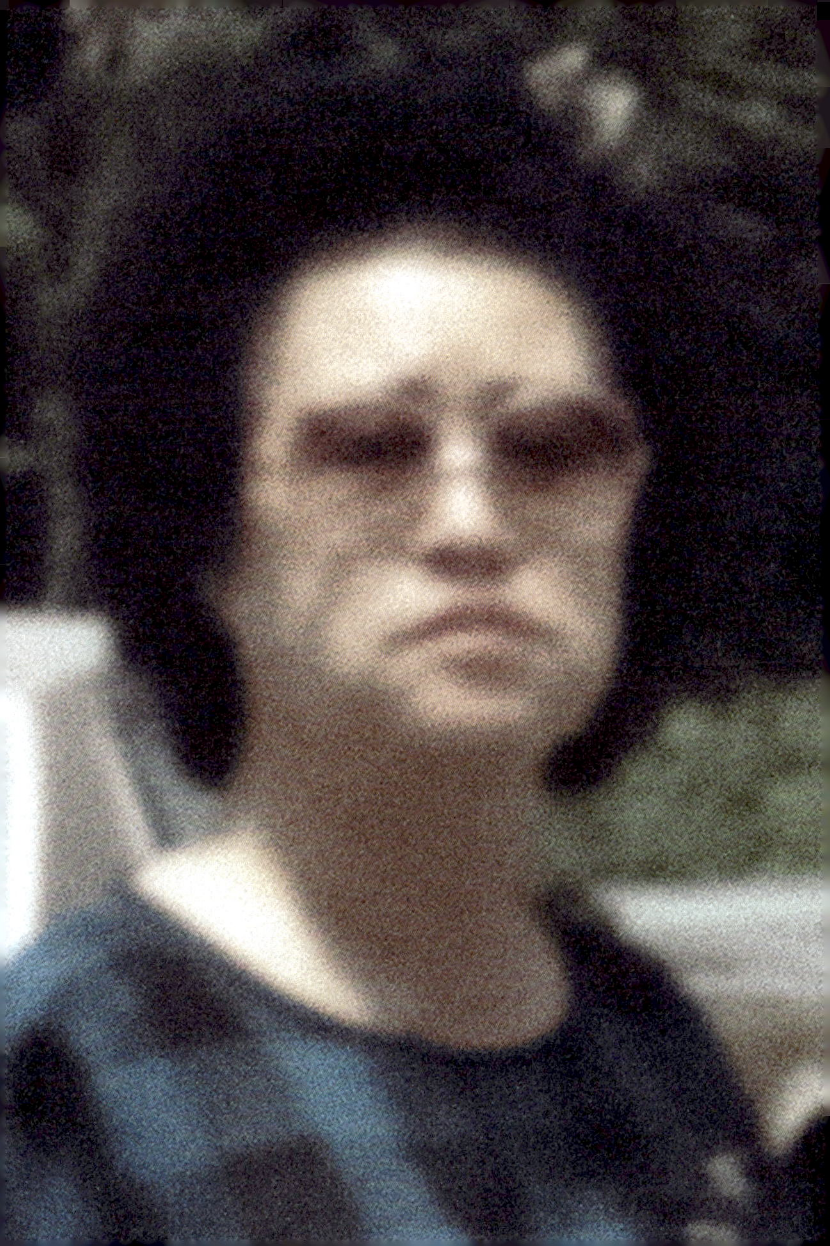

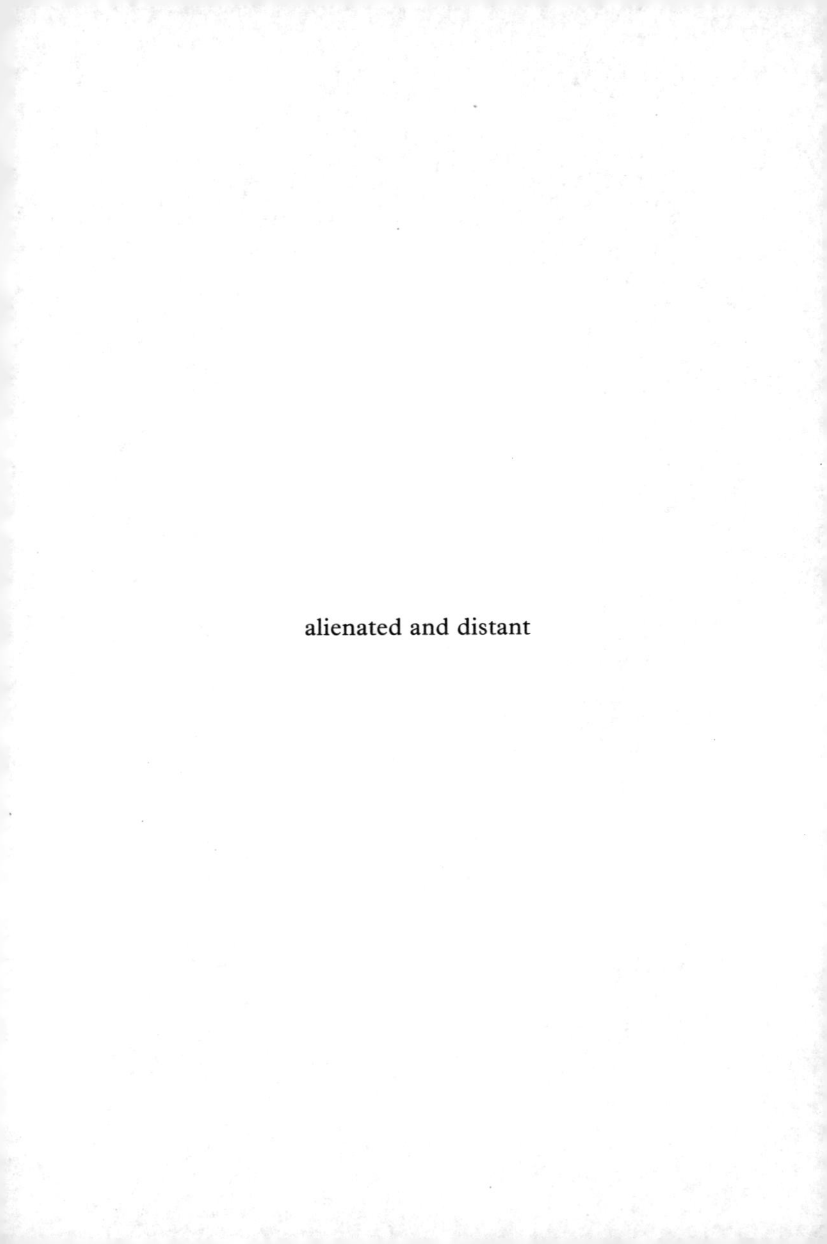

alienated and distant

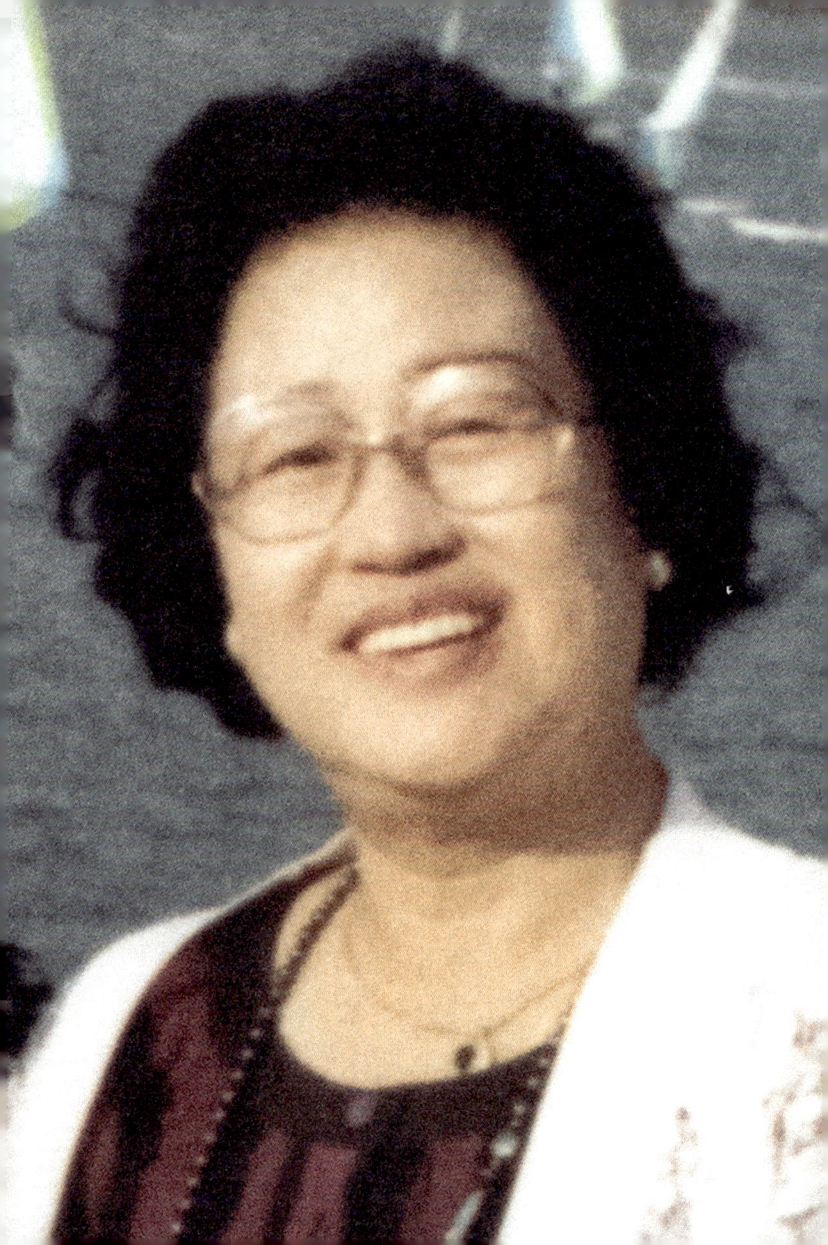

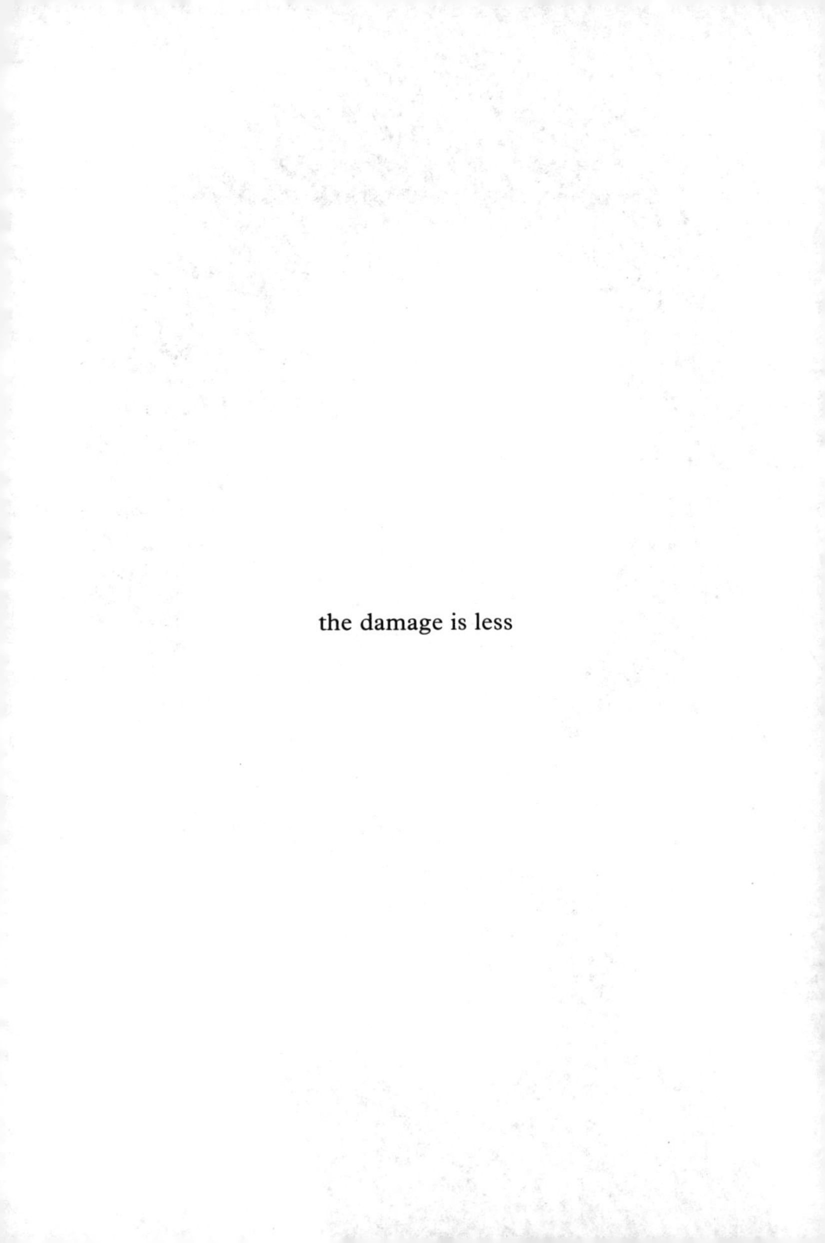

the damage is less

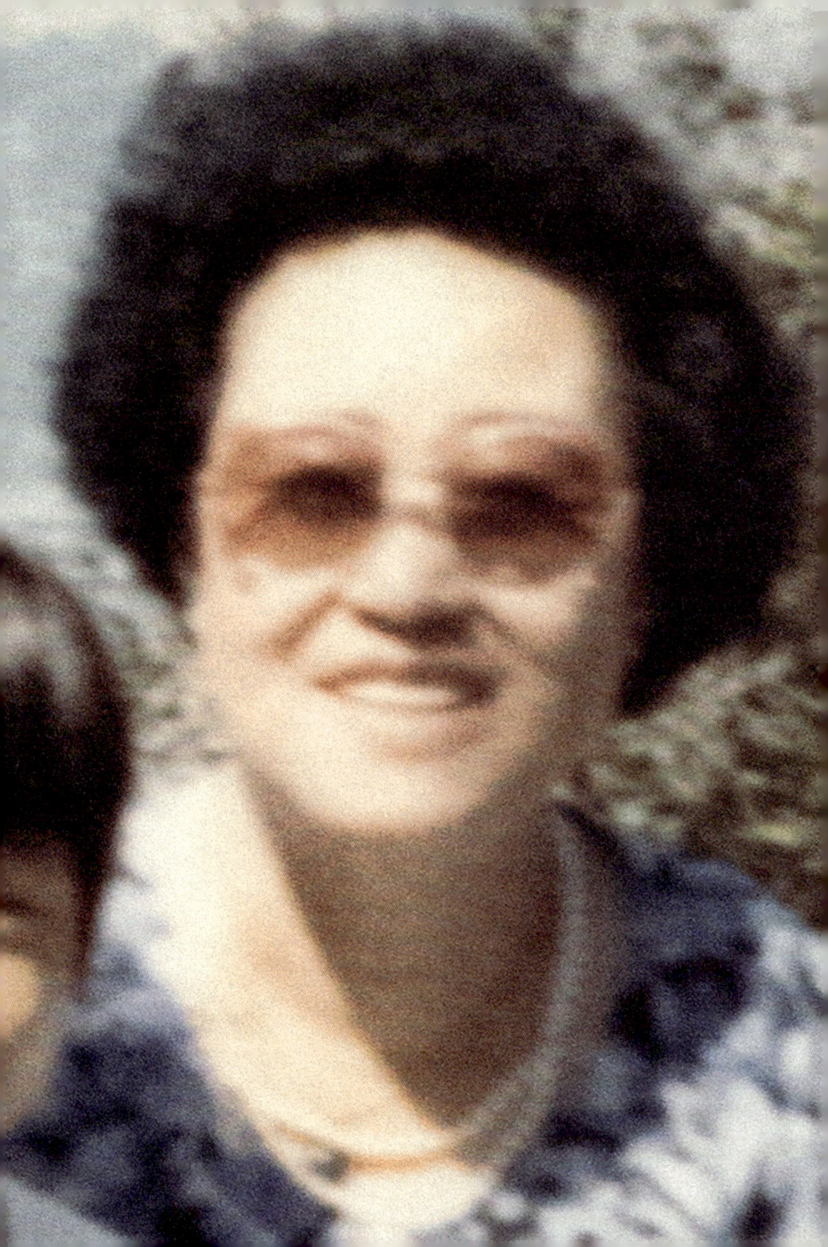

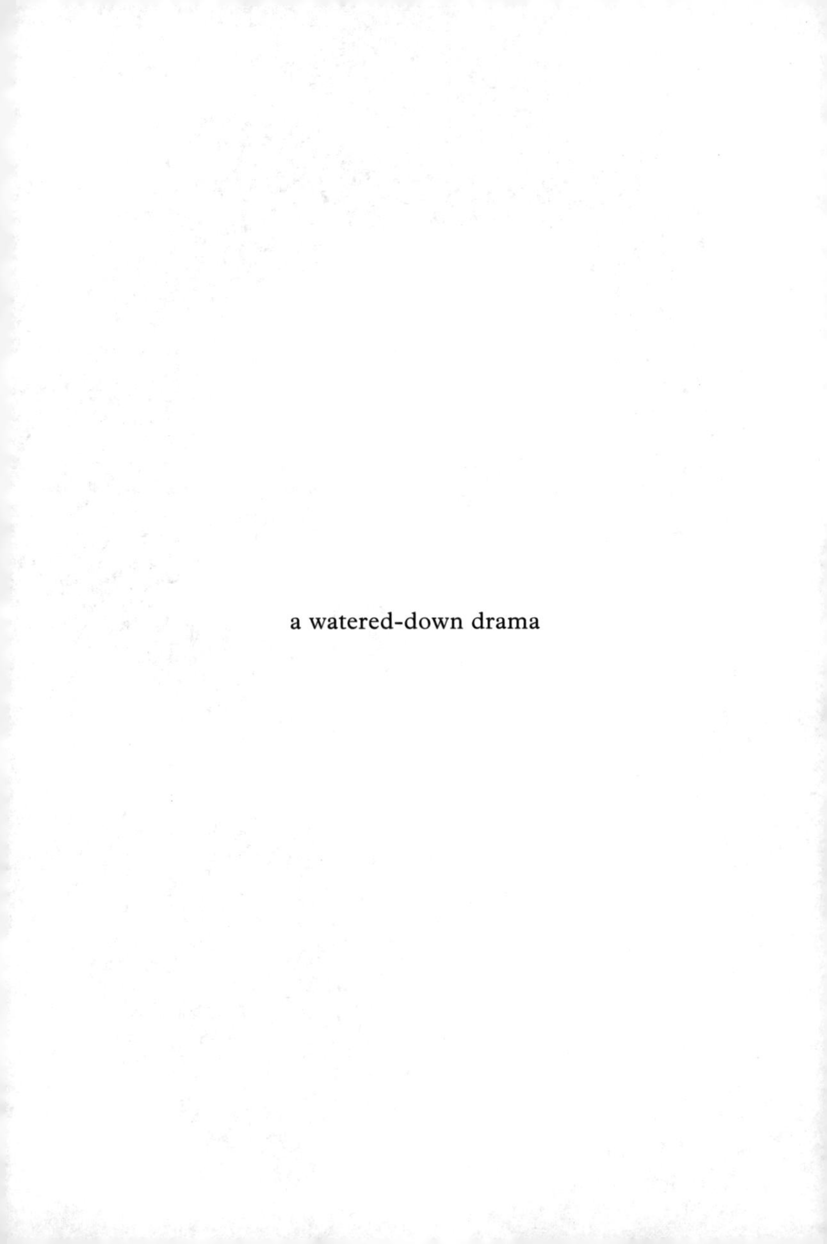

a watered-down drama

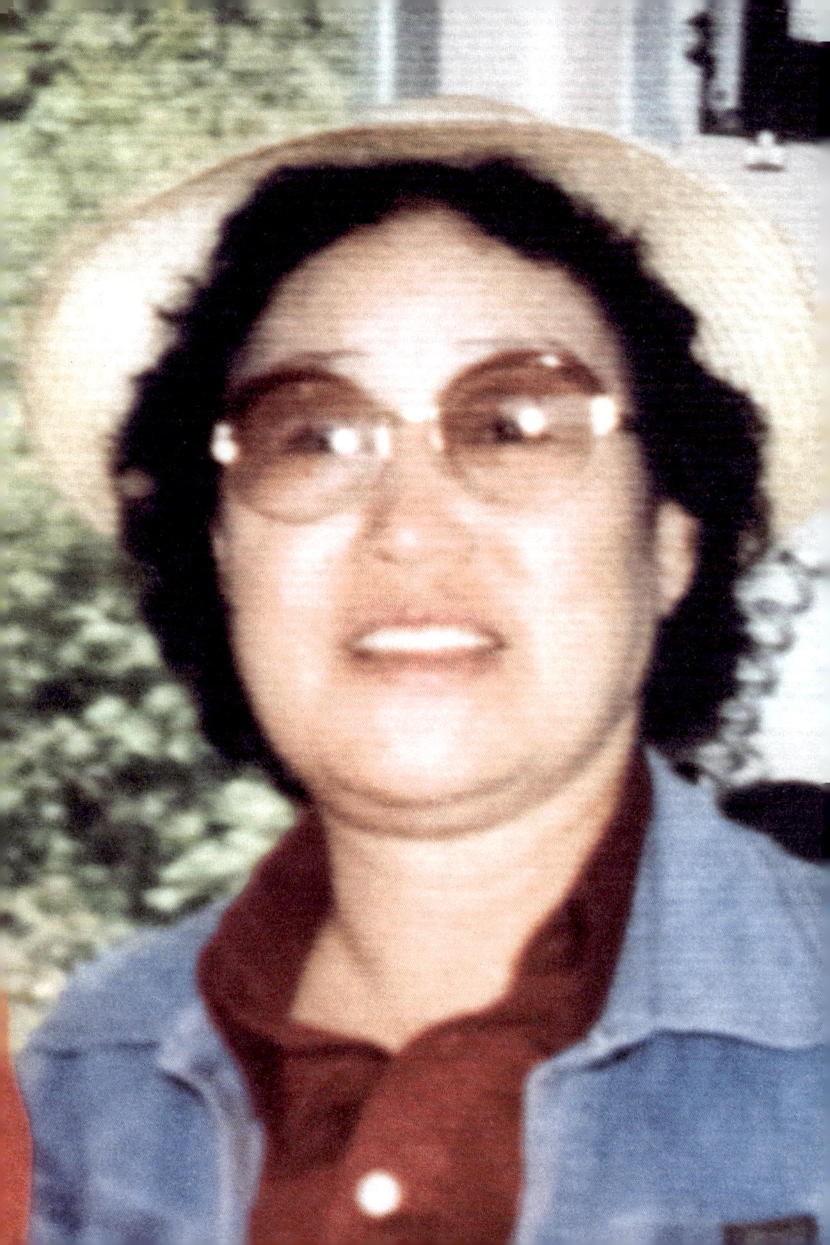

is all i got

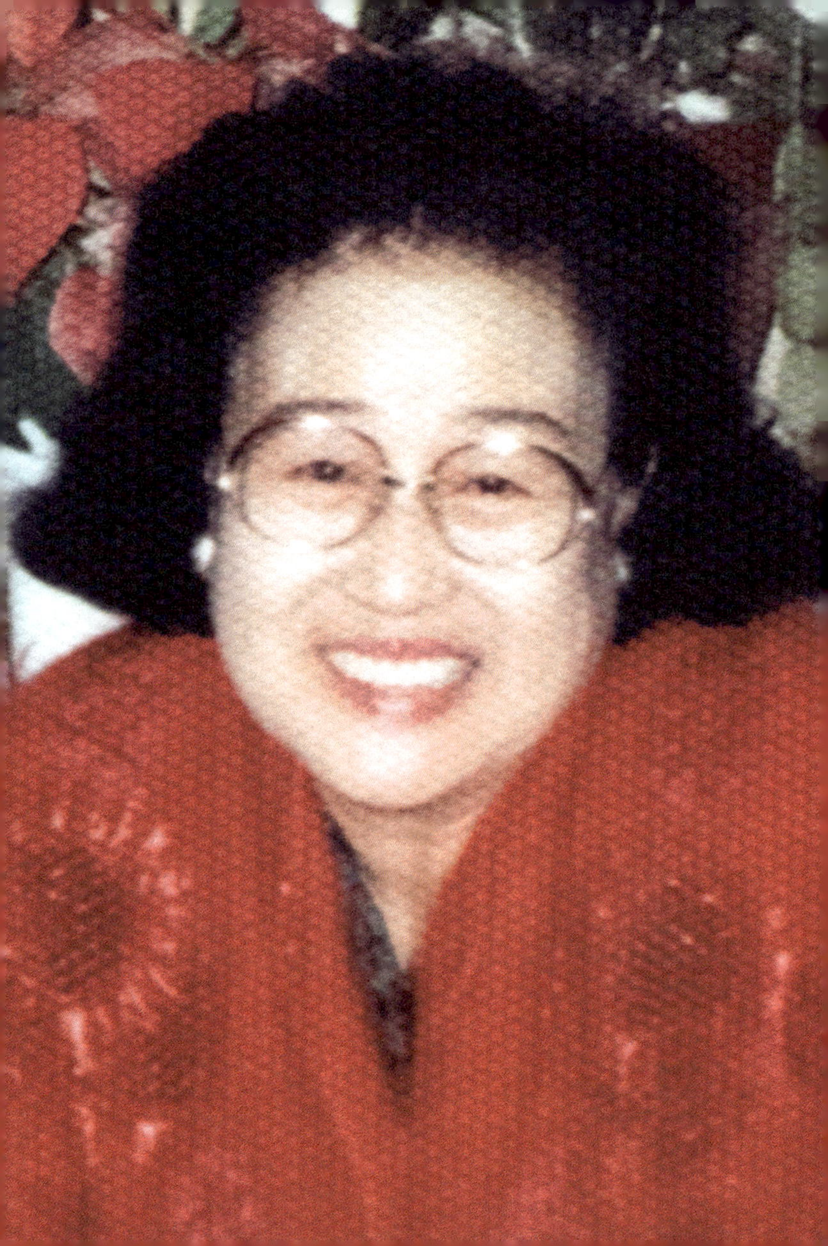

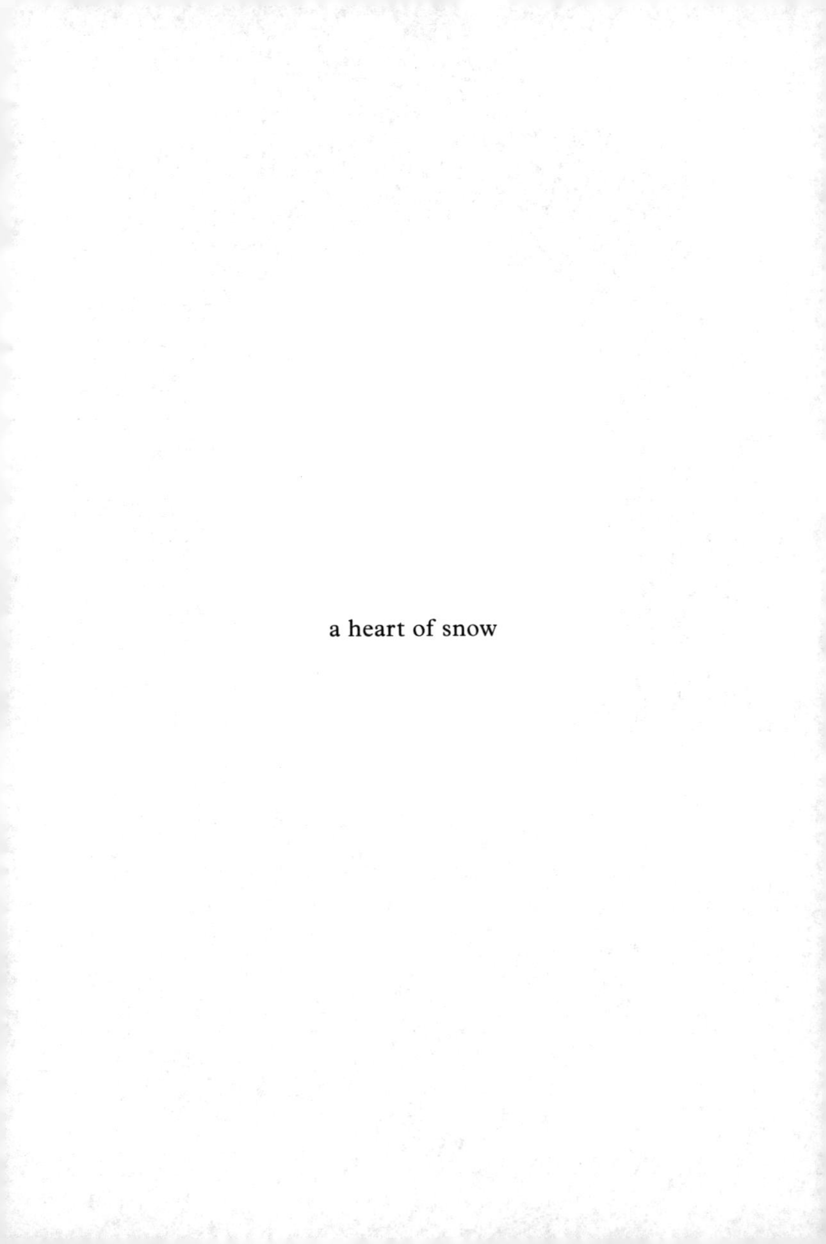

a heart of snow

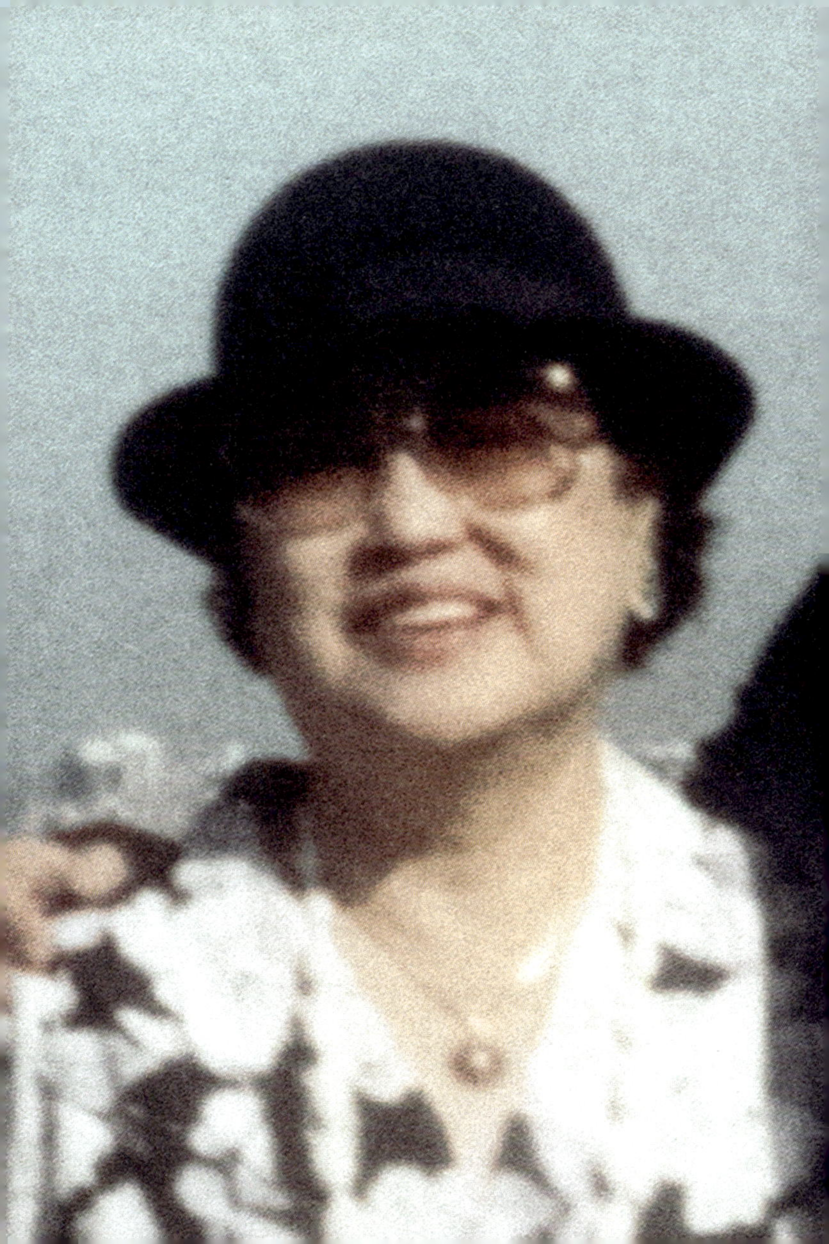

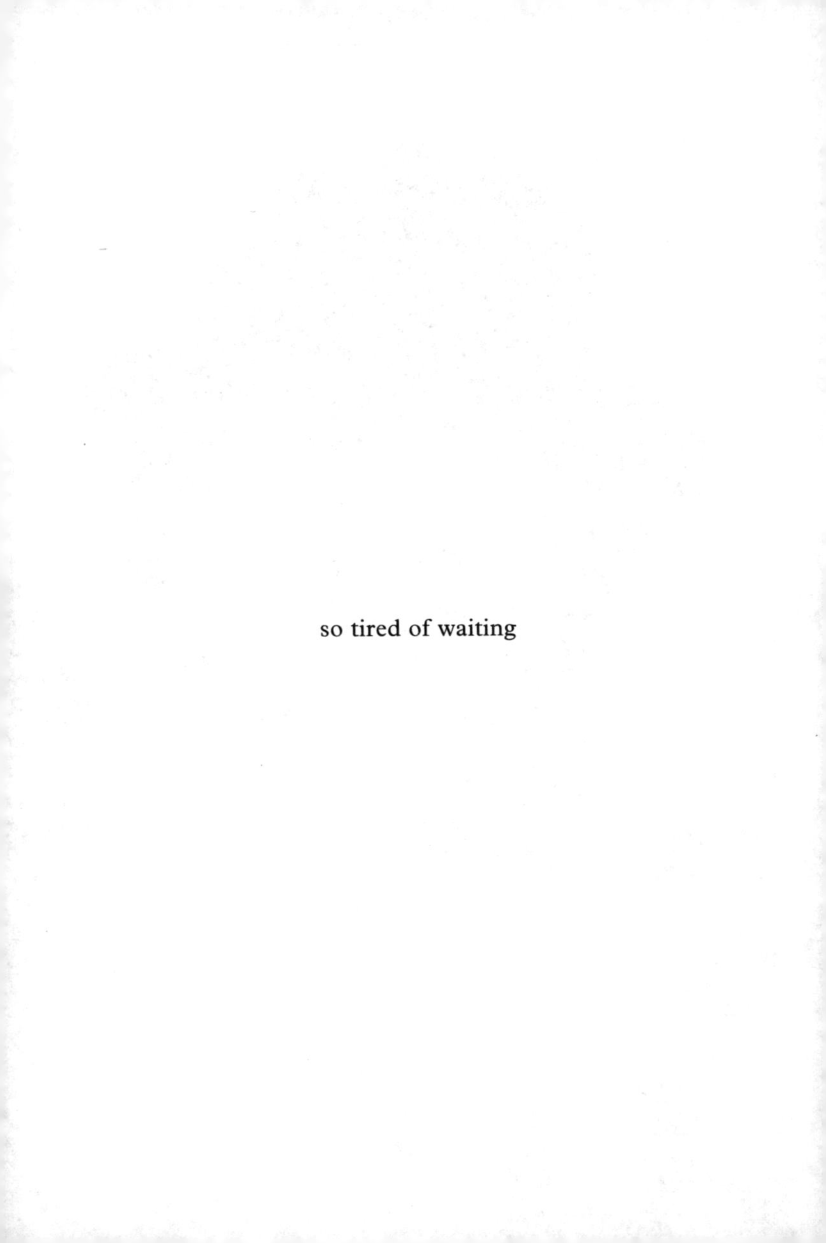

so tired of waiting

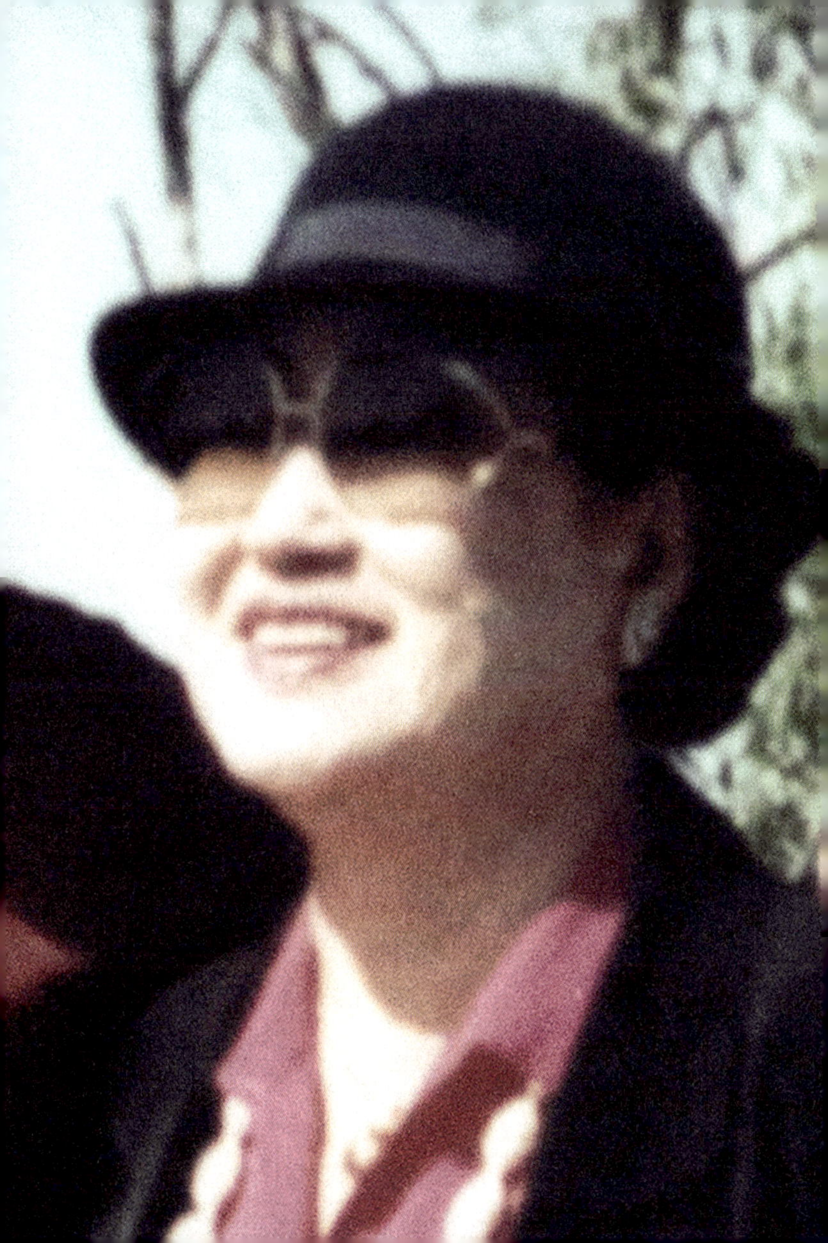

it will beat again

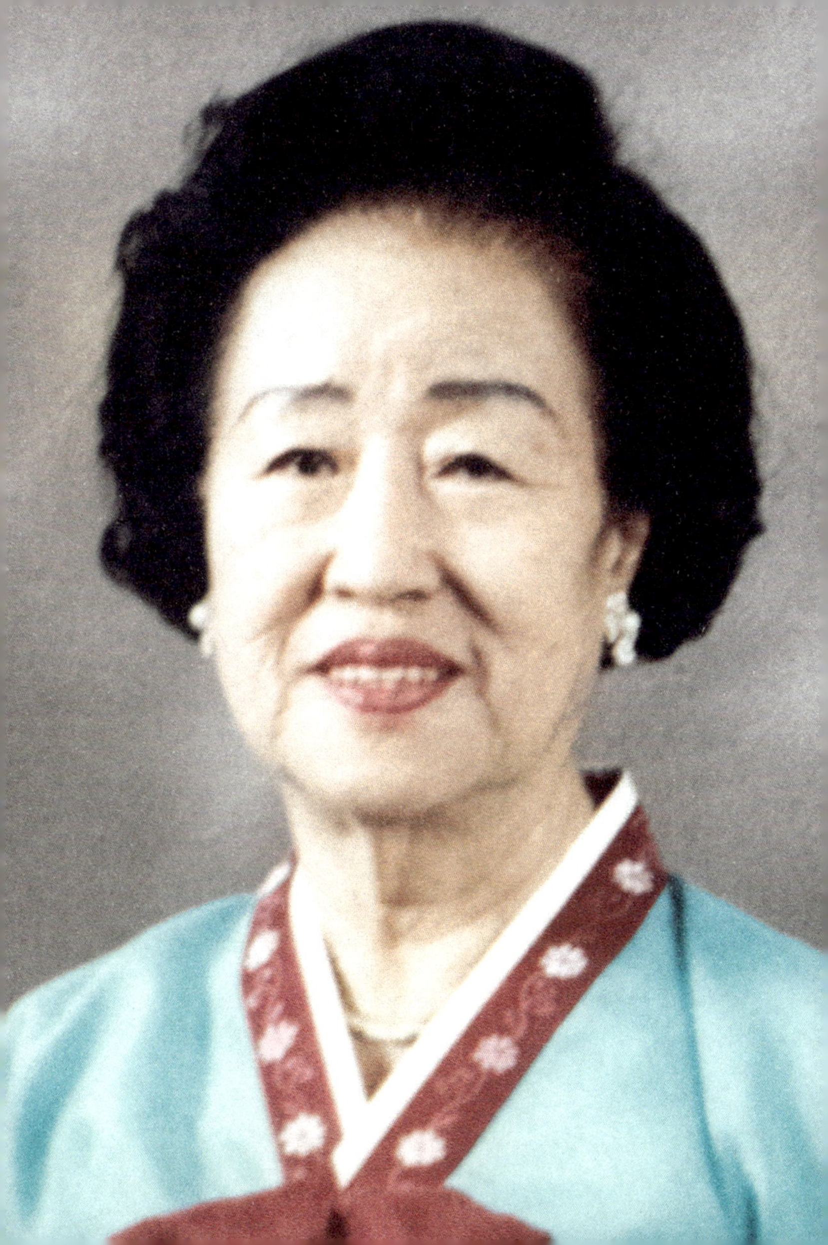

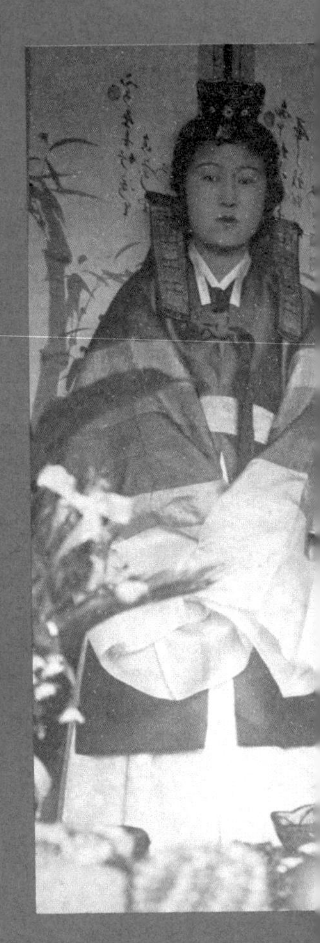

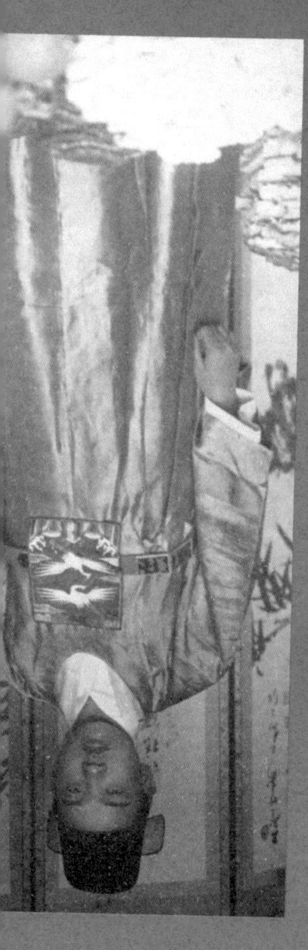

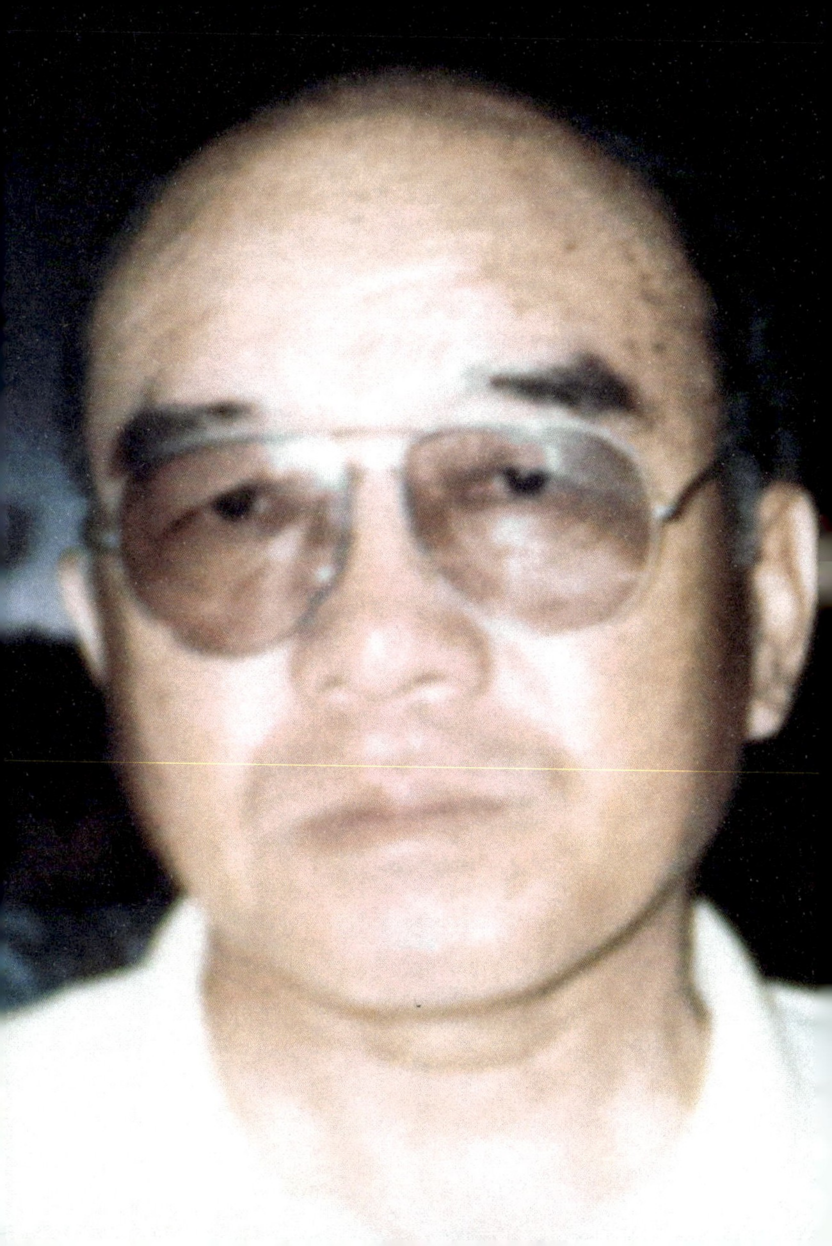

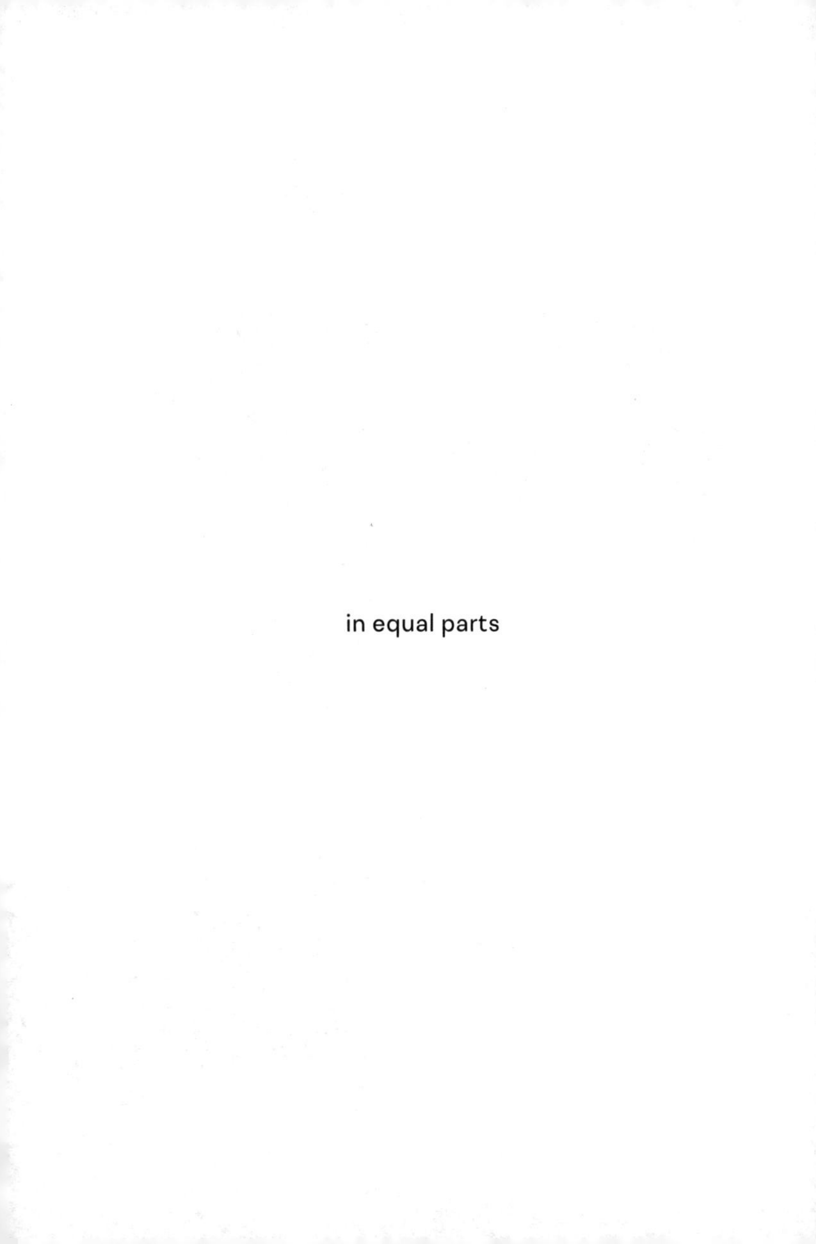

in equal parts

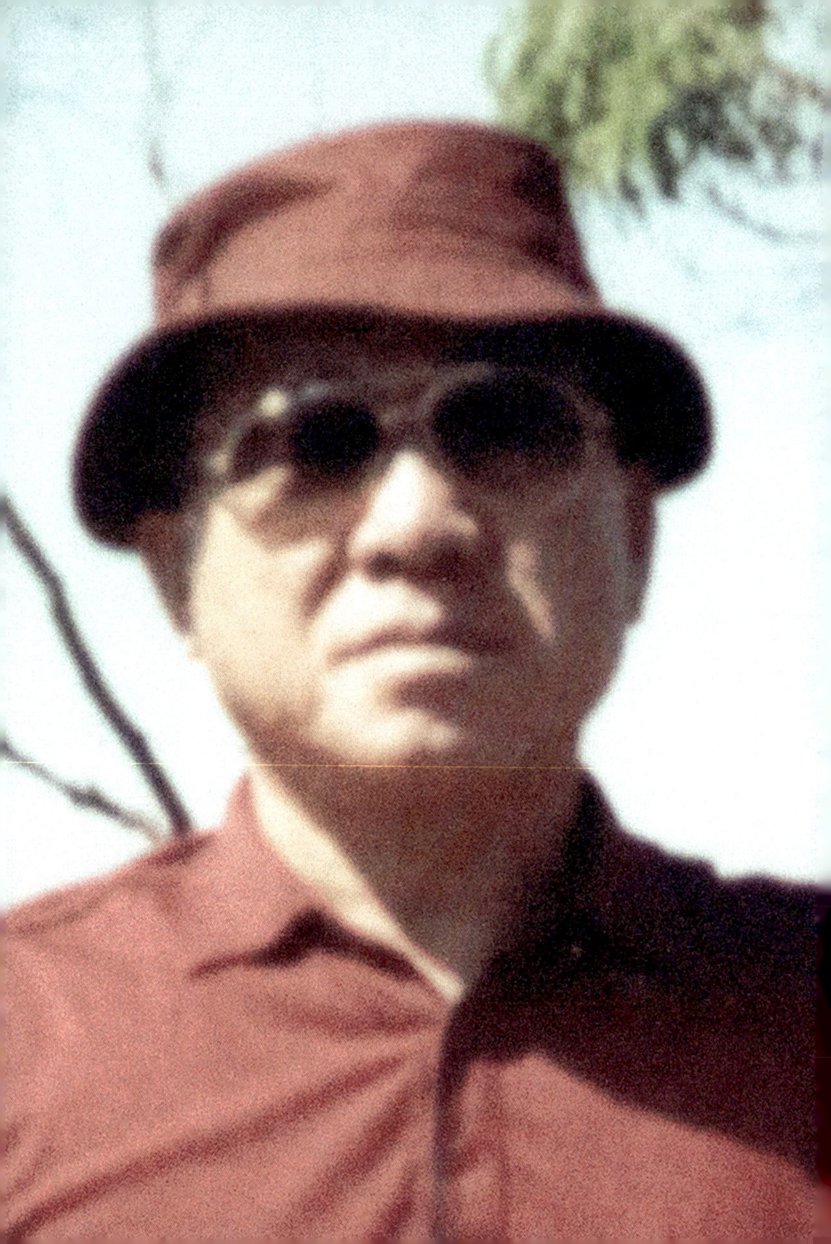

nothing

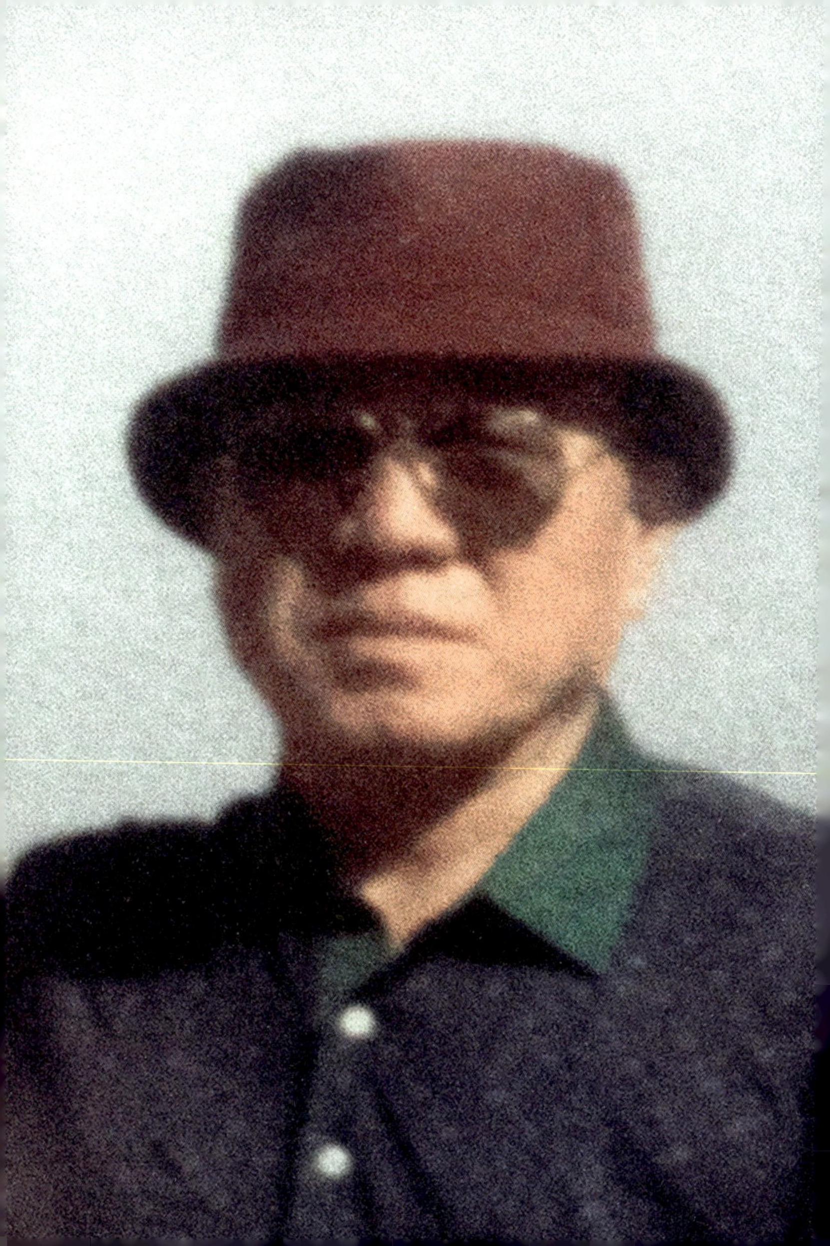

for nobody

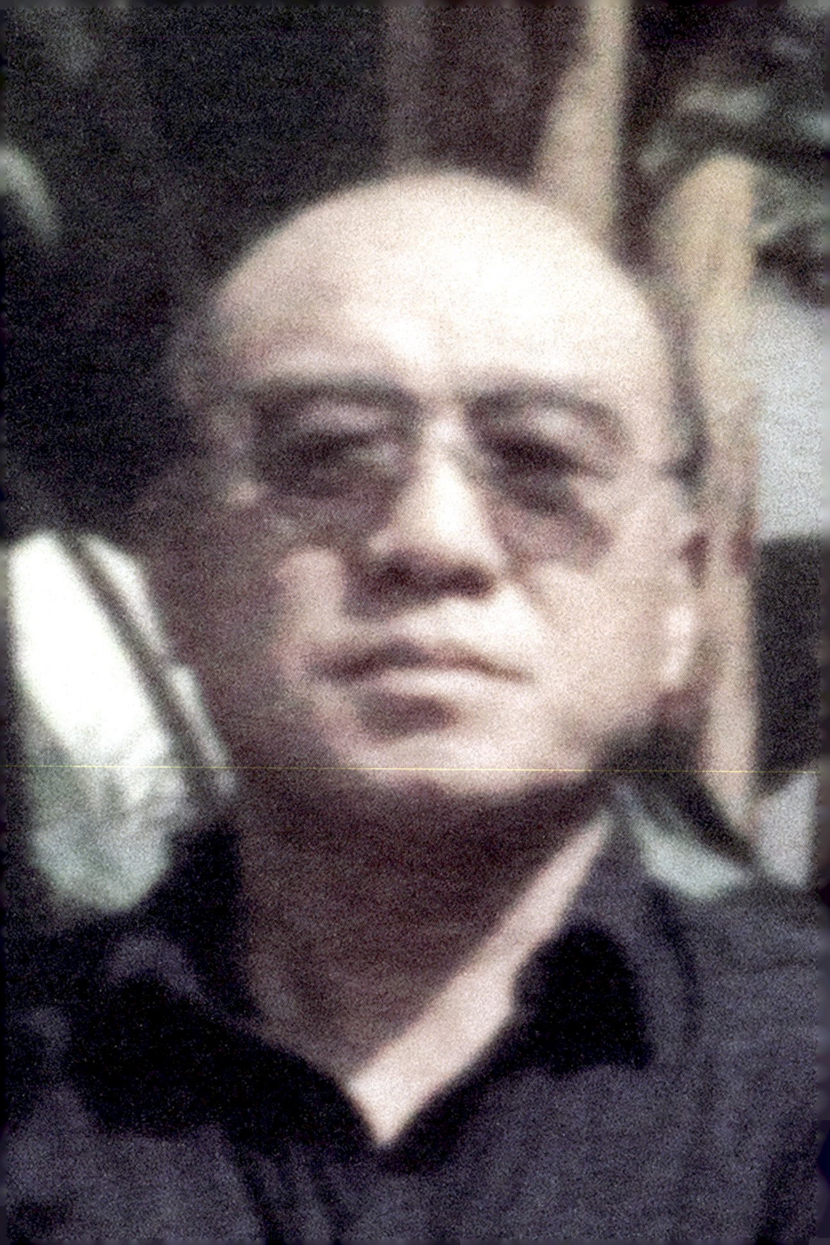

all

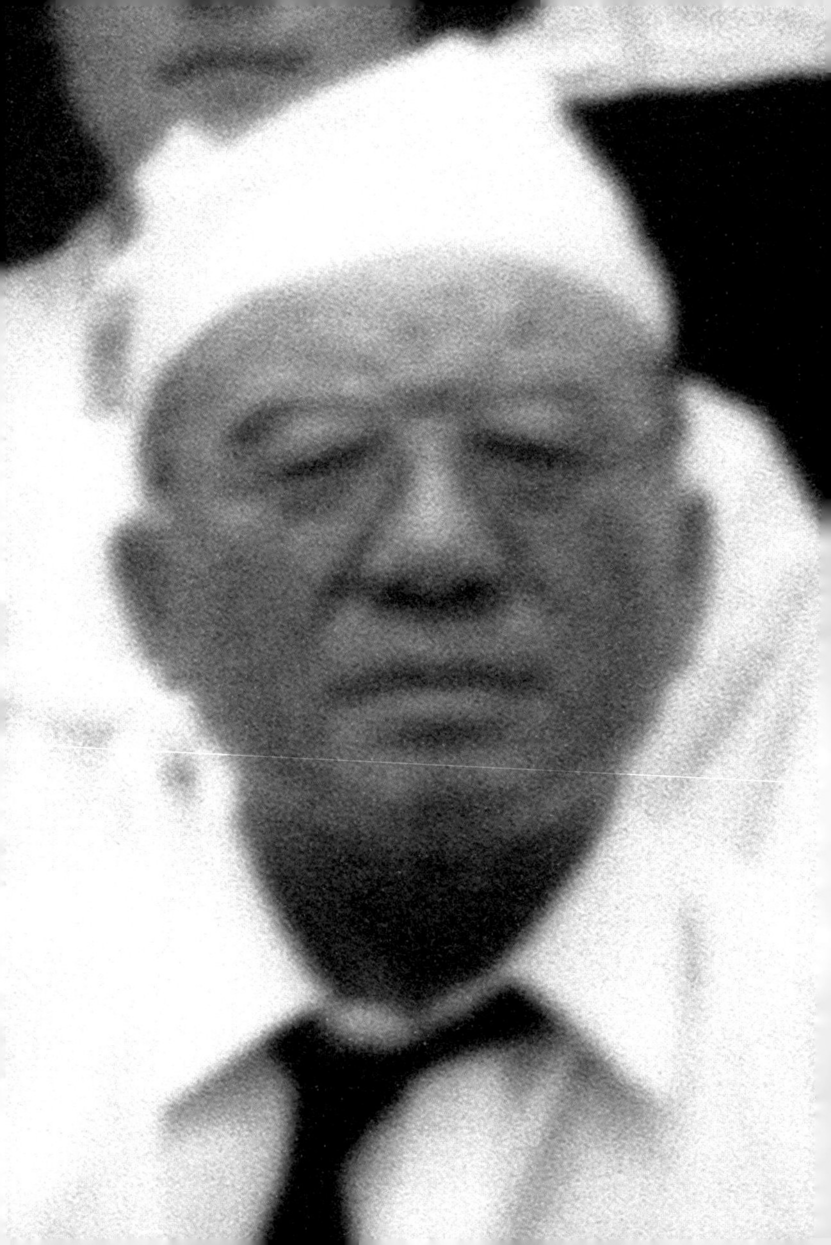

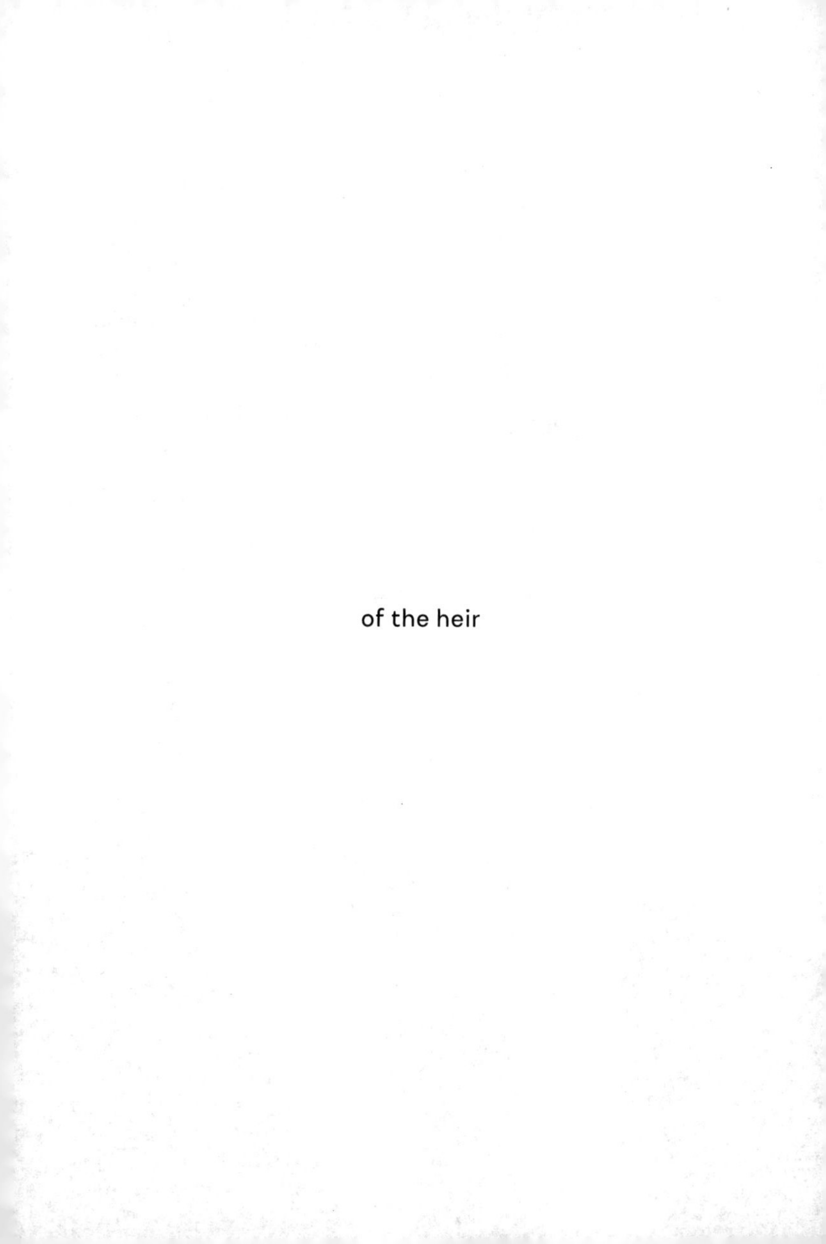

of the heir

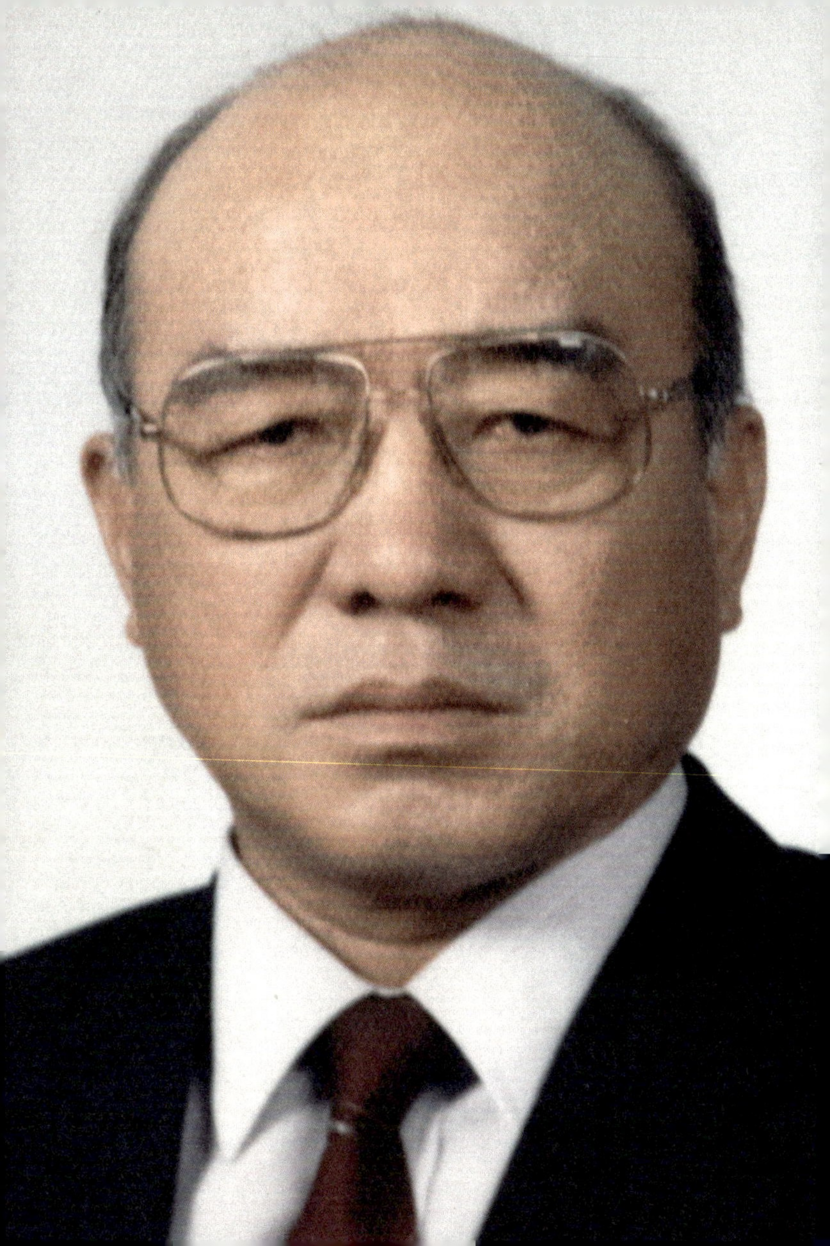

the last will

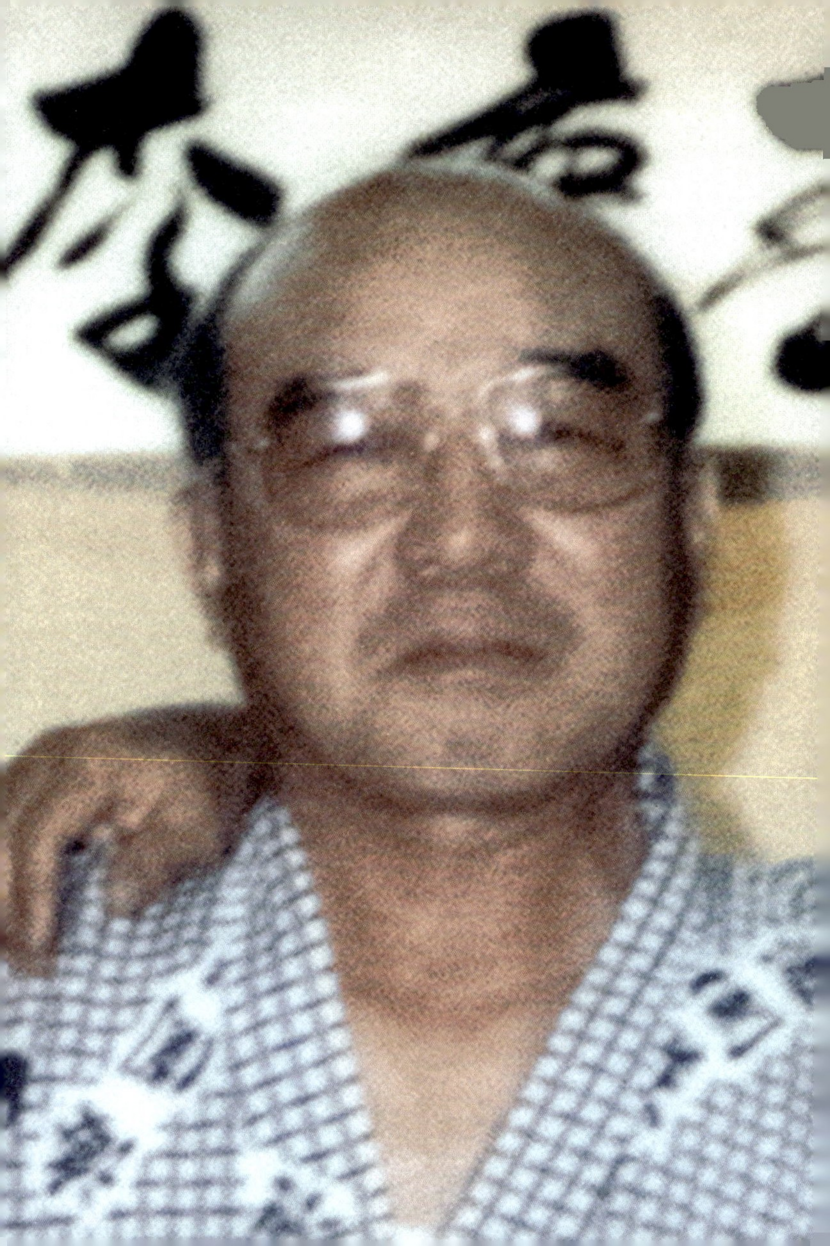

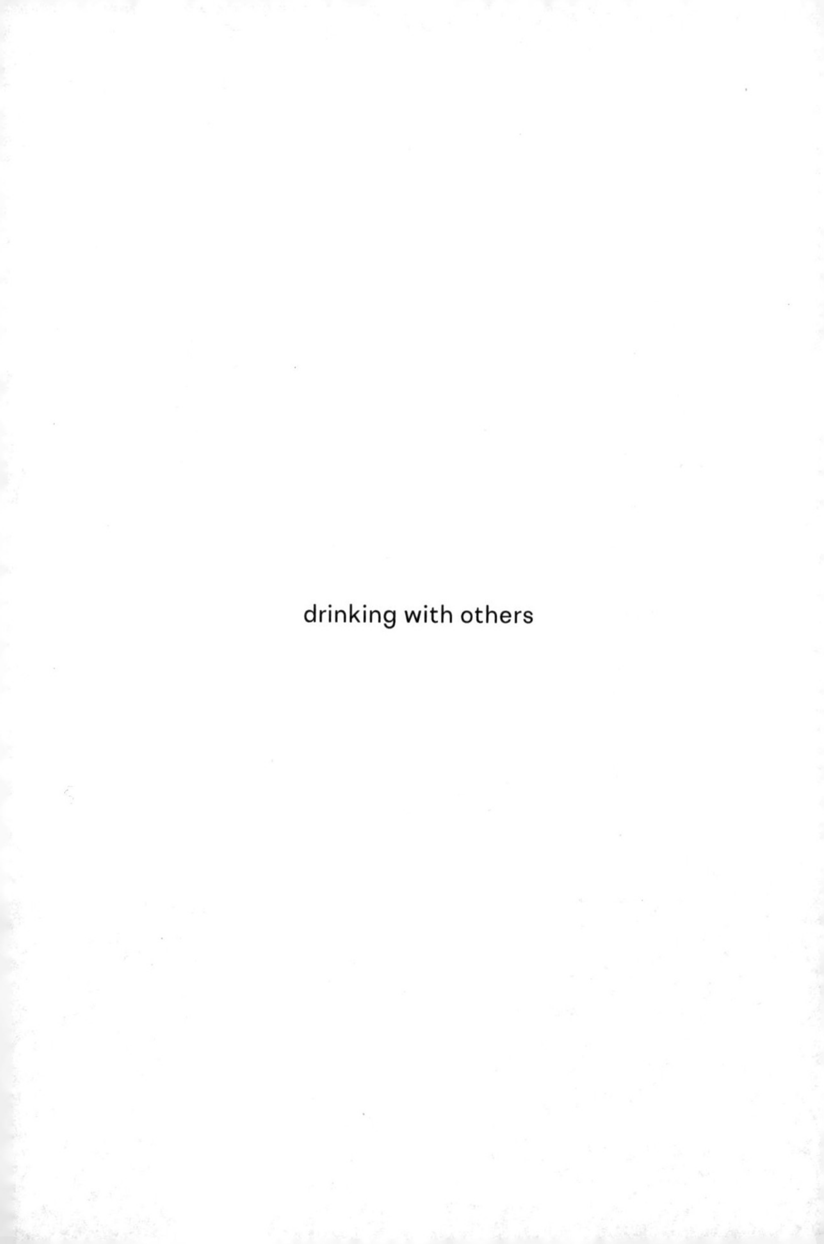

drinking with others

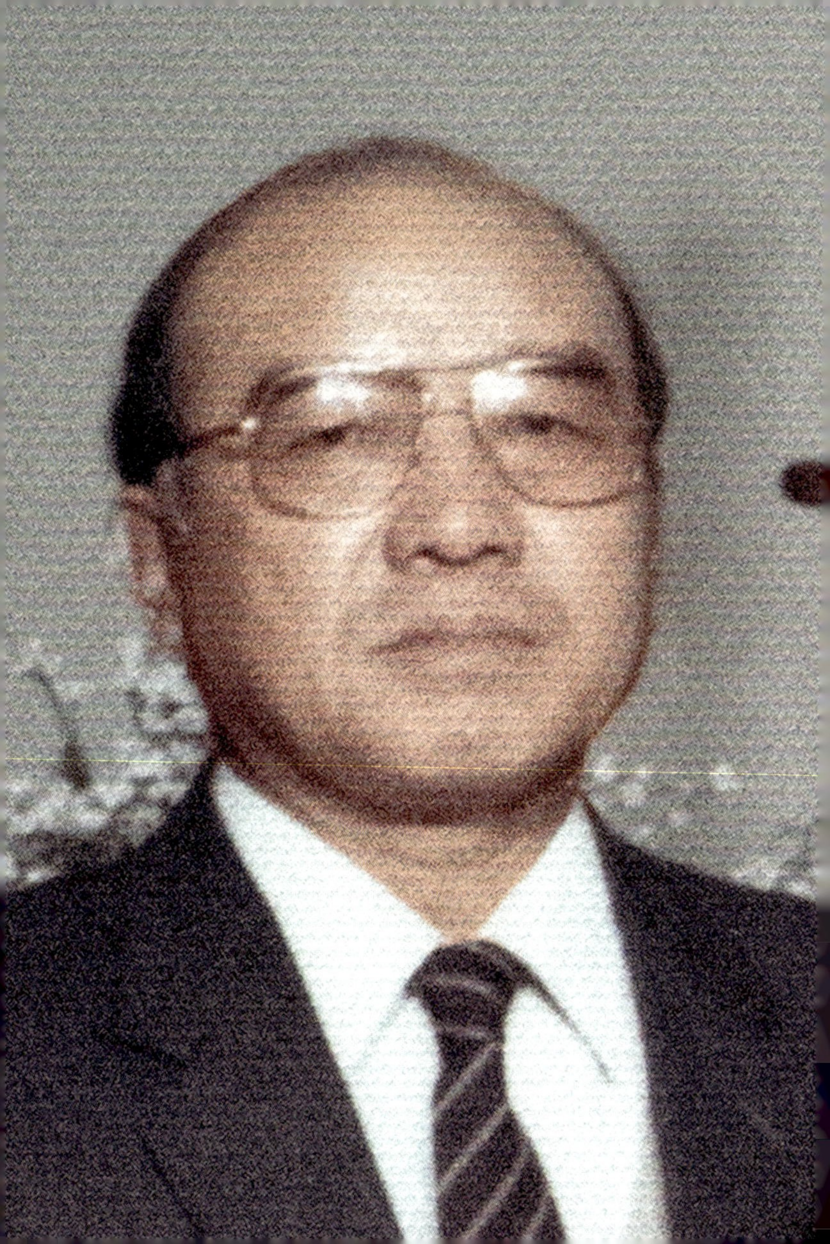

when i recall

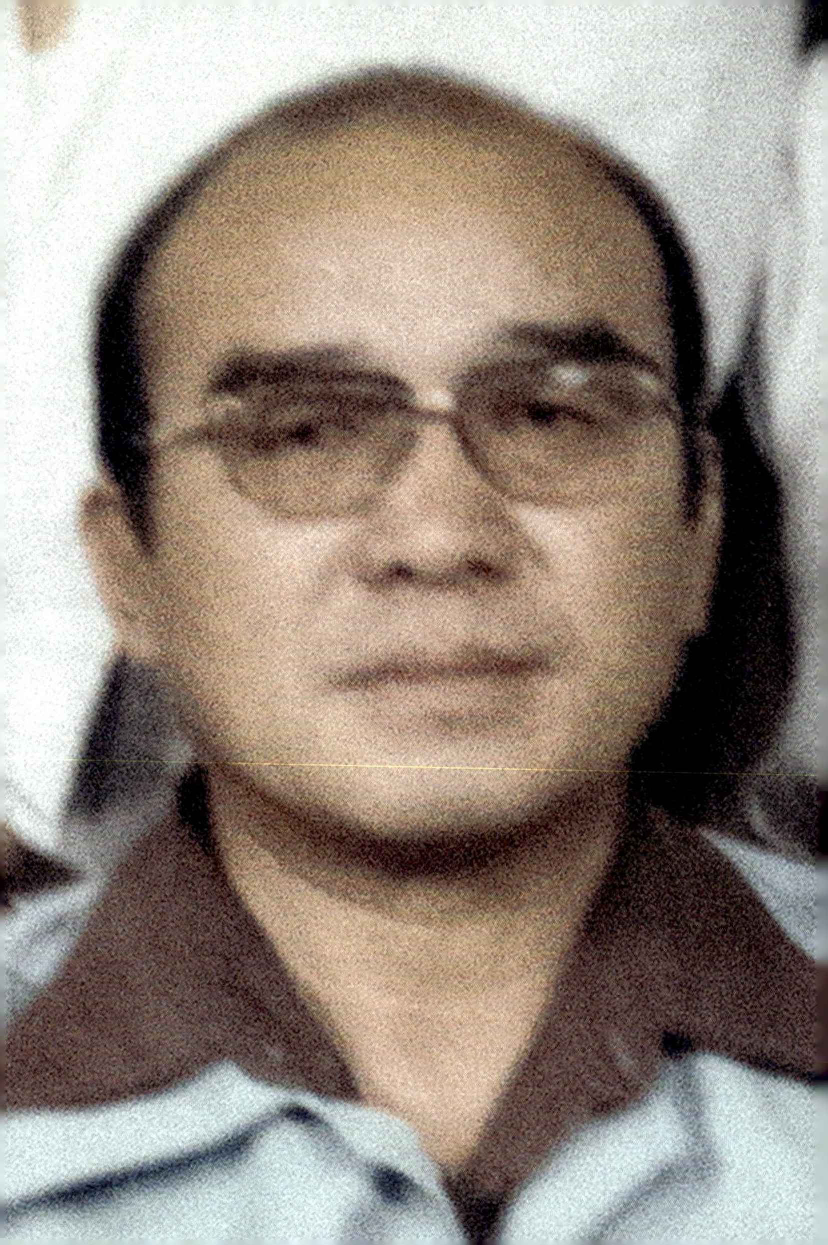

my eyes gleam

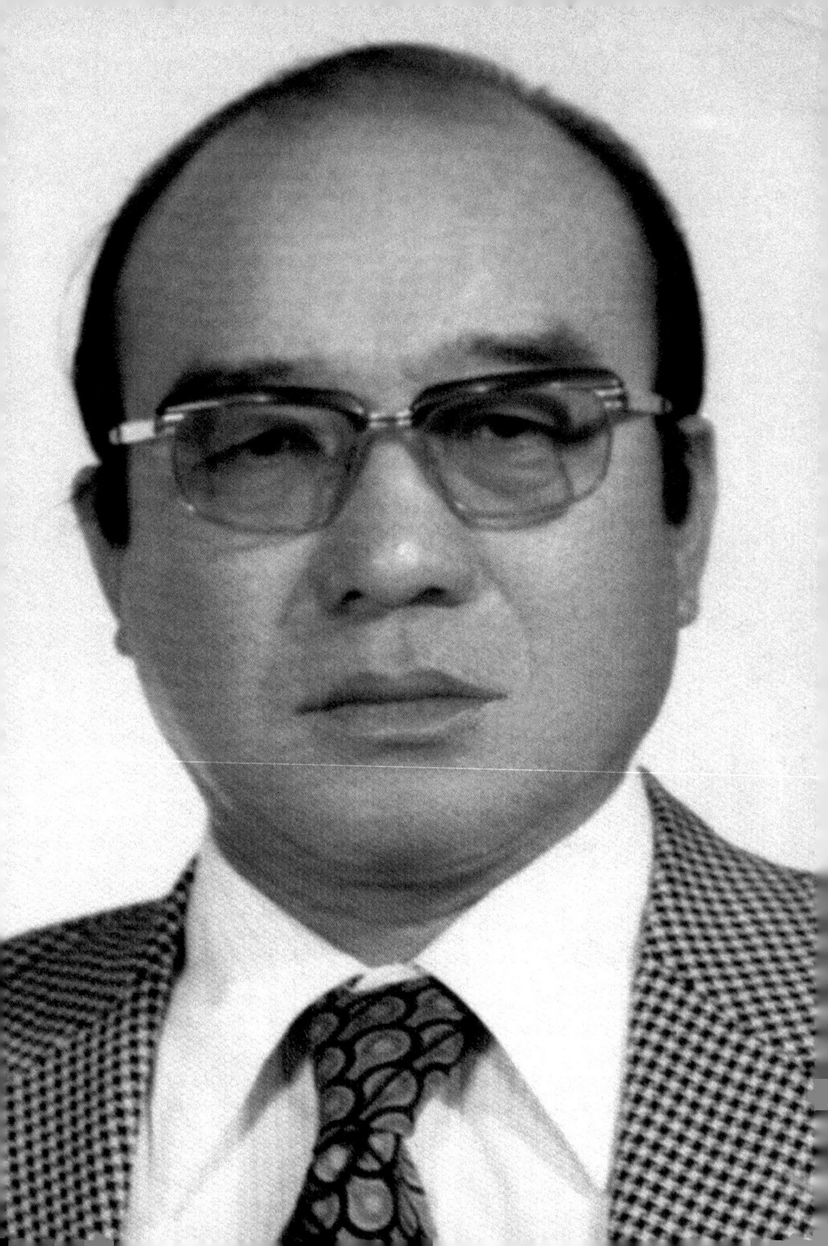

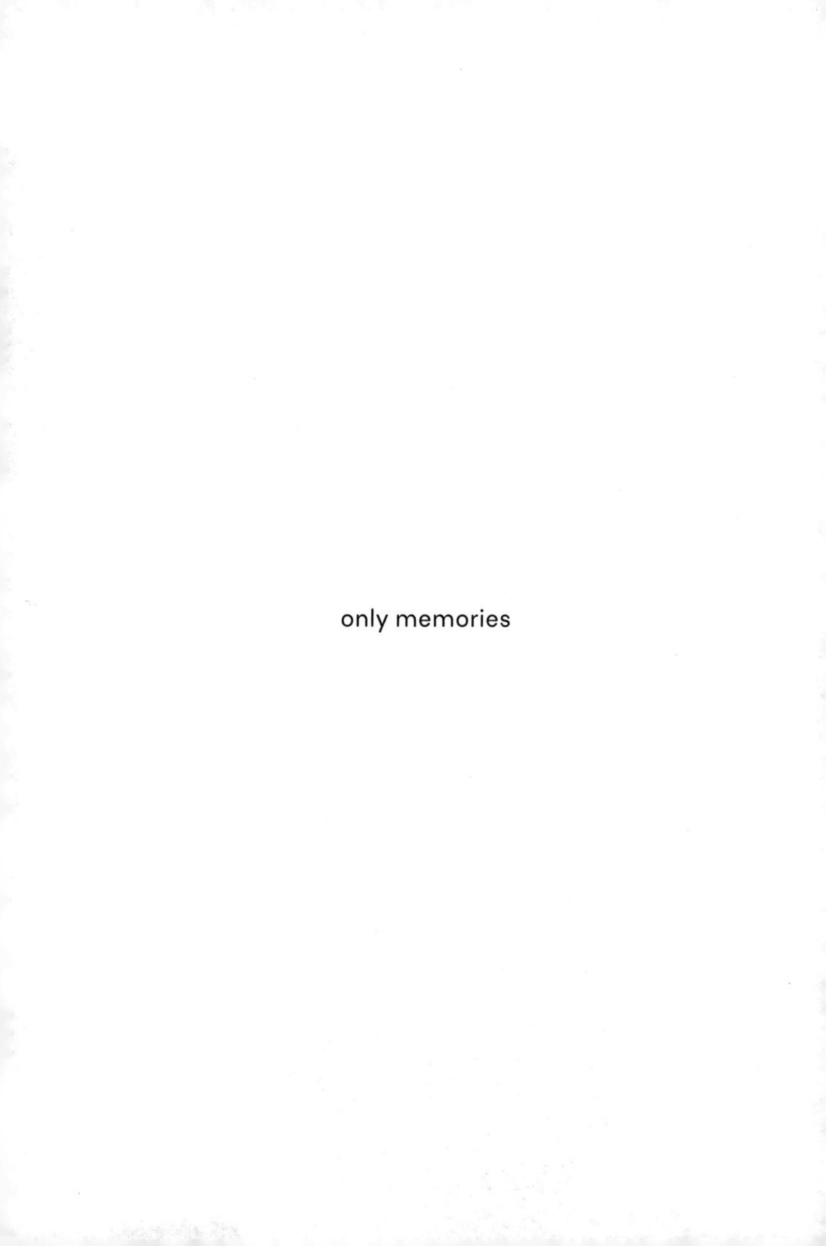

only memories

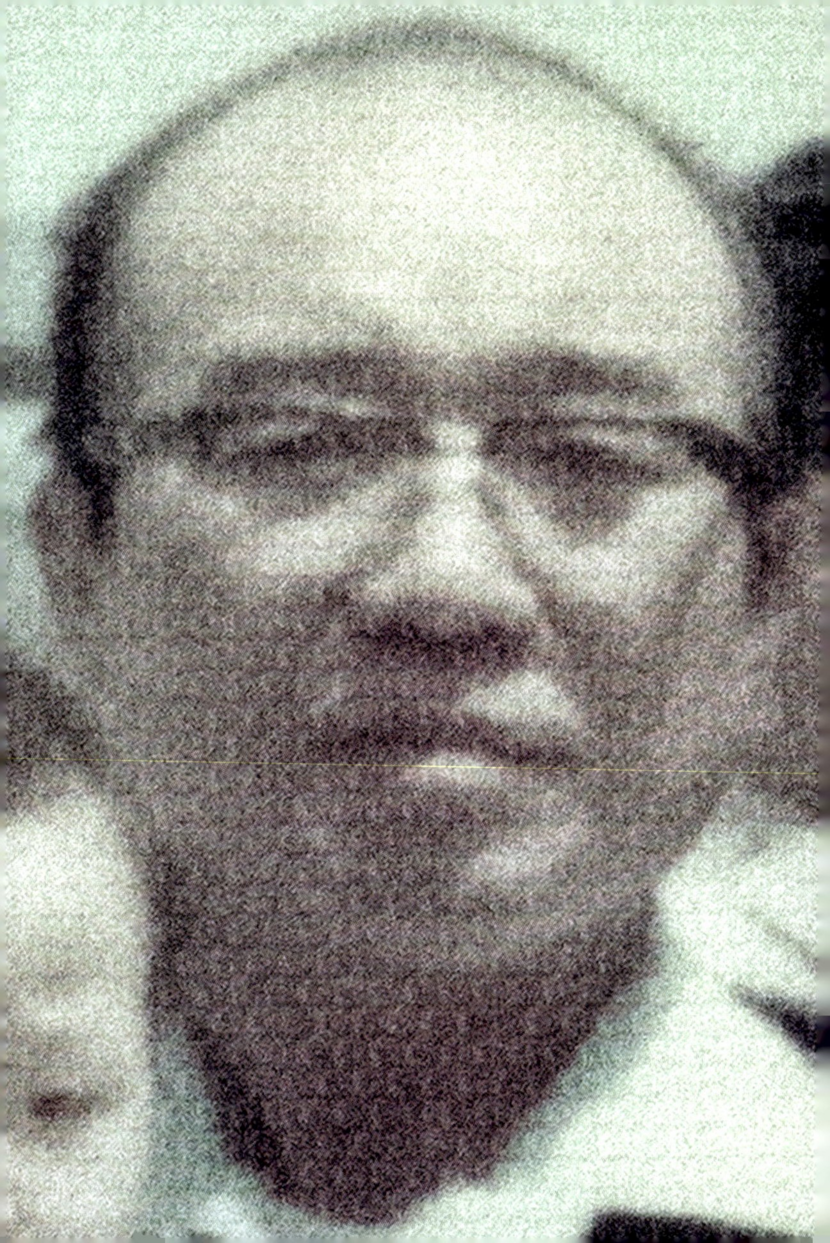

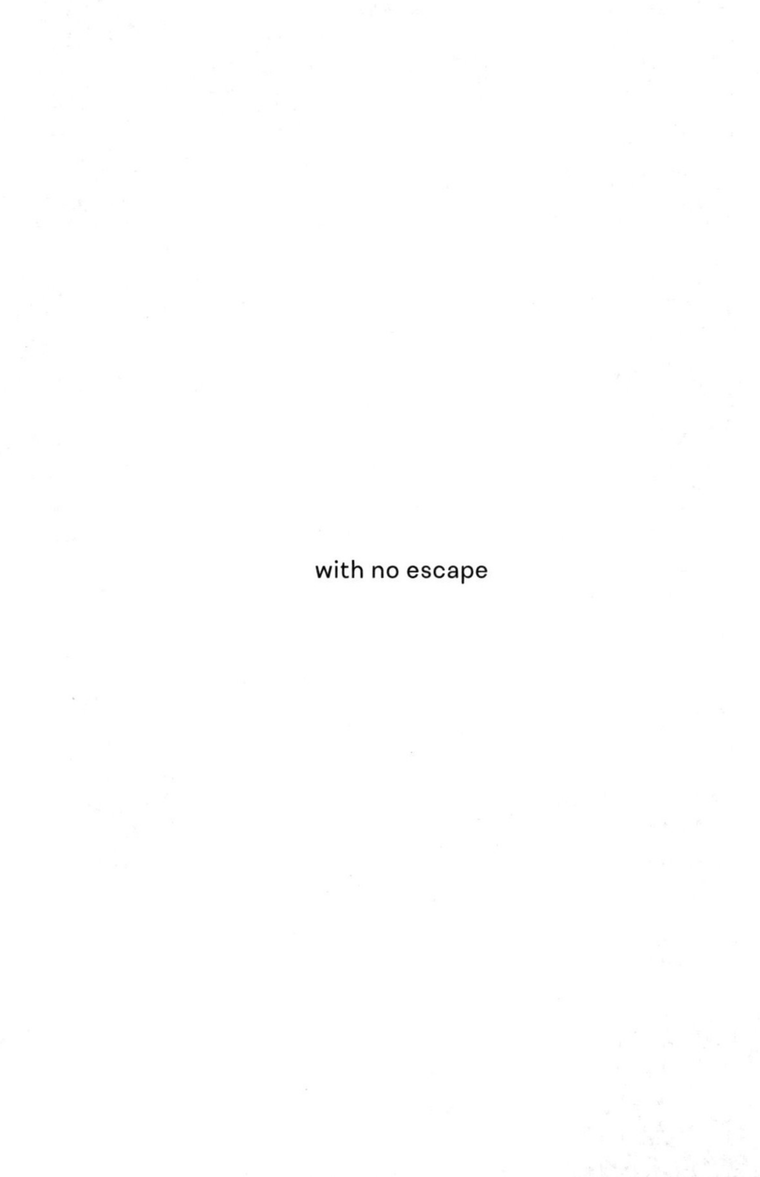
with no escape

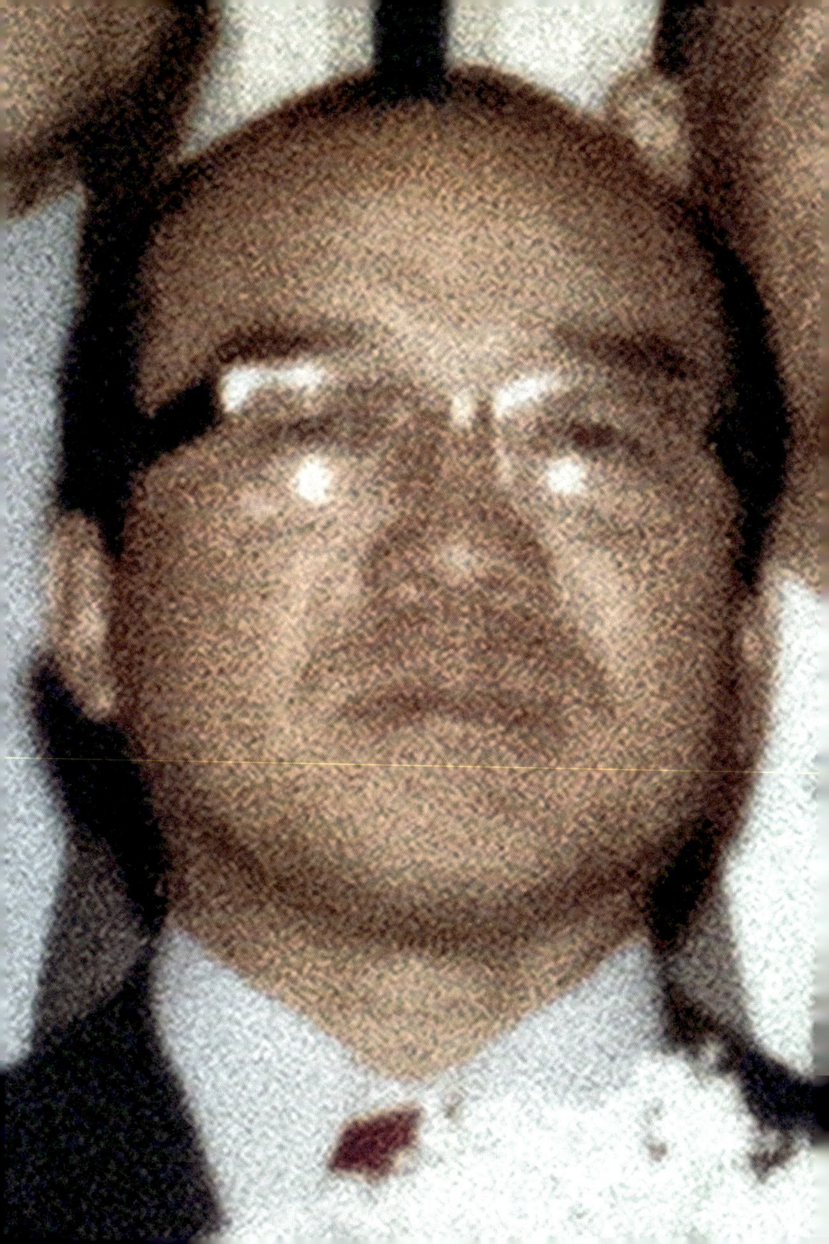

monotony

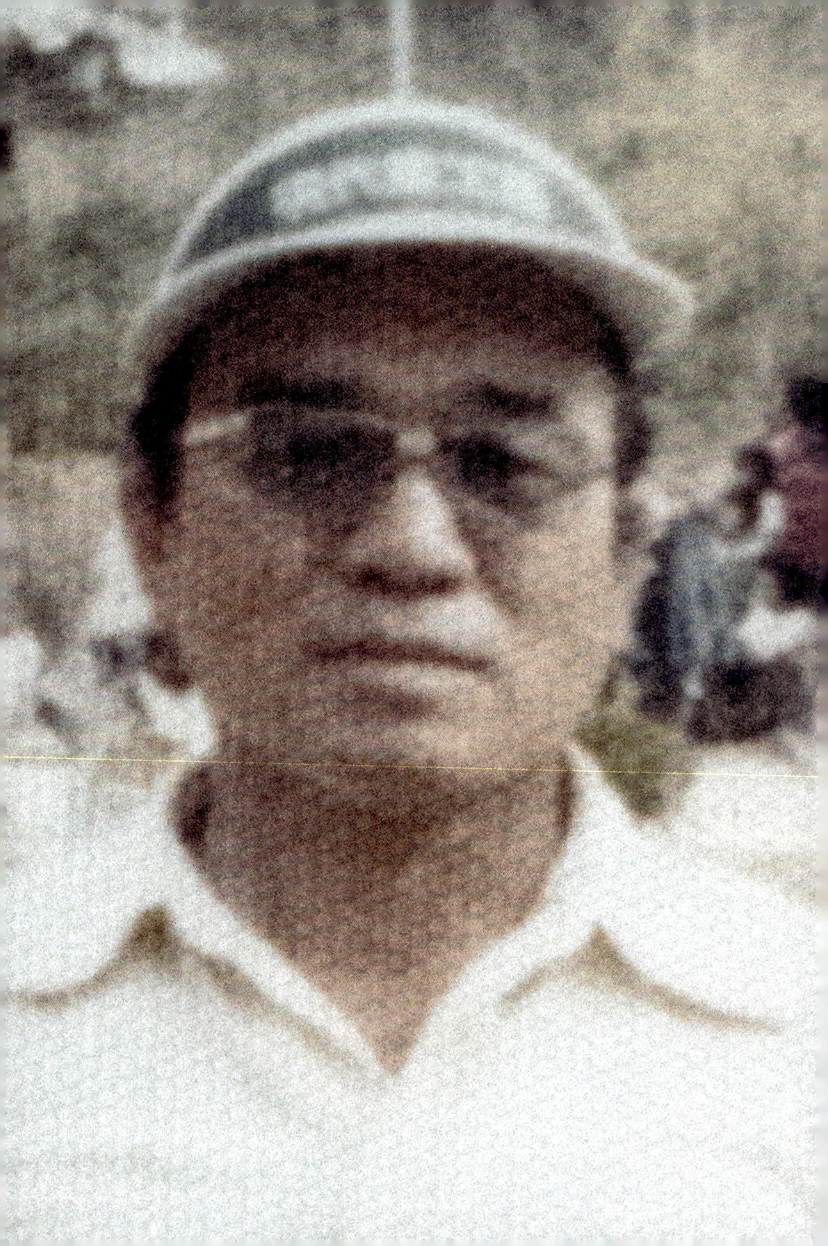

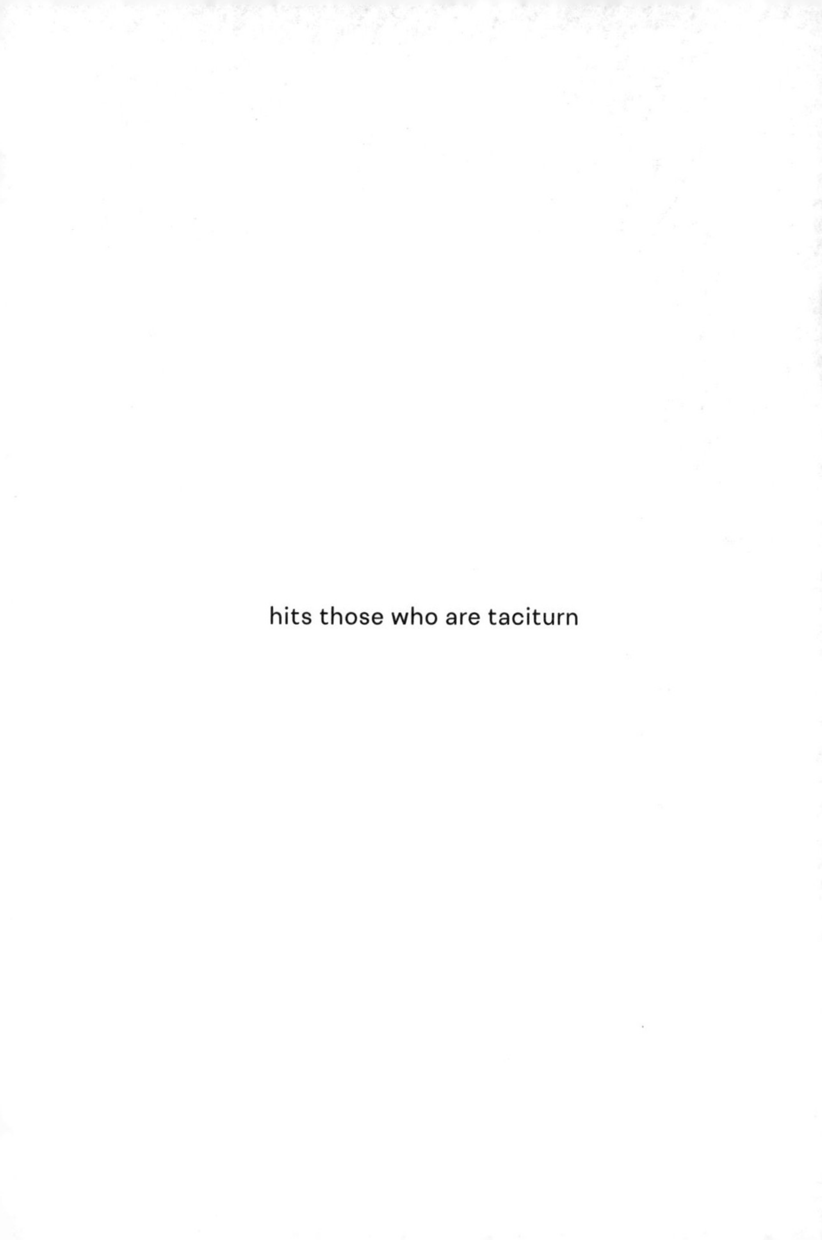
hits those who are taciturn

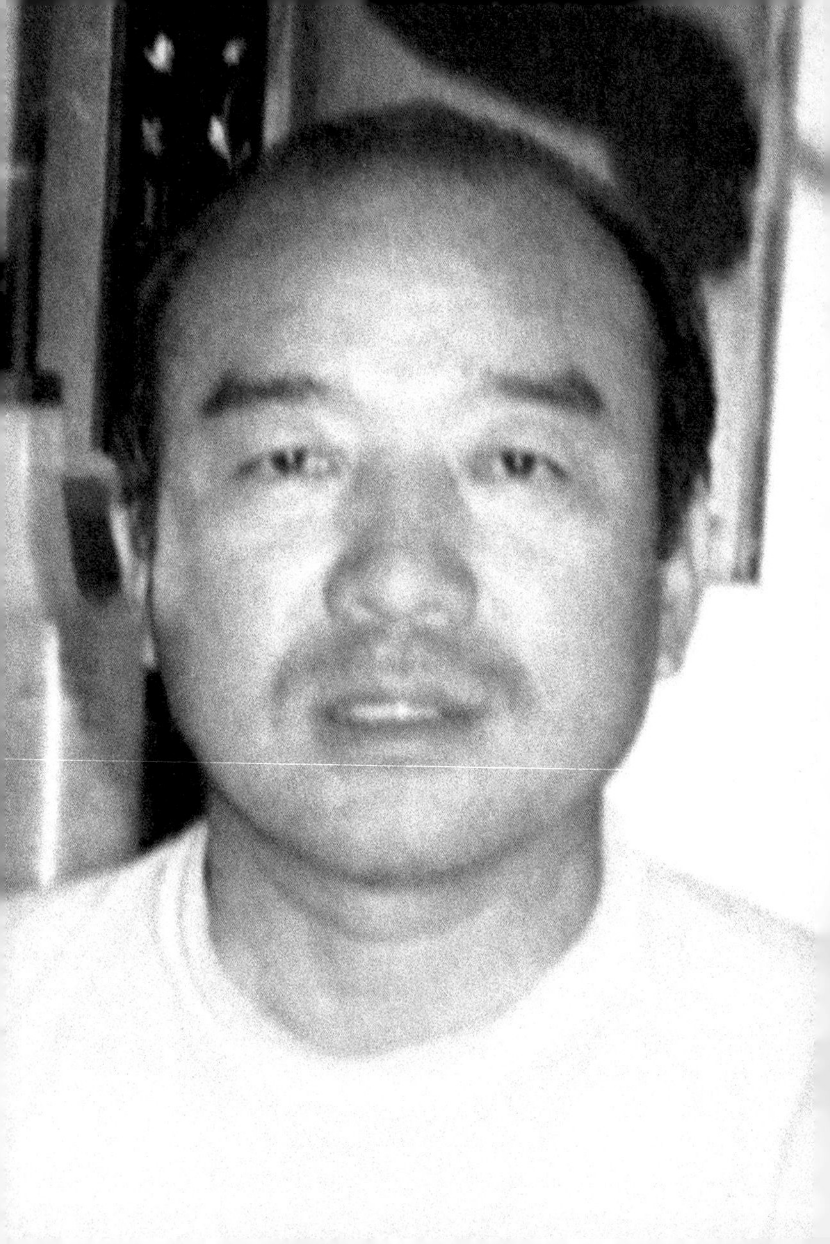

nostalgia

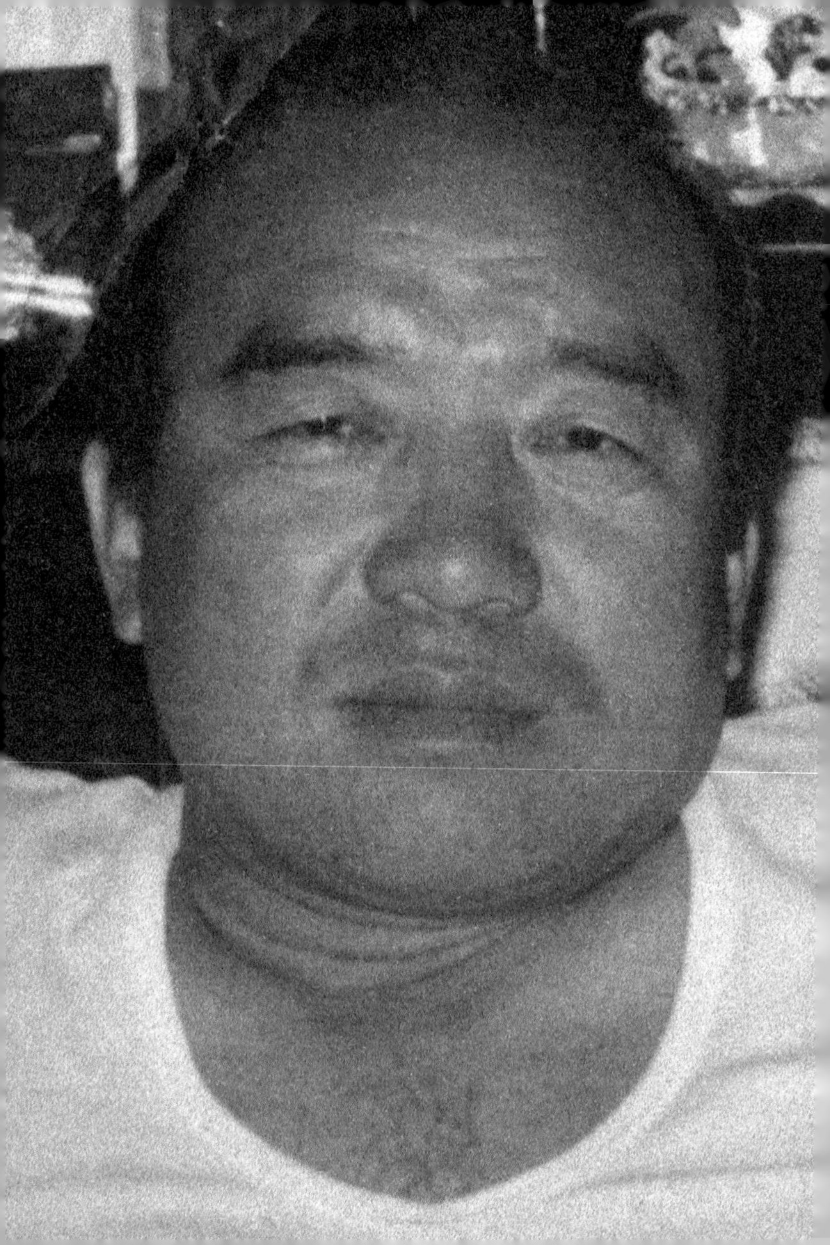

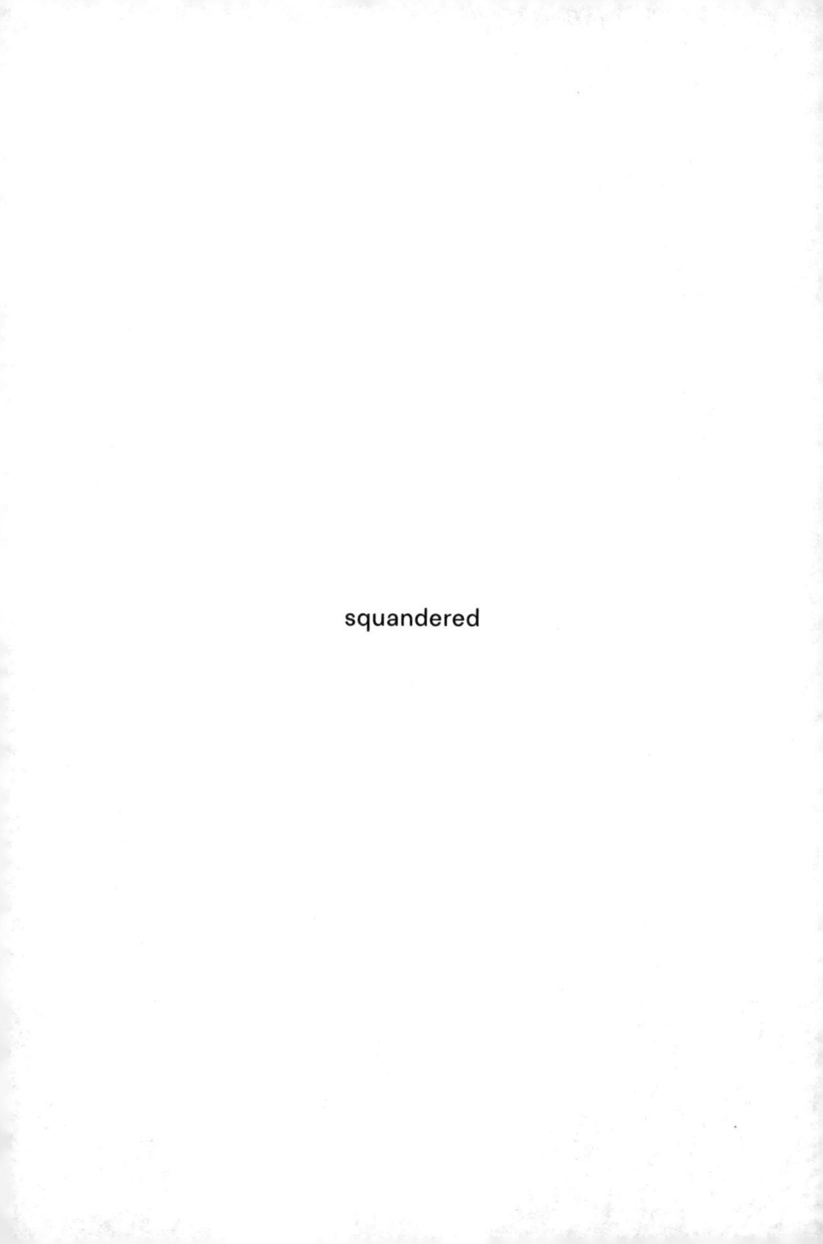

squandered

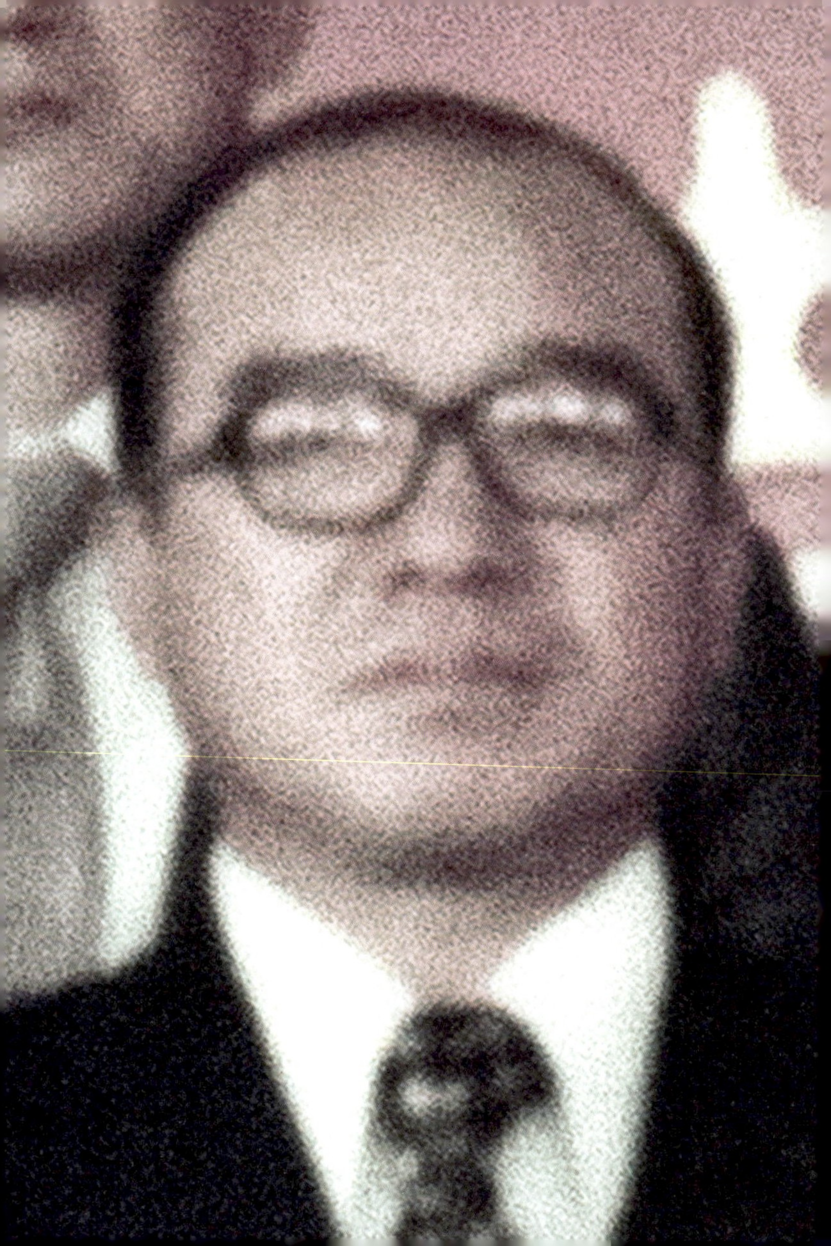

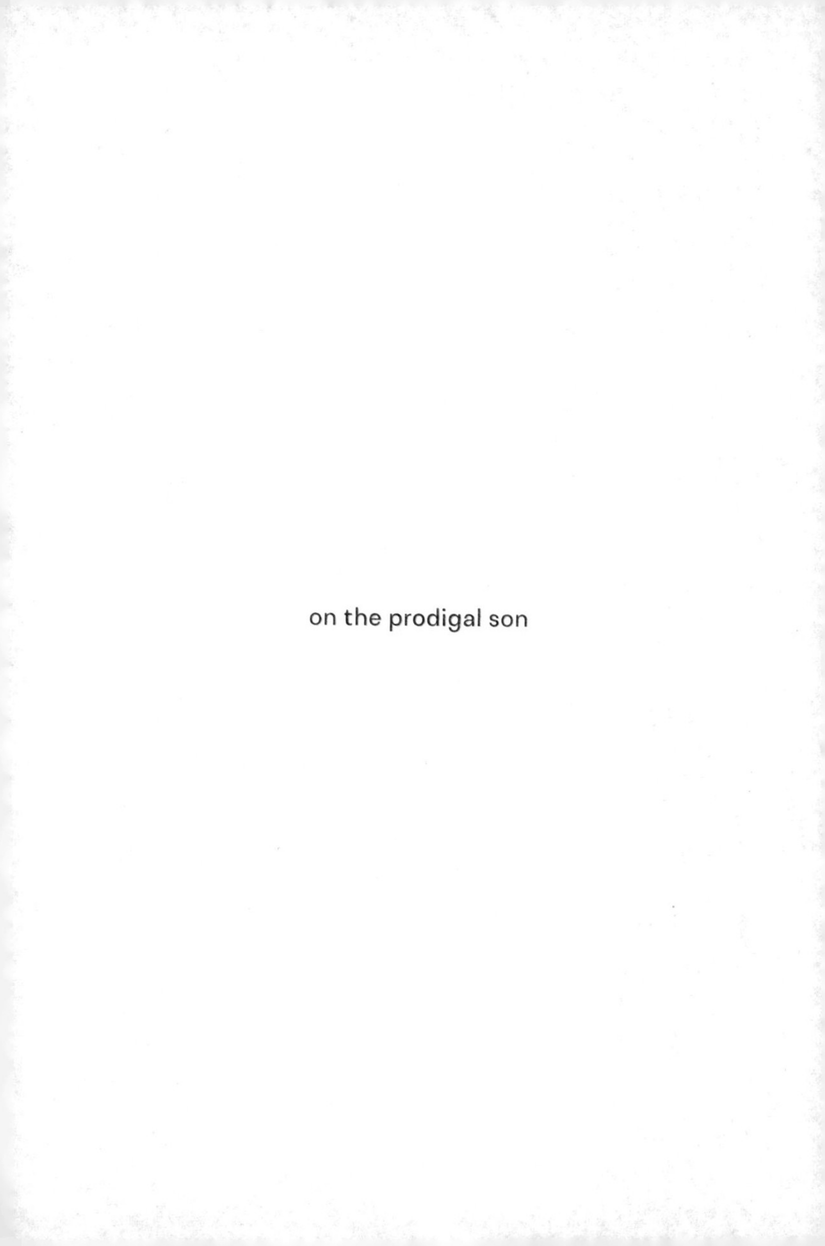

on the prodigal son

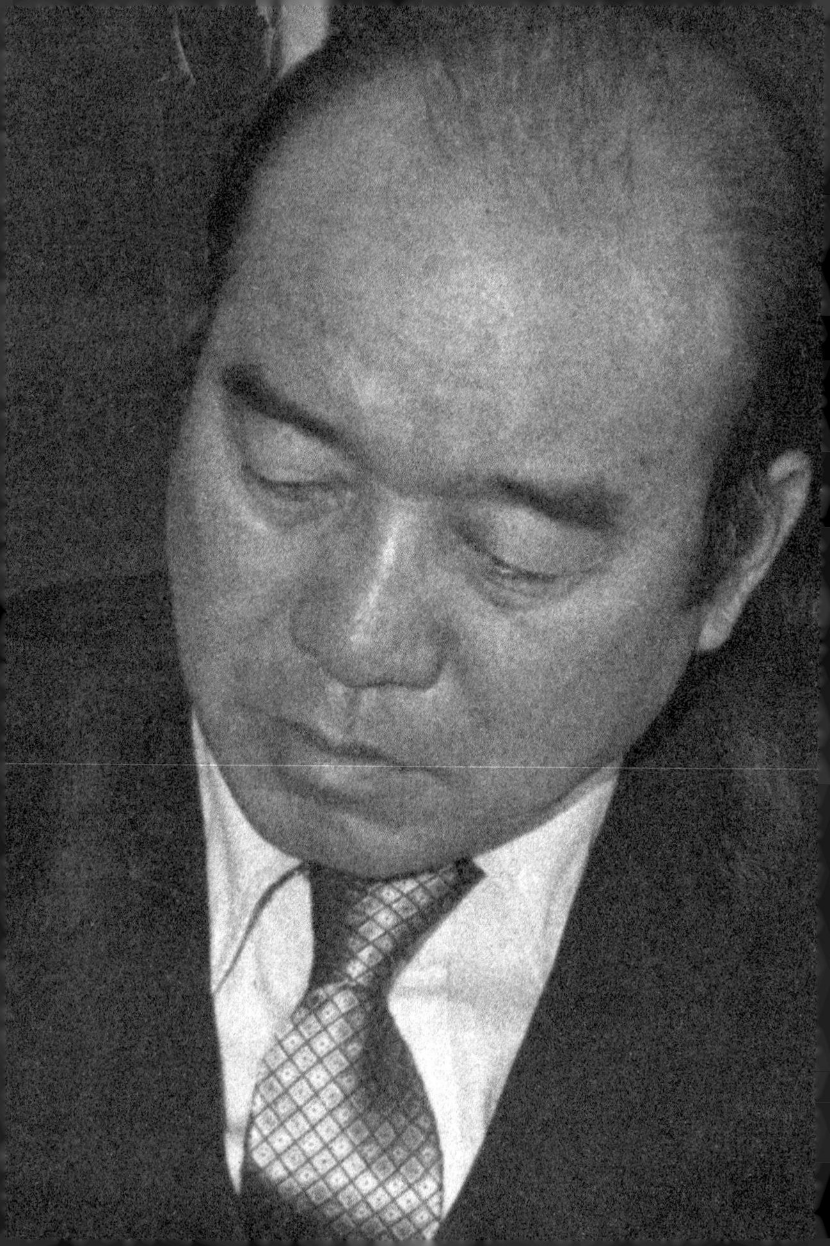

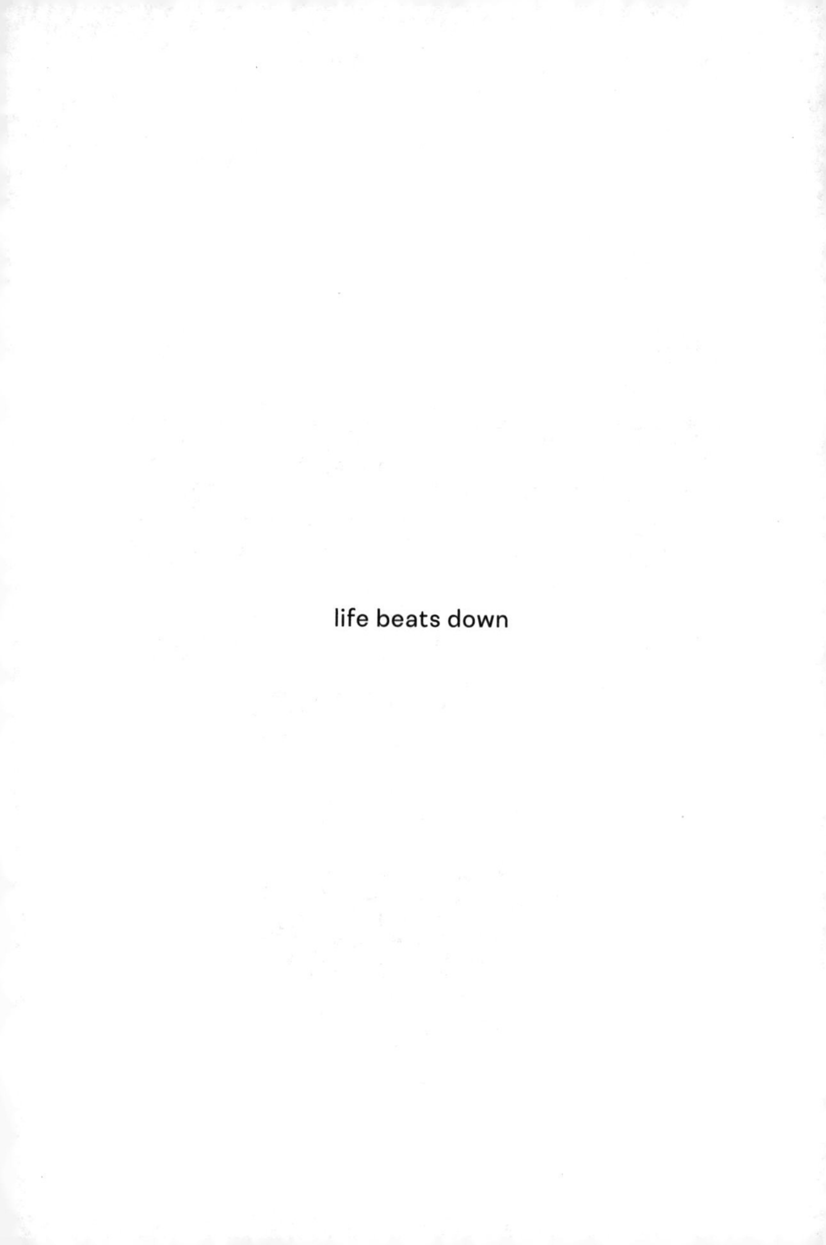

life beats down

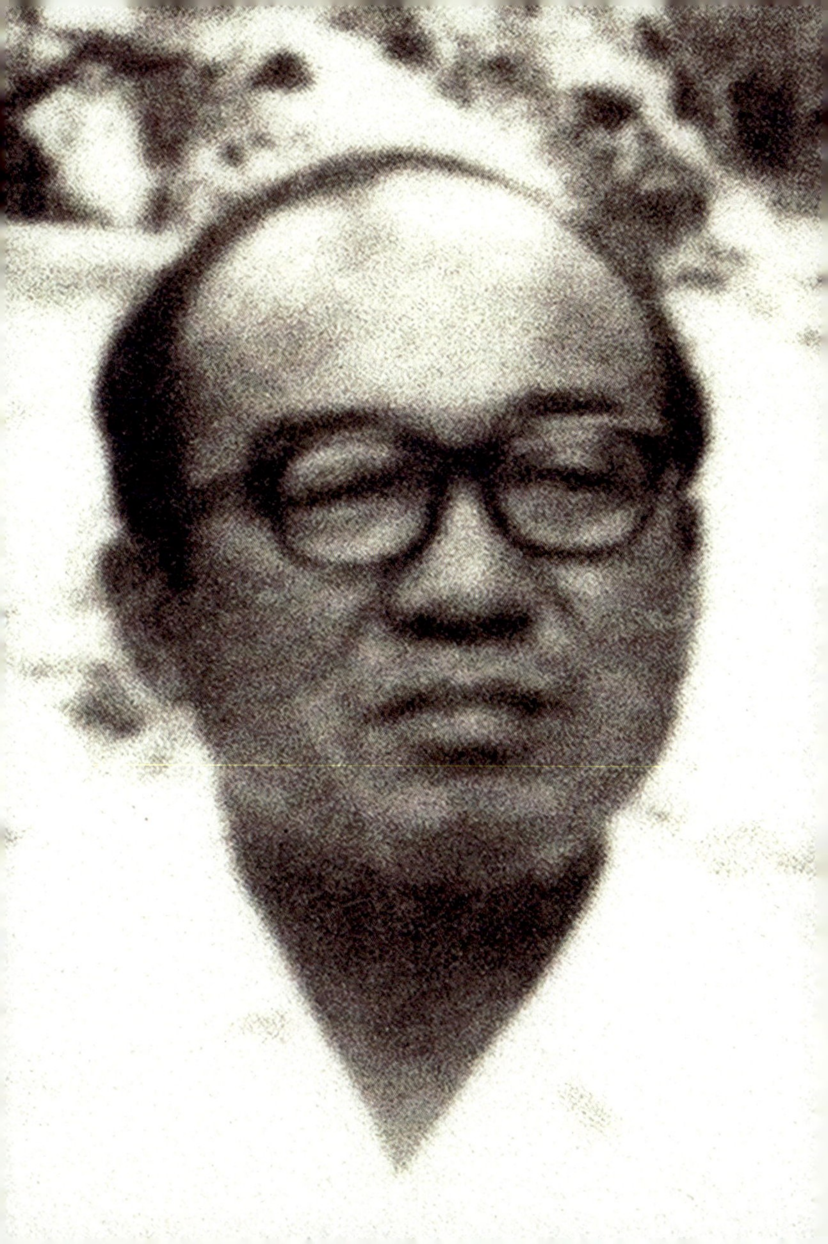

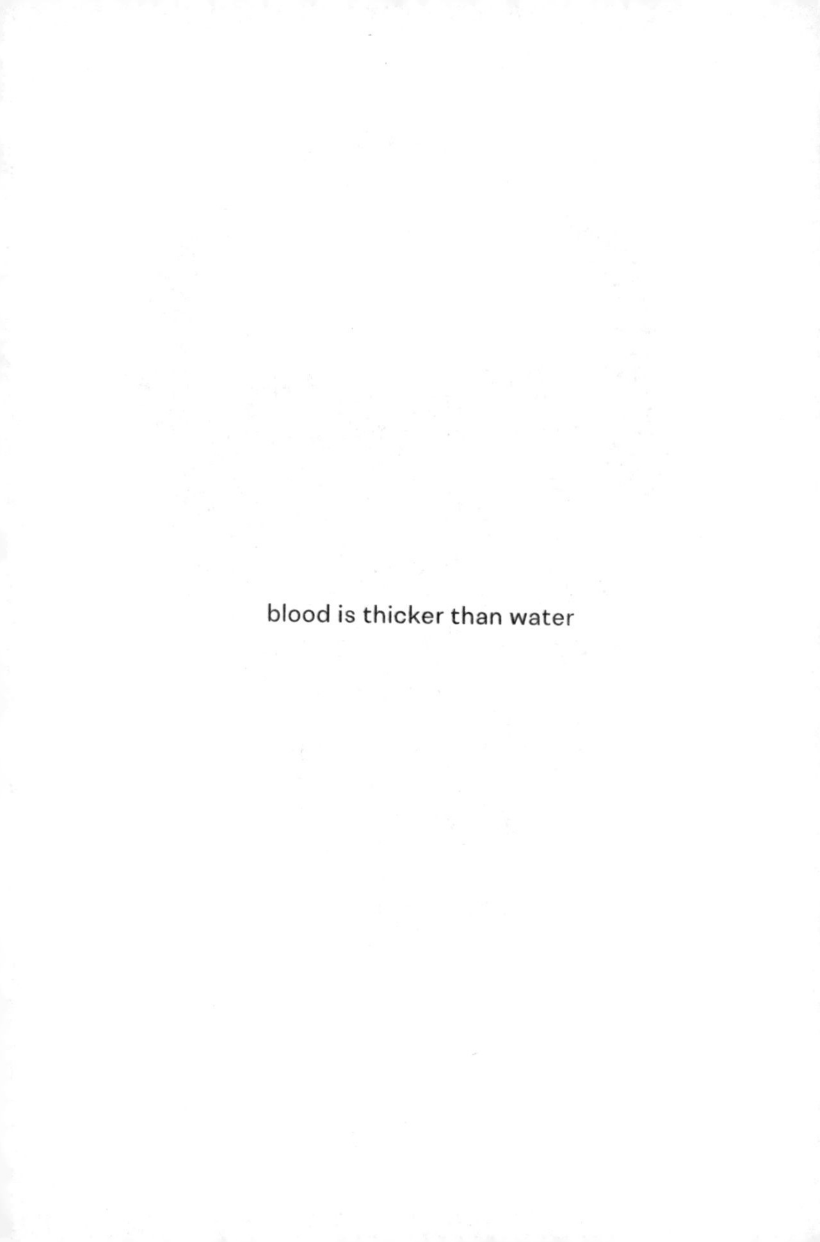

blood is thicker than water

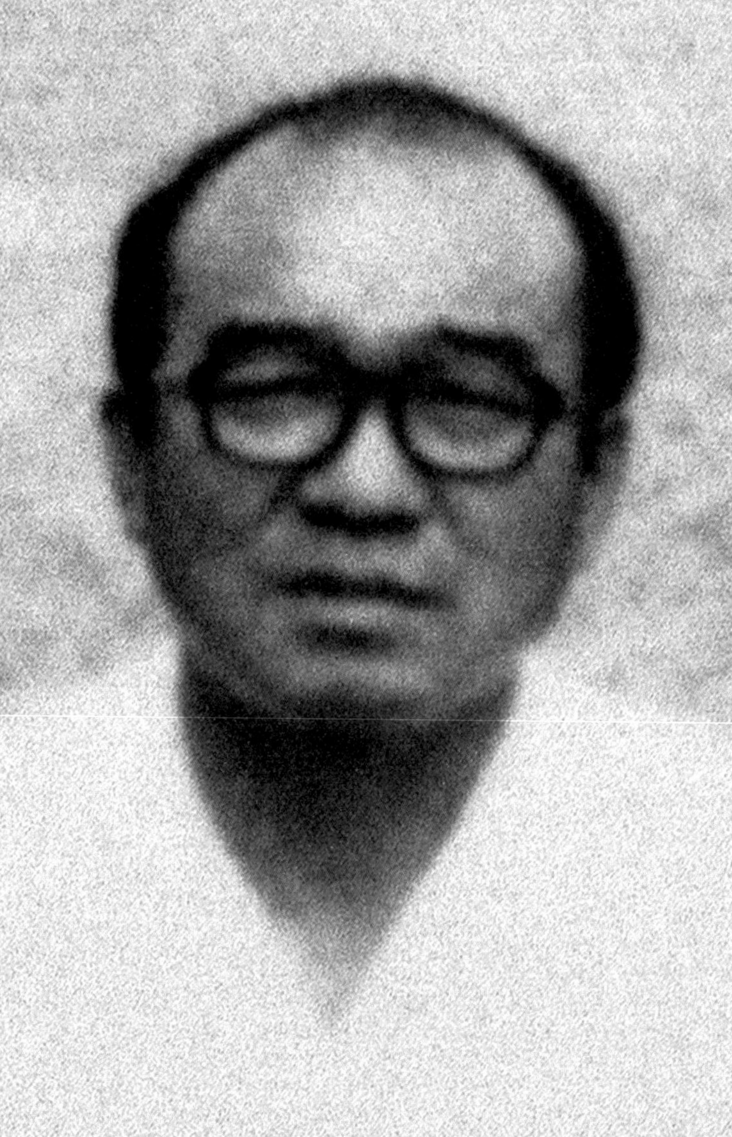

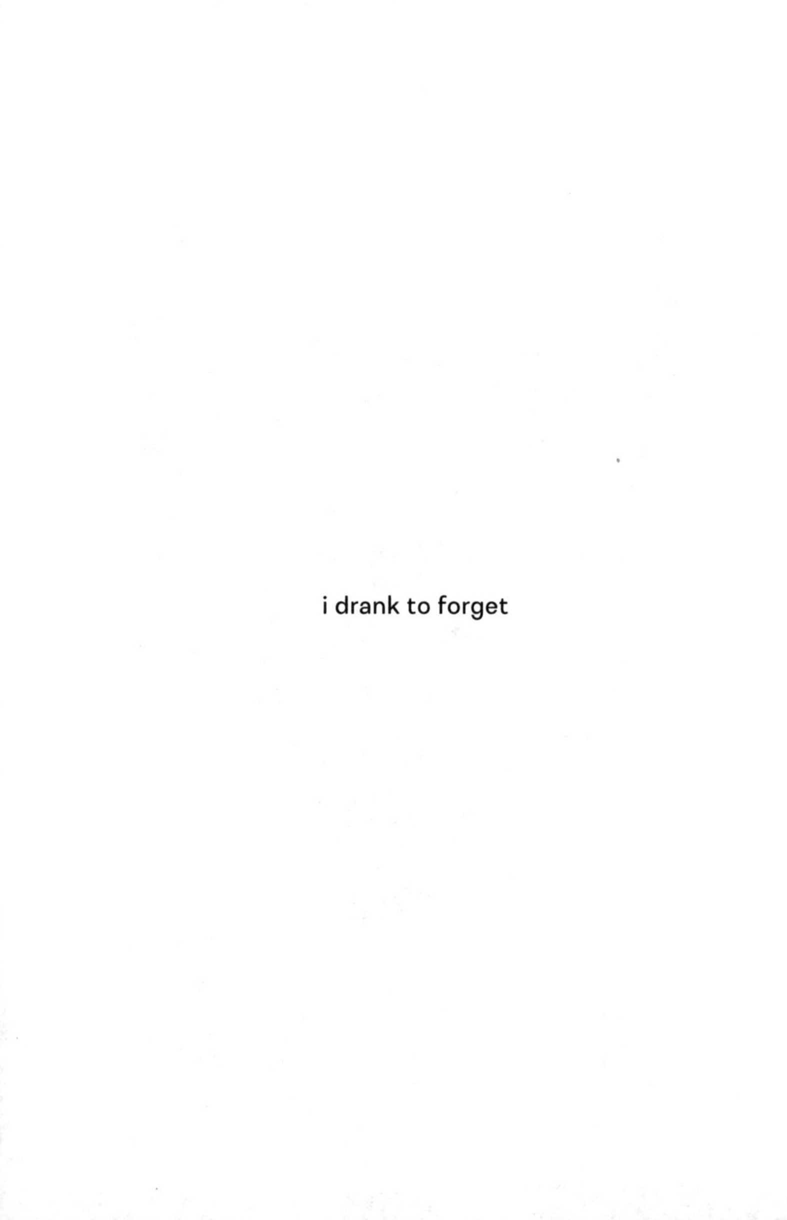

i drank to forget

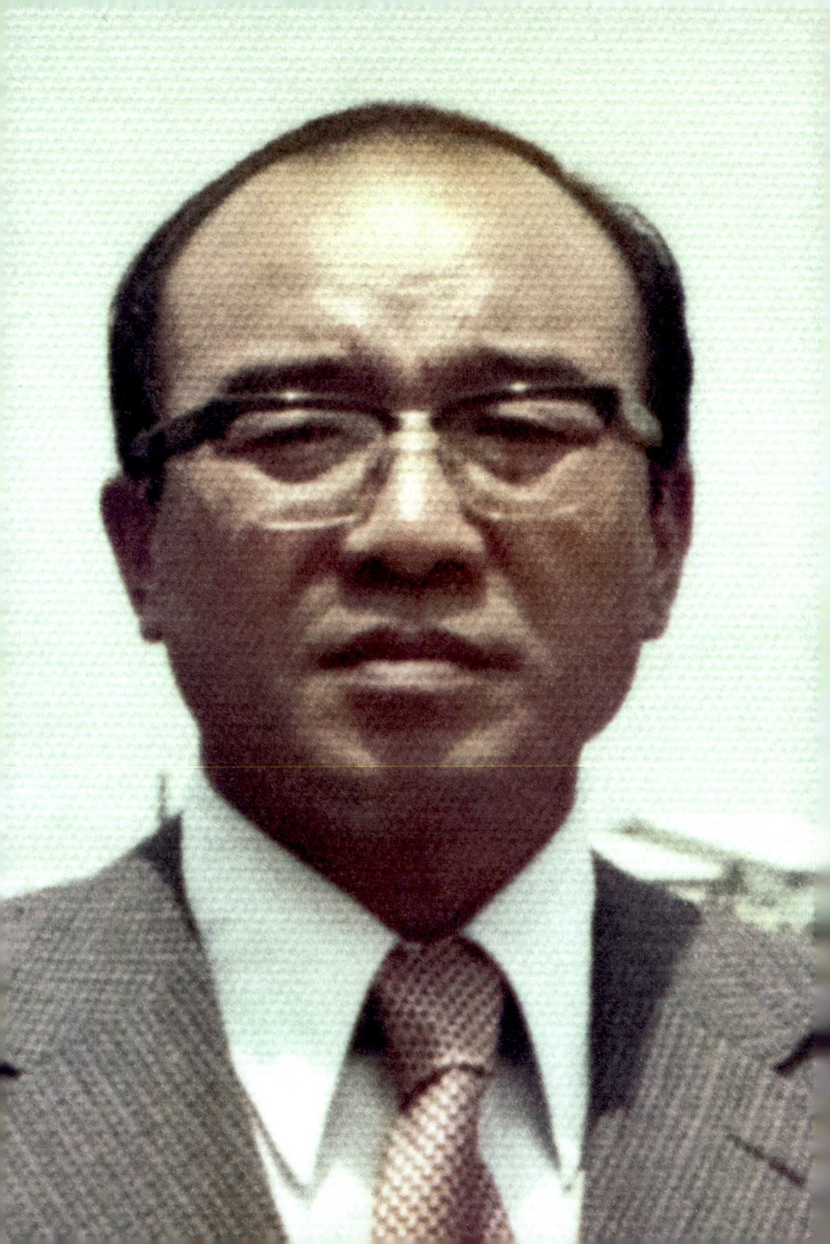

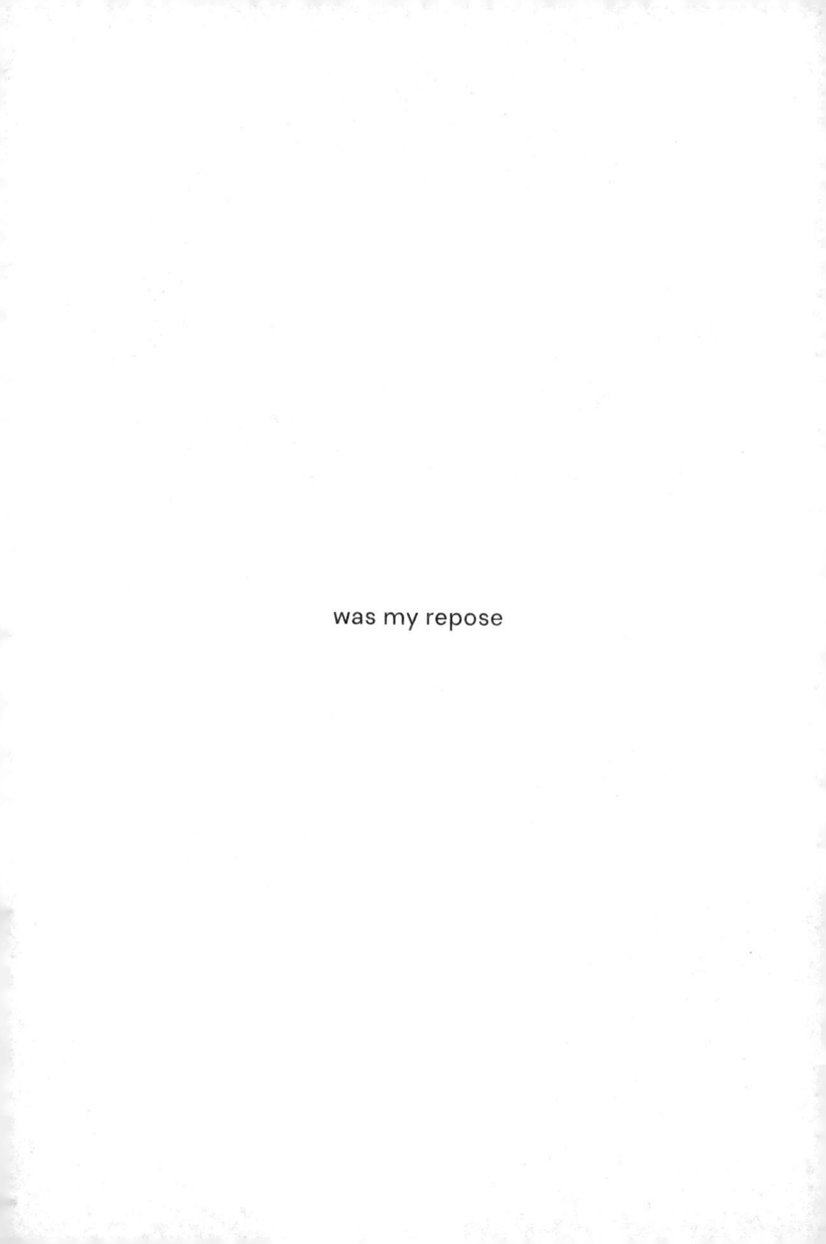

was my repose

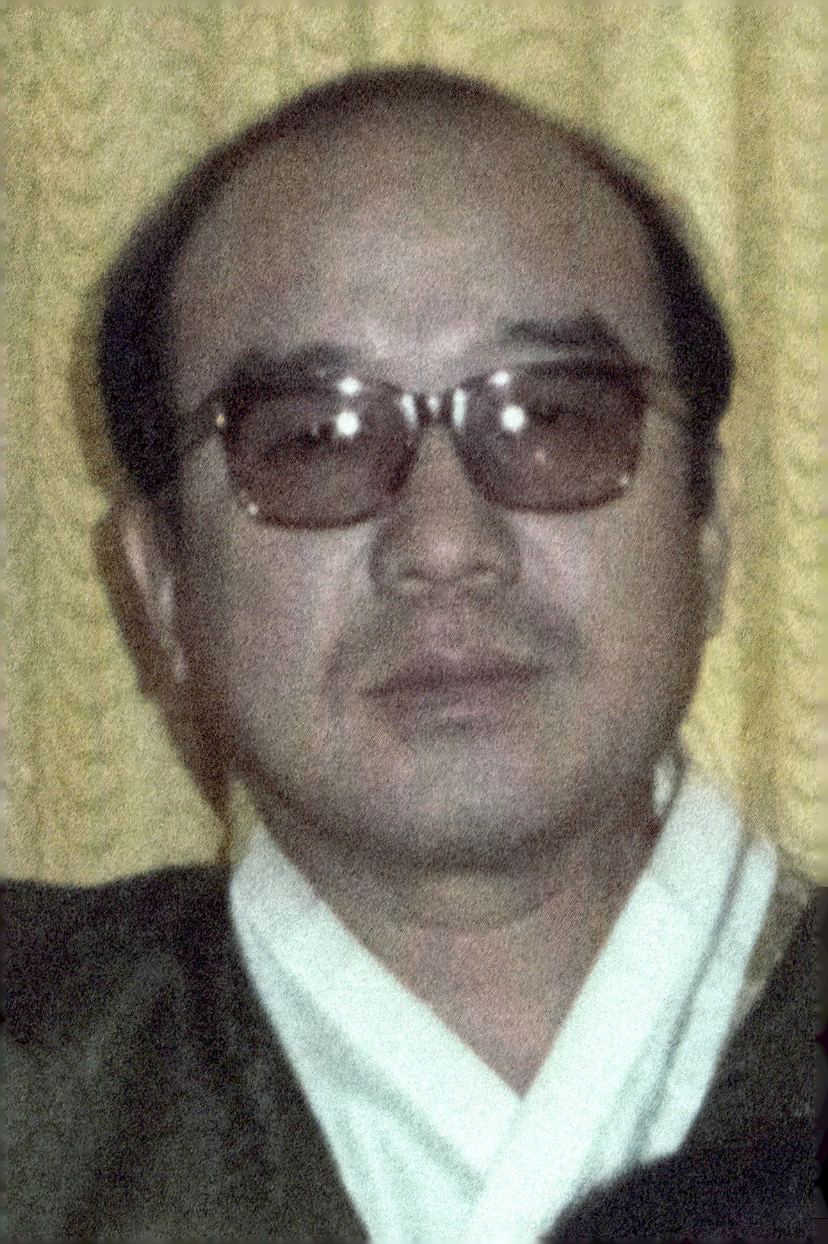

my work

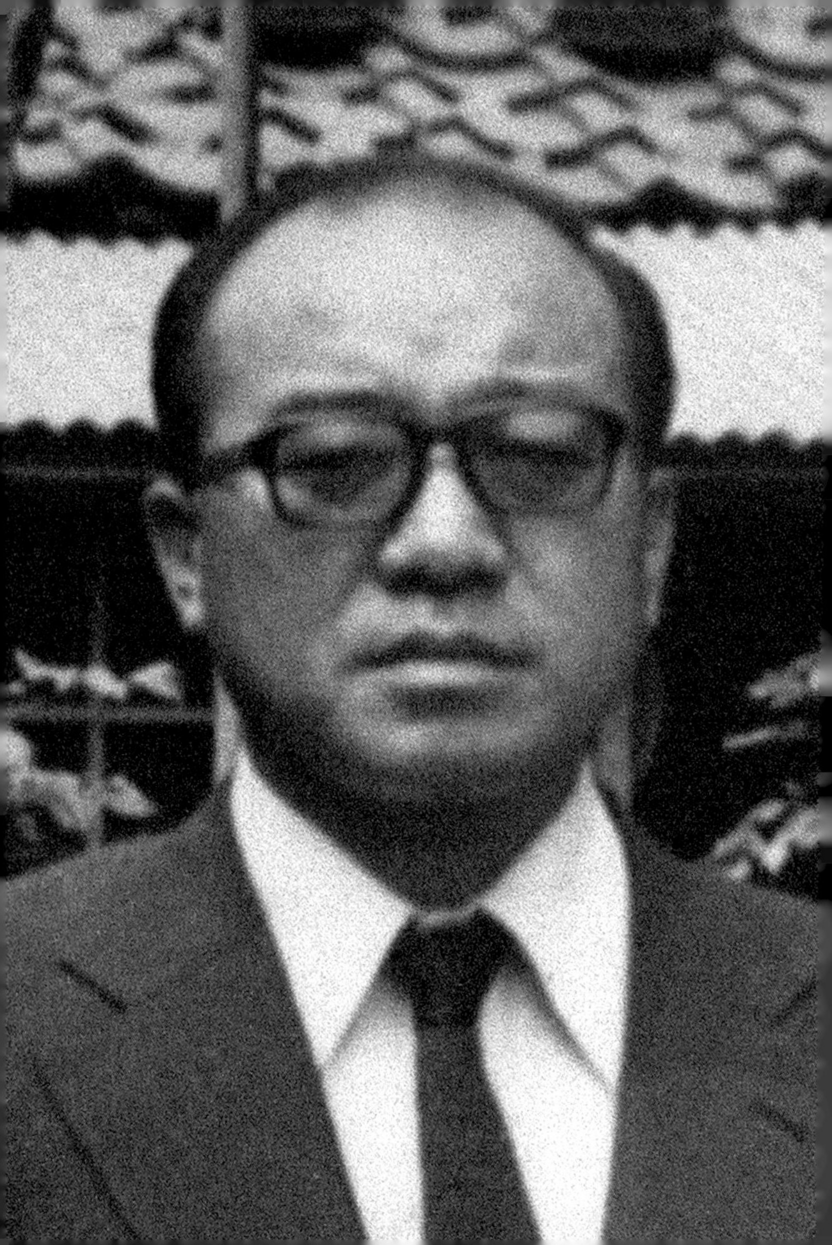

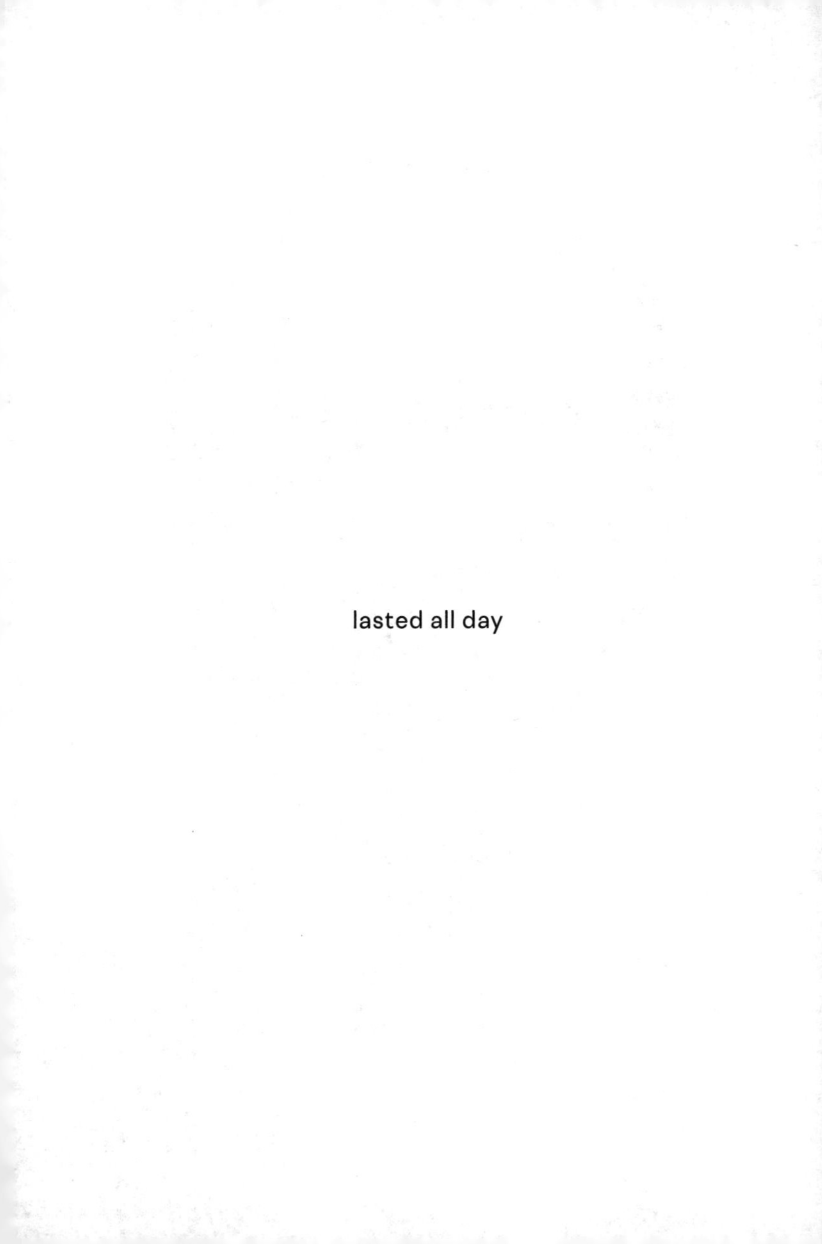
lasted all day

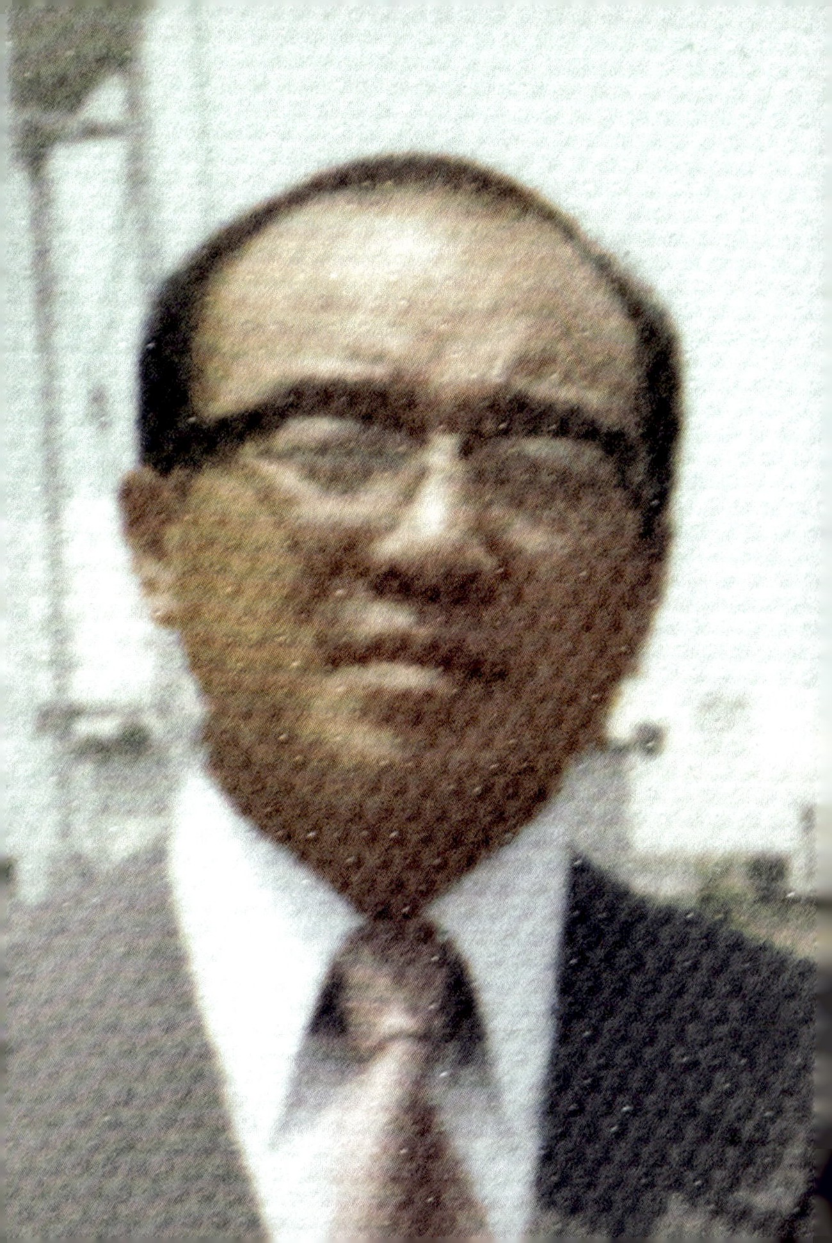

duty time

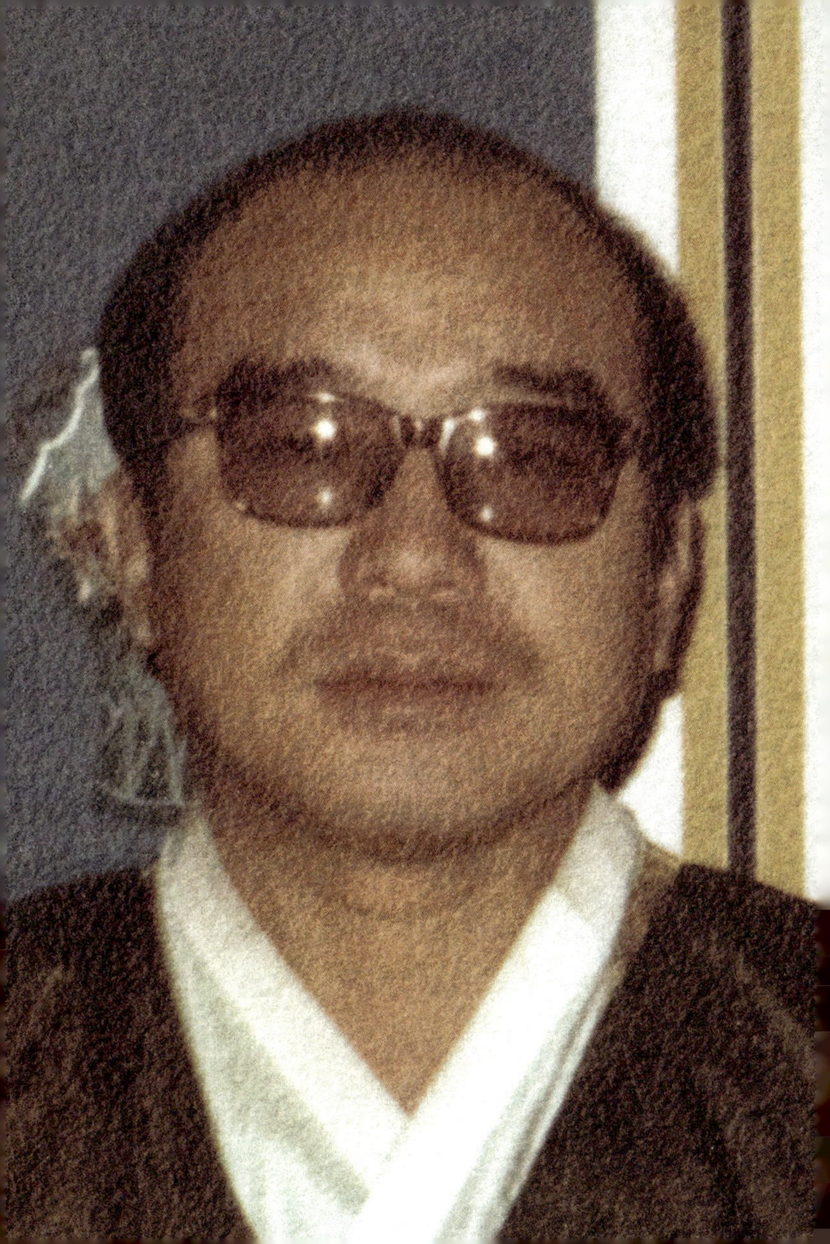

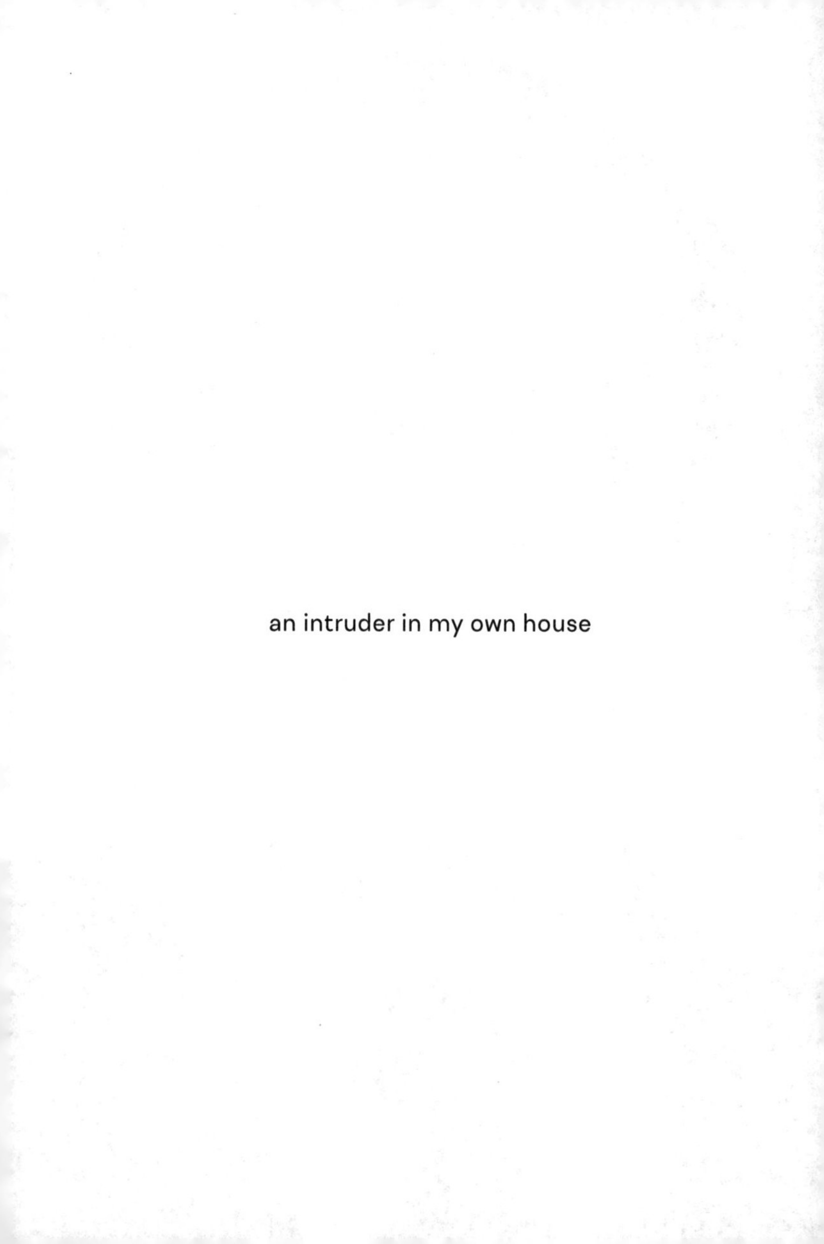

an intruder in my own house

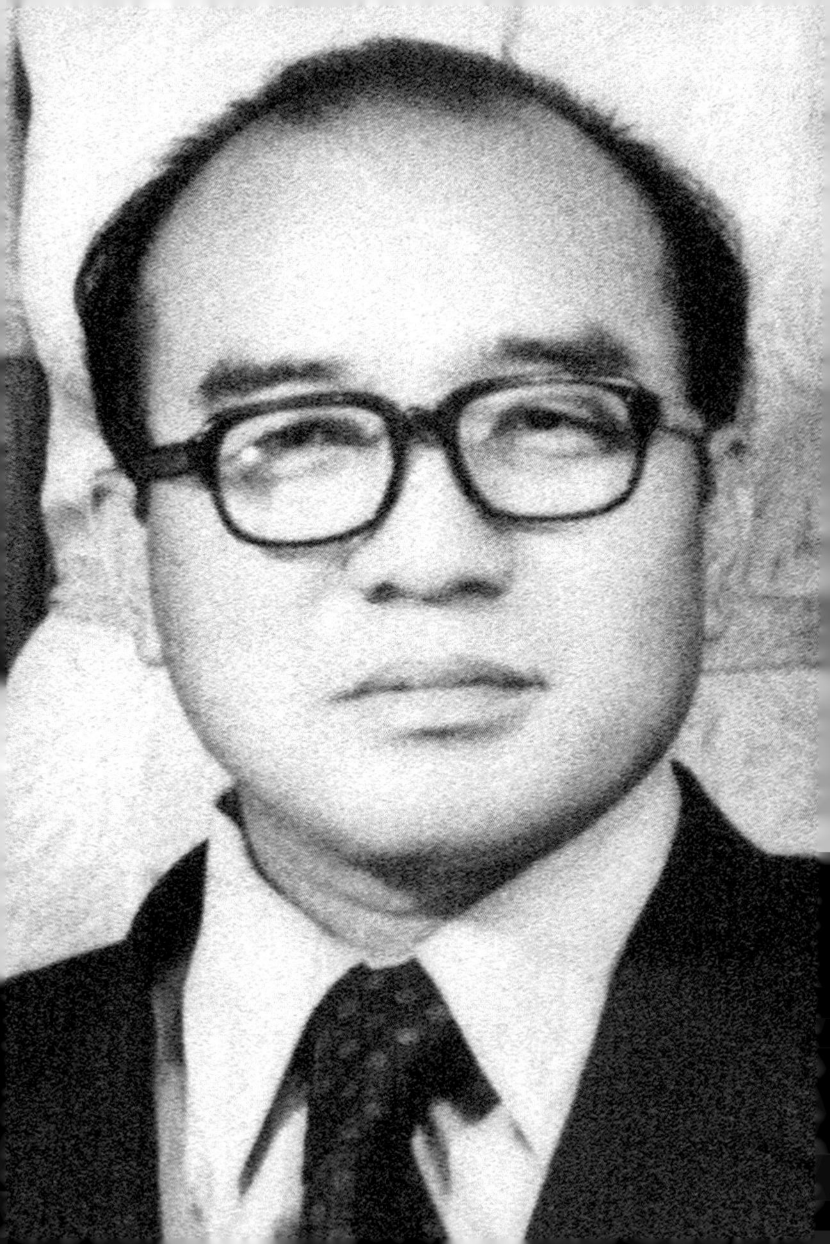

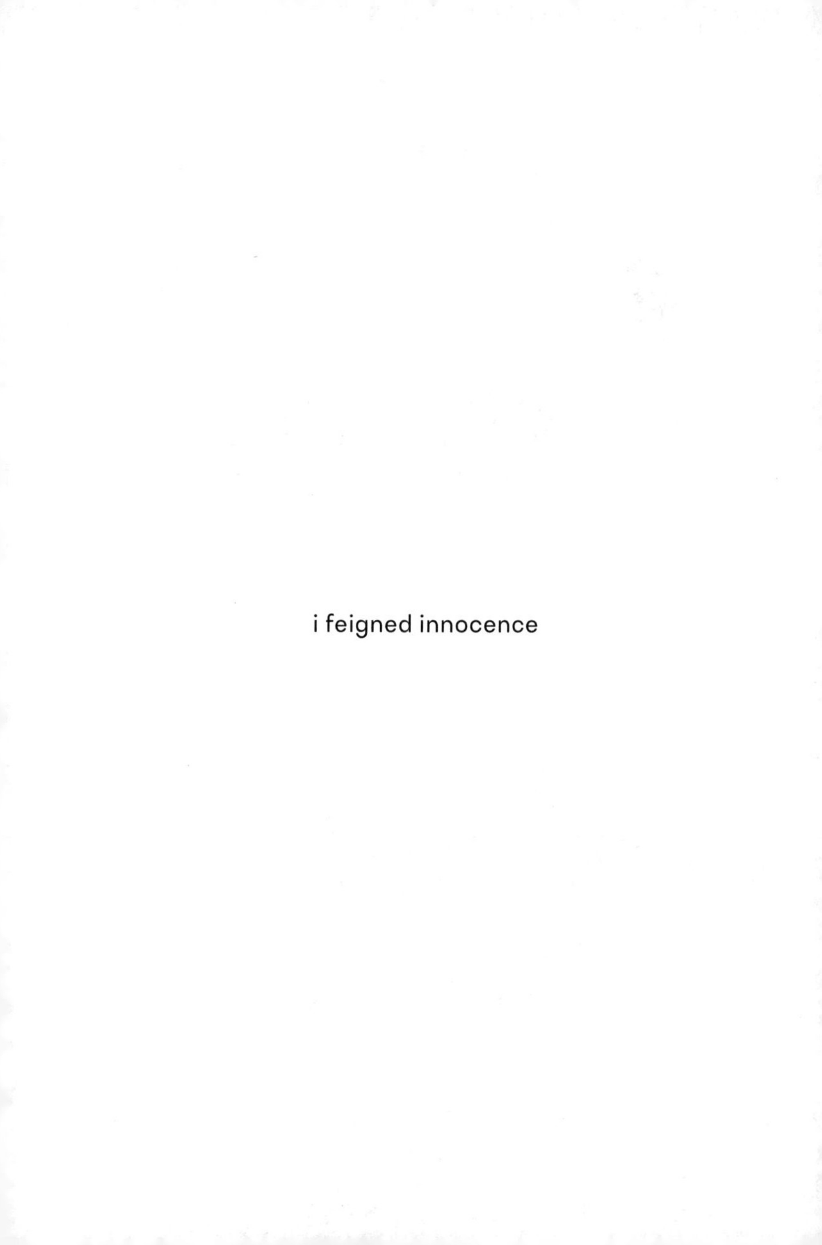

i feigned innocence

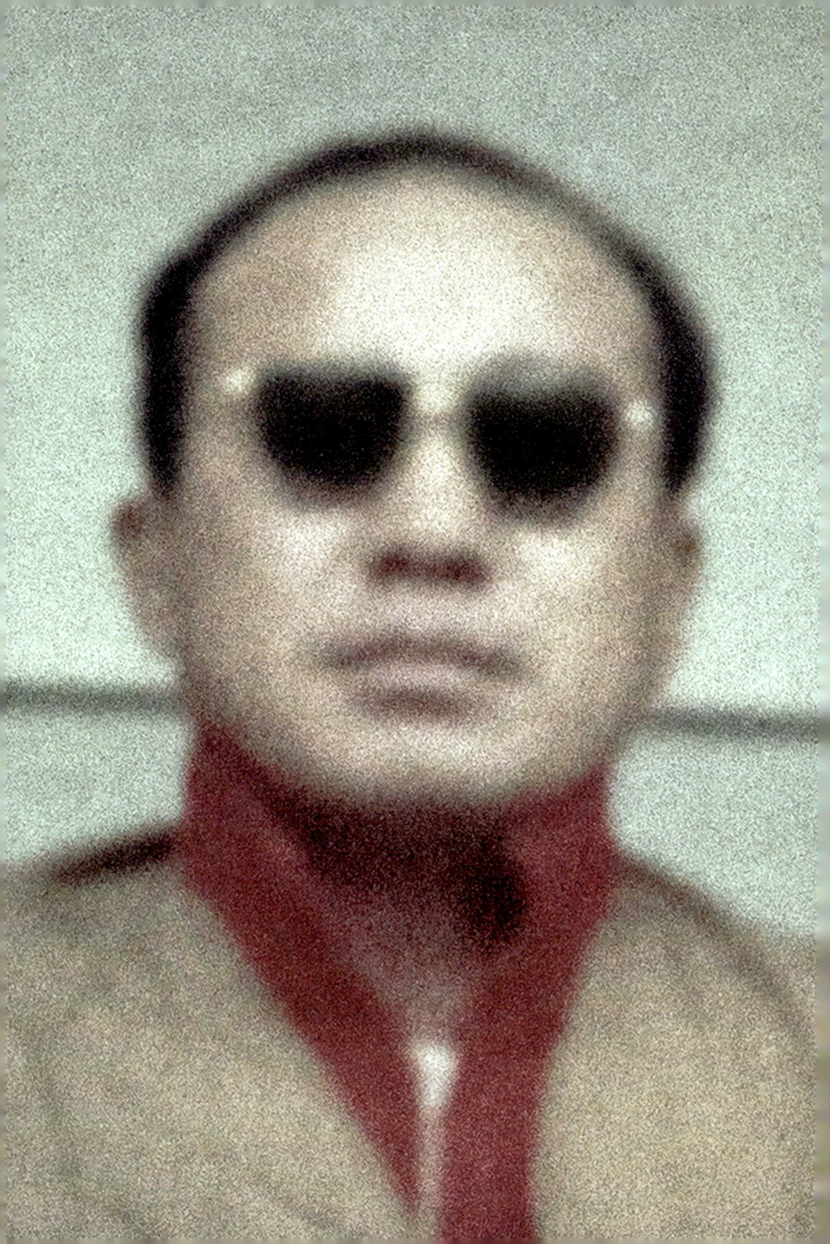

i hid

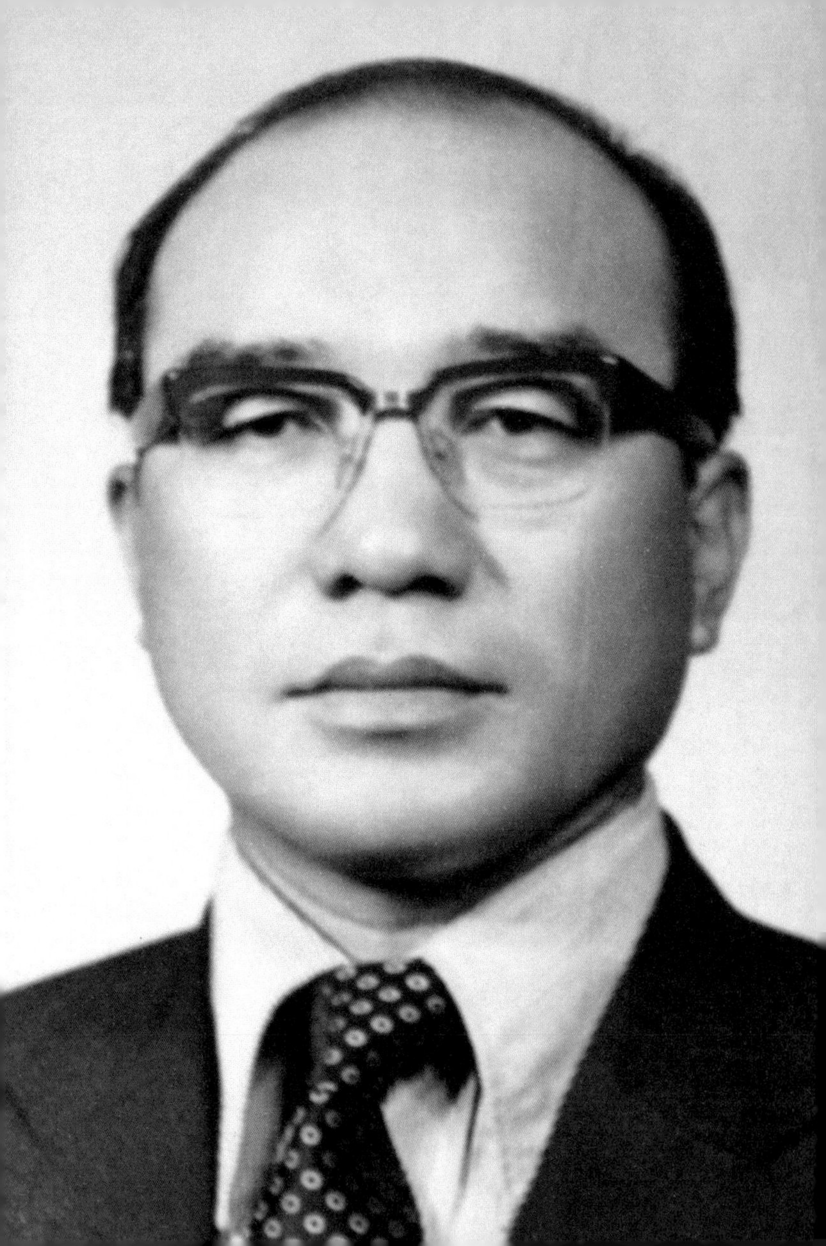

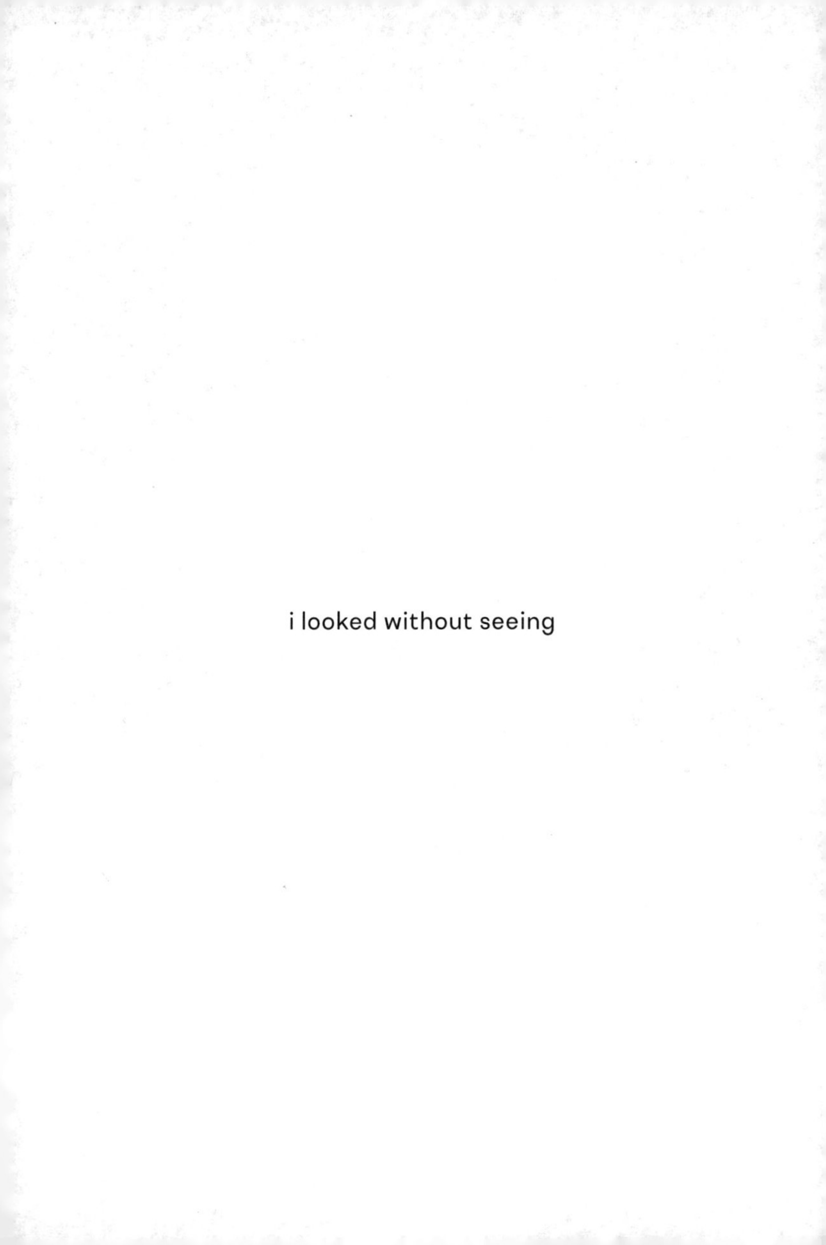

i looked without seeing

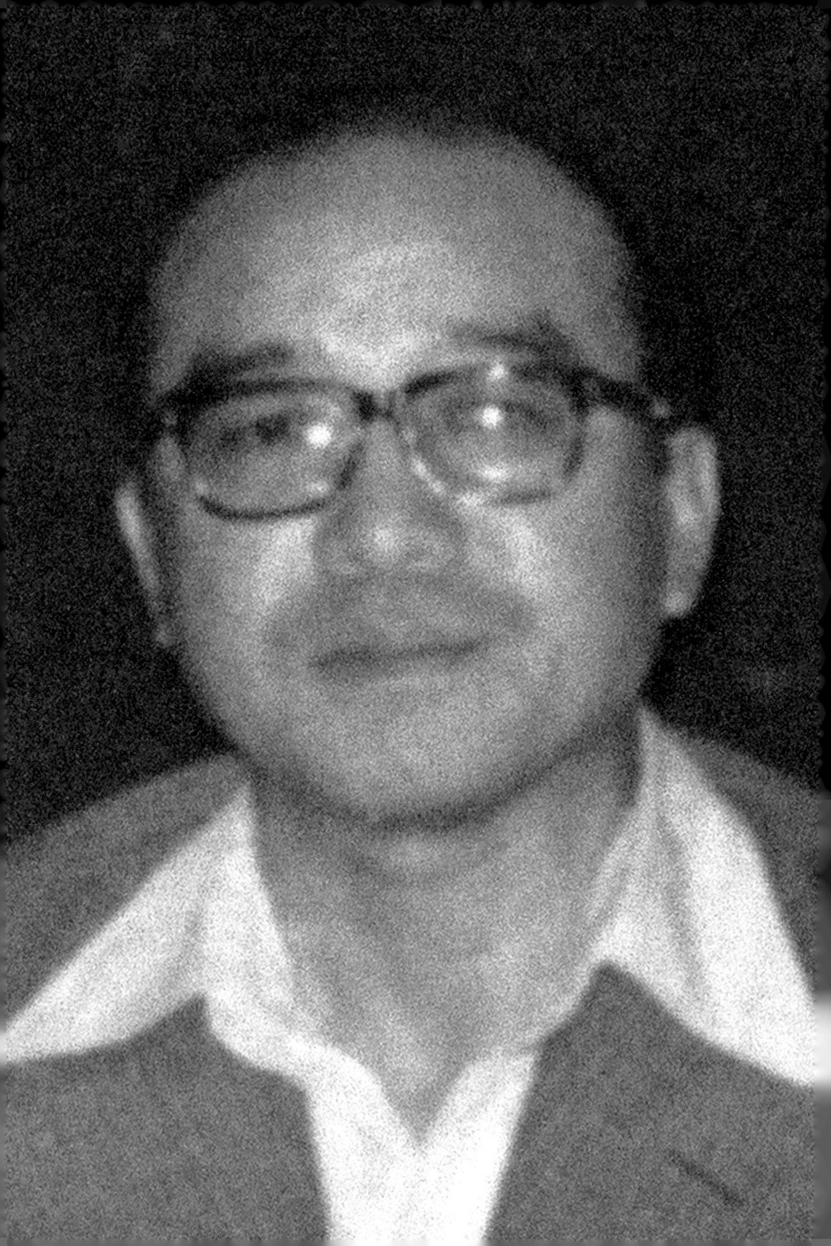

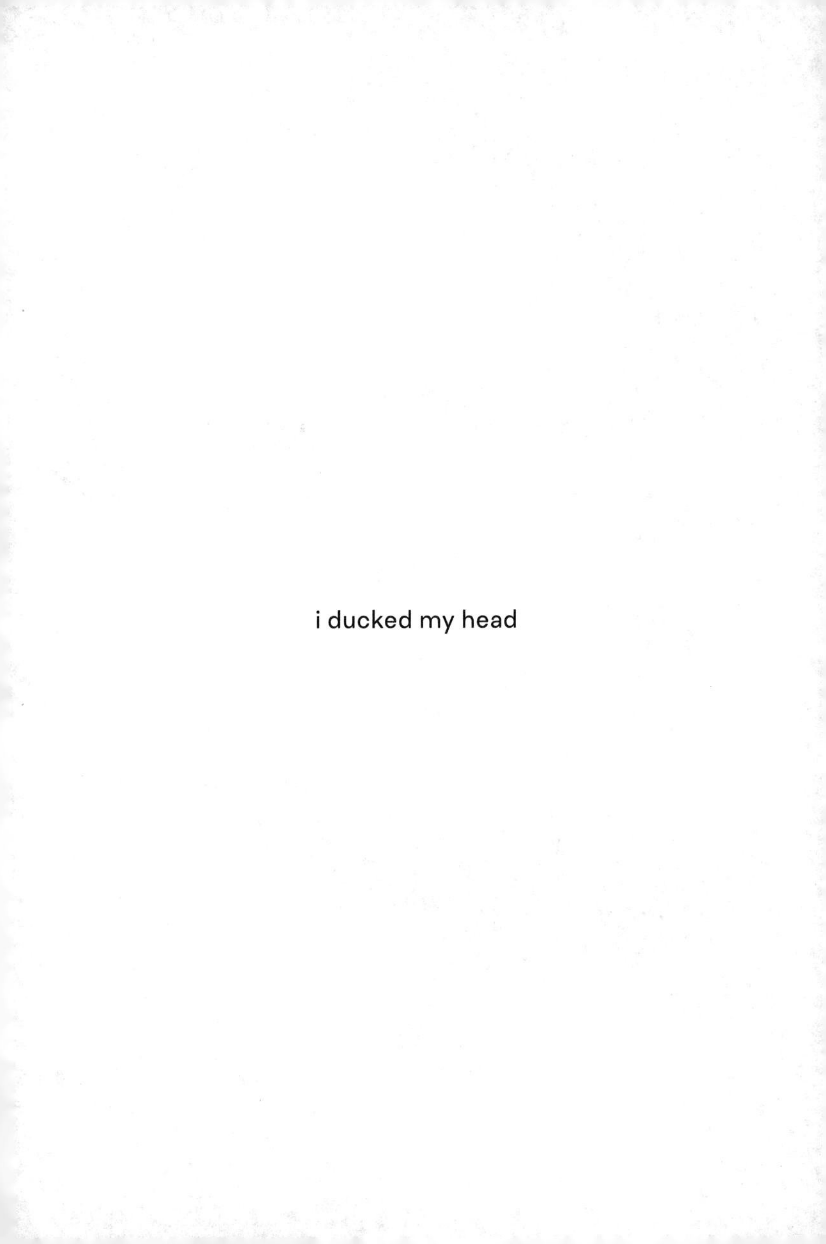

i ducked my head

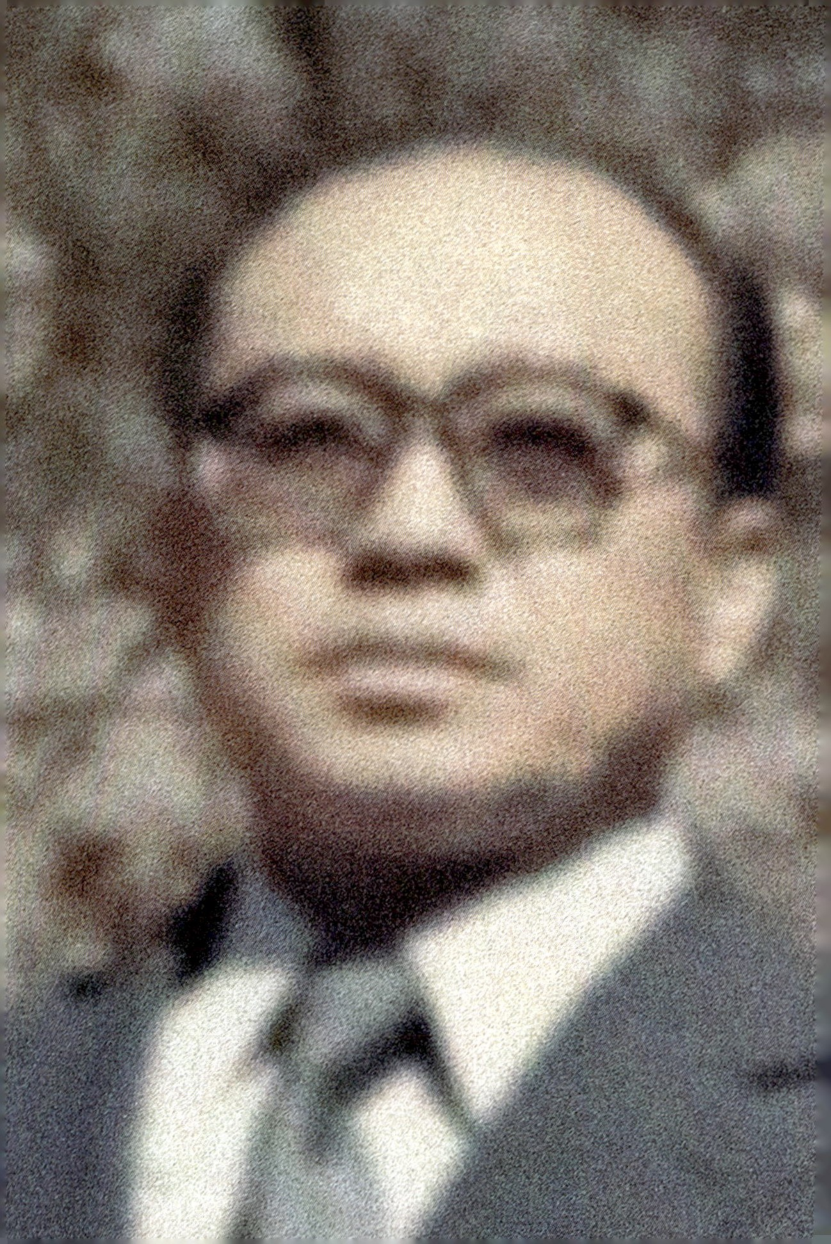

i owed everything

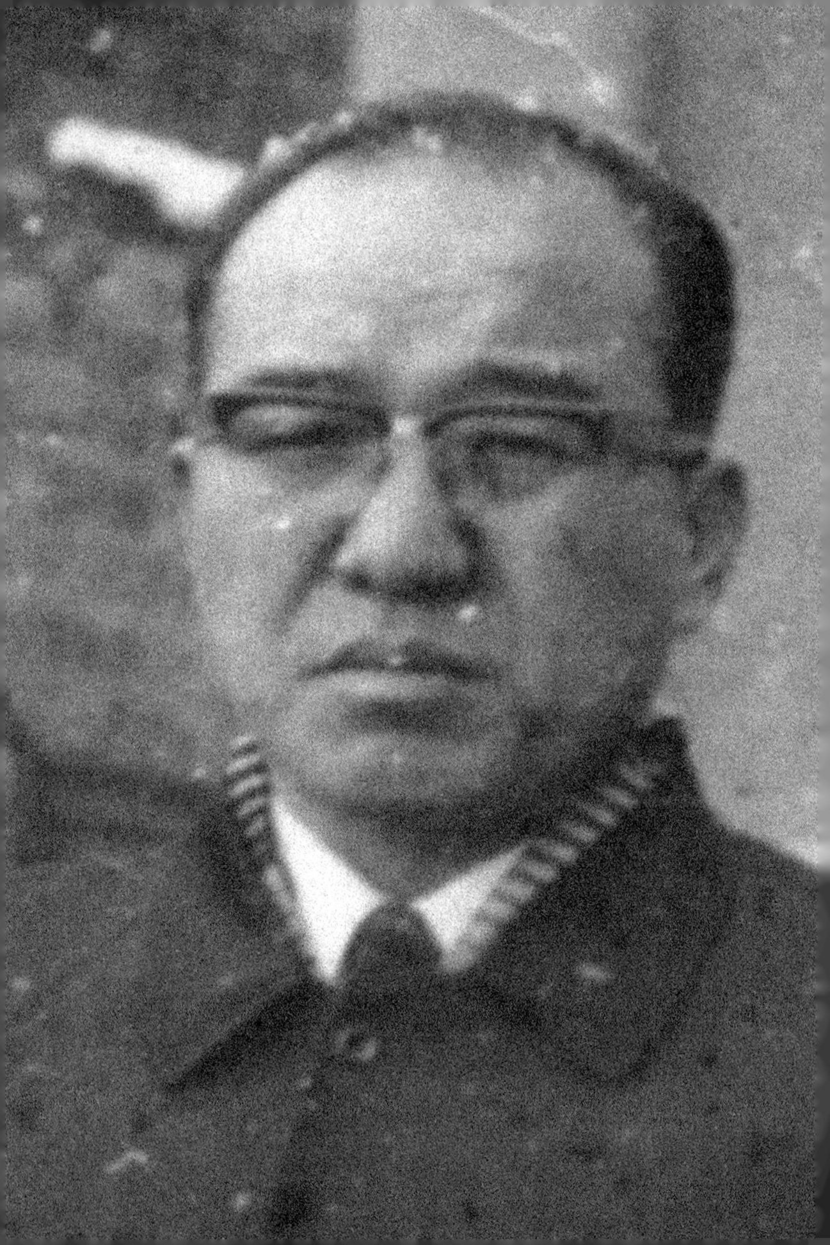

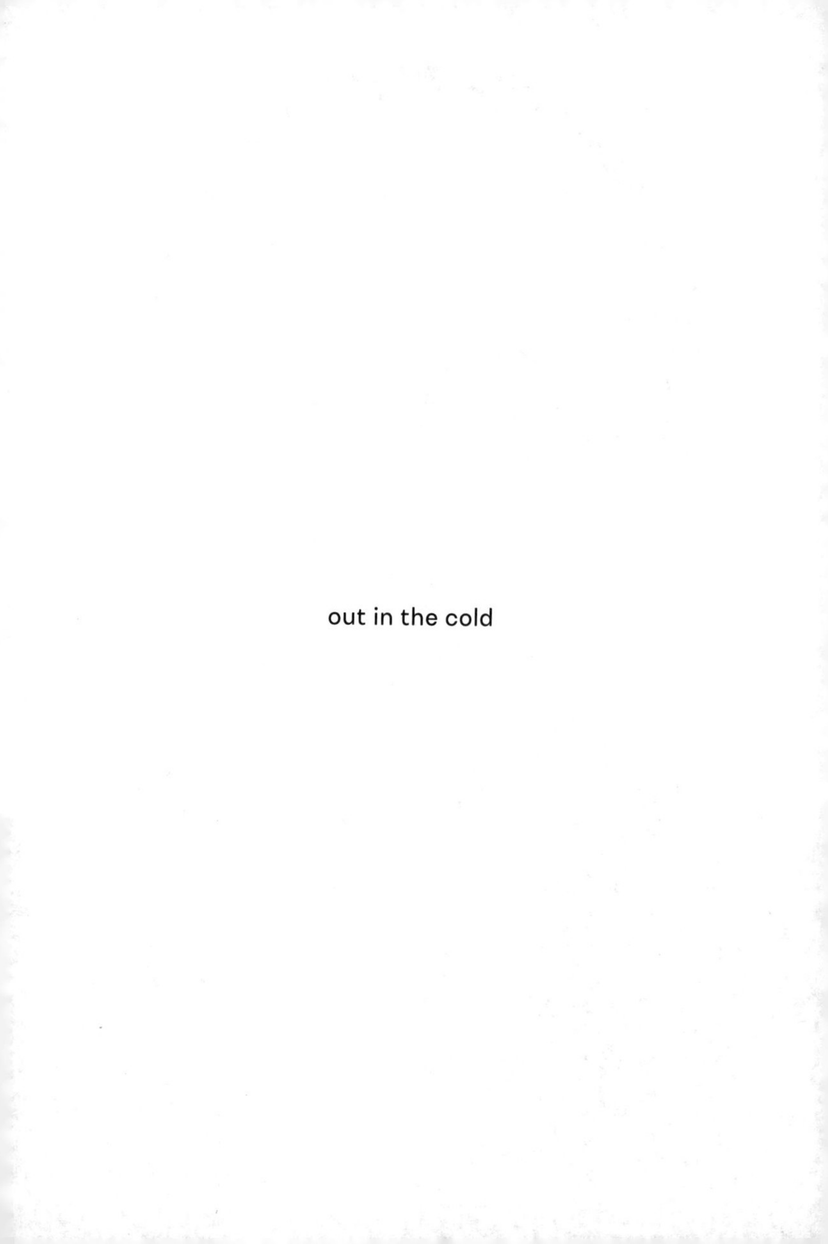

out in the cold

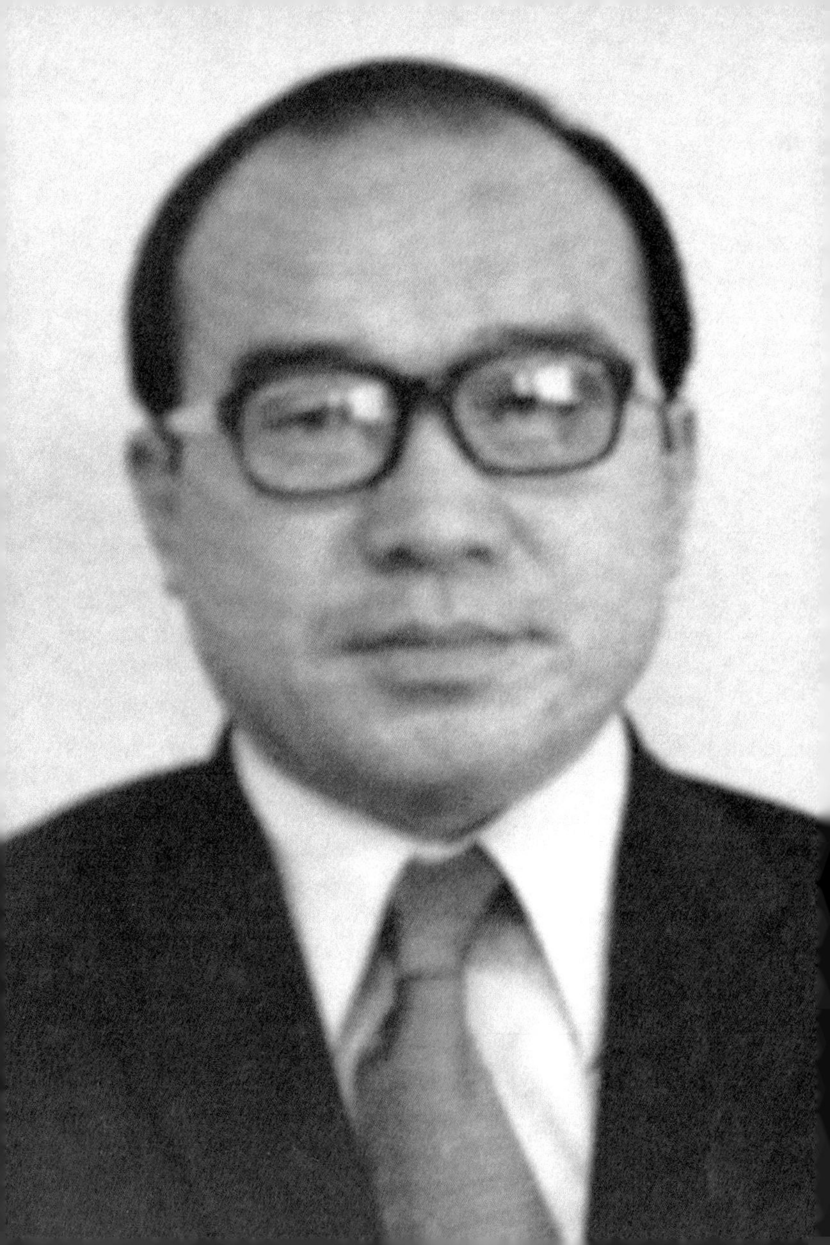

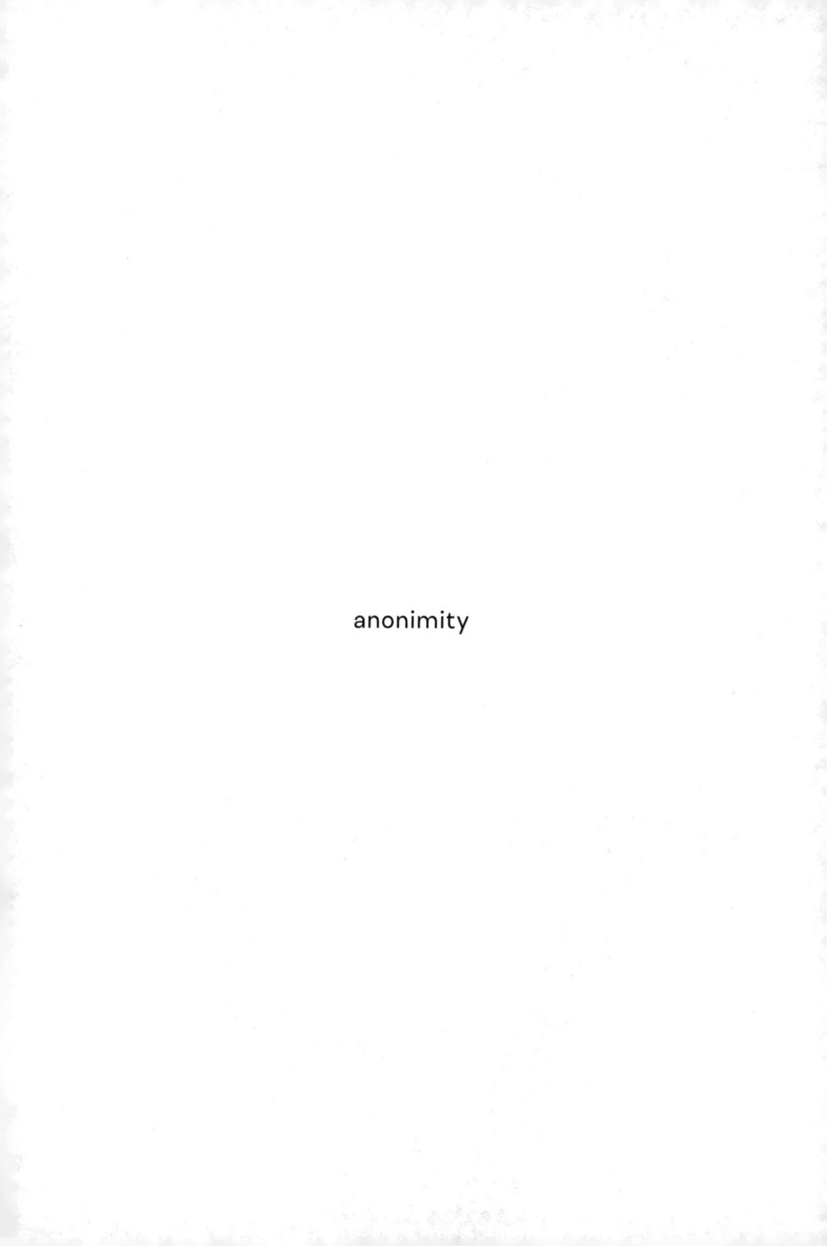

anonimity

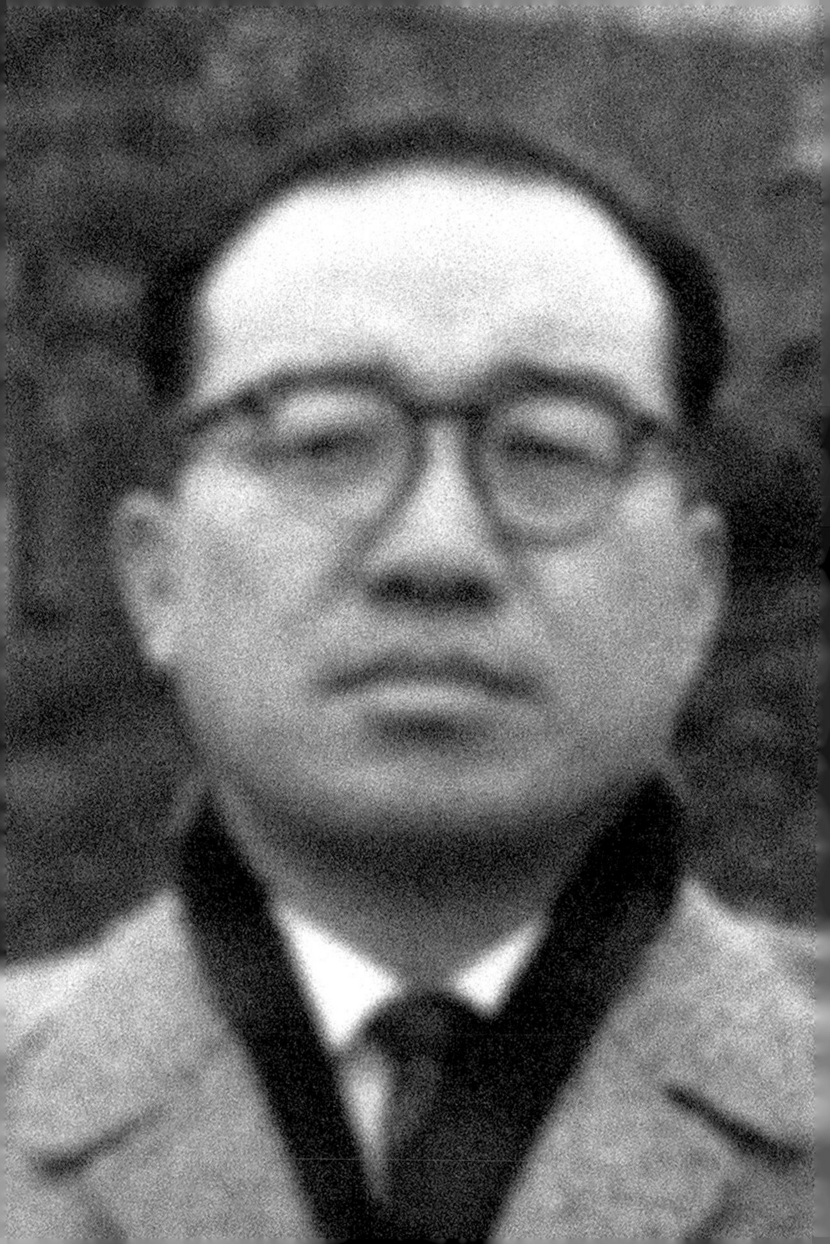

servitude

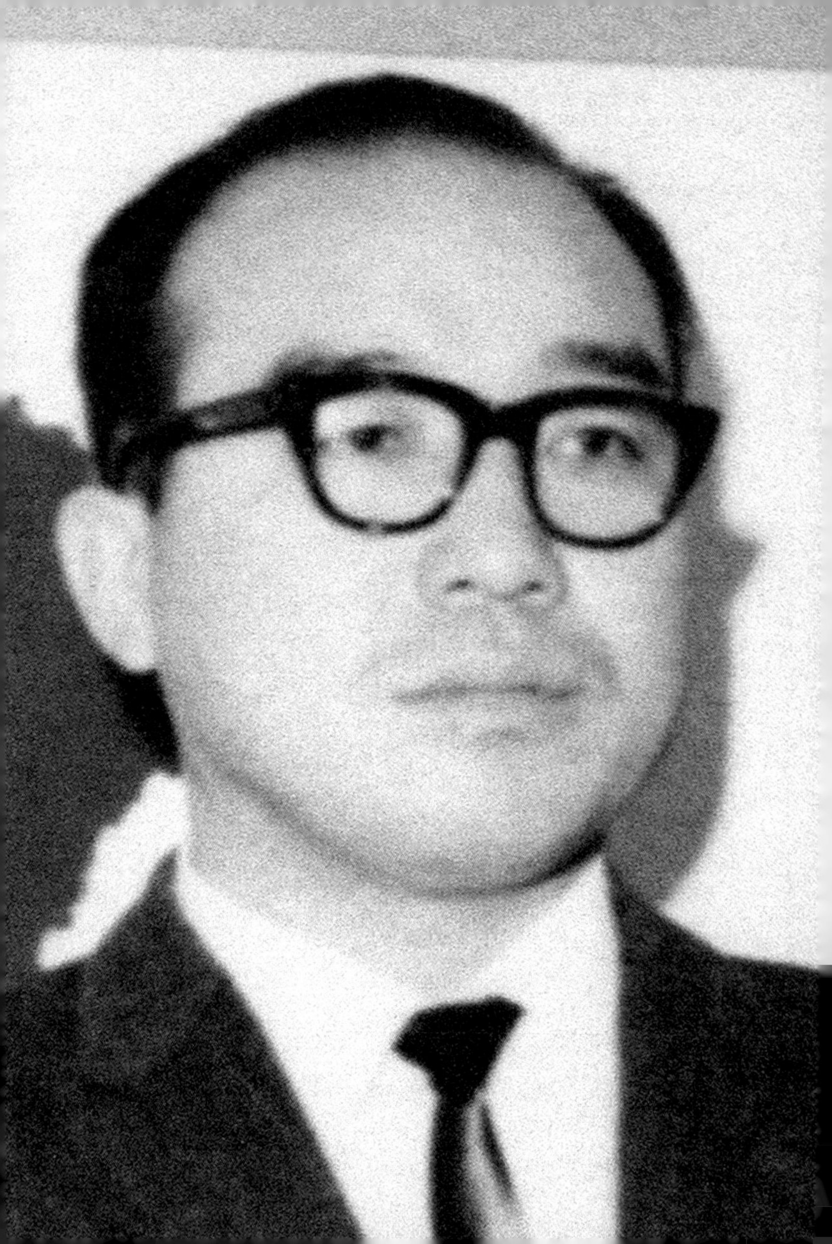

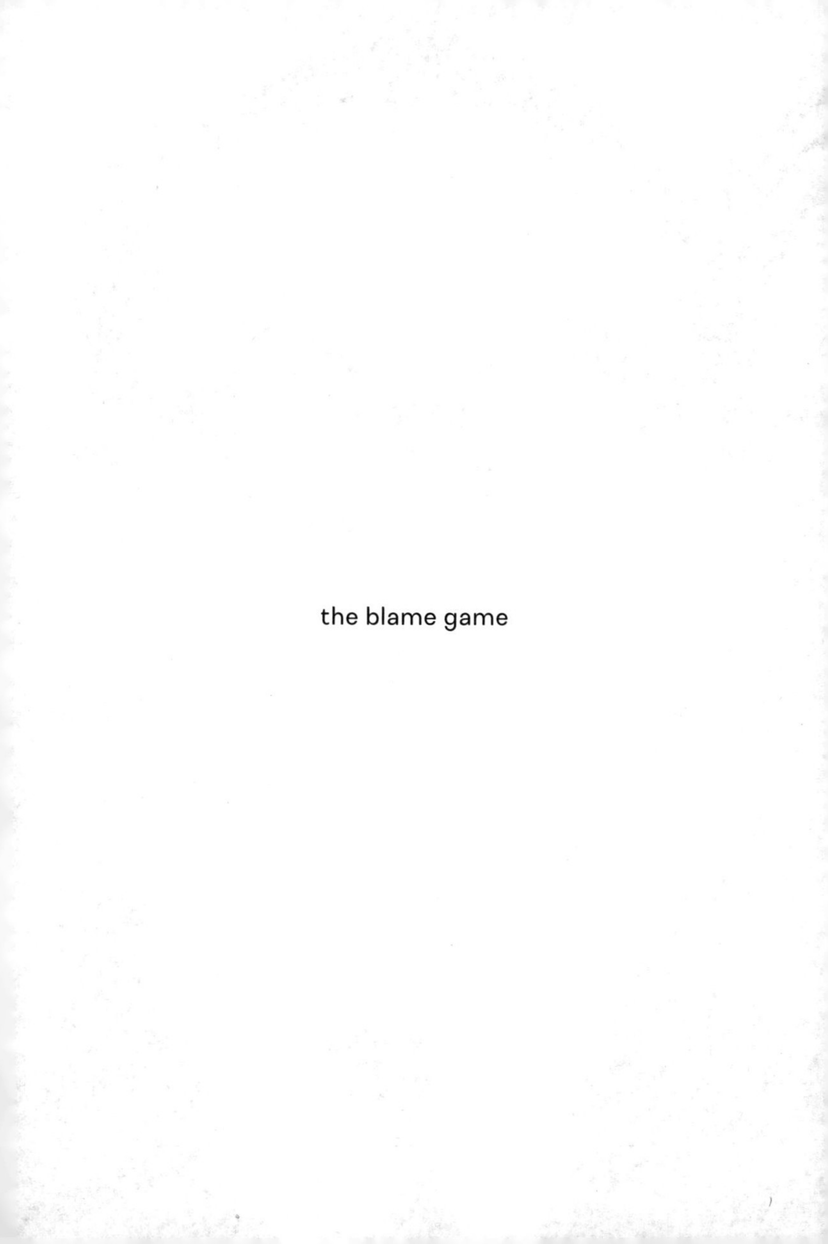

the blame game

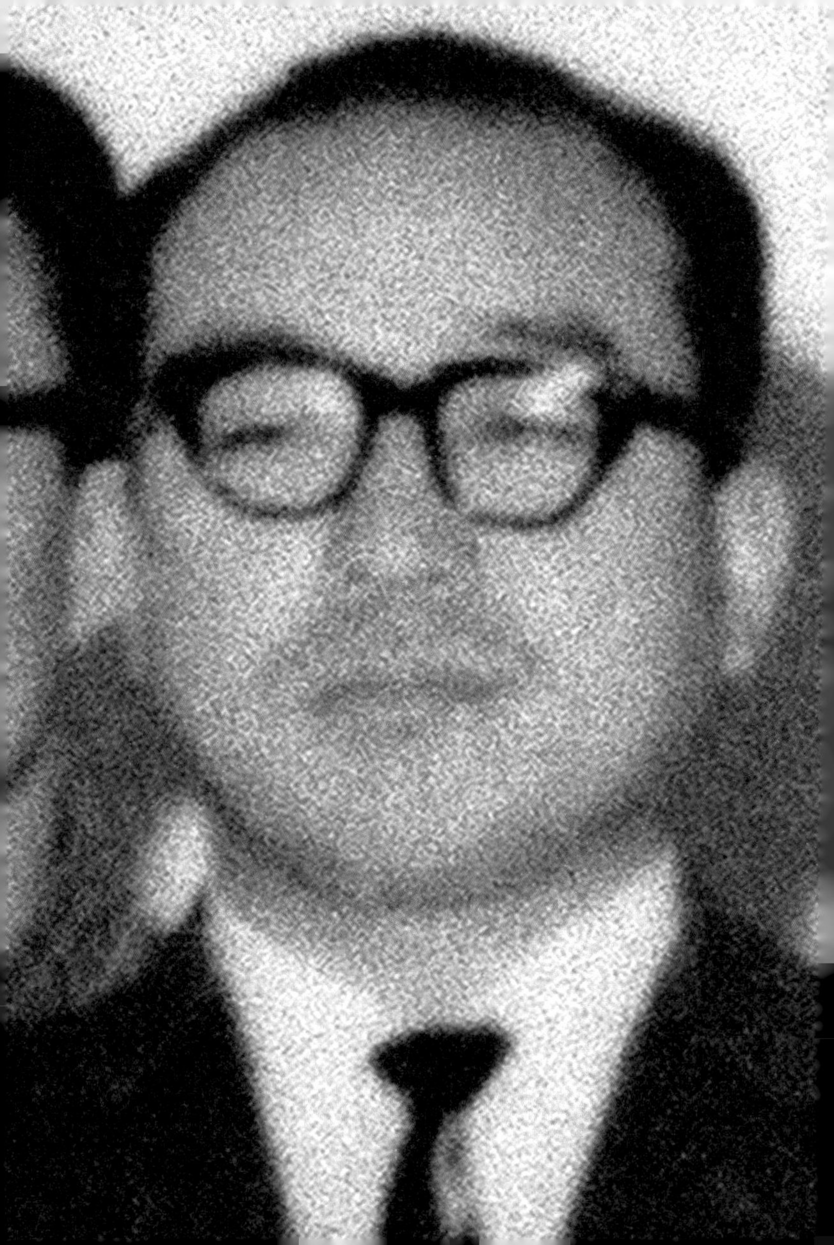

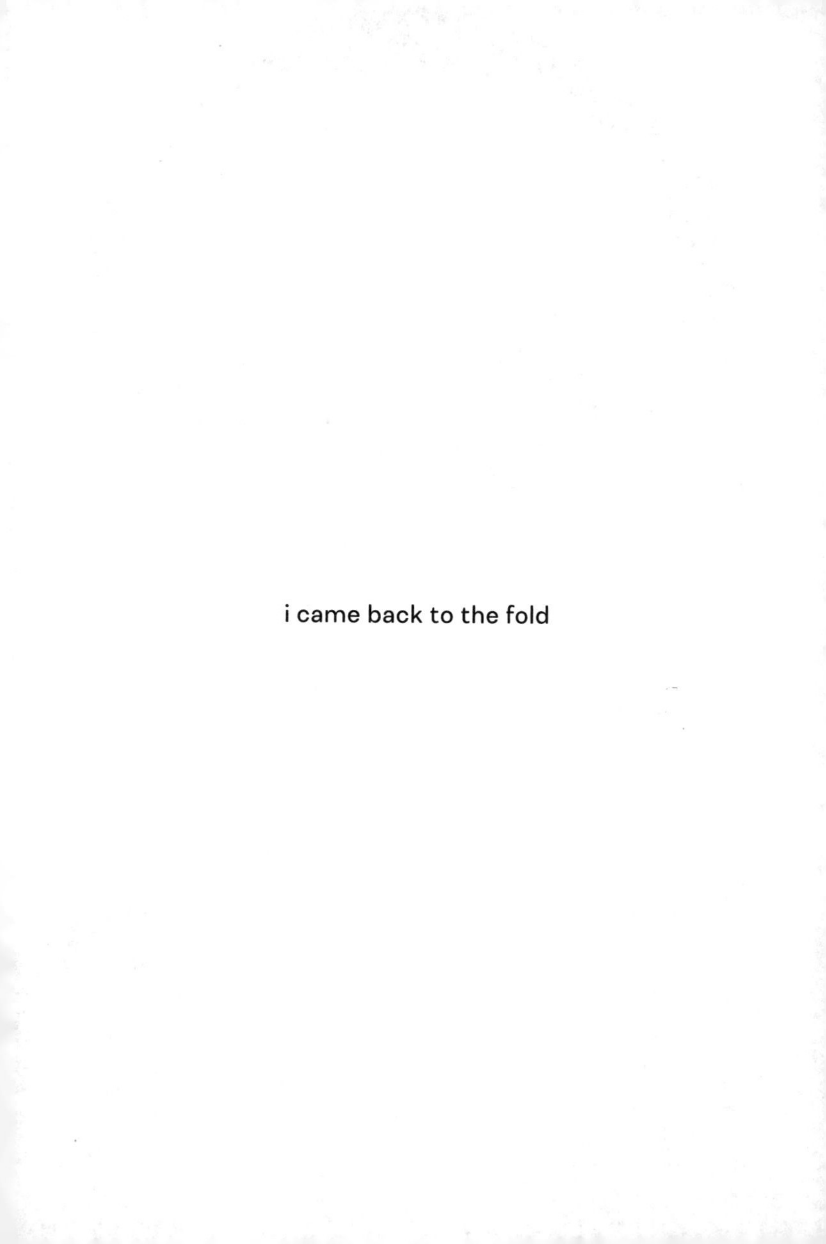

i came back to the fold

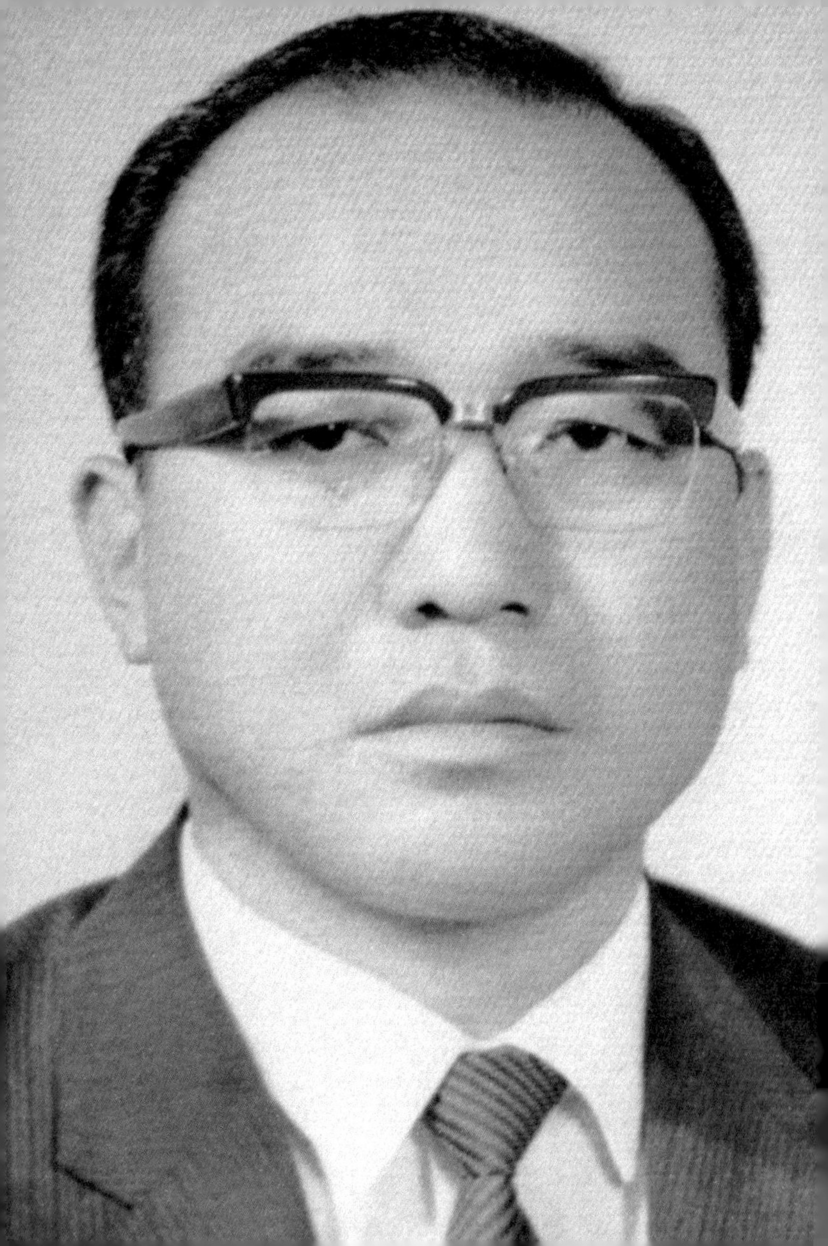

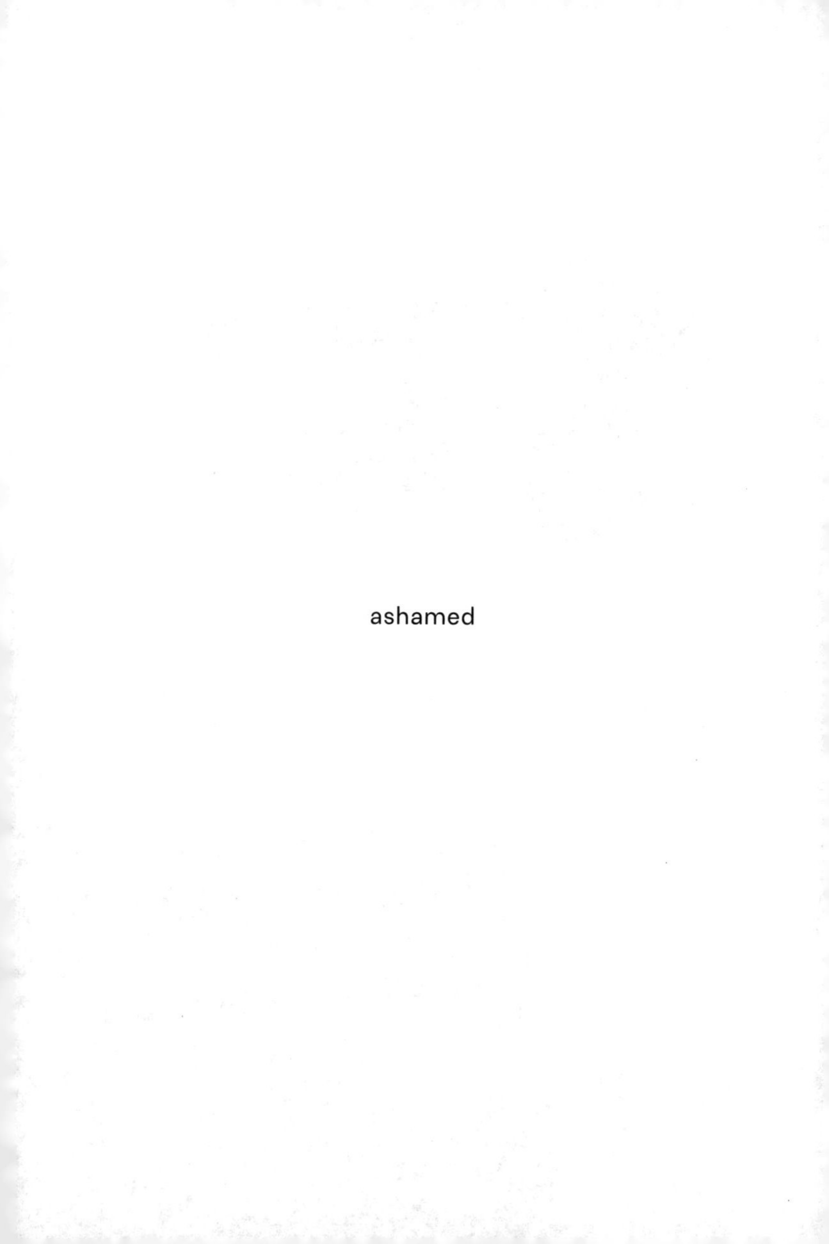

ashamed

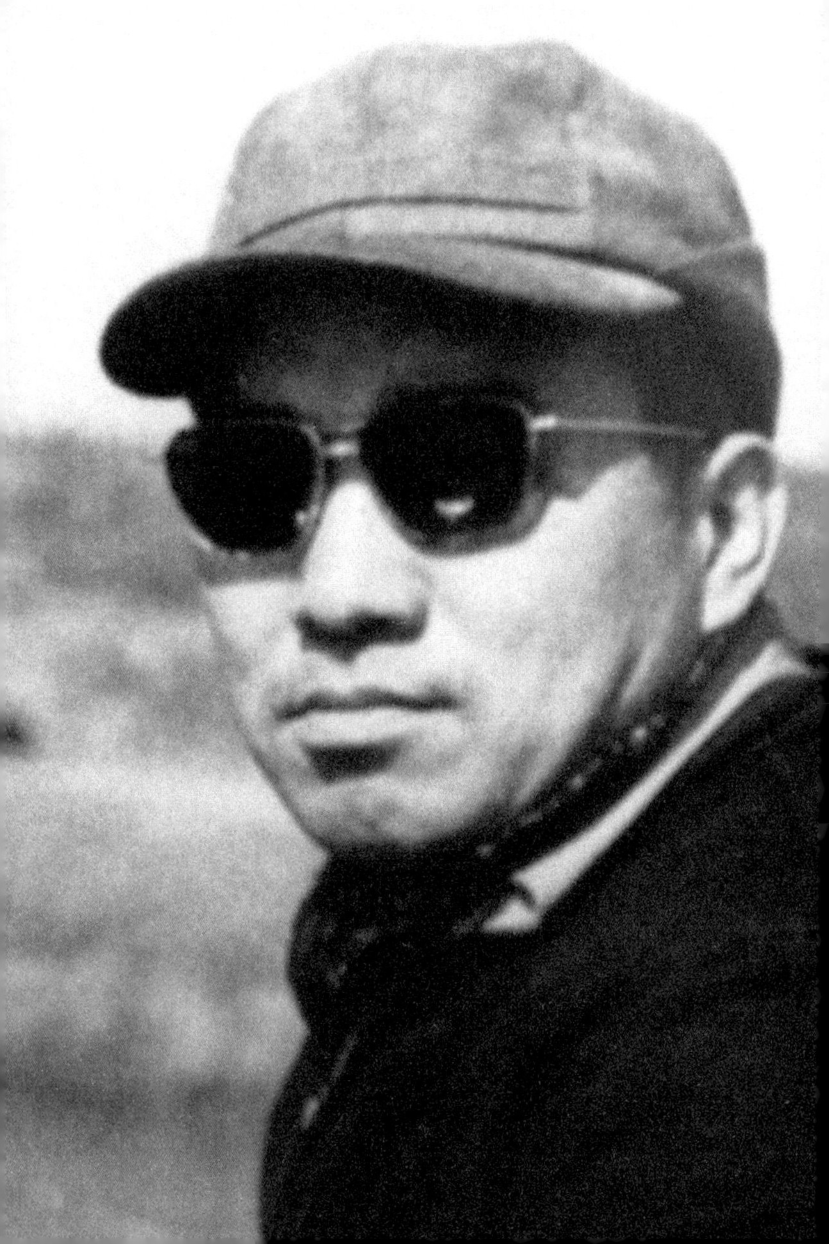

i came back home

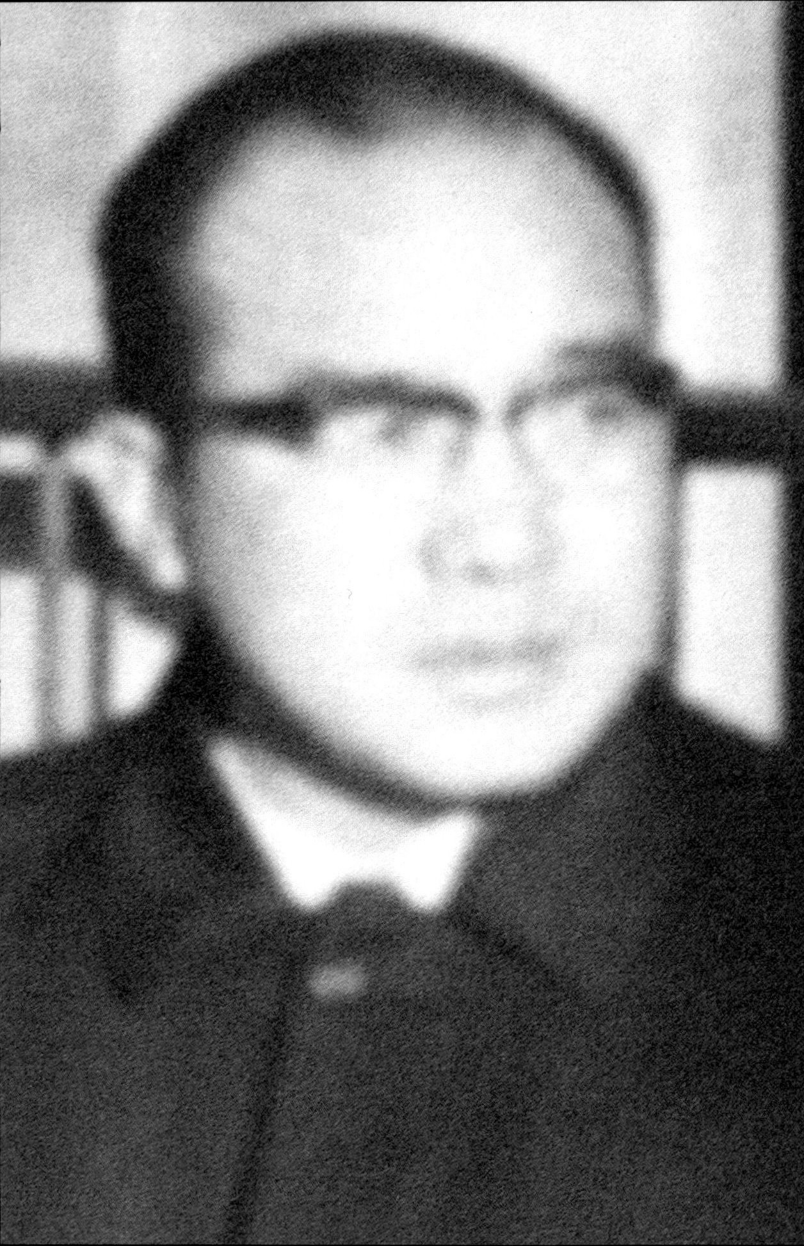

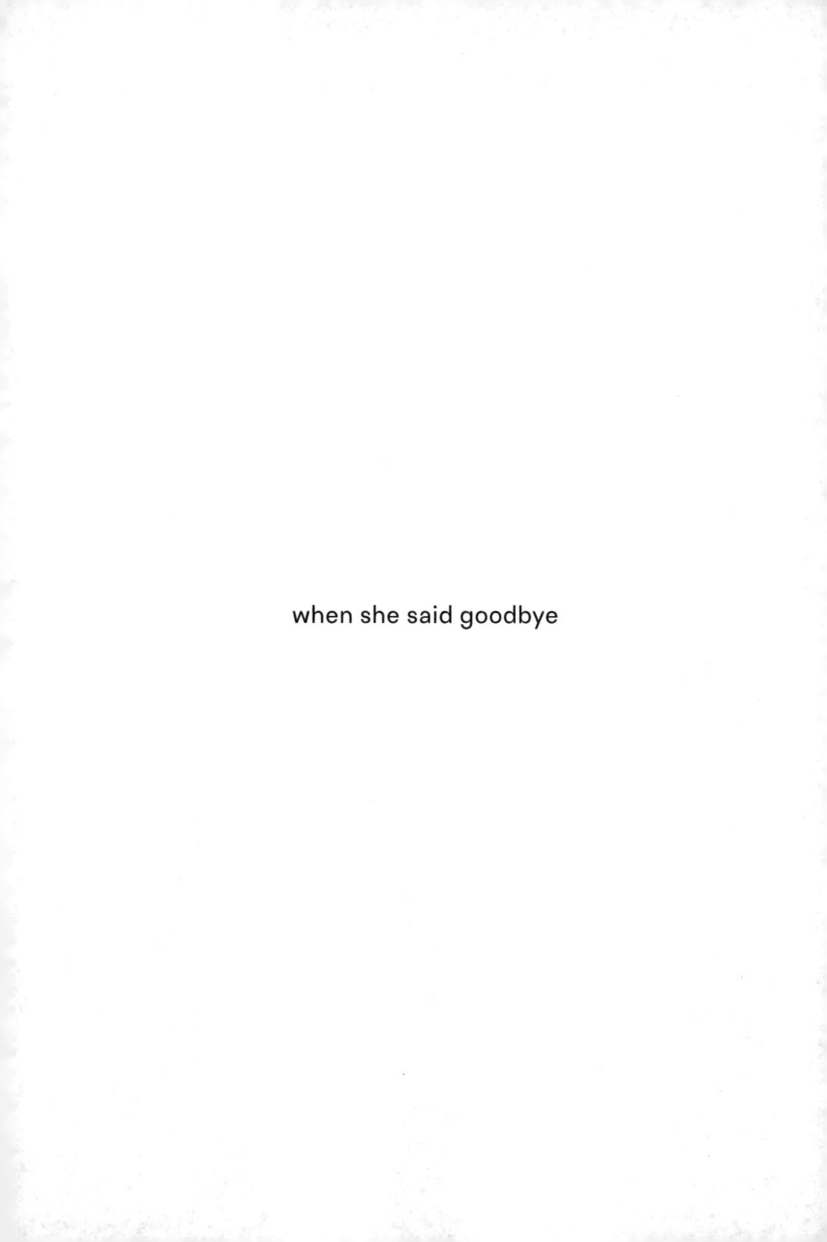

when she said goodbye

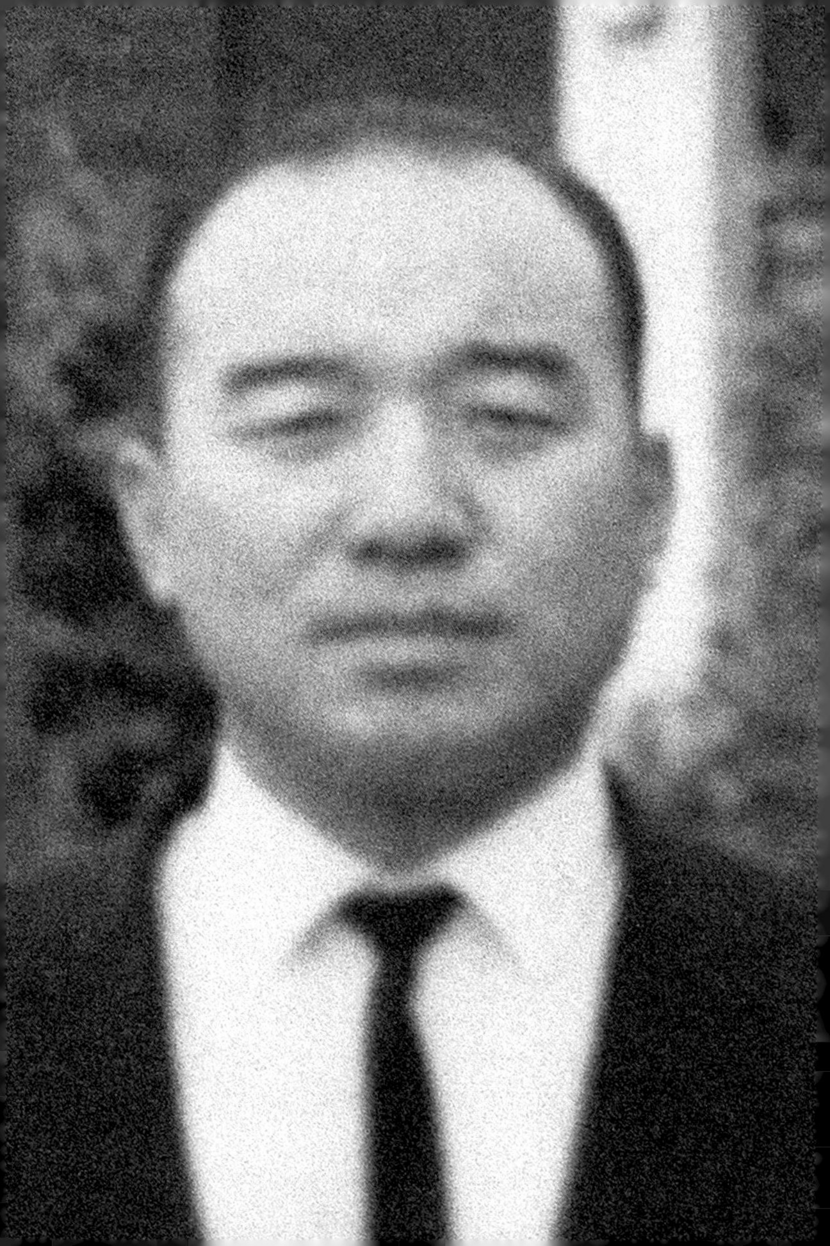

nothing lasts that long

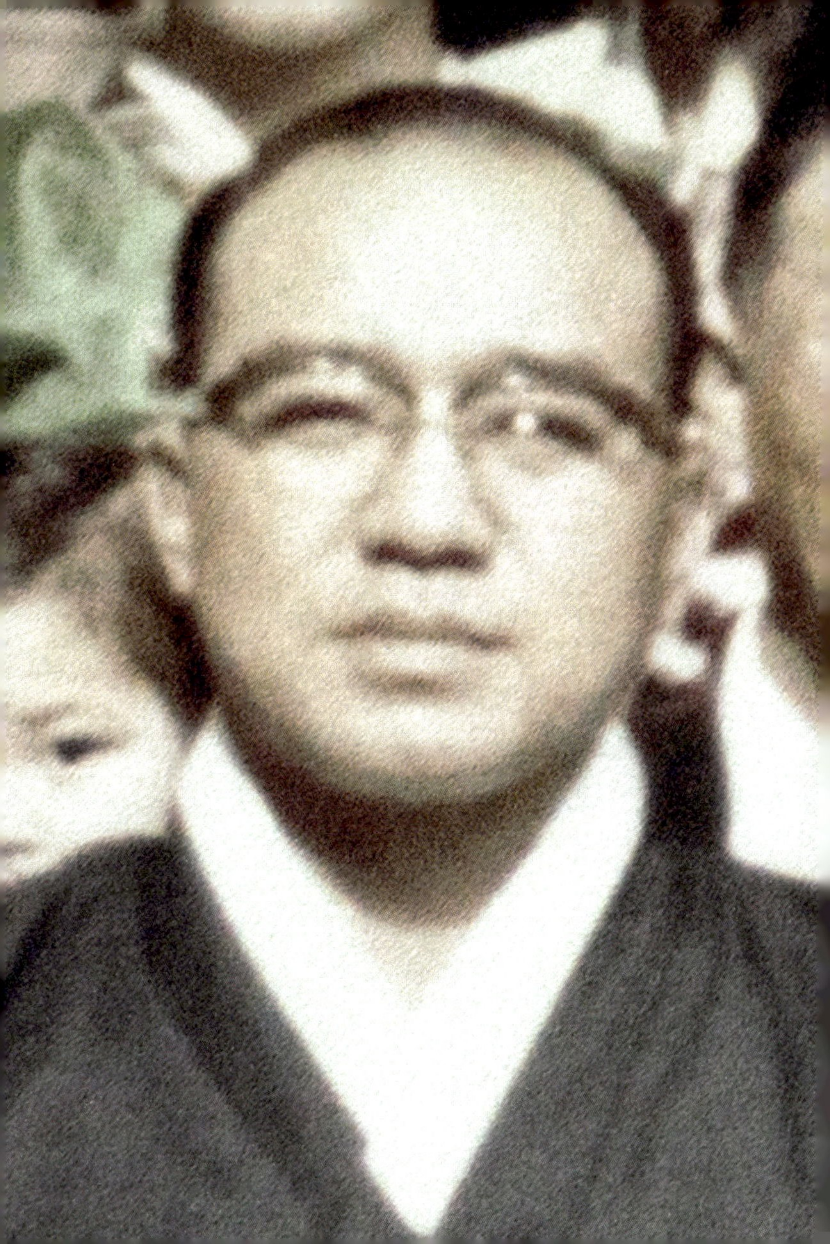

forever

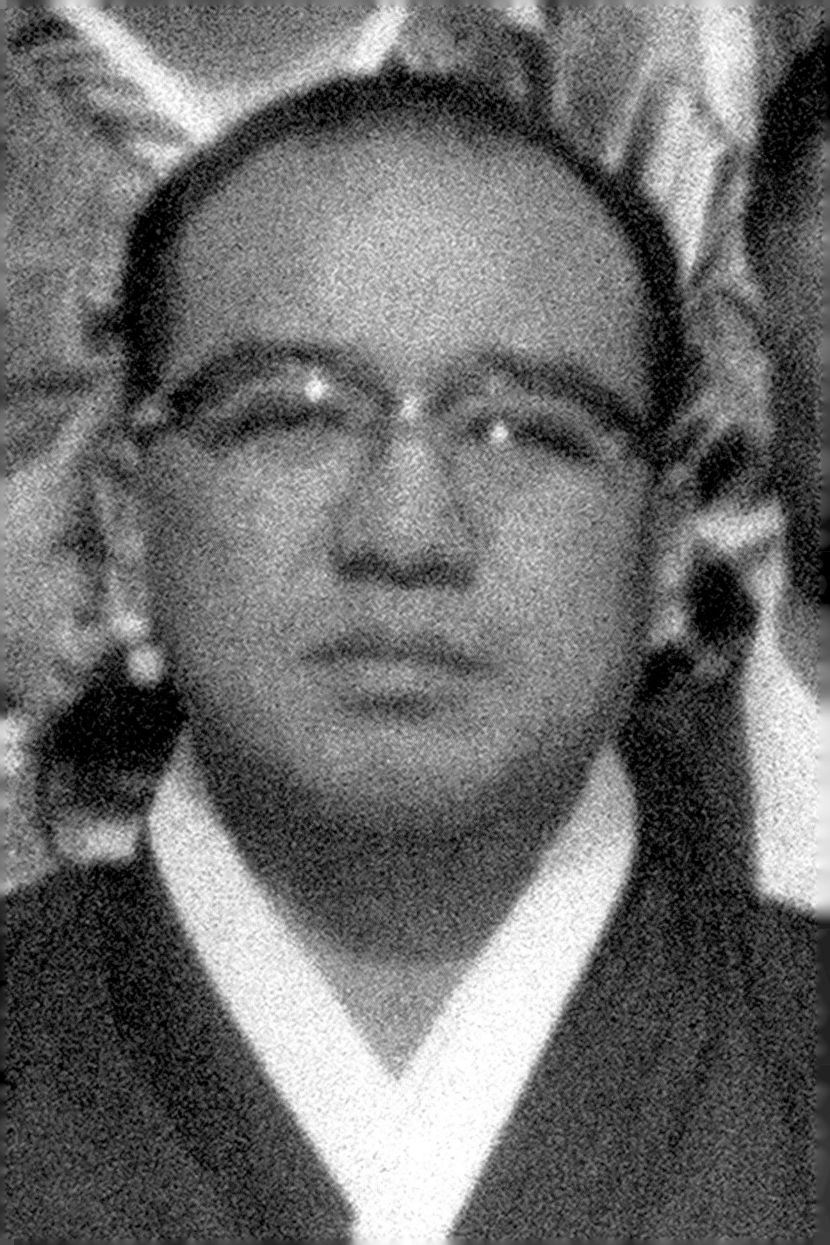

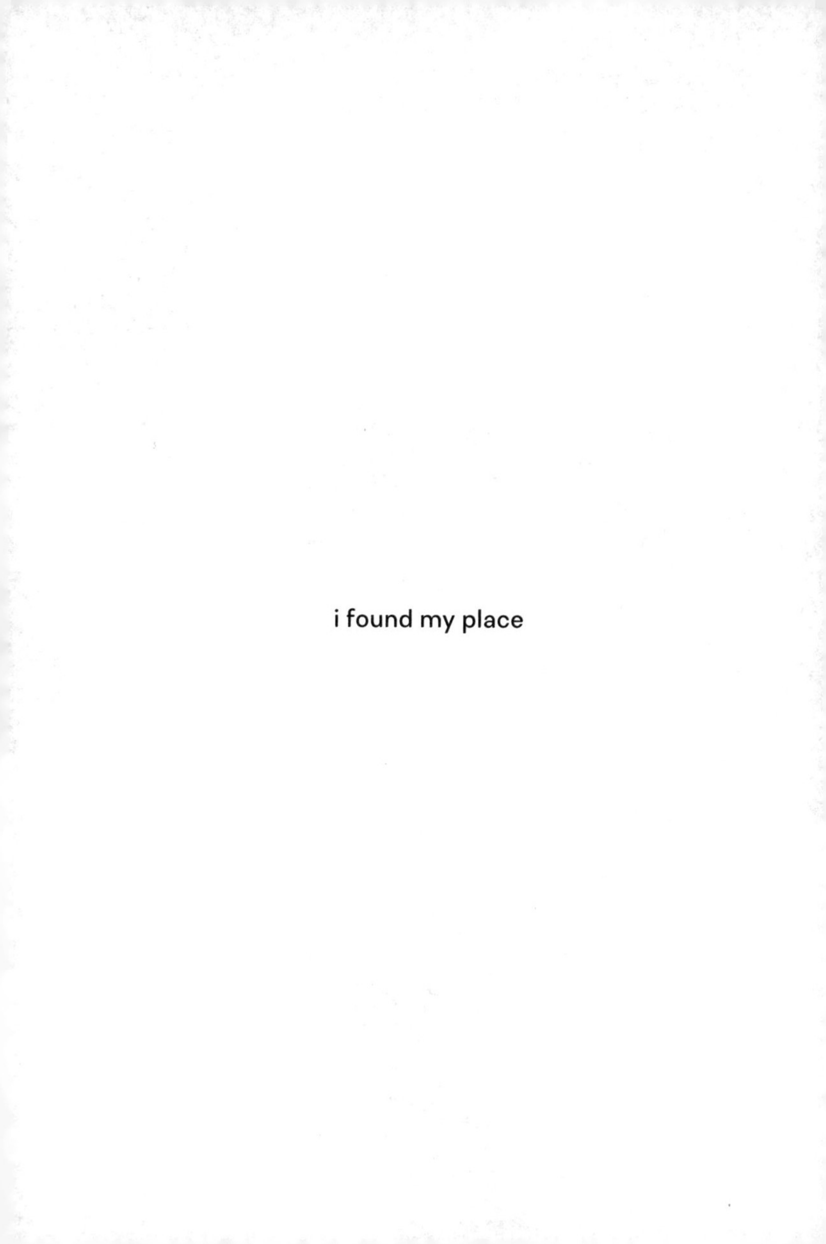

i found my place

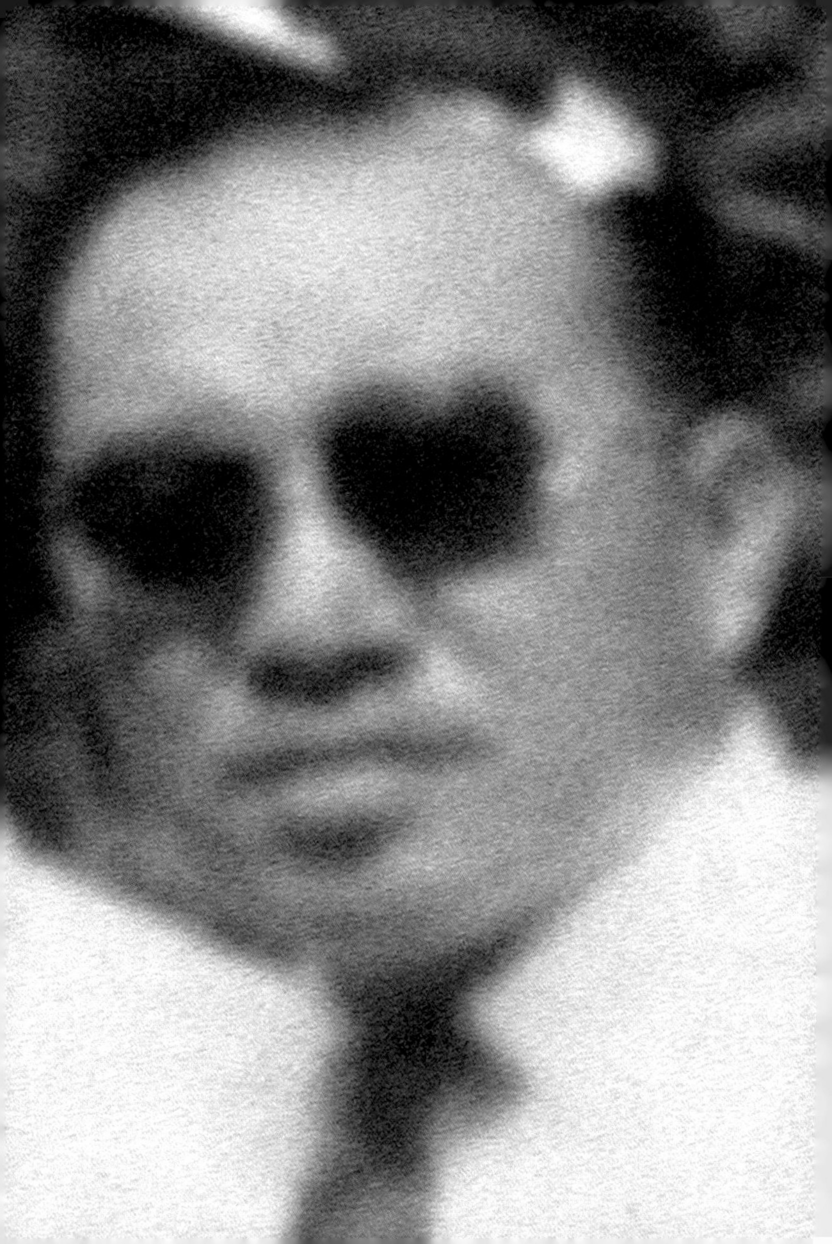

i broke my moorings

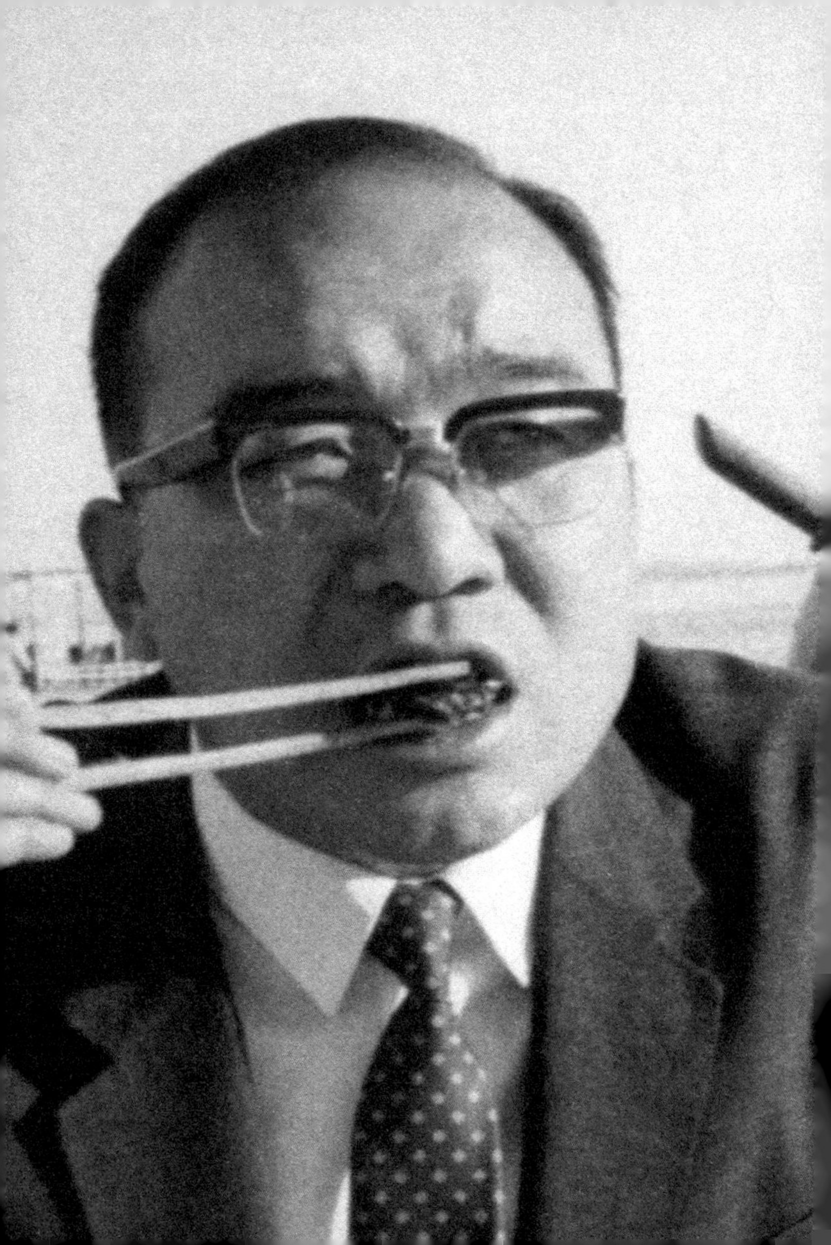

i made the most of it

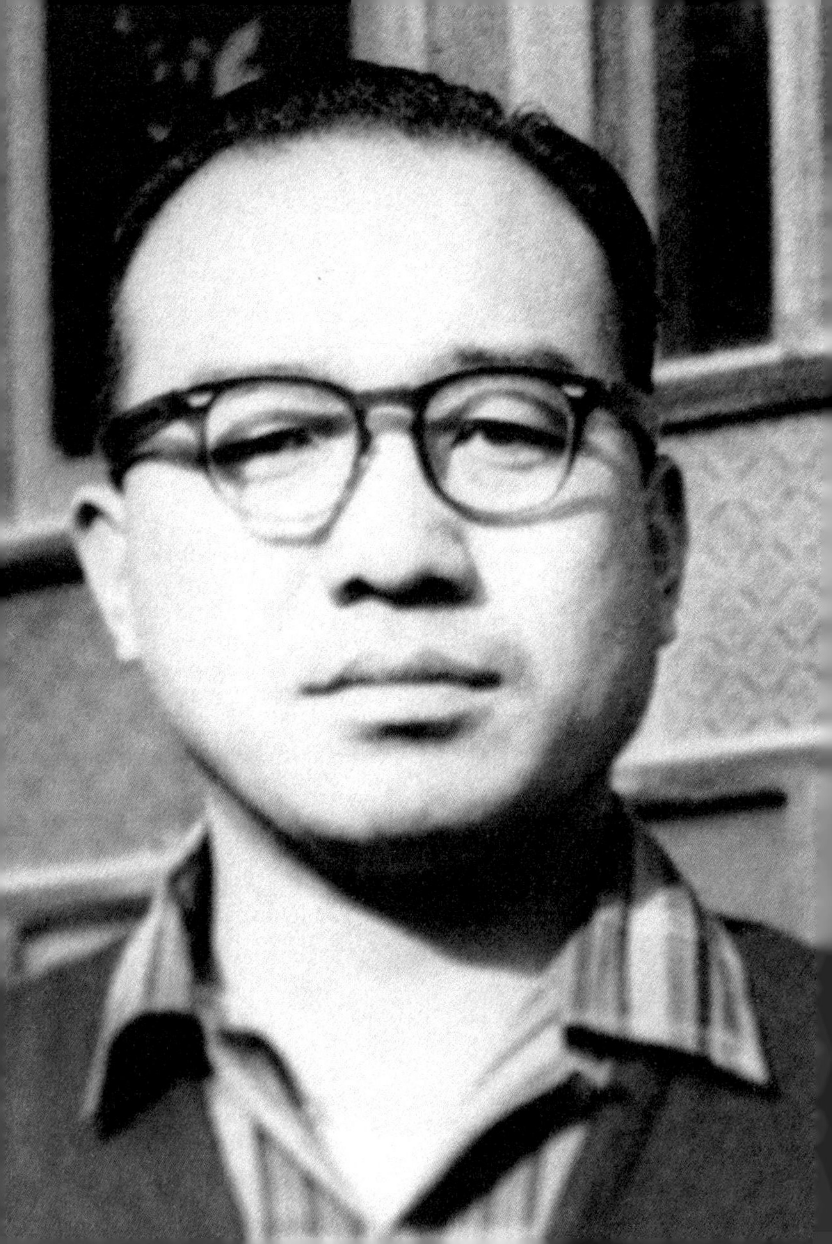

i flew without a net

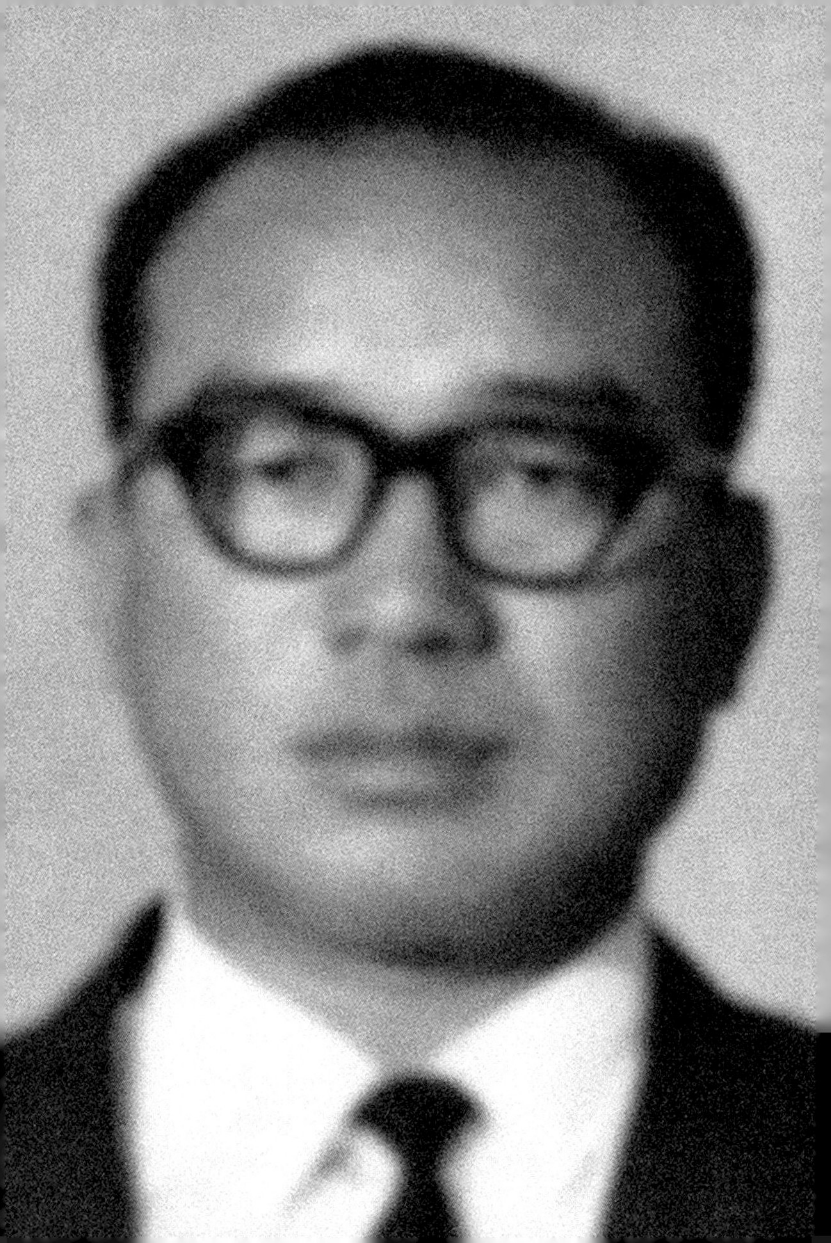

without counting on anyone

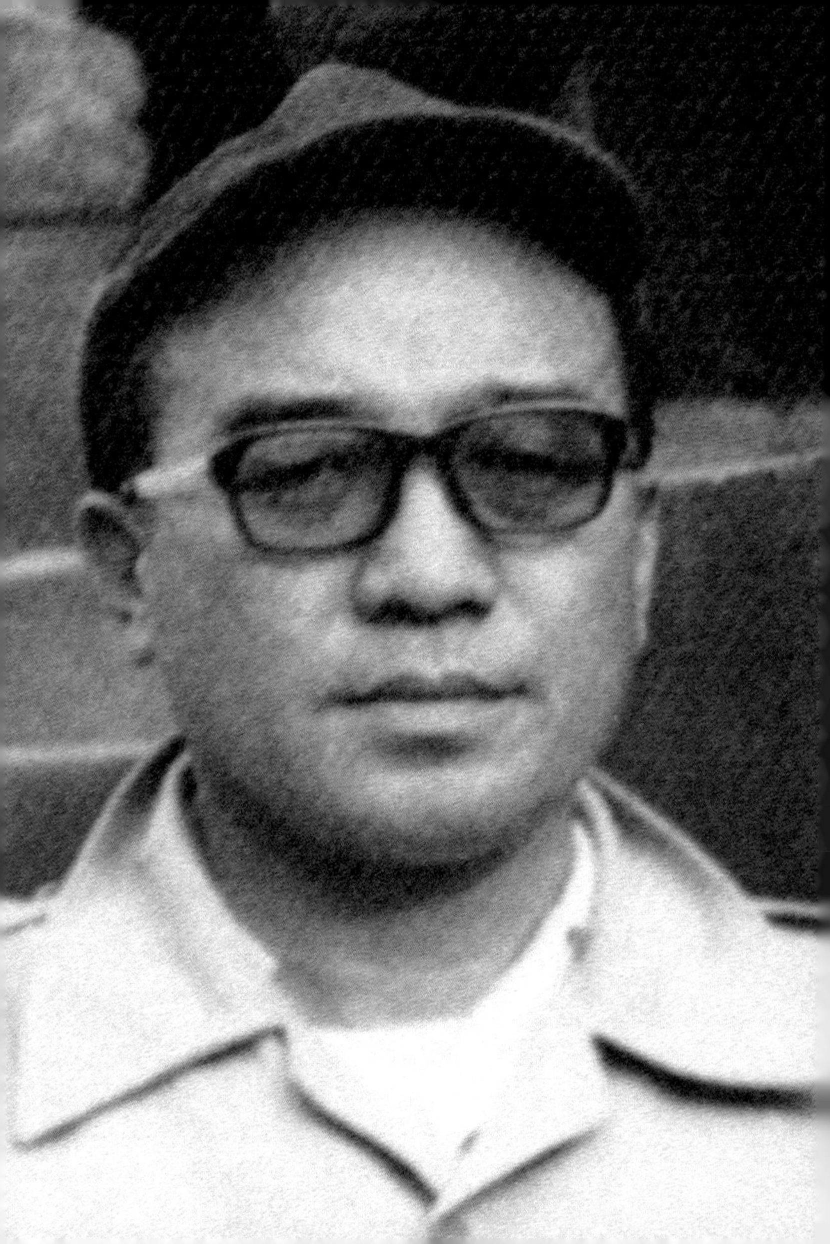

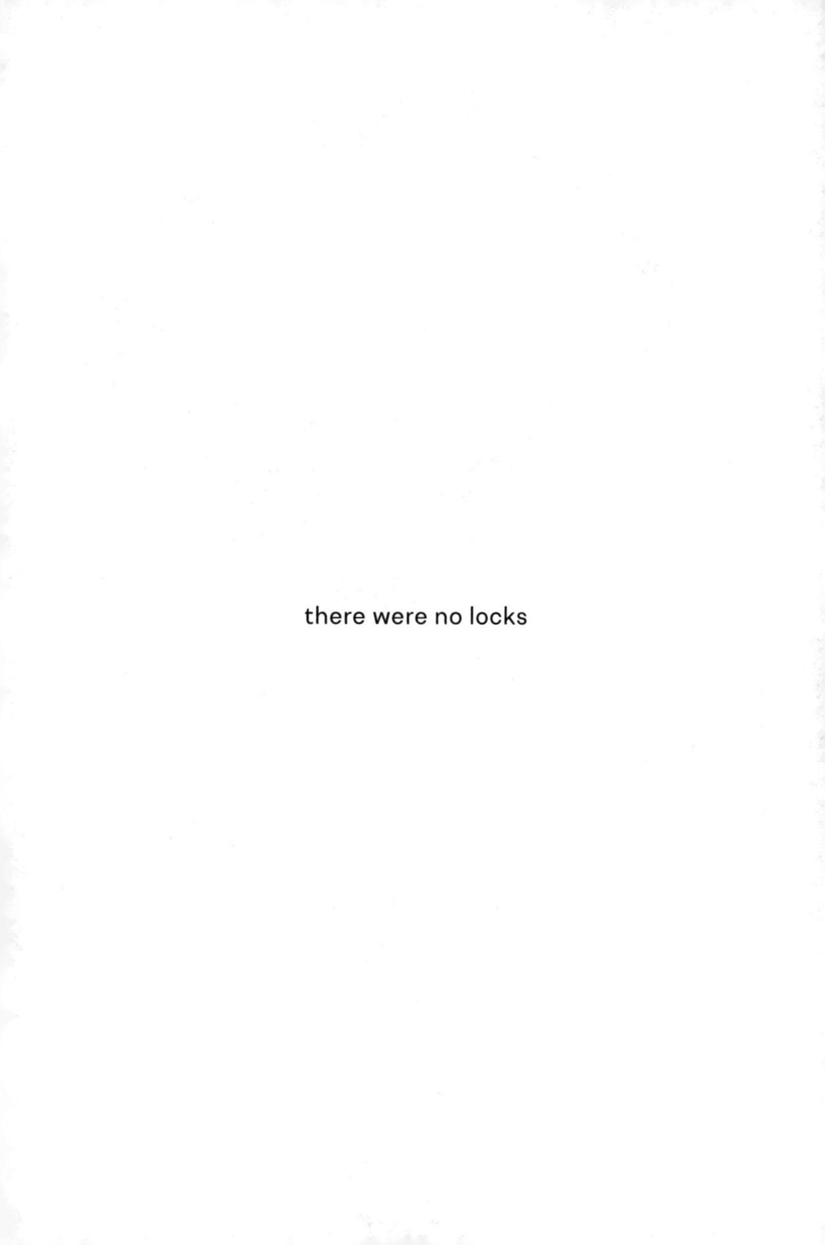

there were no locks

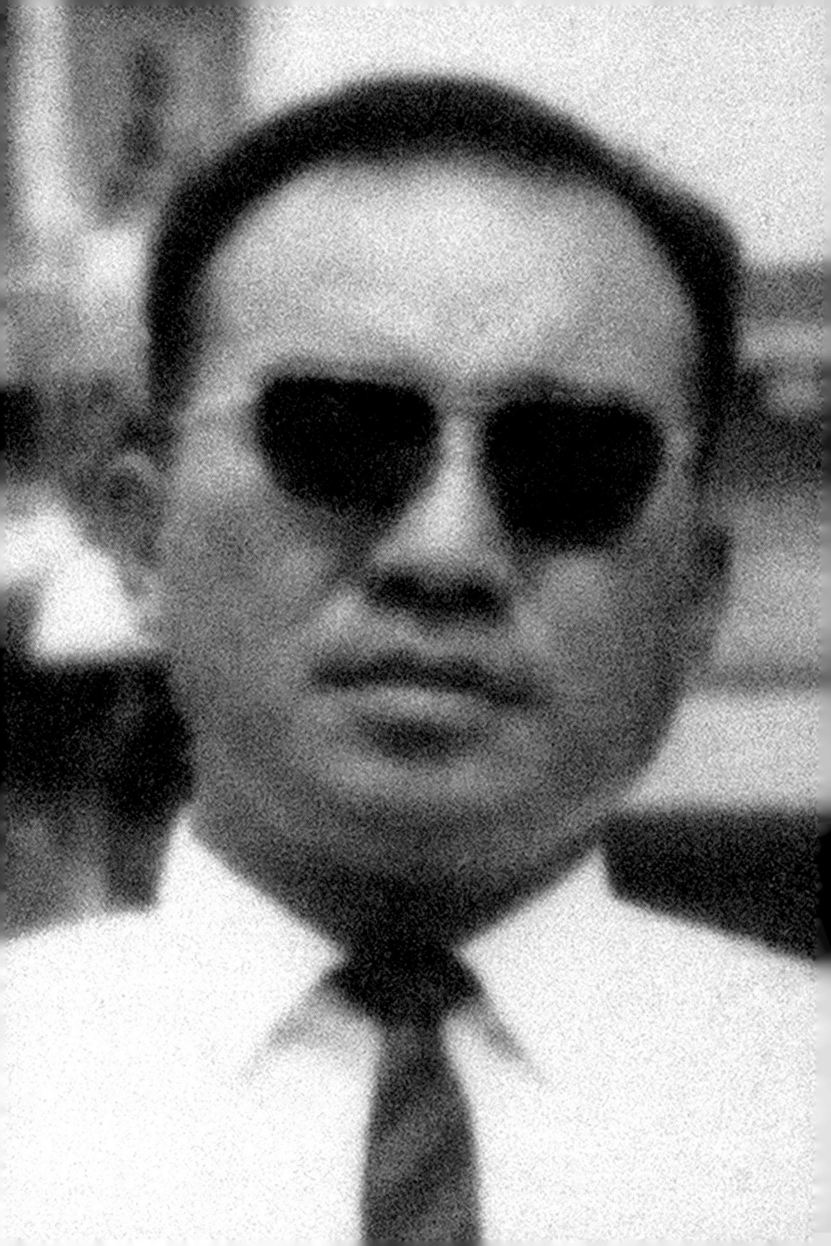

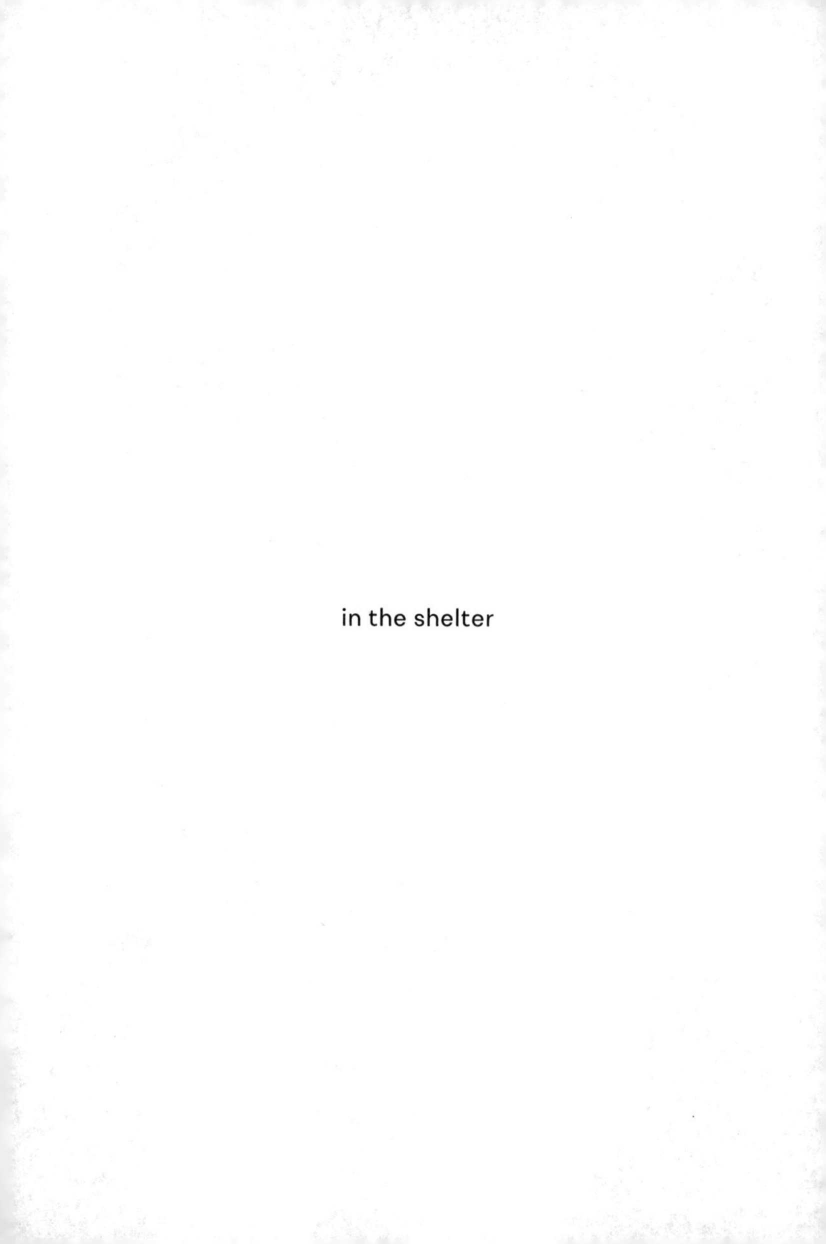

in the shelter

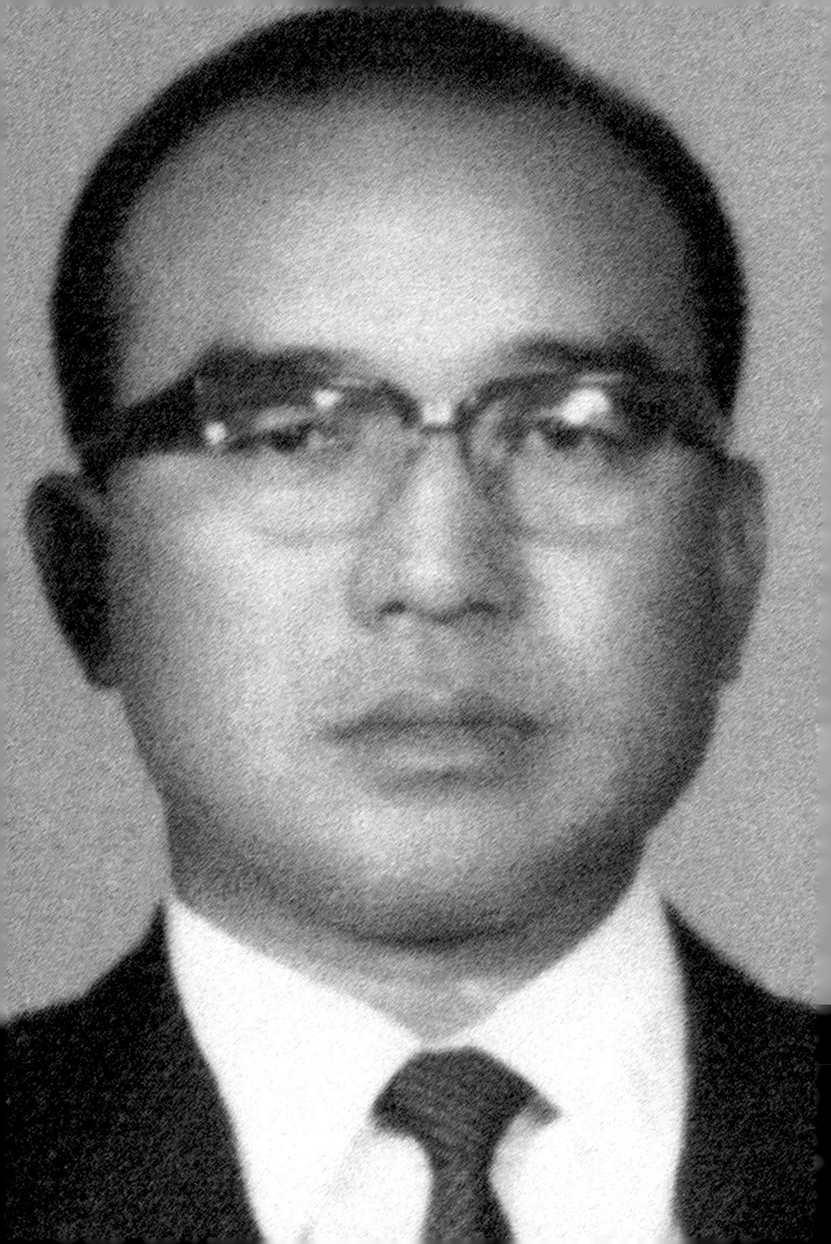

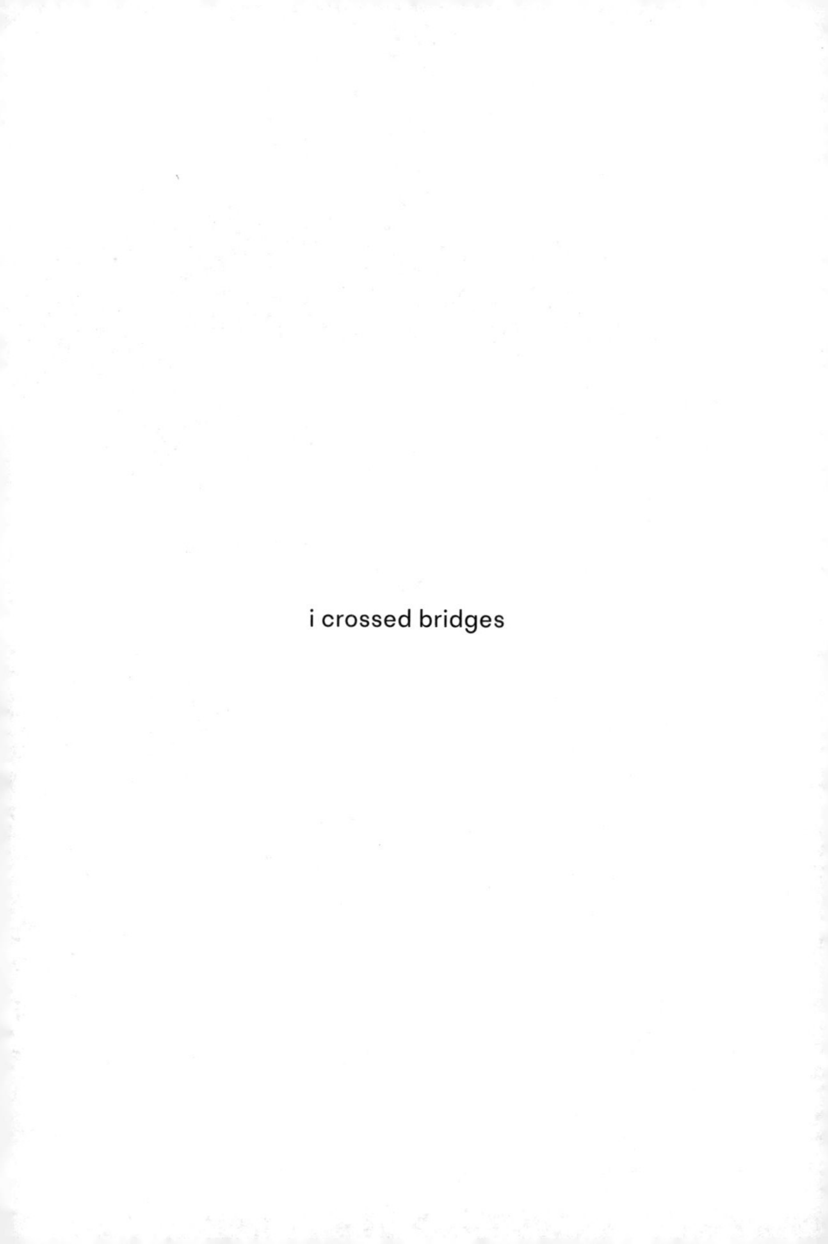

i crossed bridges

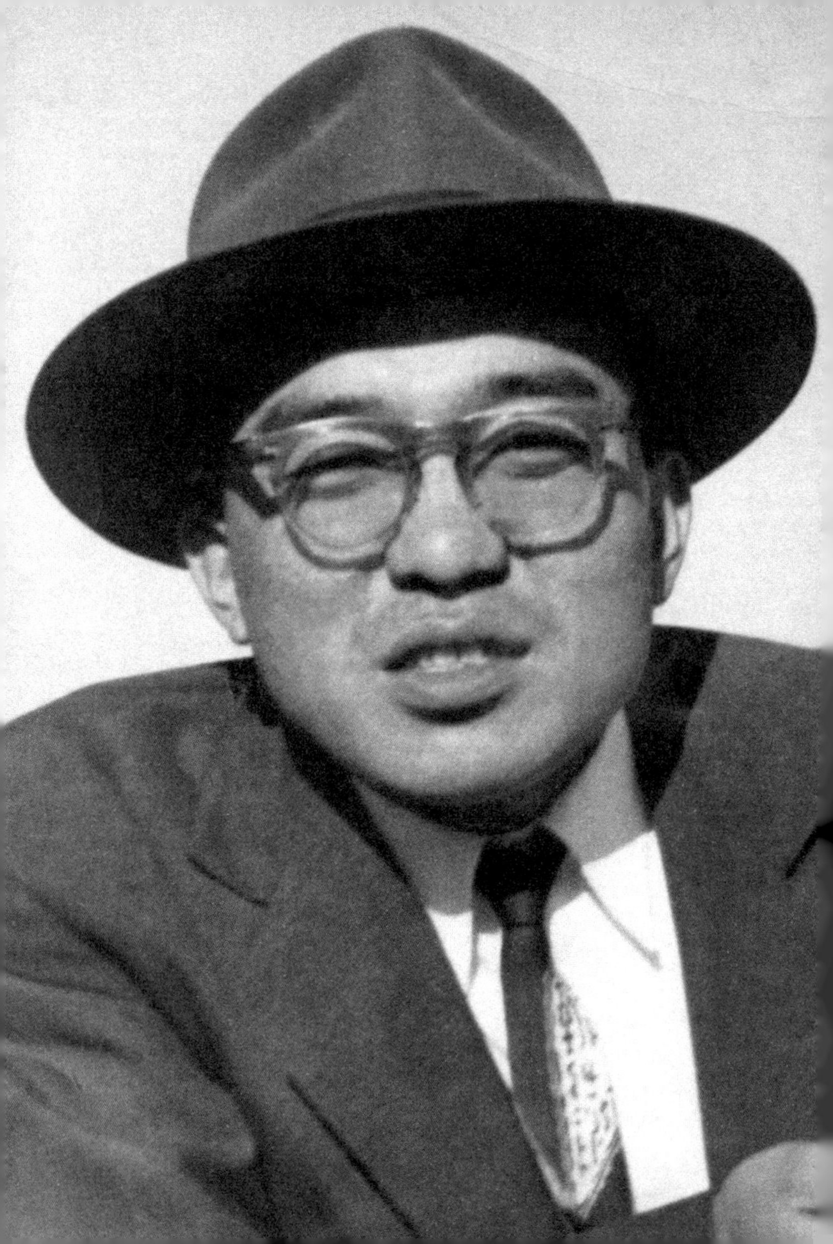

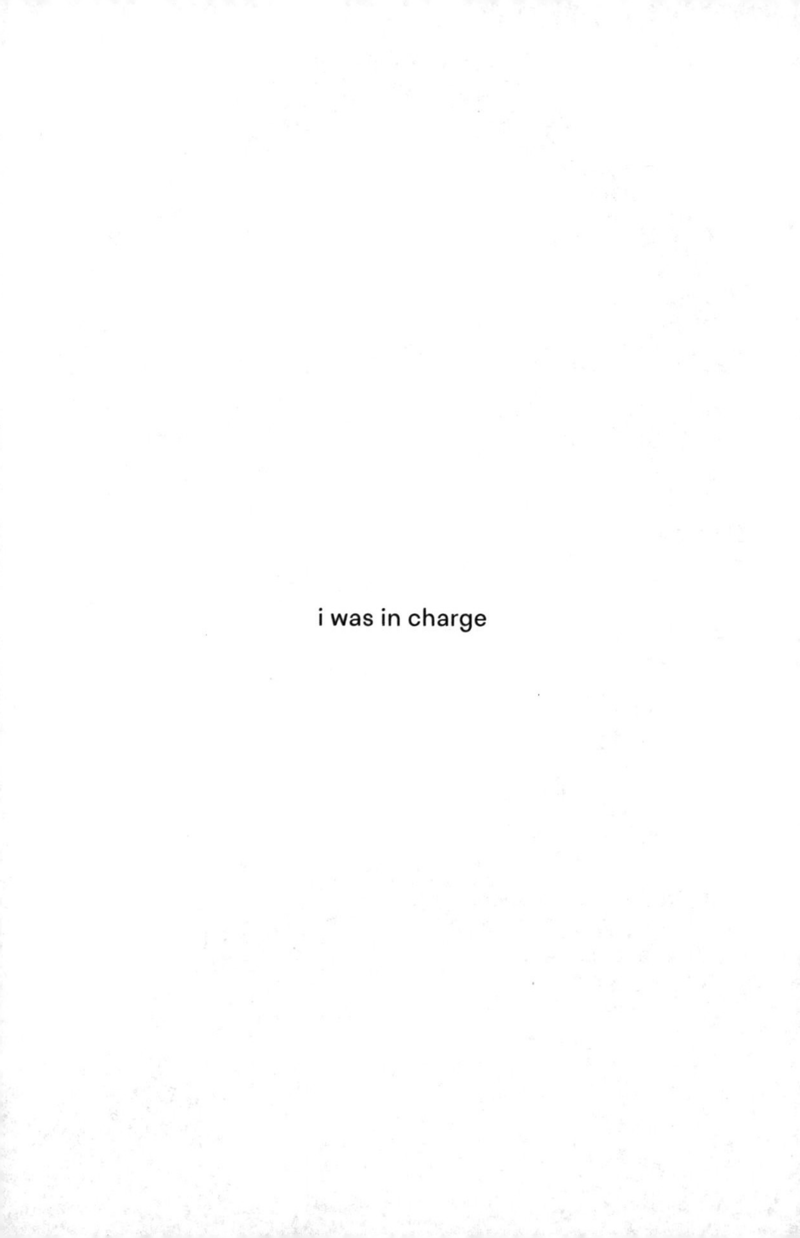

i was in charge

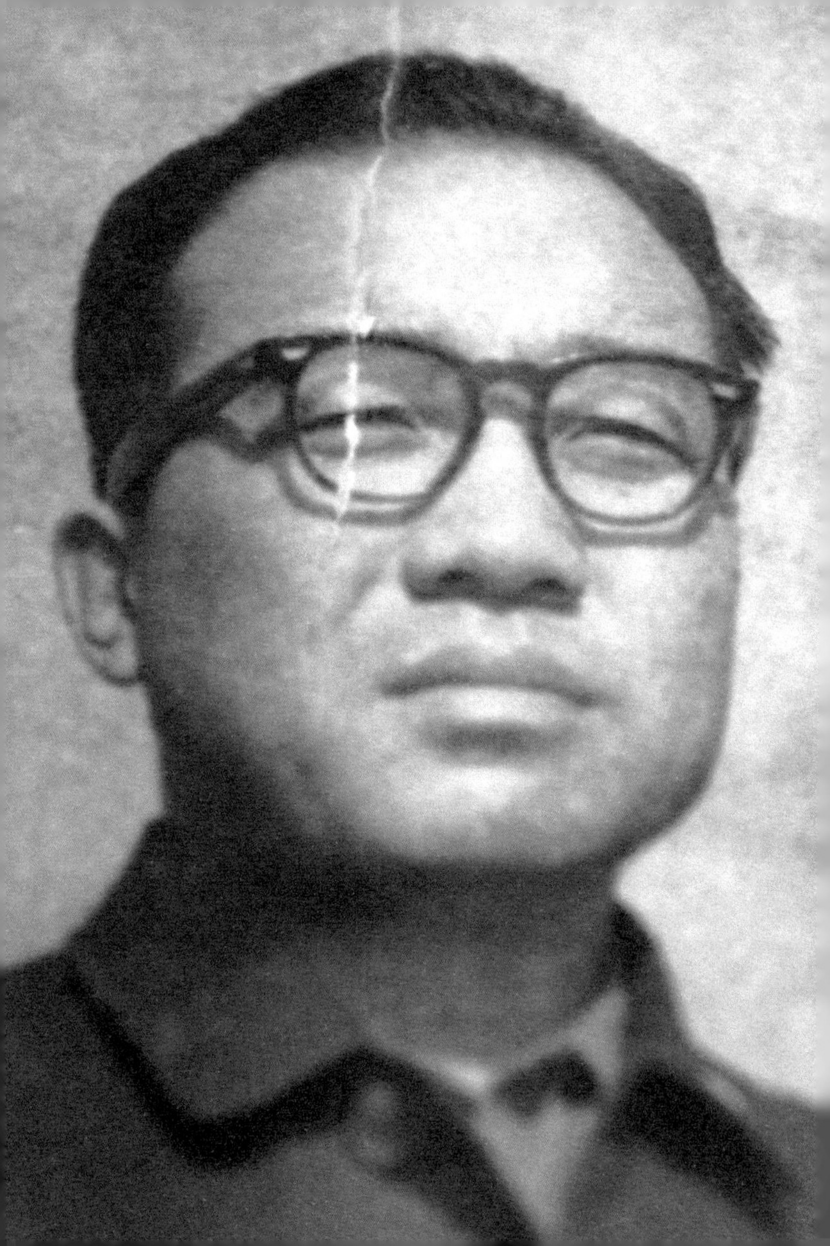

my will

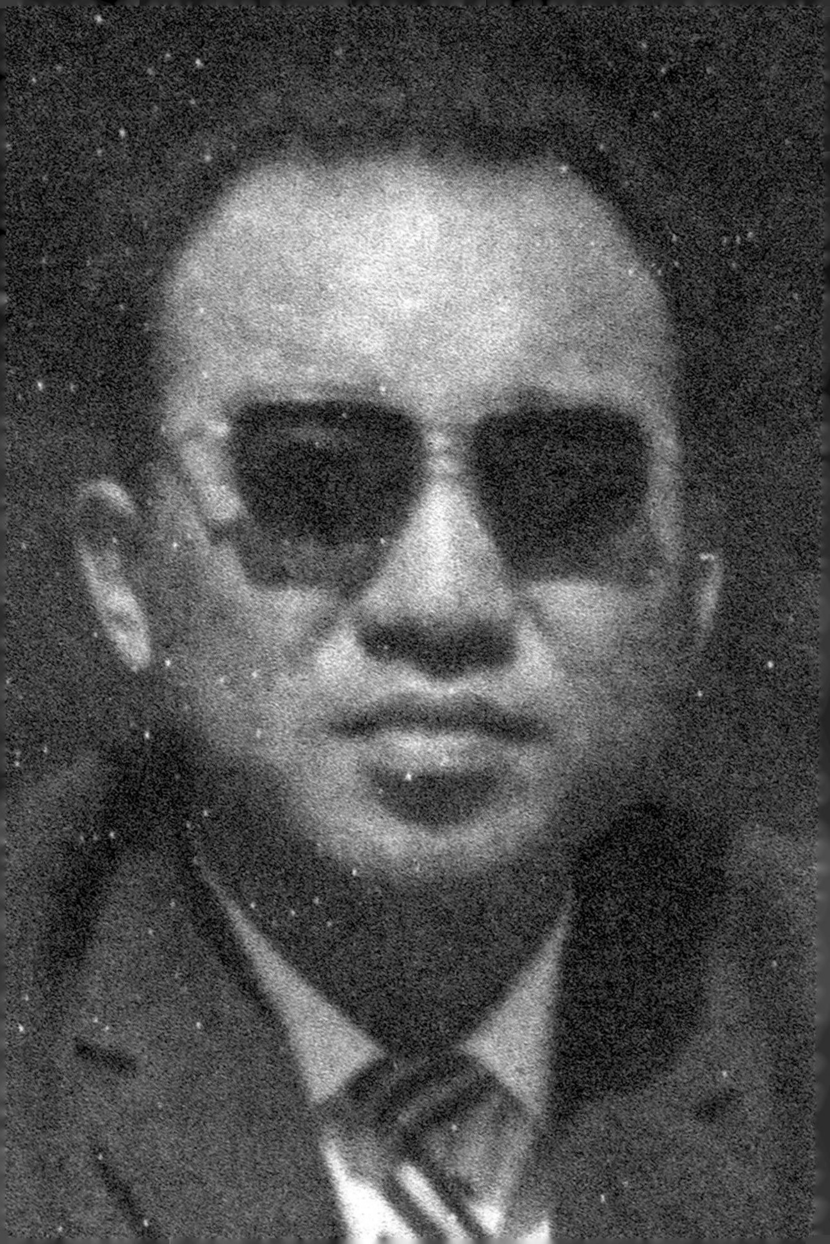

i obeyed

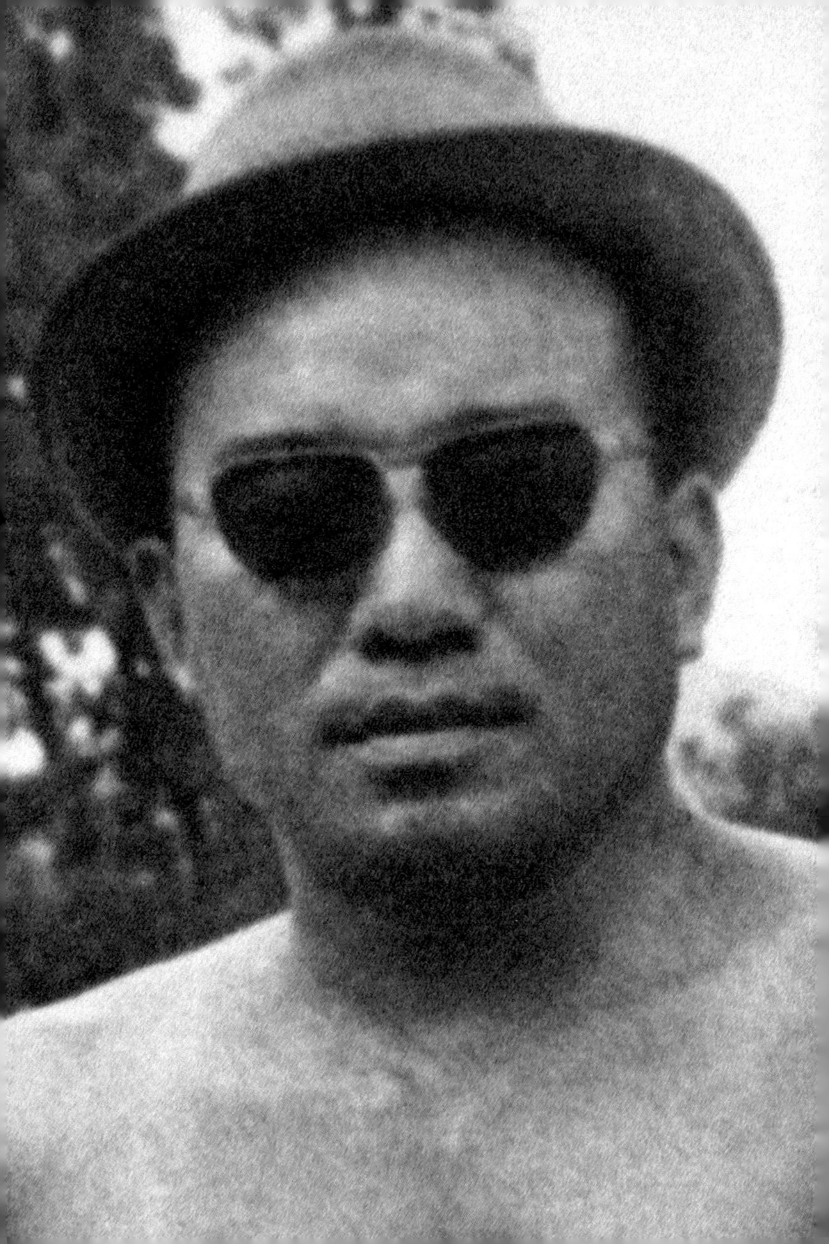

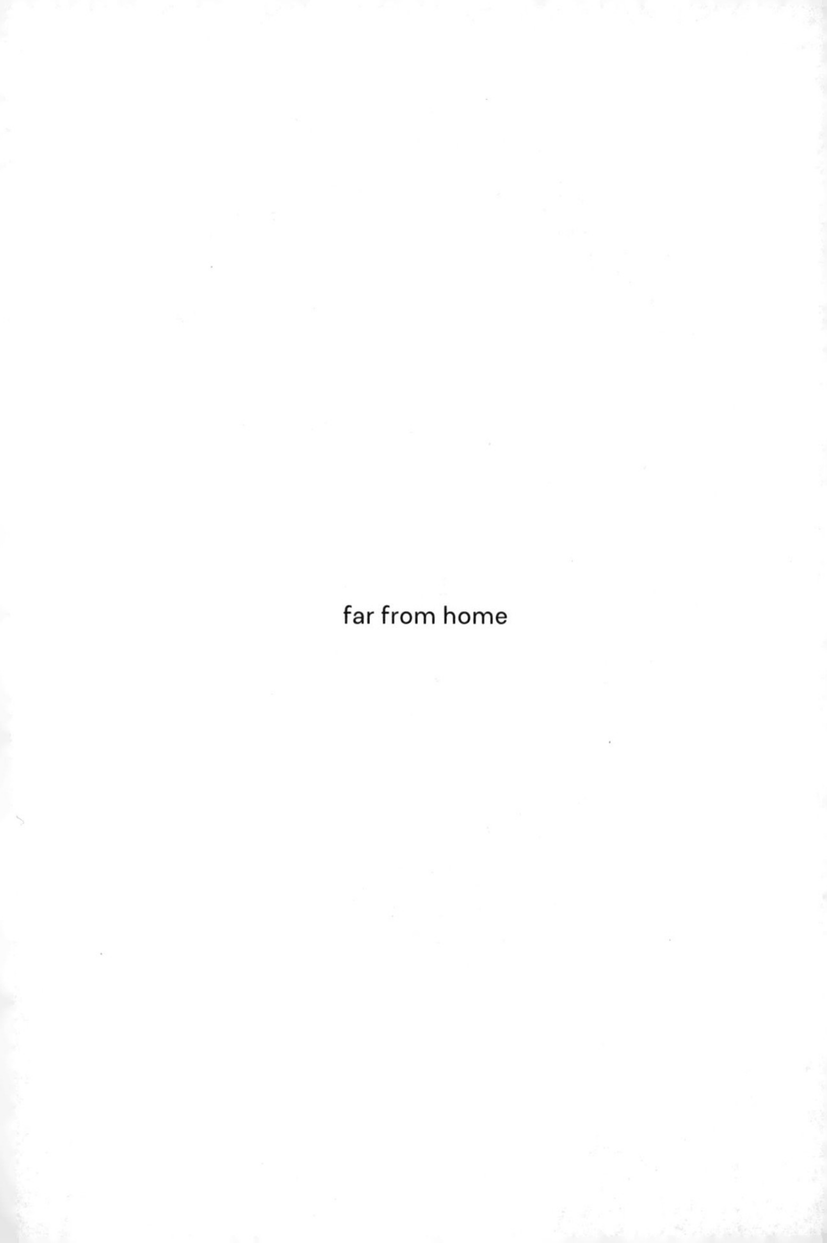

far from home

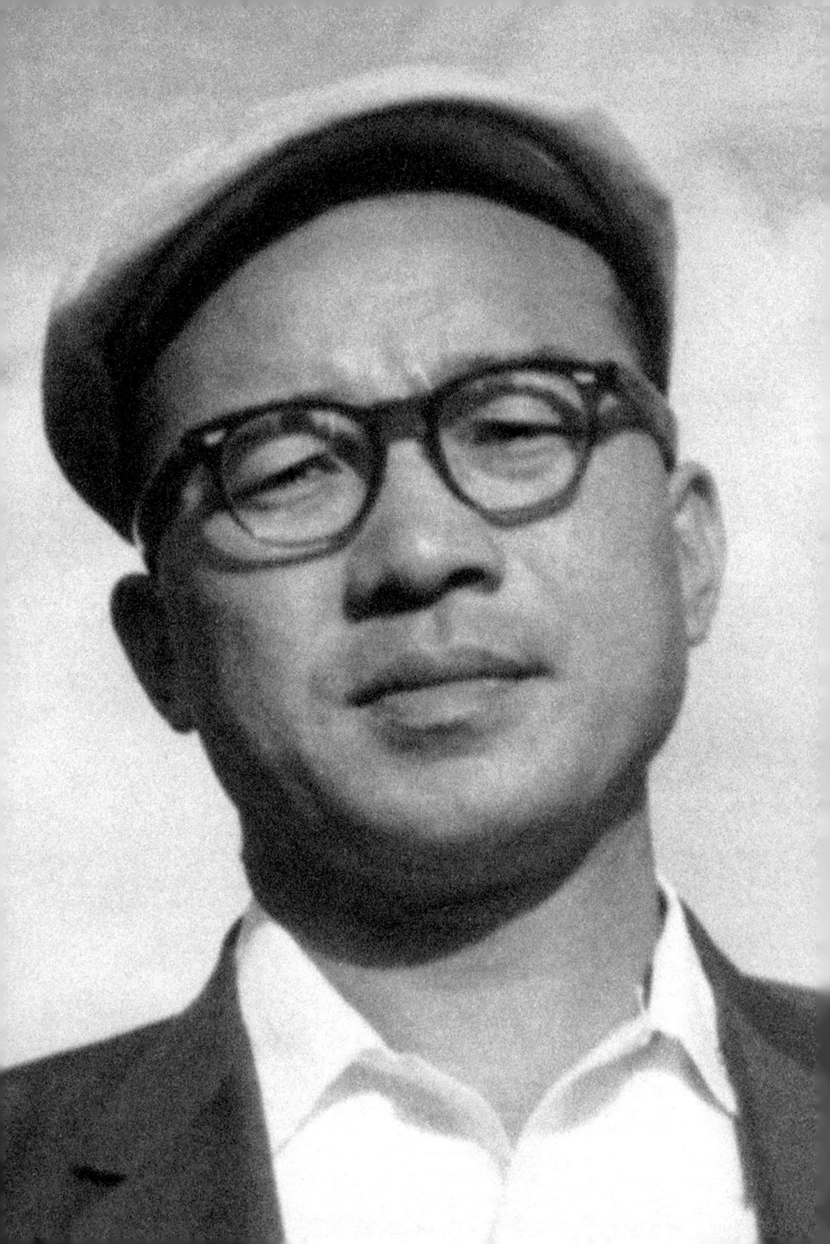

new life

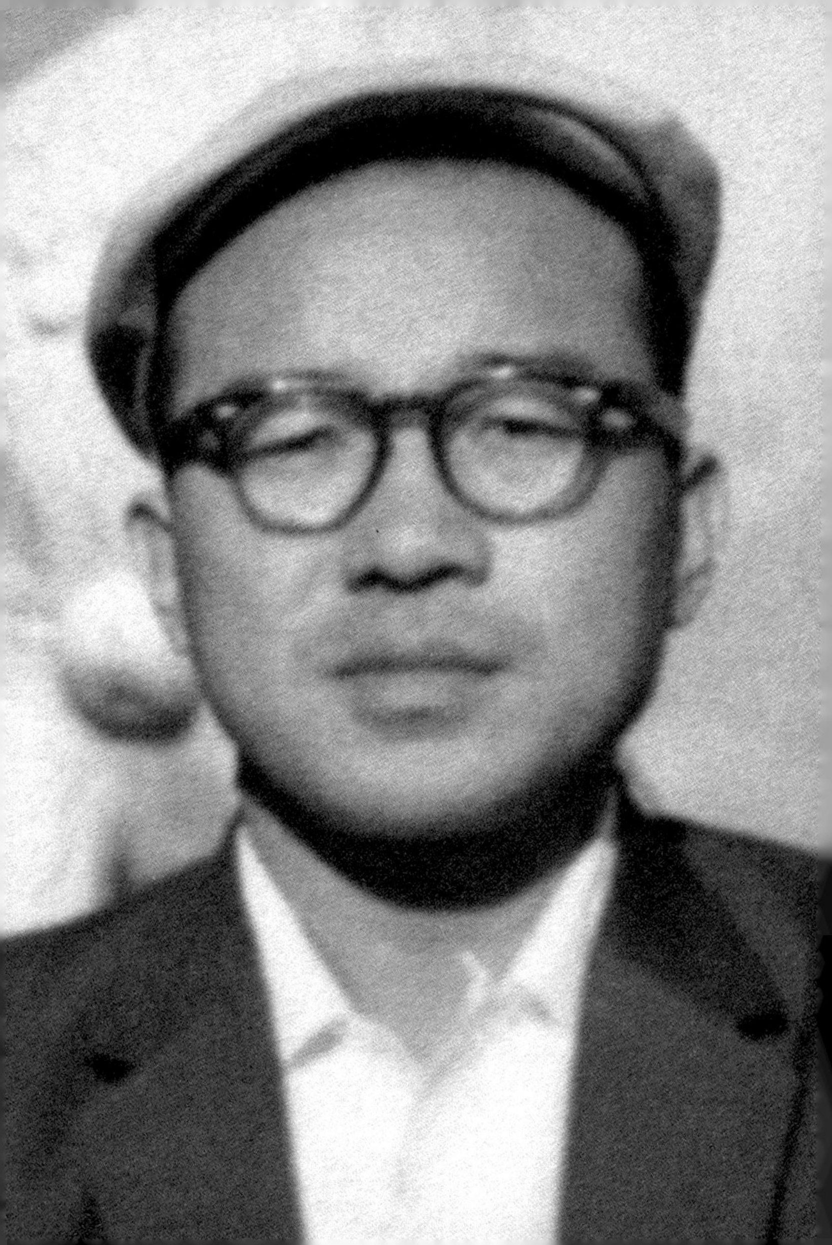

new cave

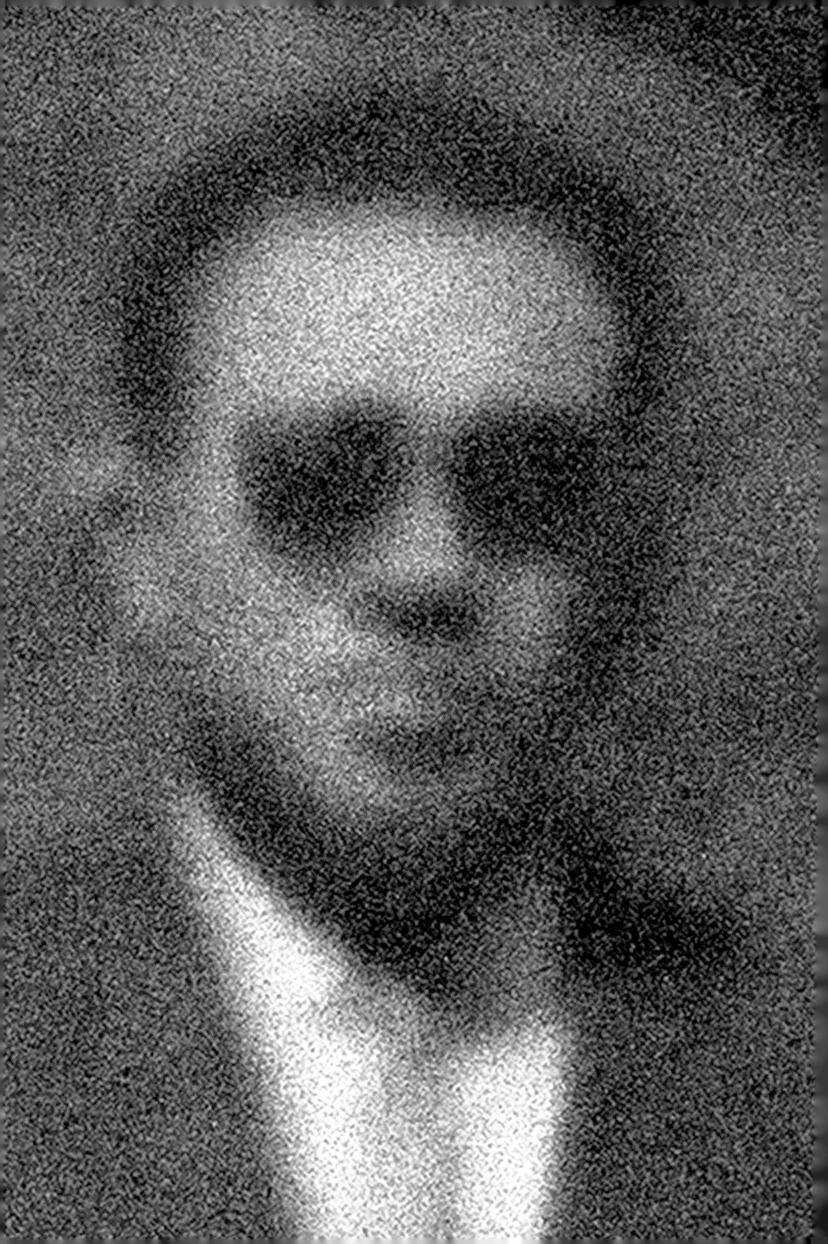

nor forward

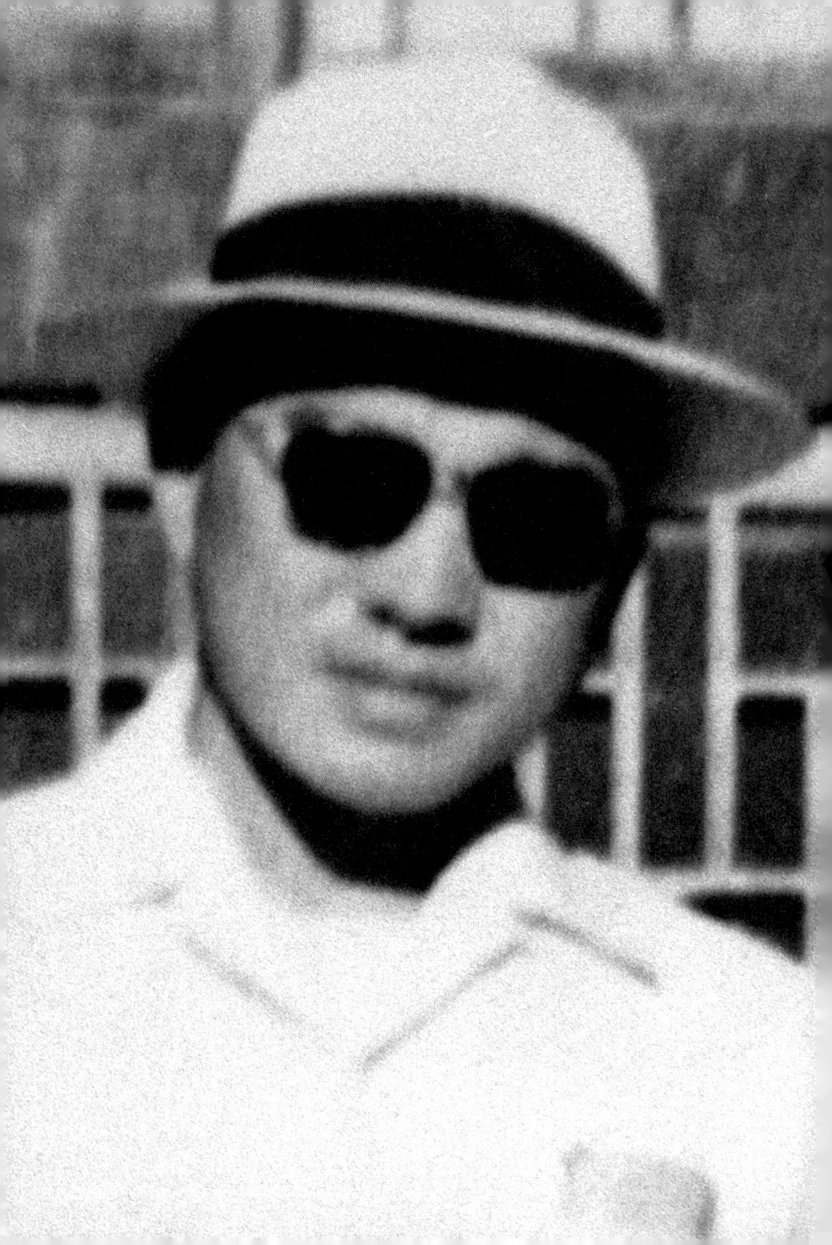

without looking back

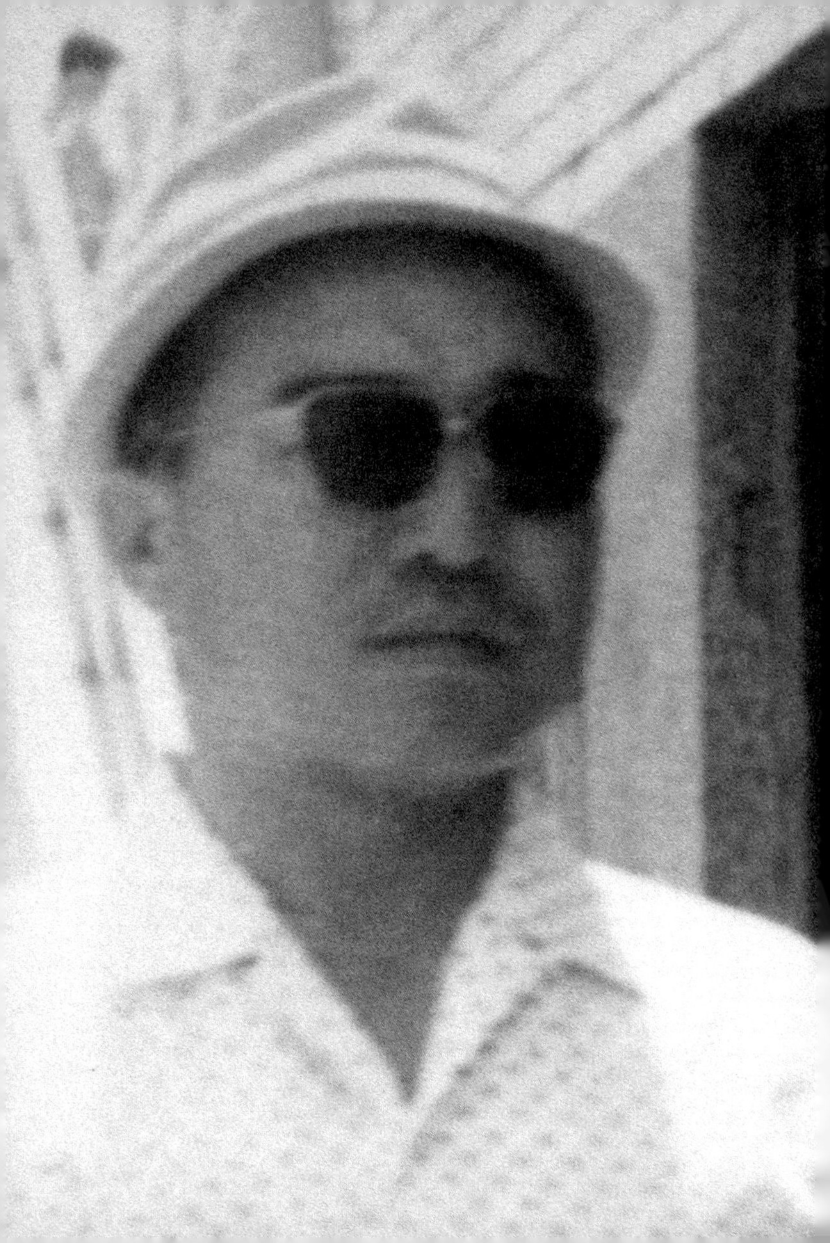

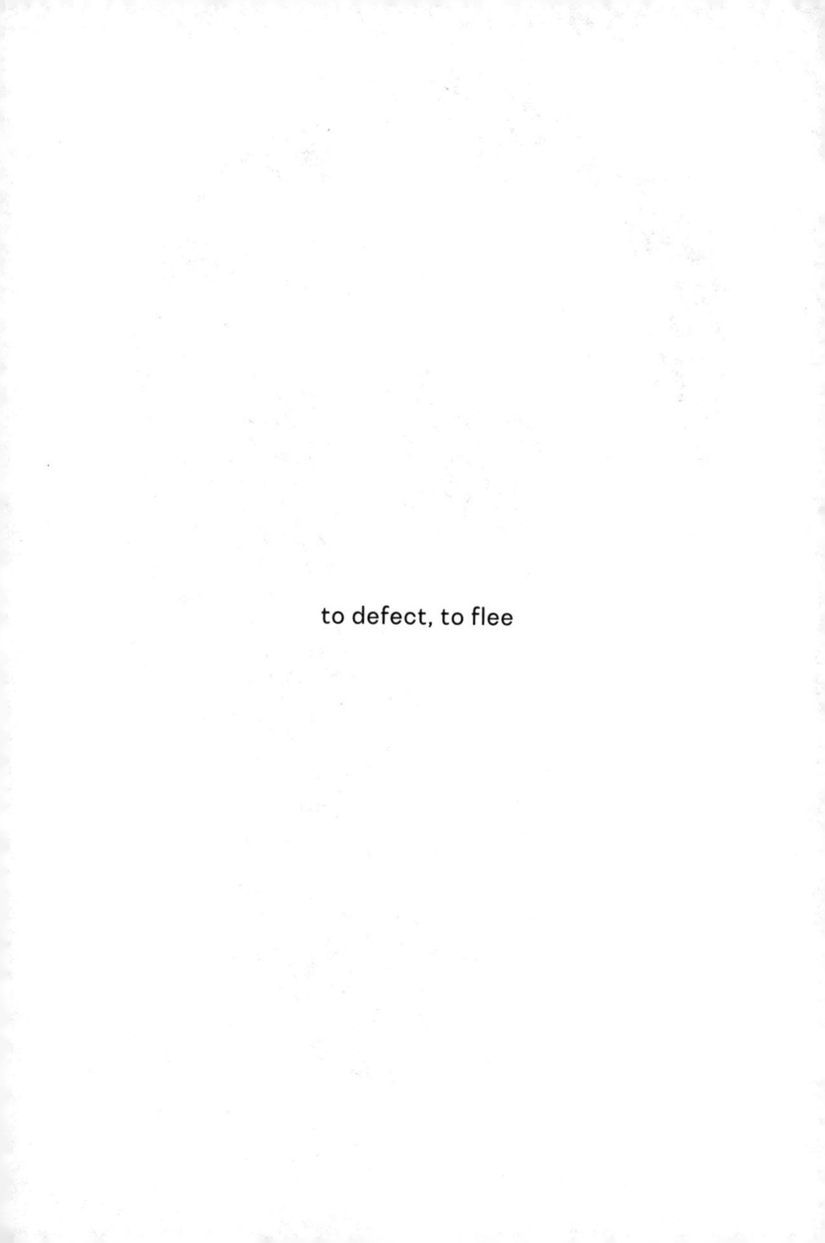

to defect, to flee

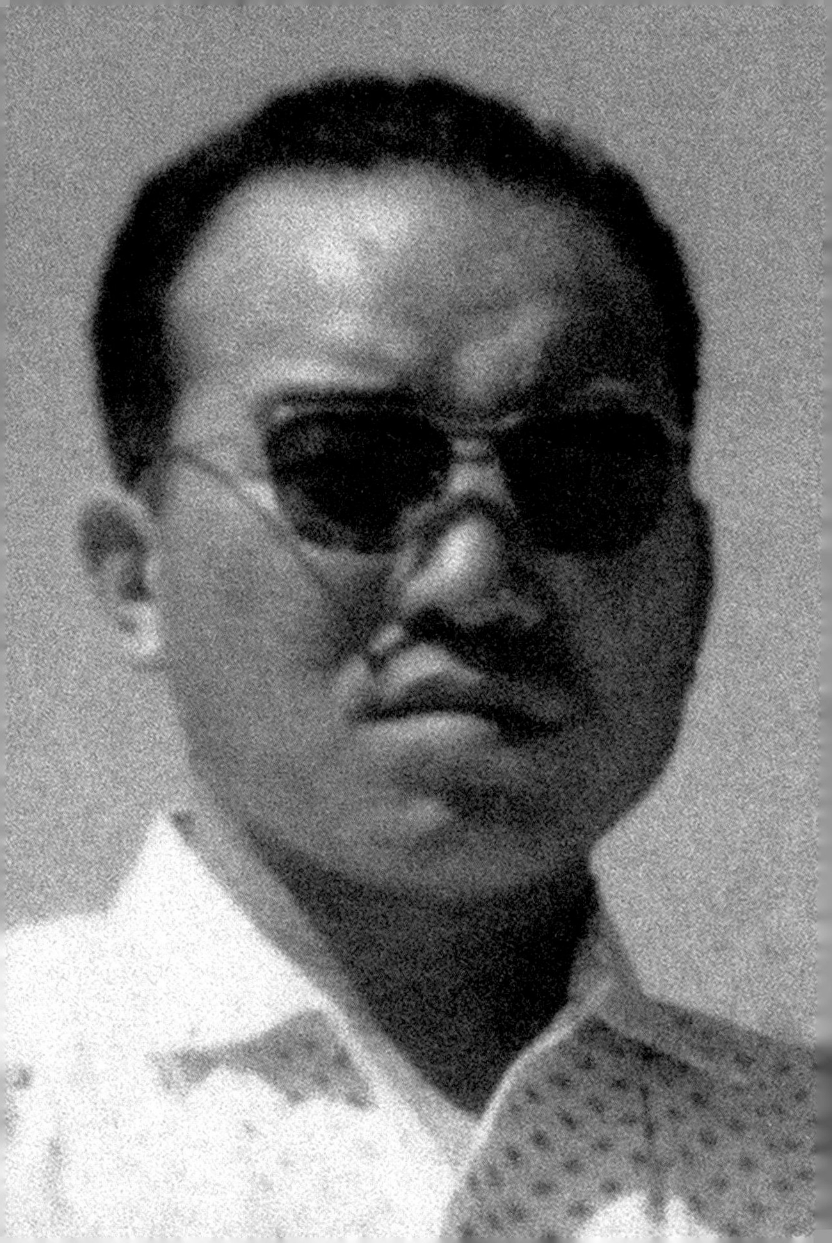

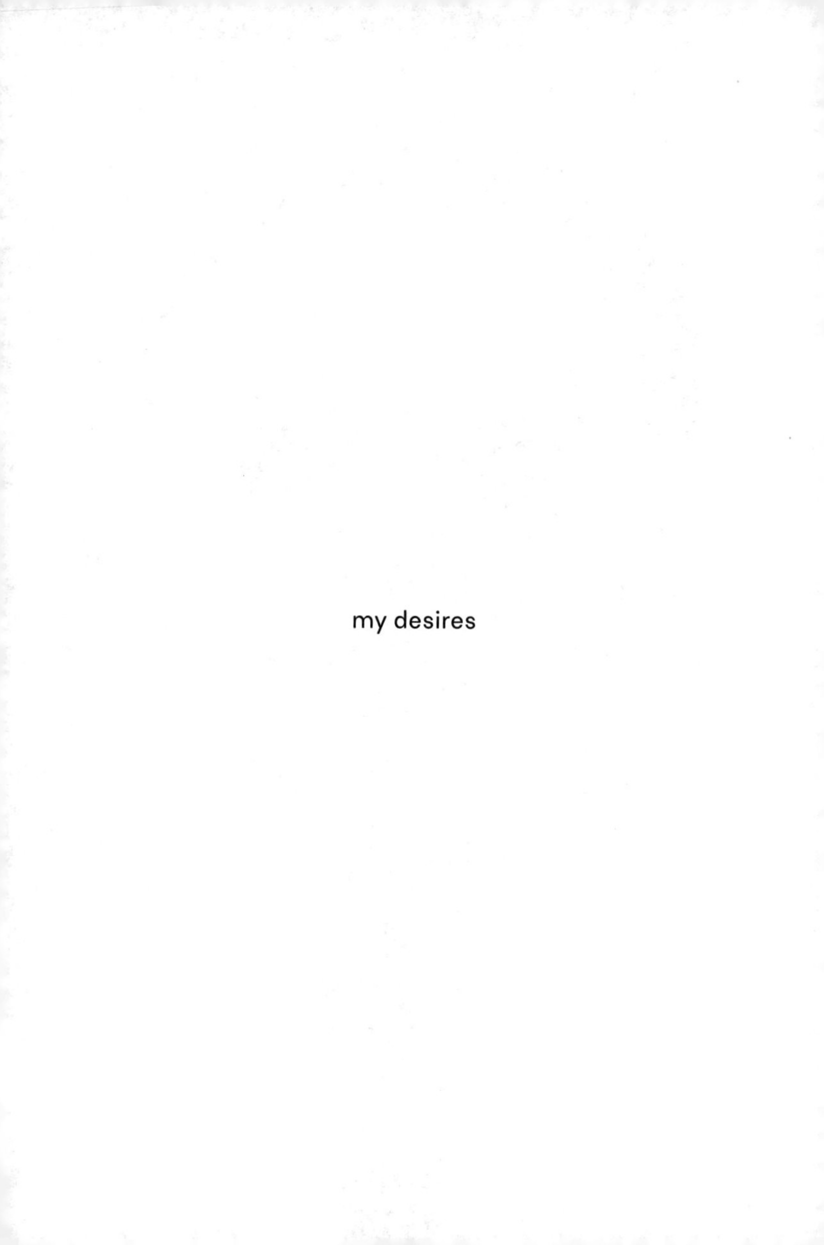

my desires

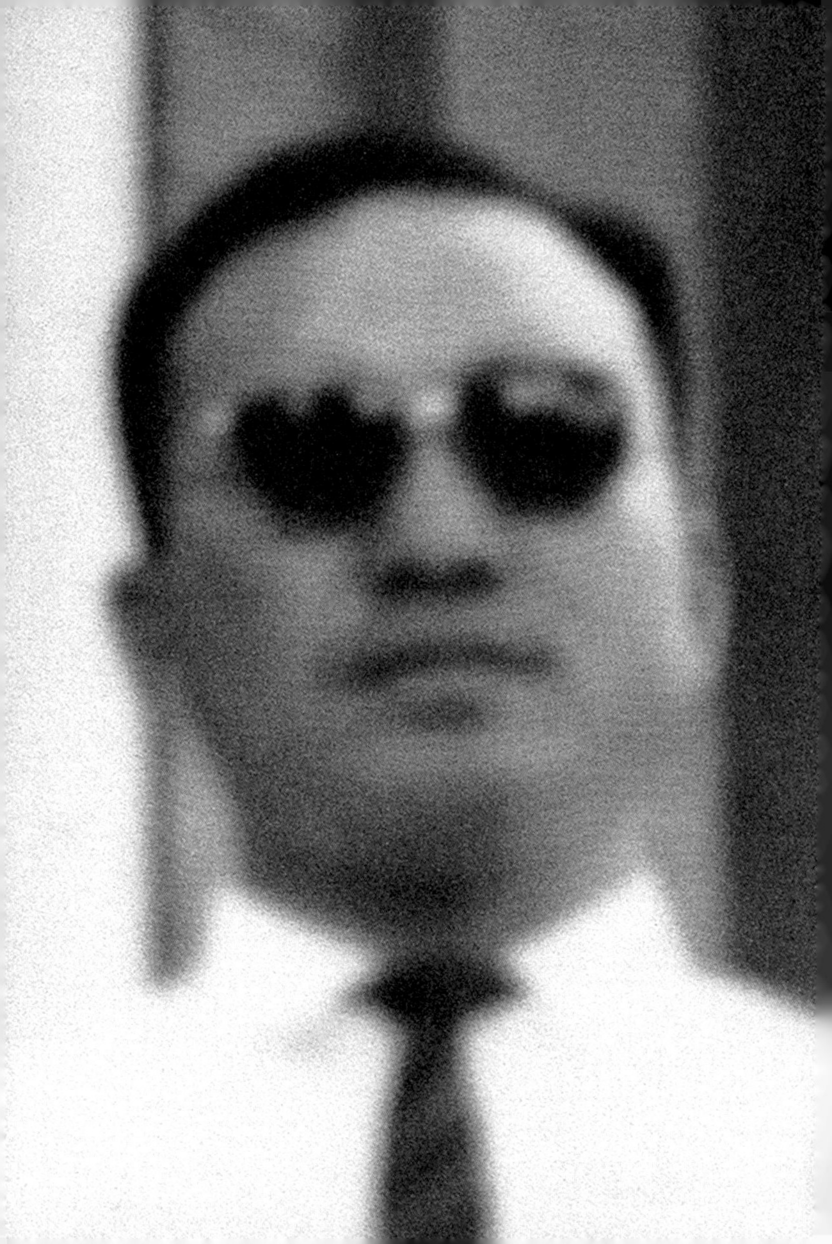

i learned to quiet

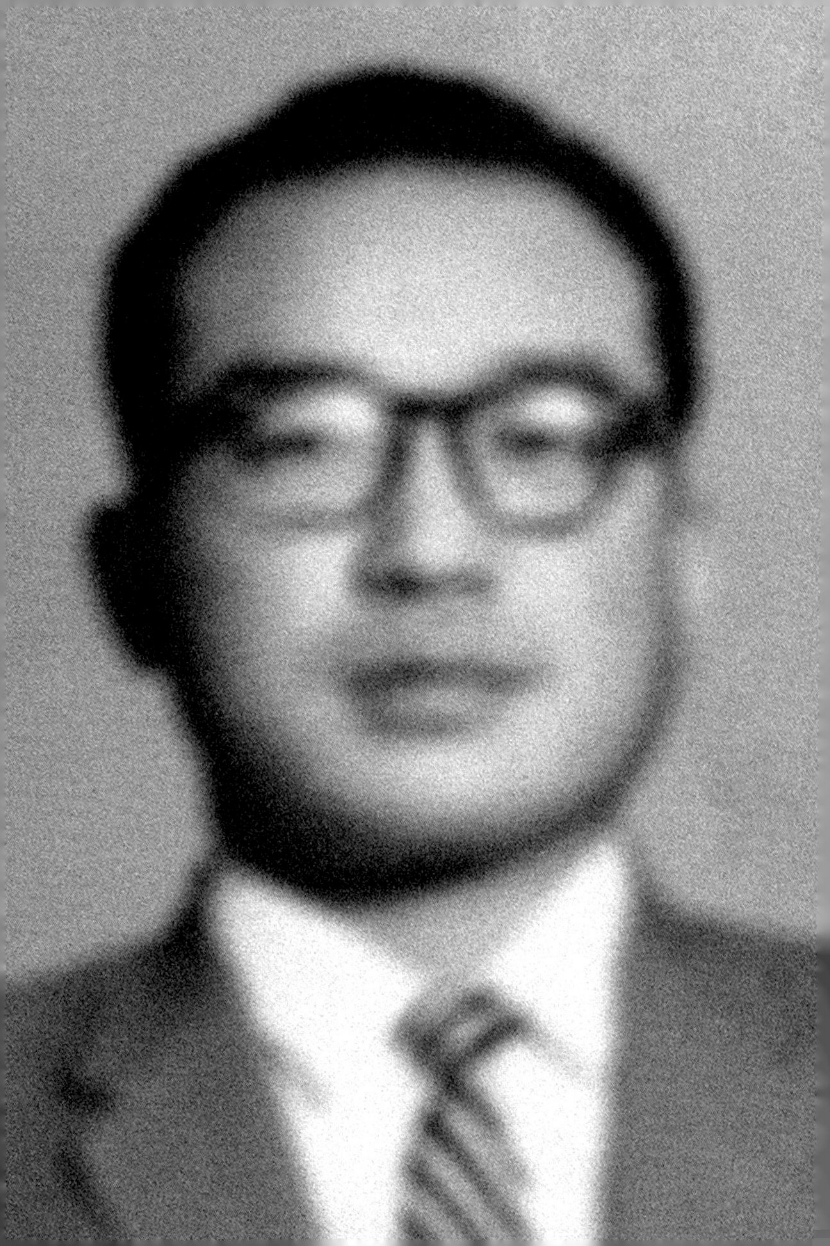

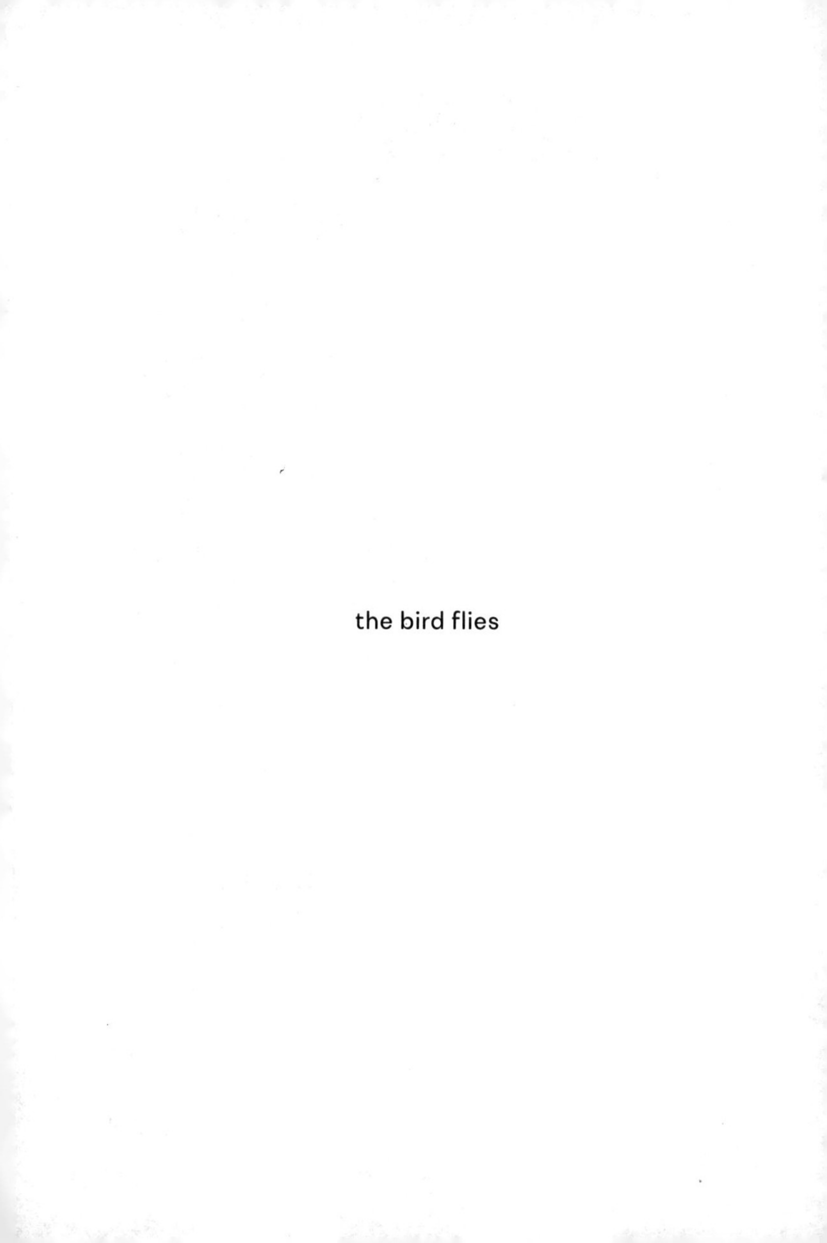

the bird flies

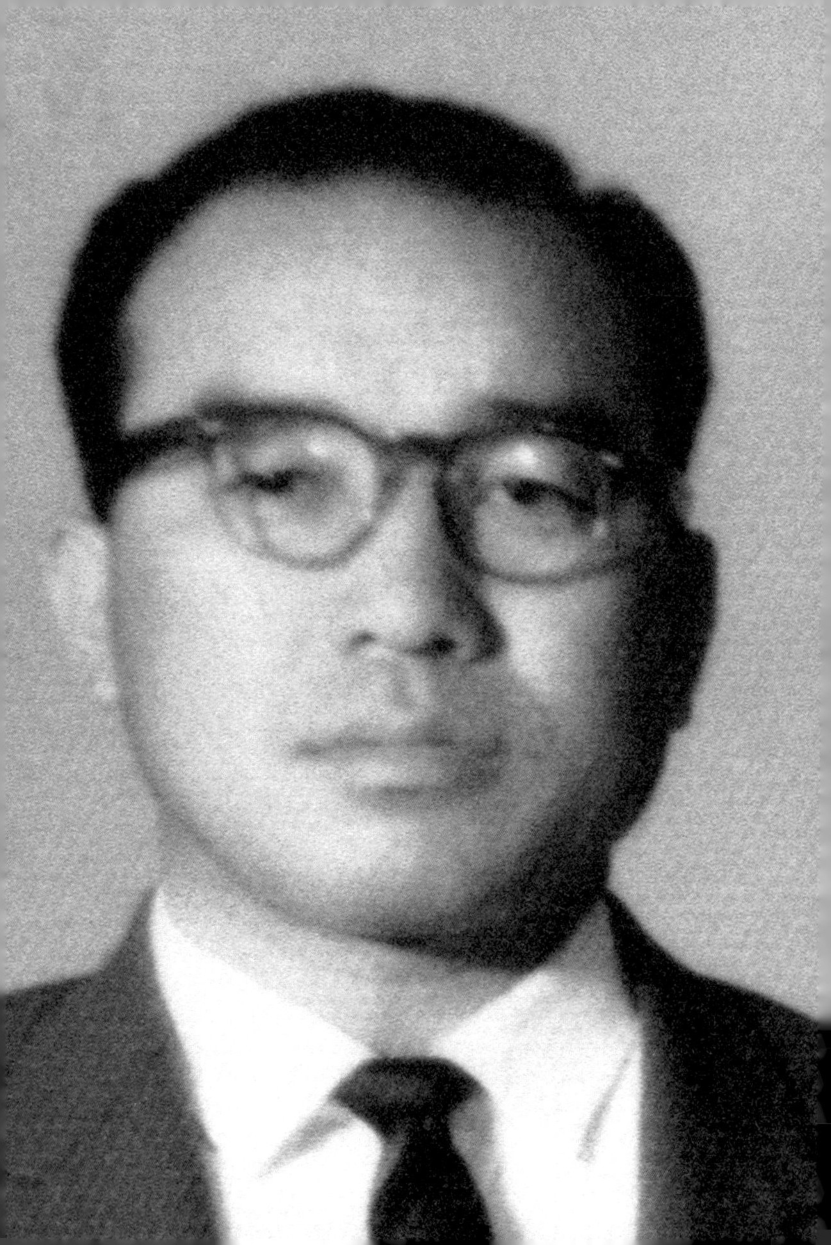

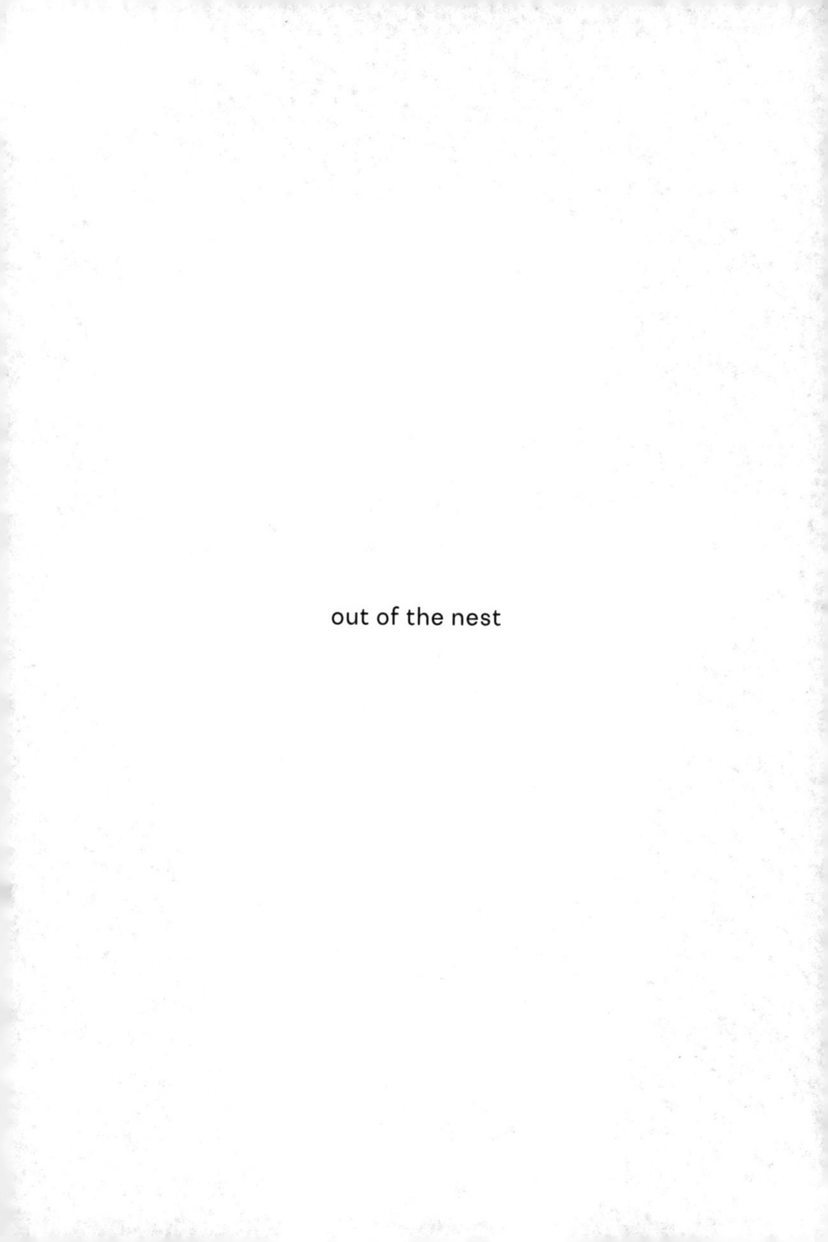

out of the nest

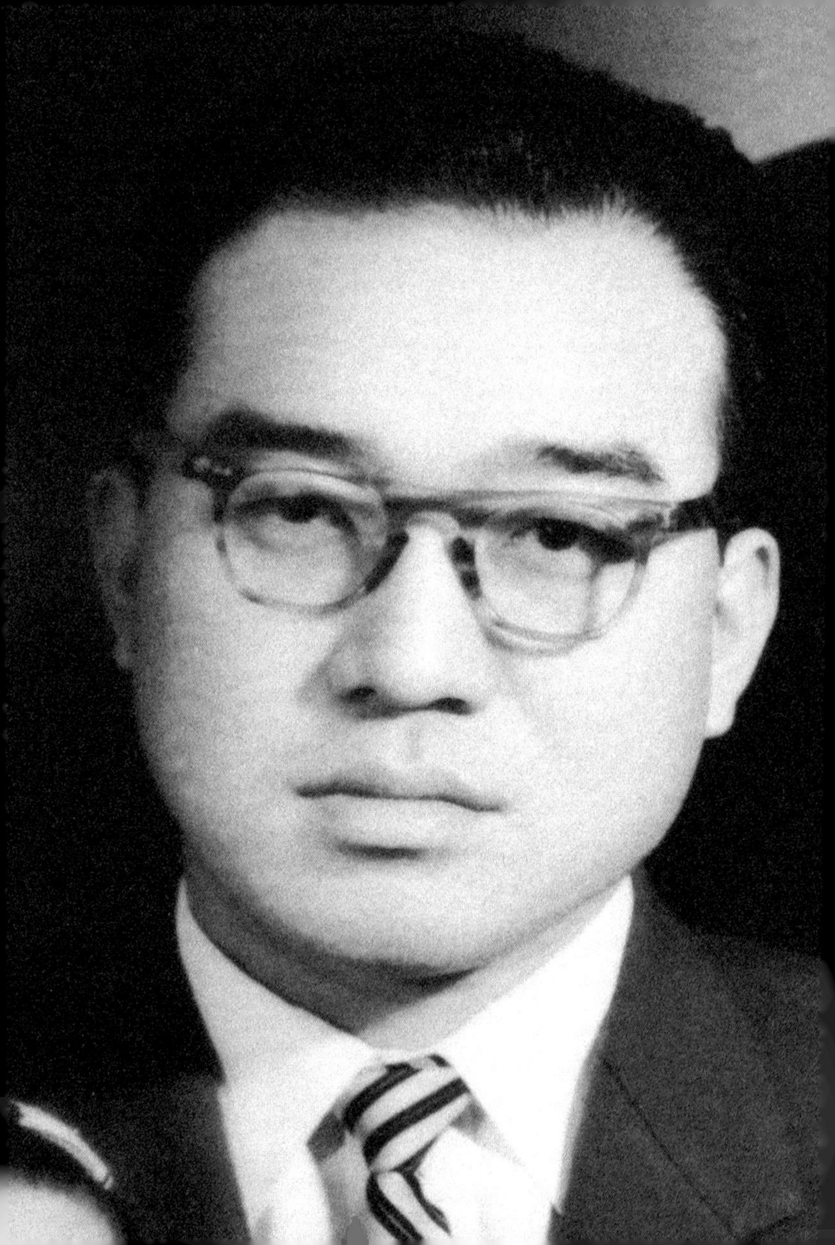

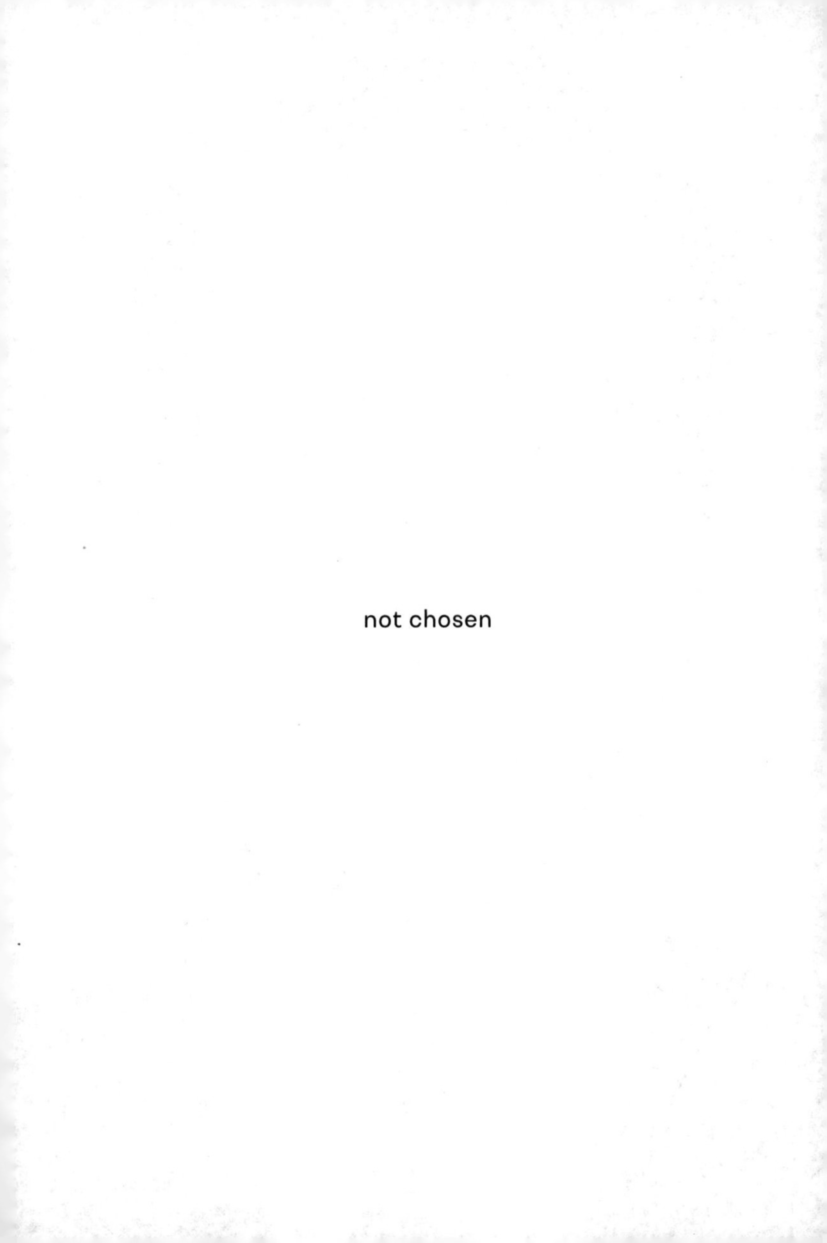

not chosen

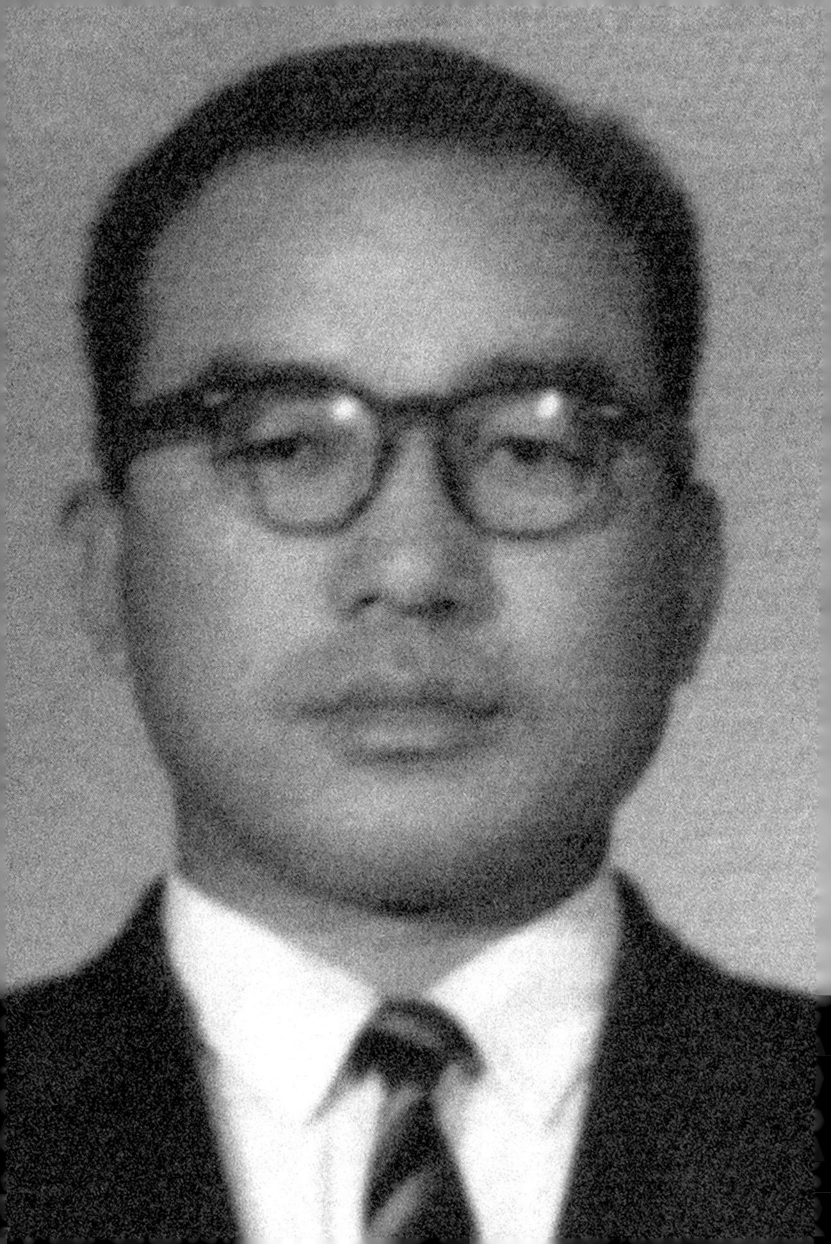

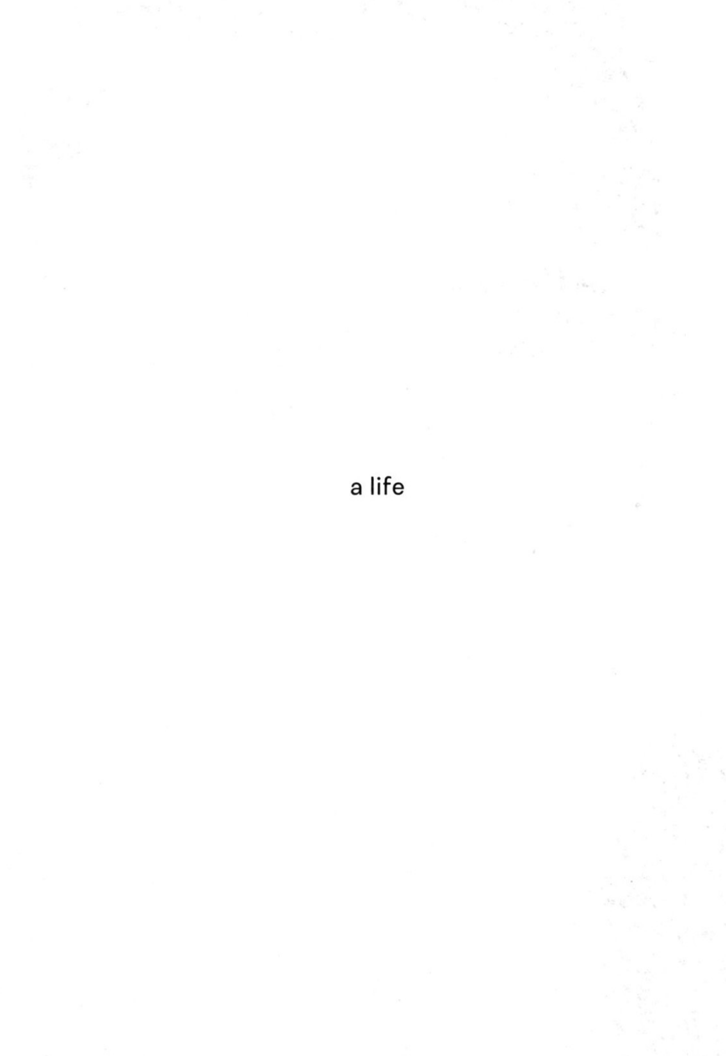

a life

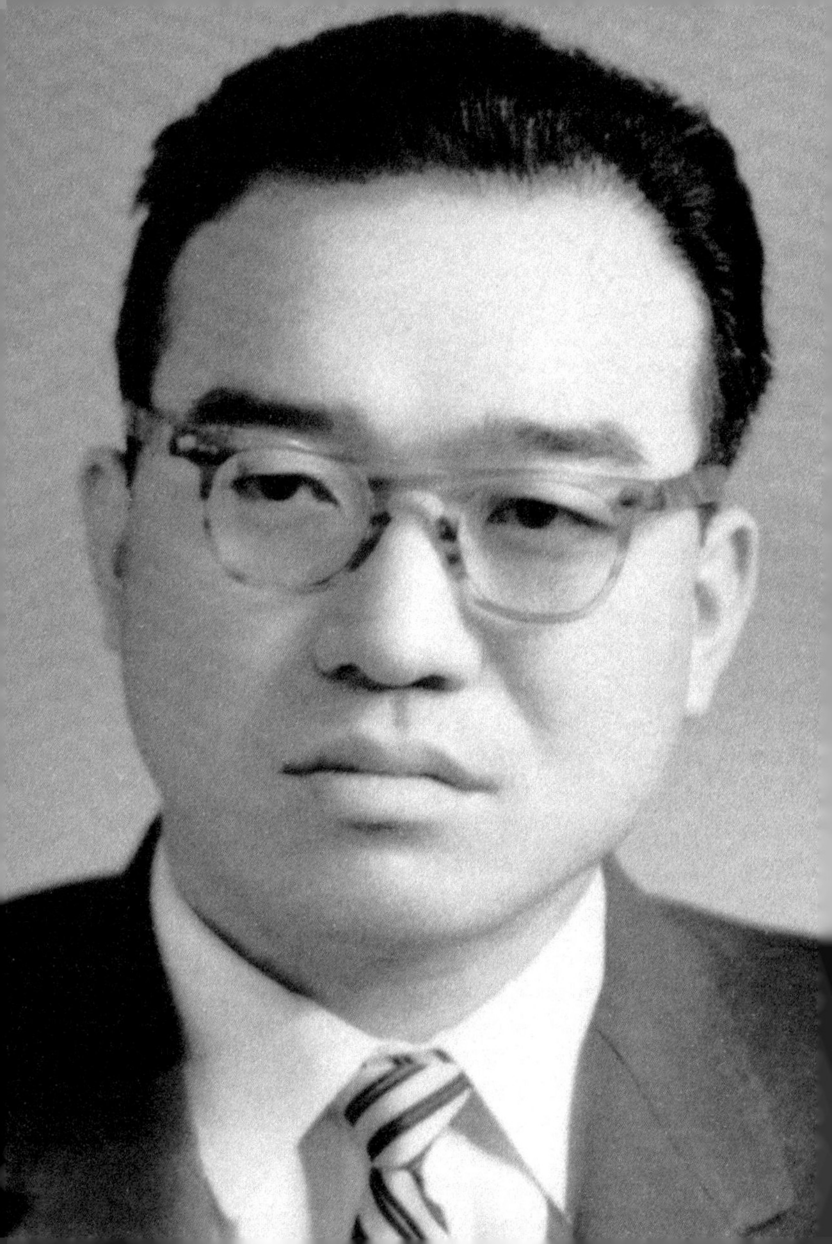

to forget

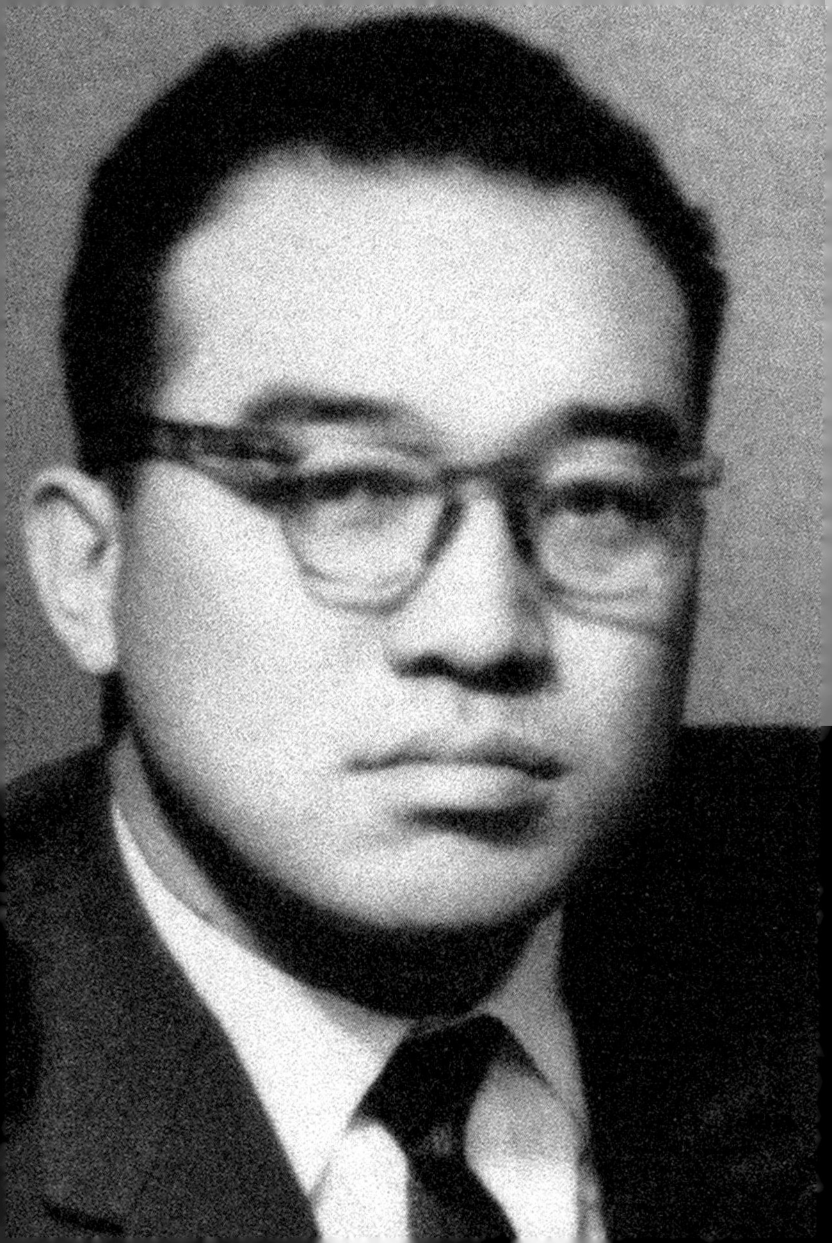

i worked hard

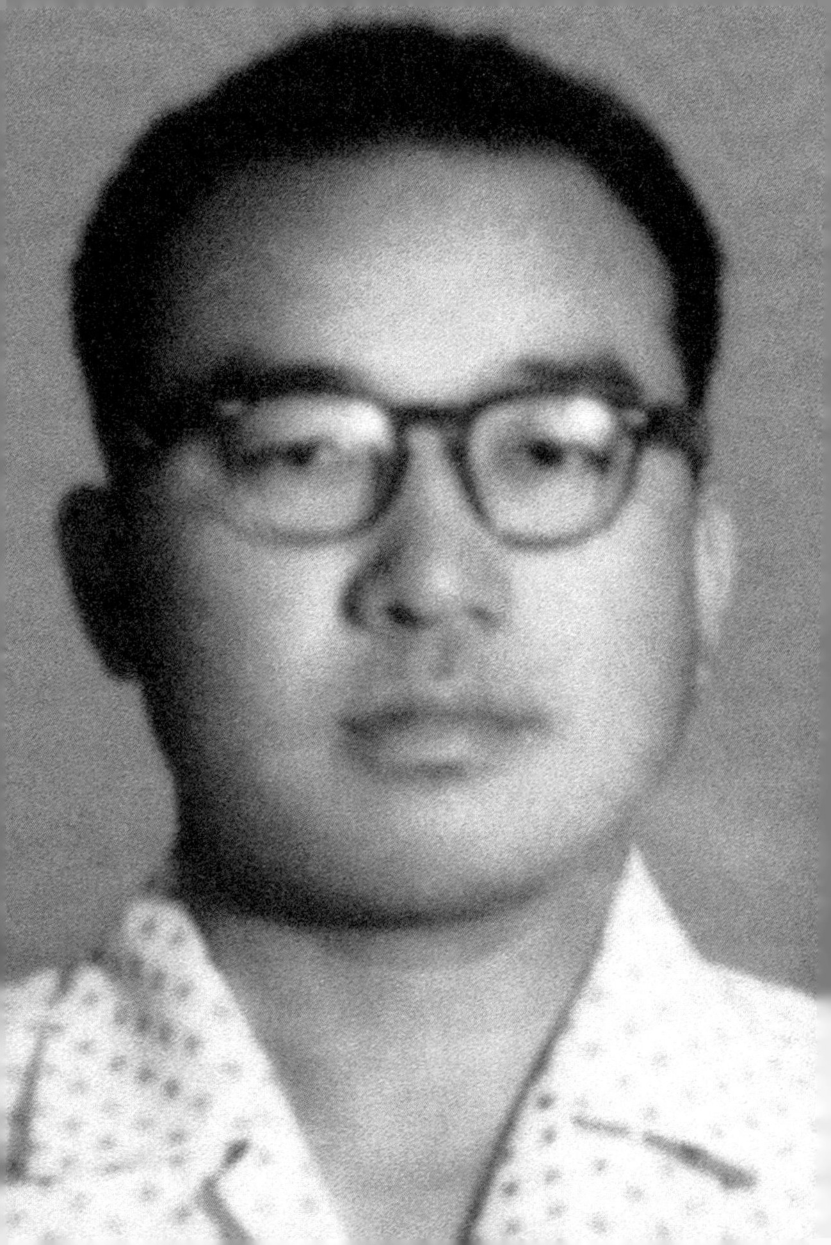

they give in

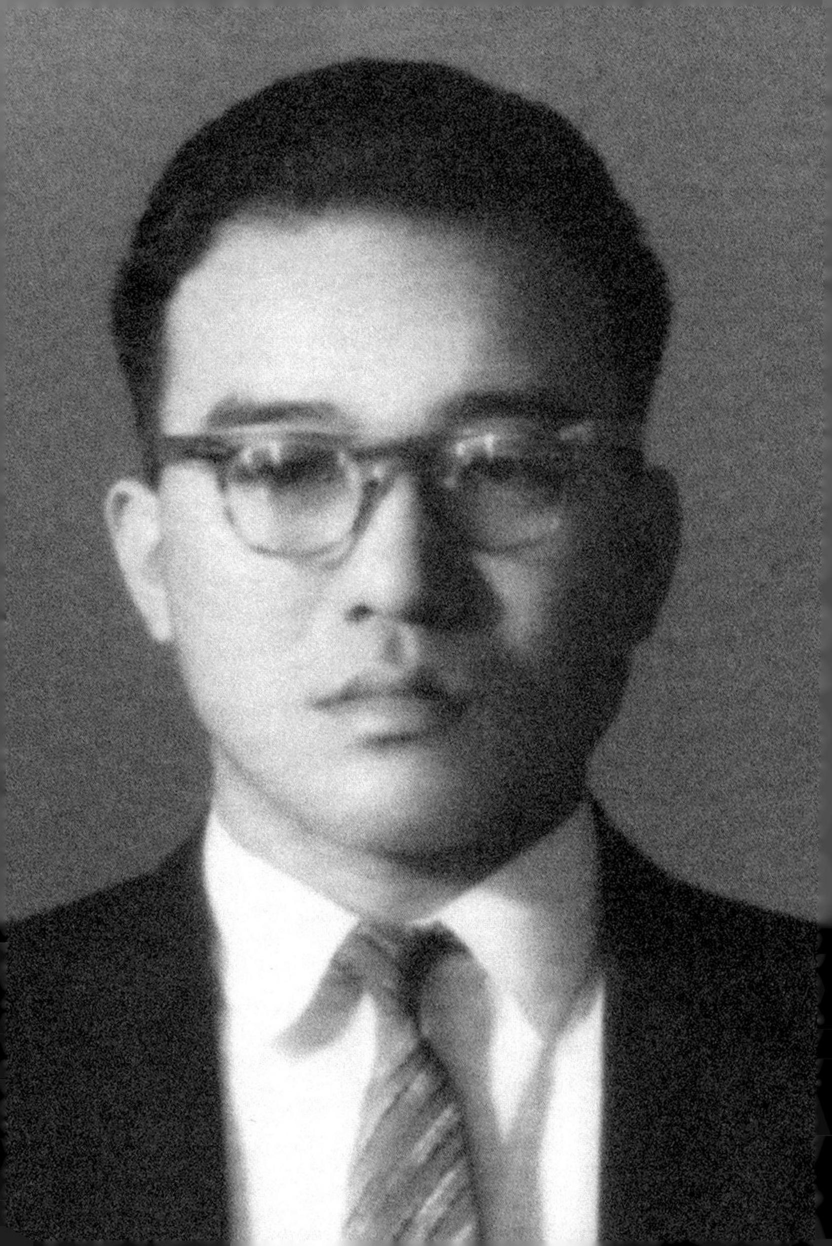

they crave respect

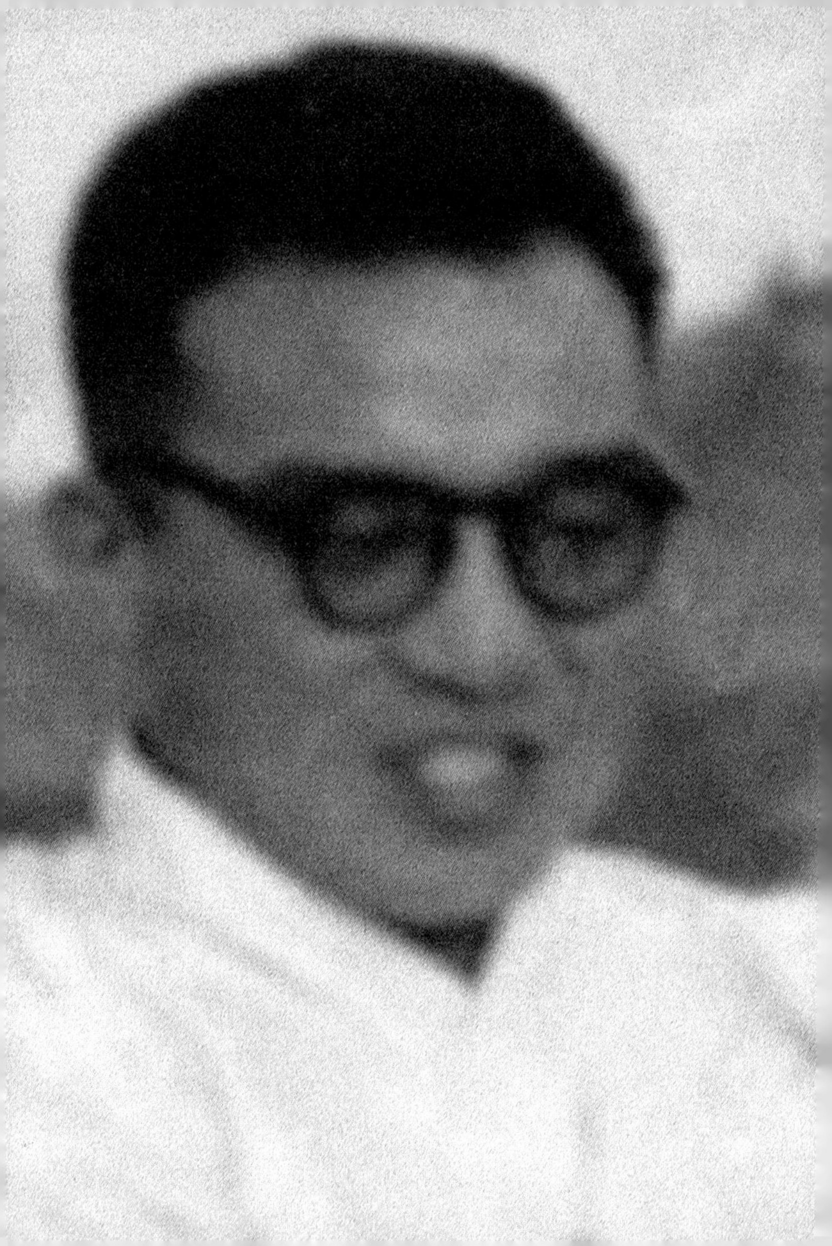

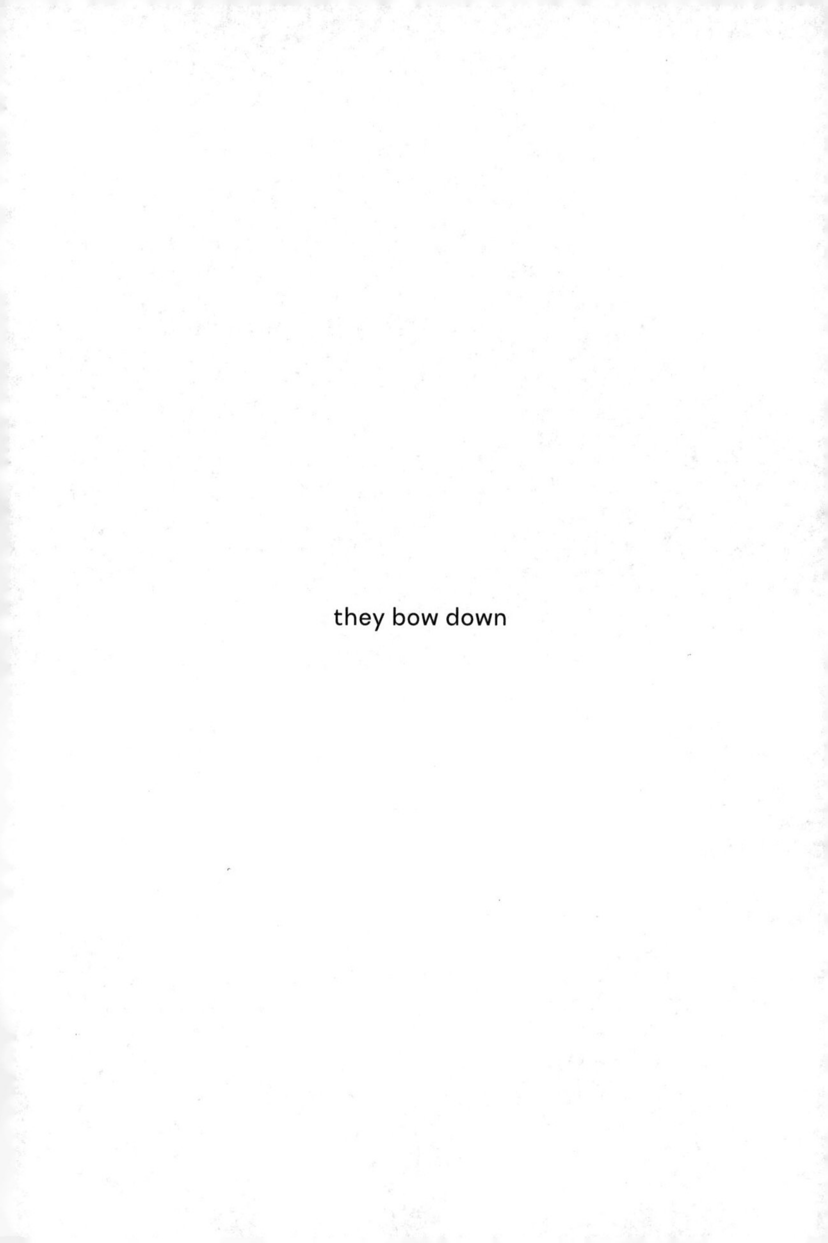

they bow down

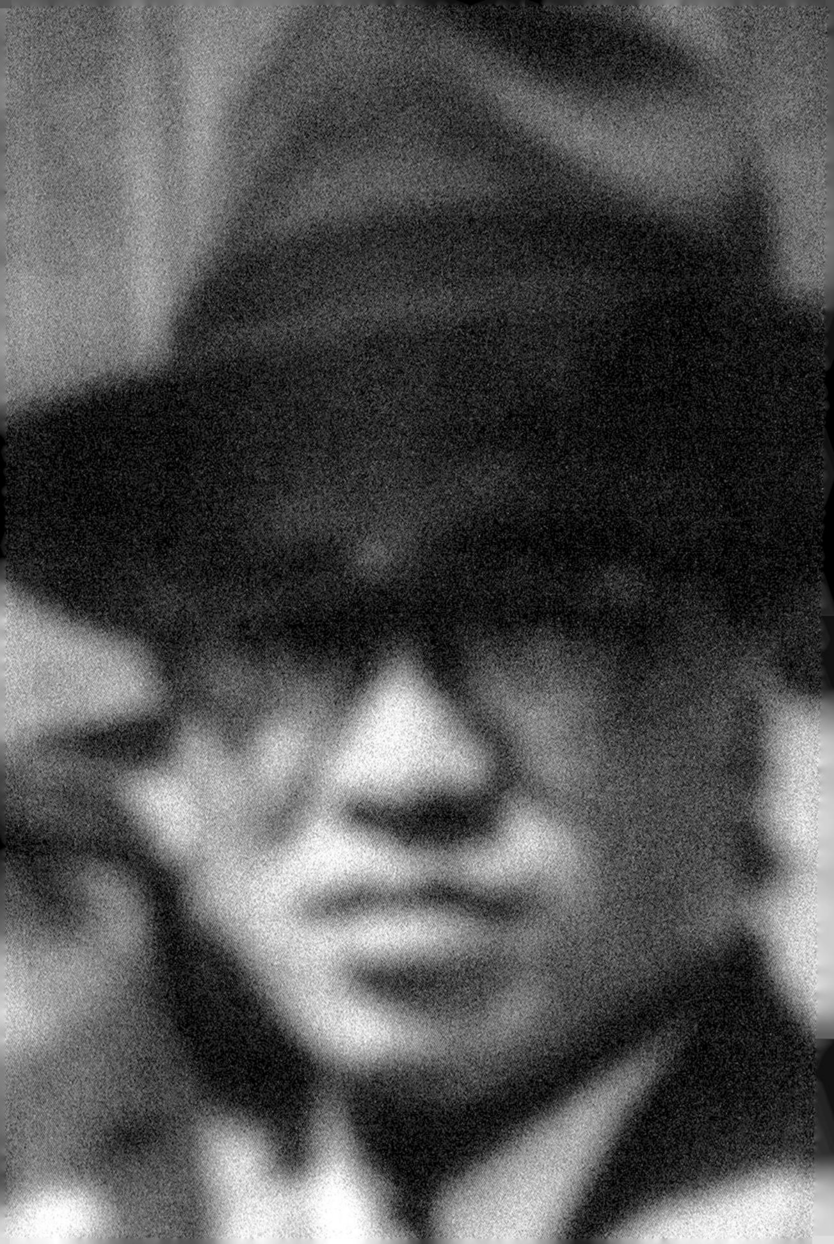

on the sly

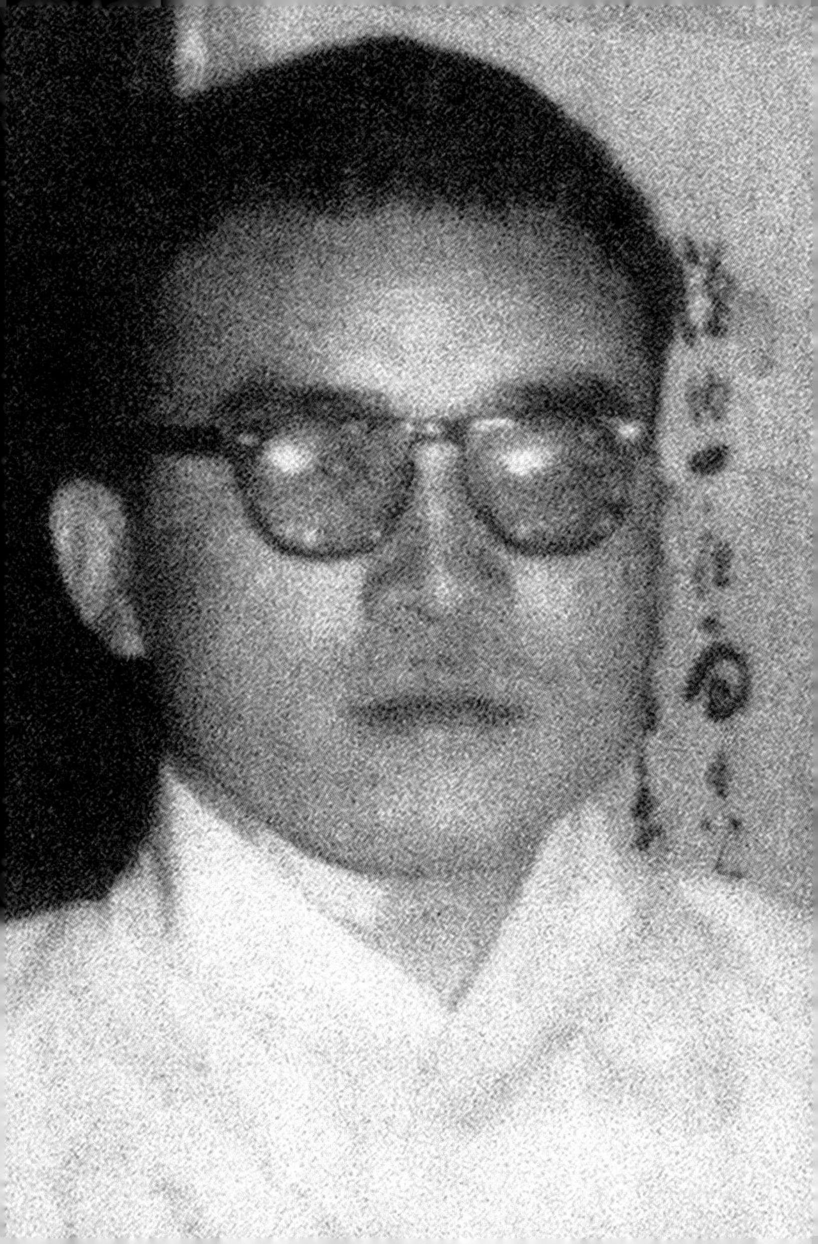

they look sideways

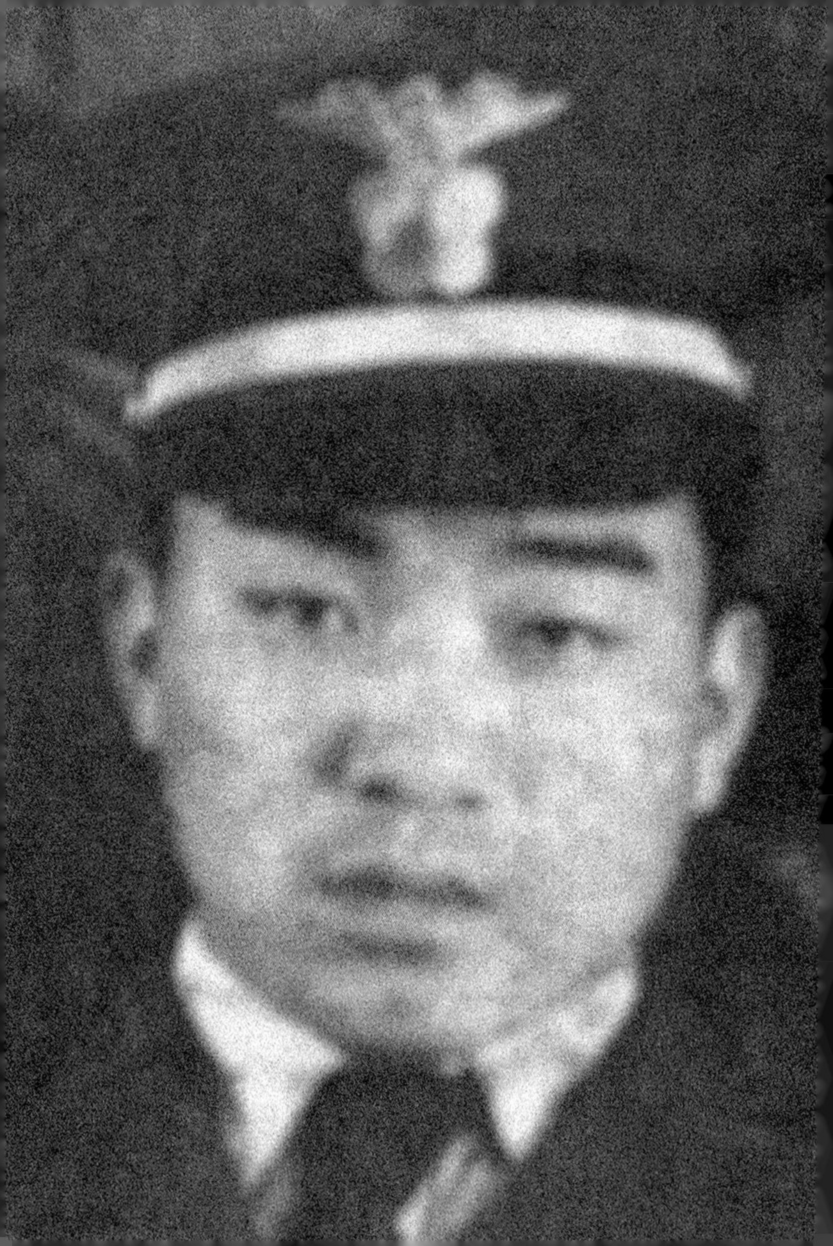

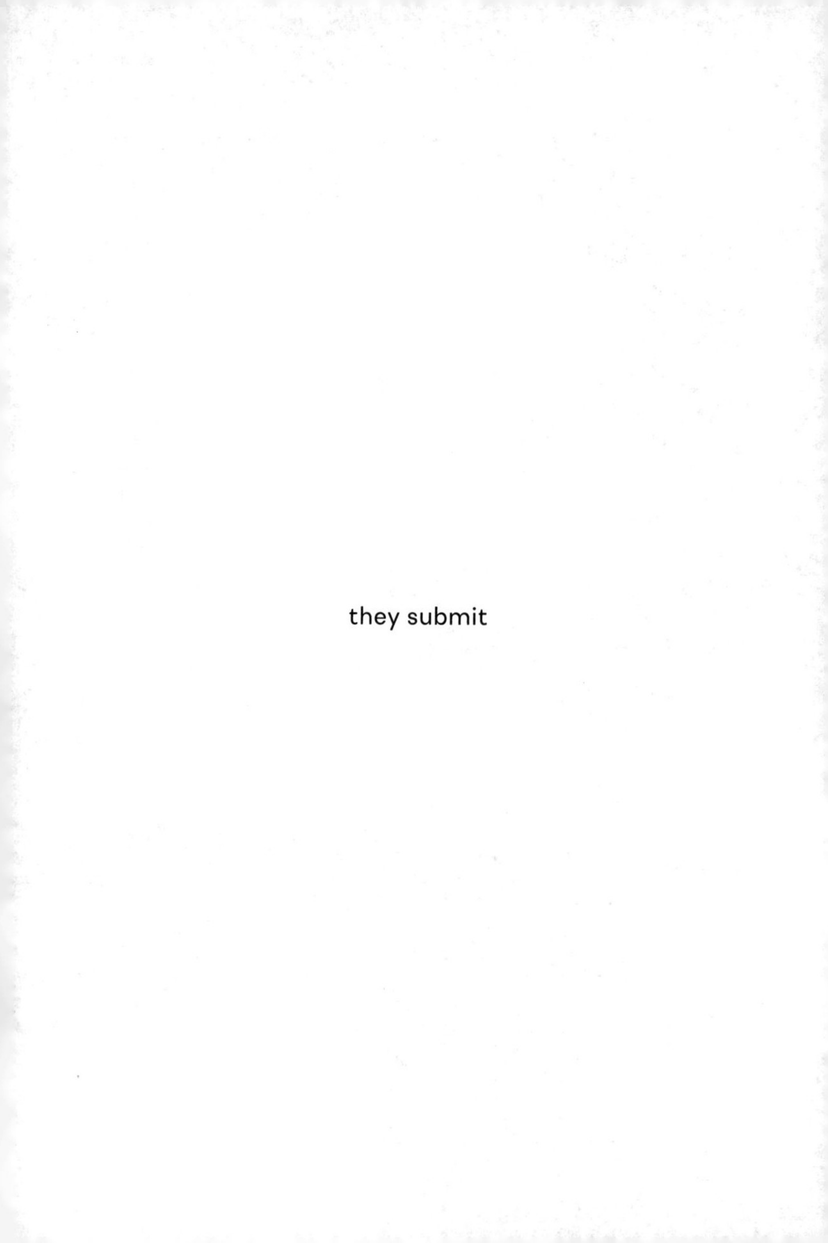

they submit

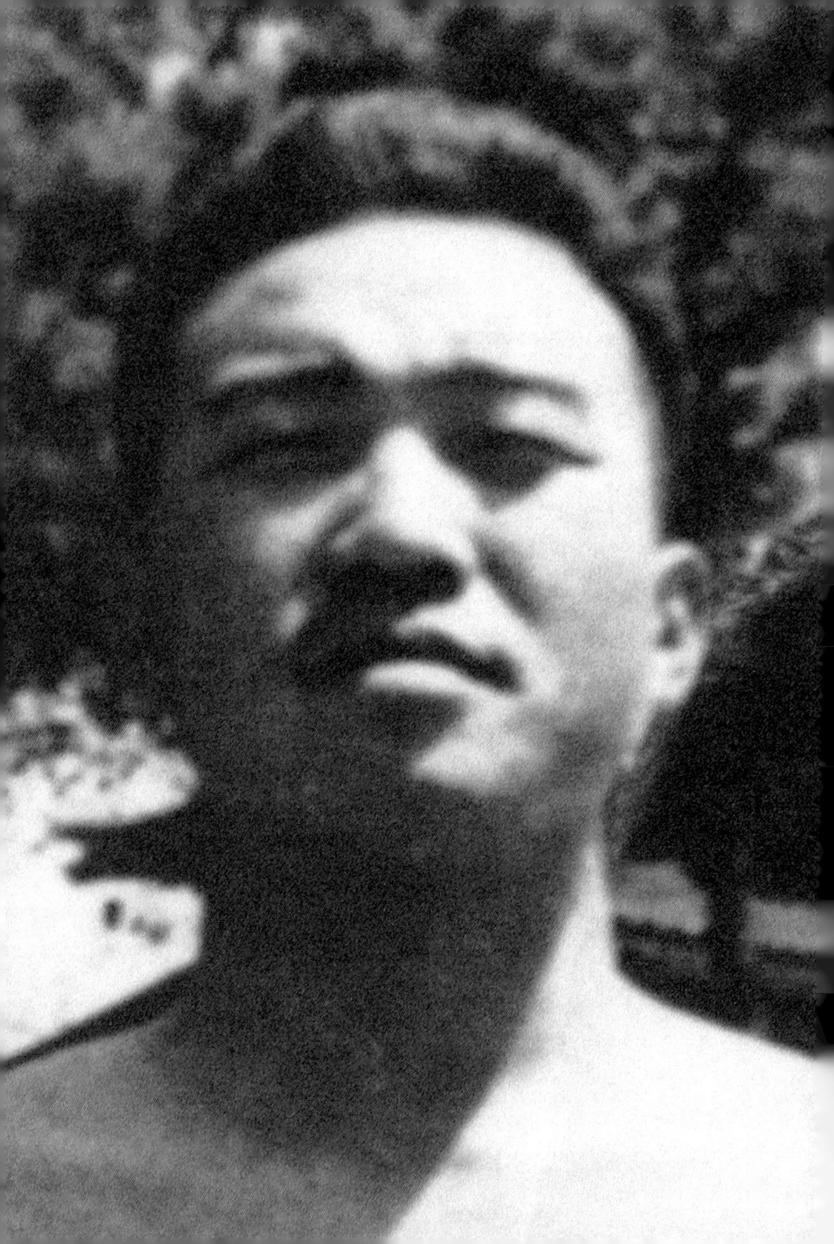

they follow the rules

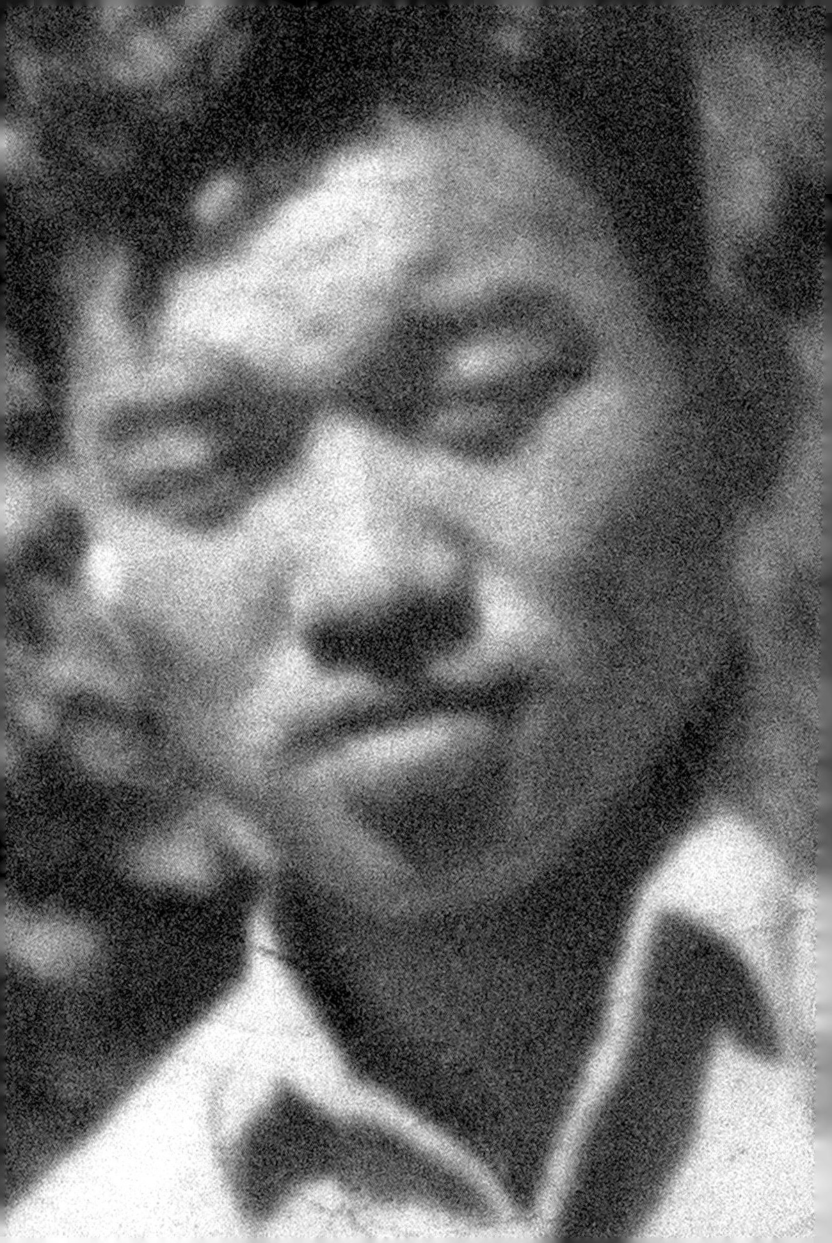

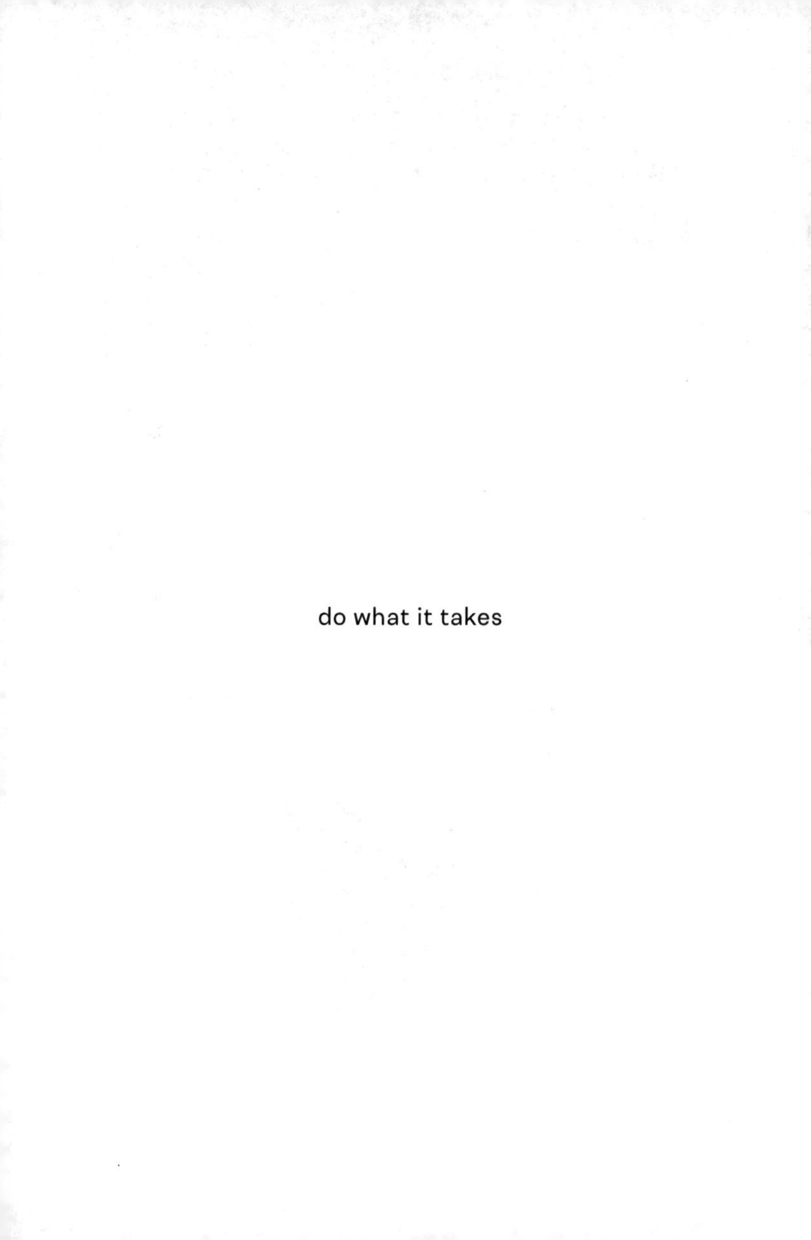

do what it takes

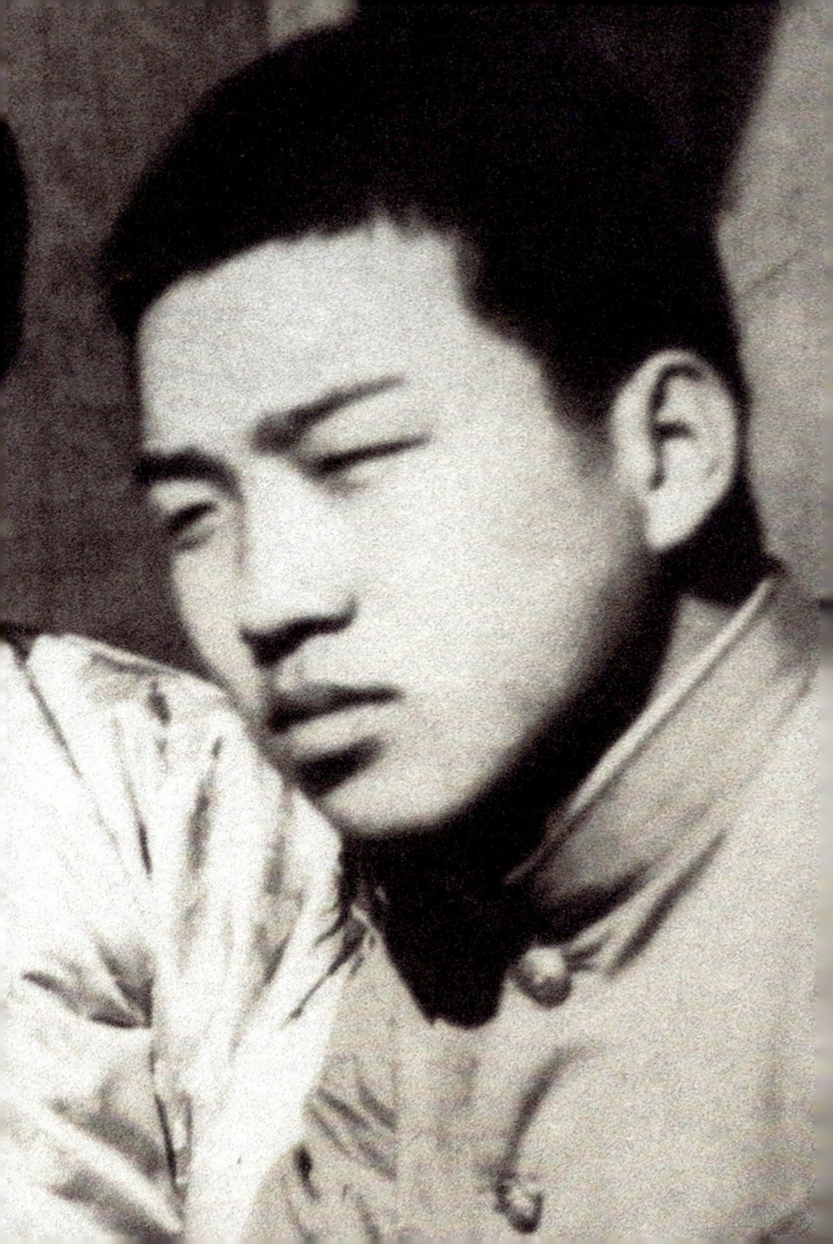

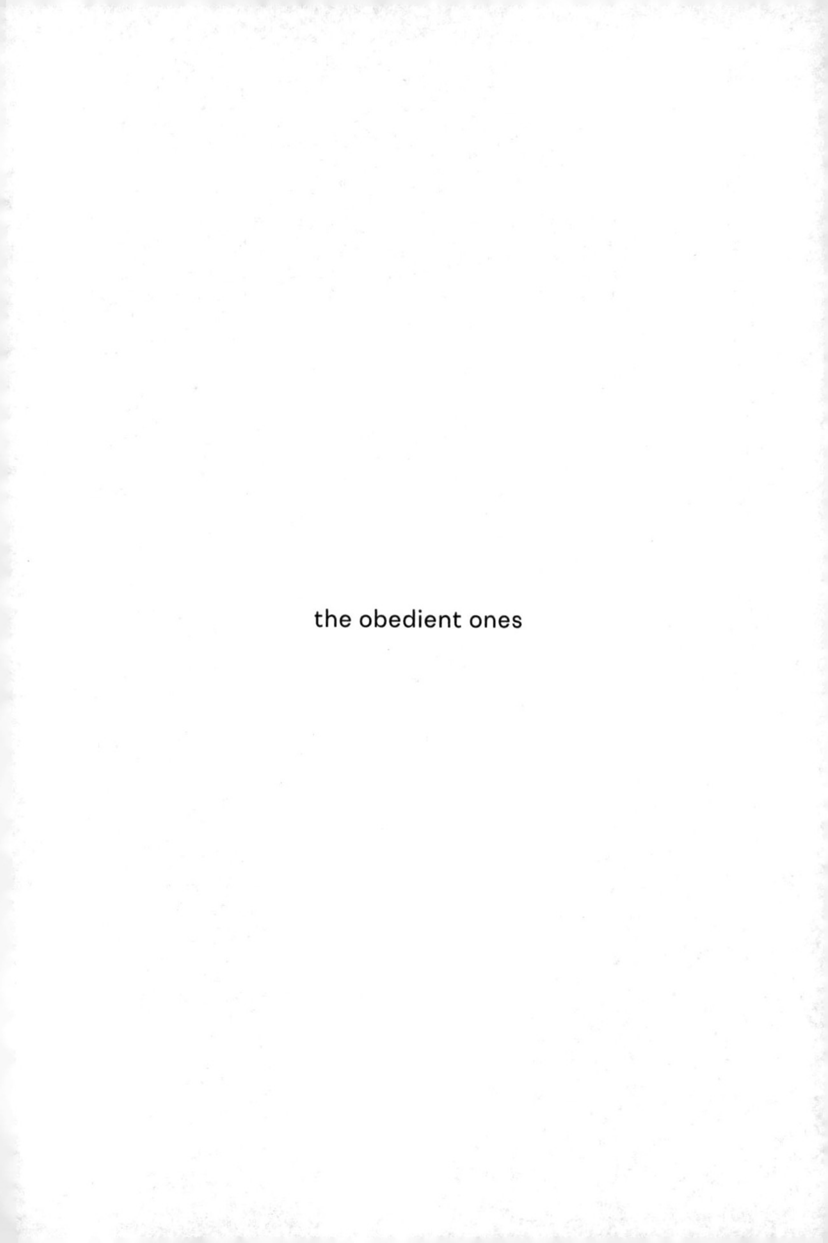

the obedient ones

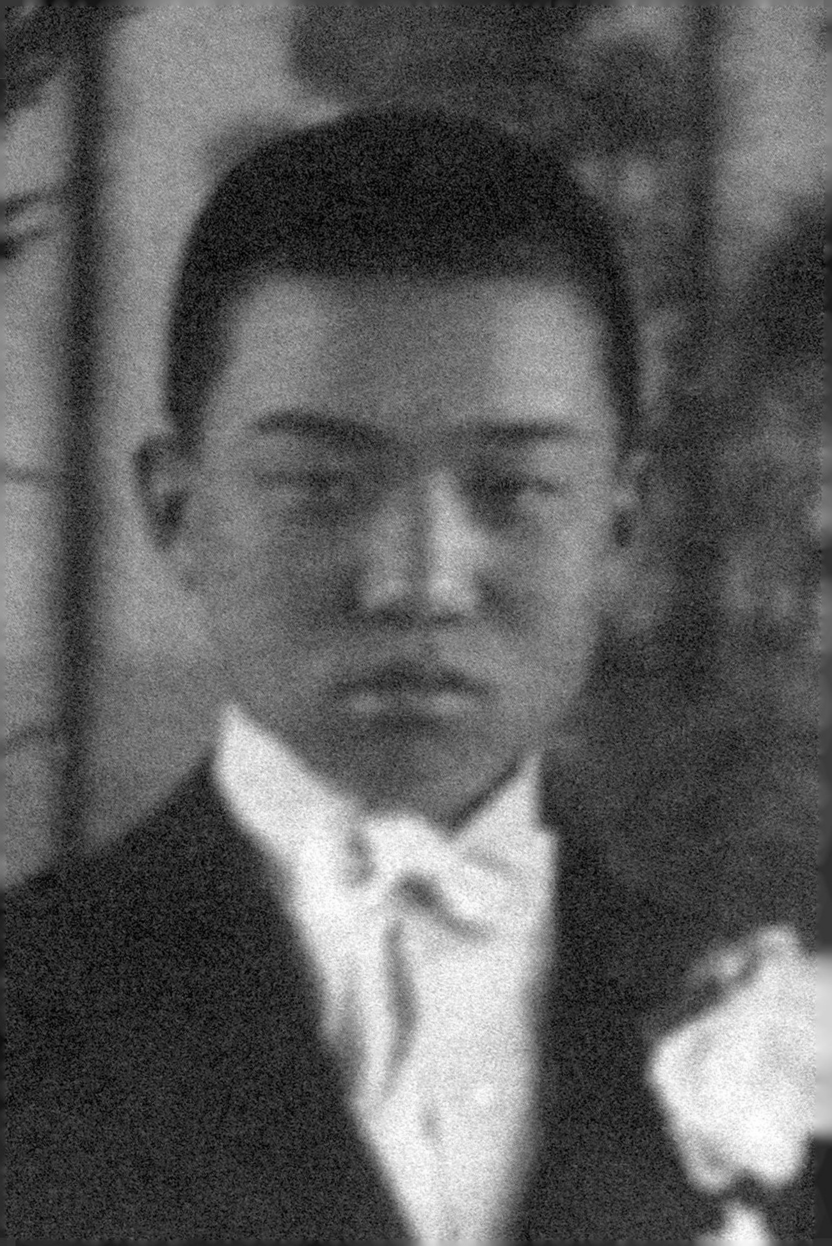

for my own good

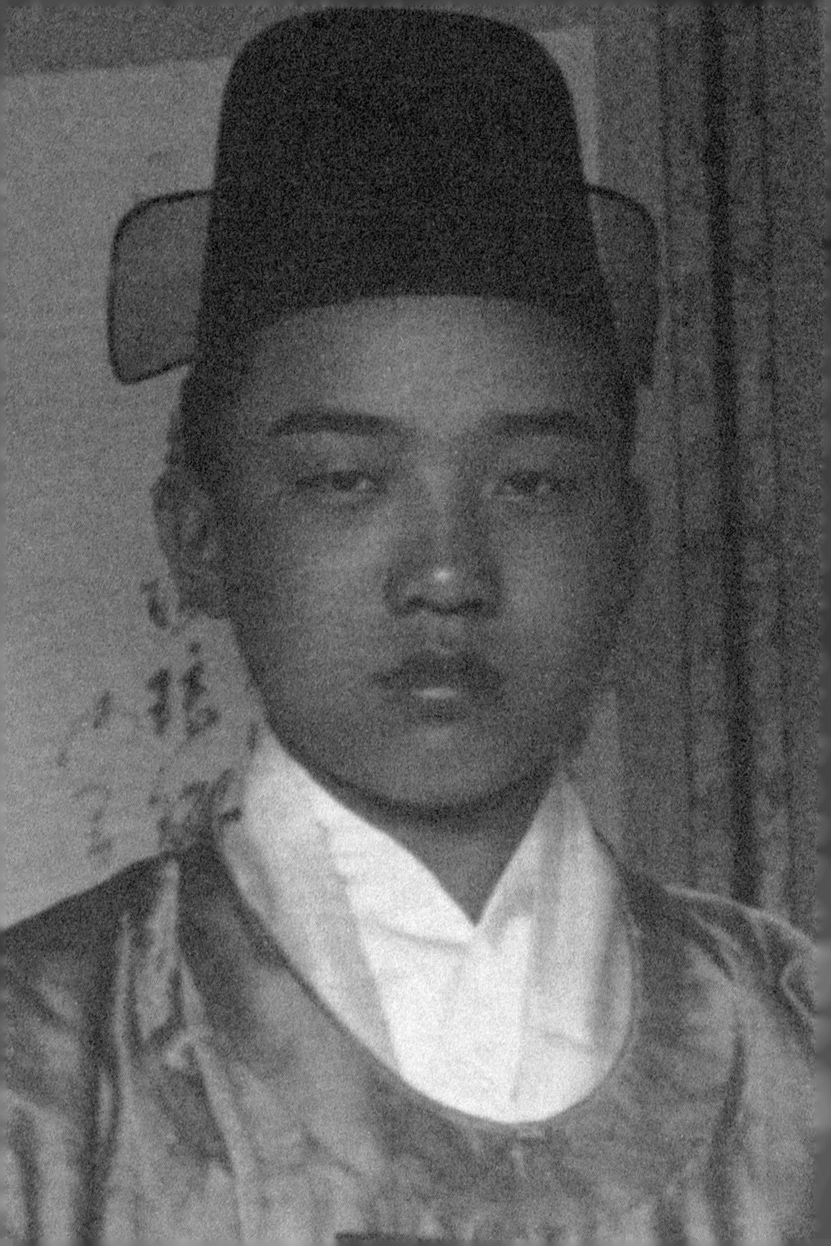

when they married me

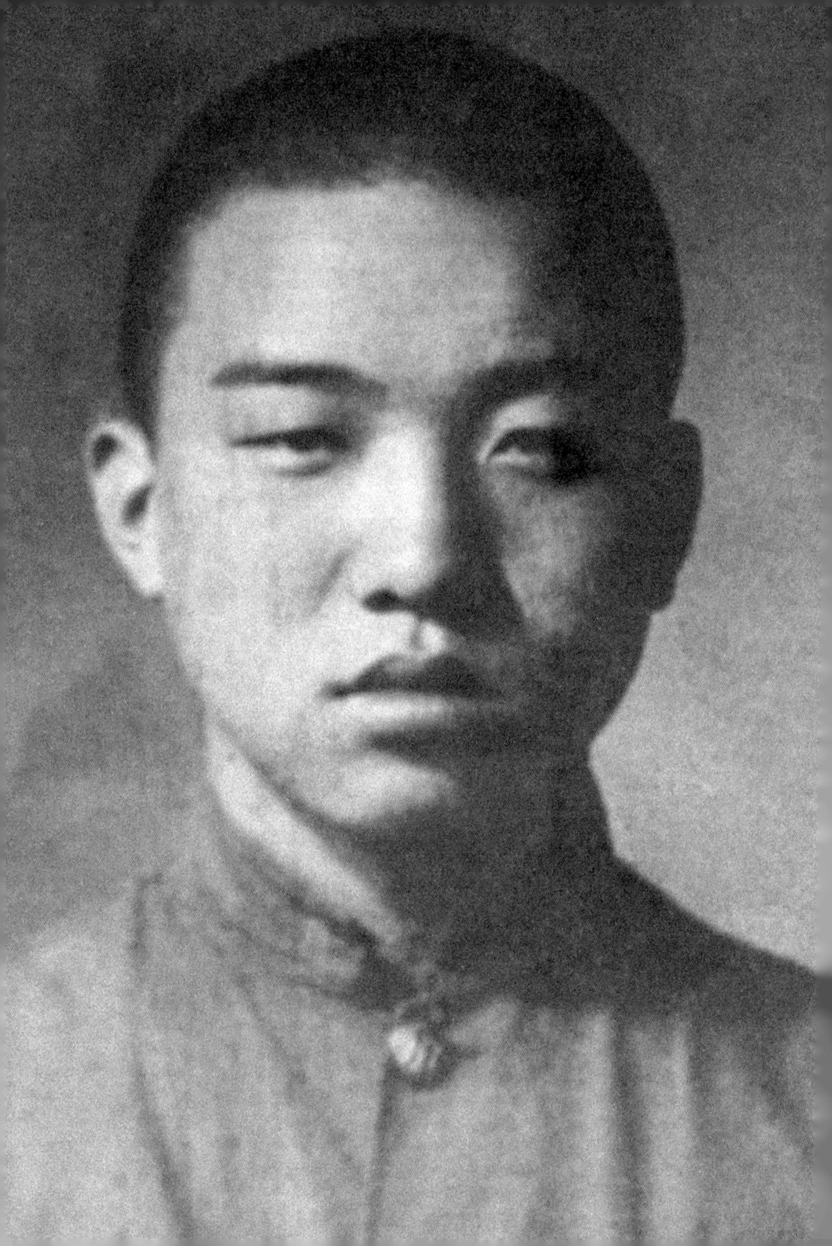

i was just a kid

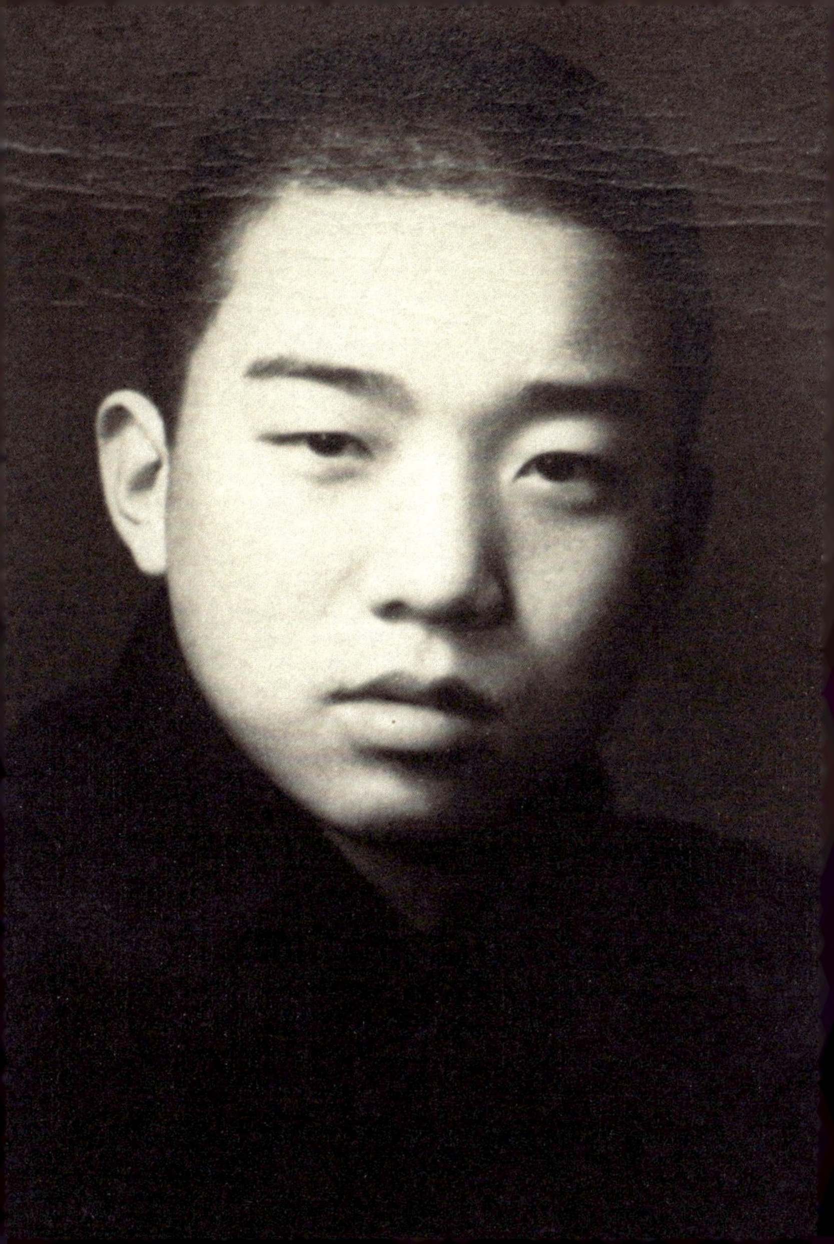

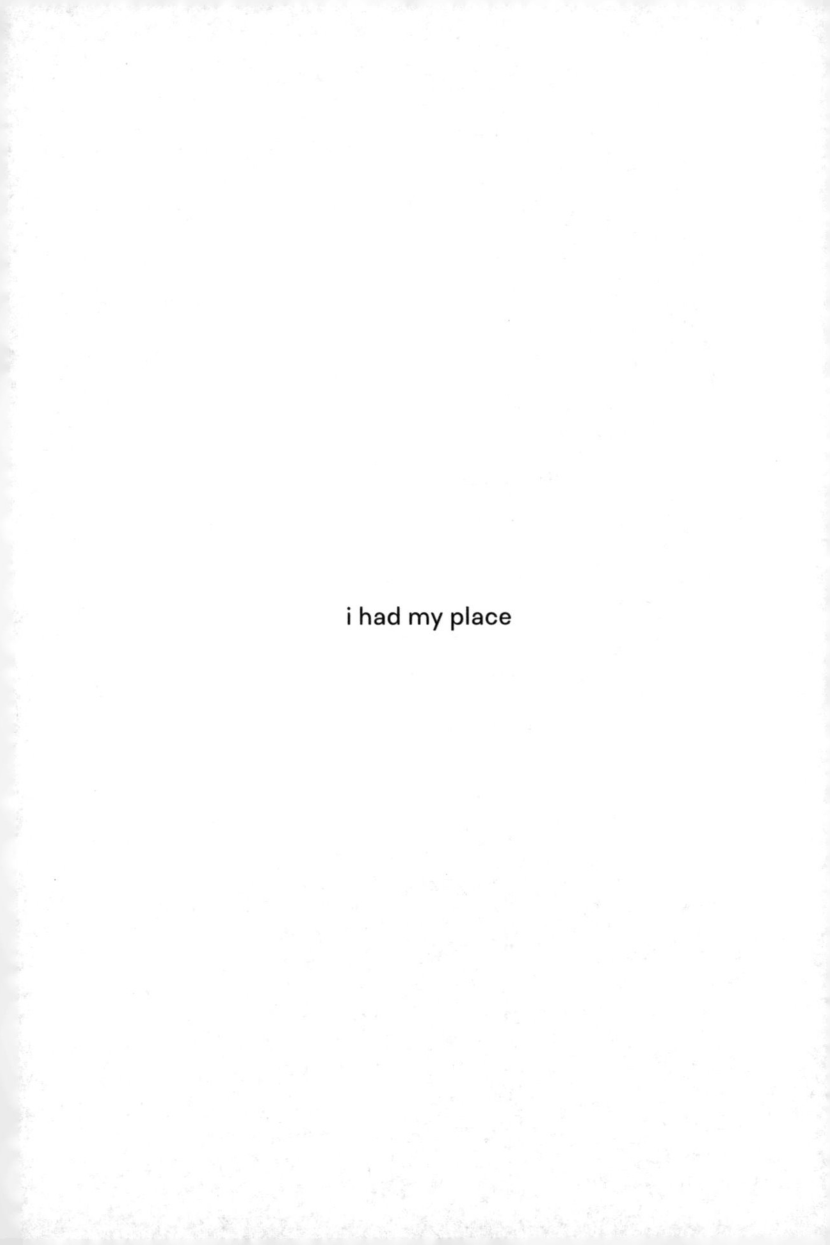

i had my place

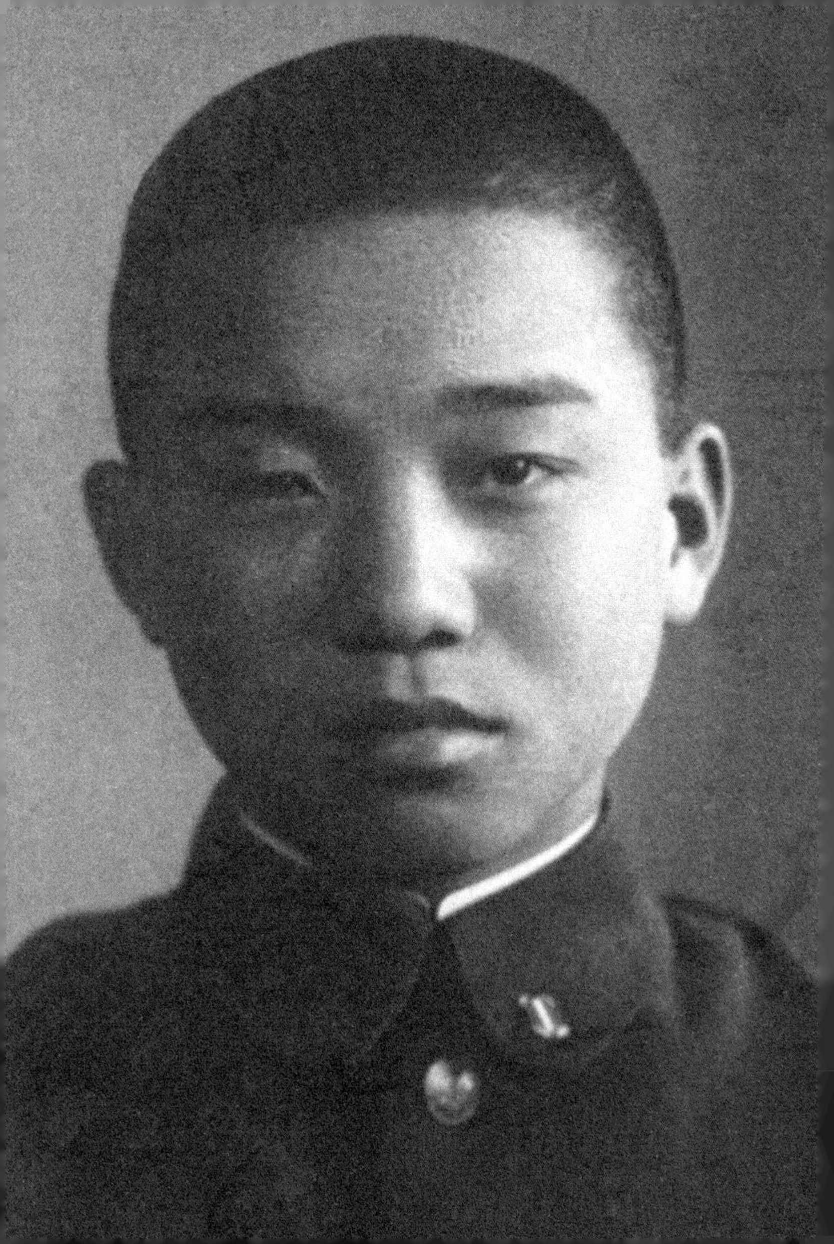

everything would change

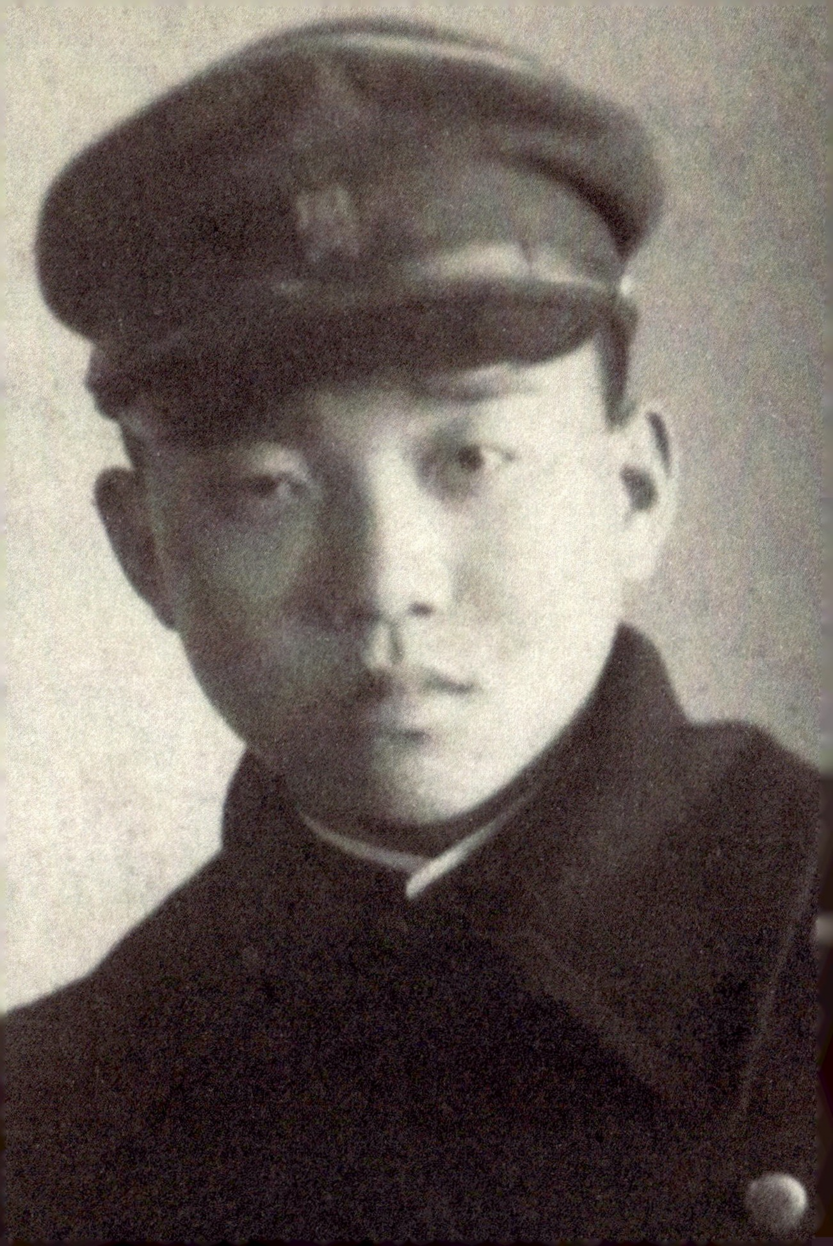

in uniform

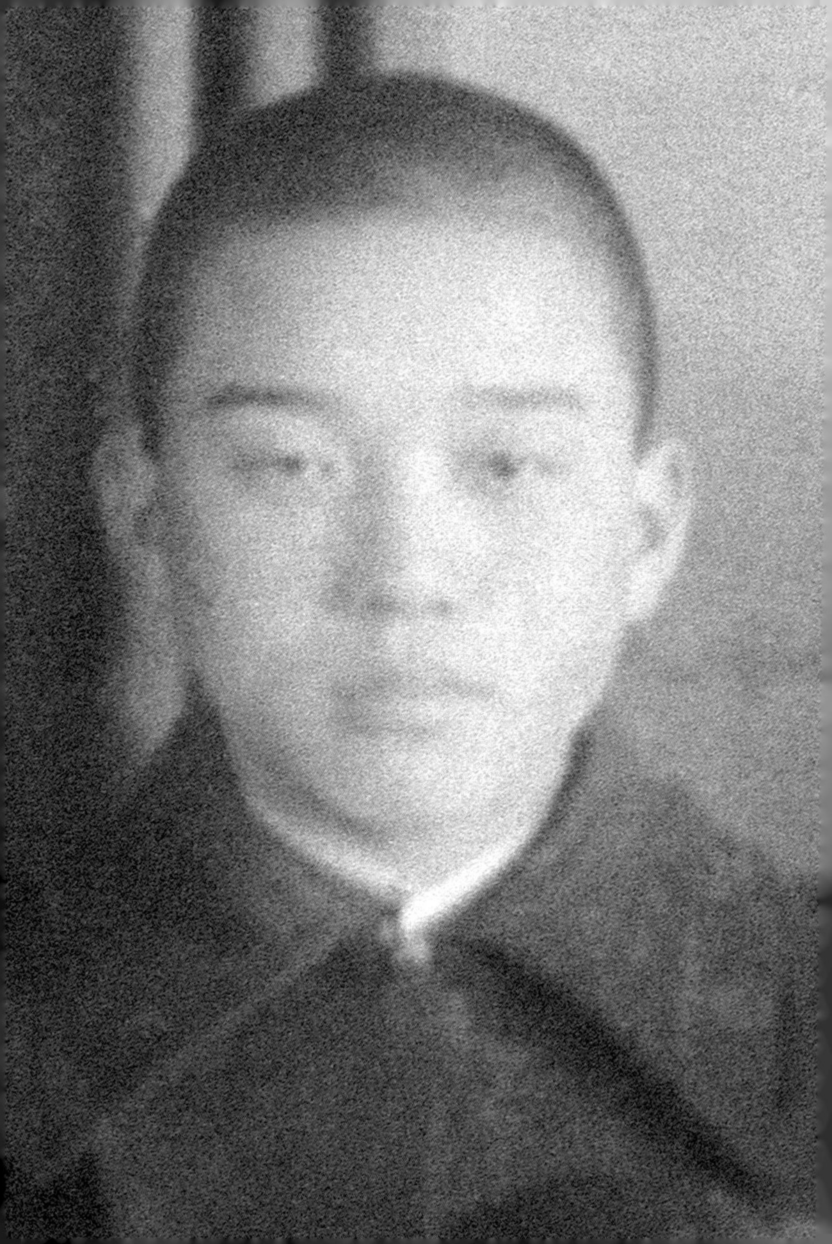

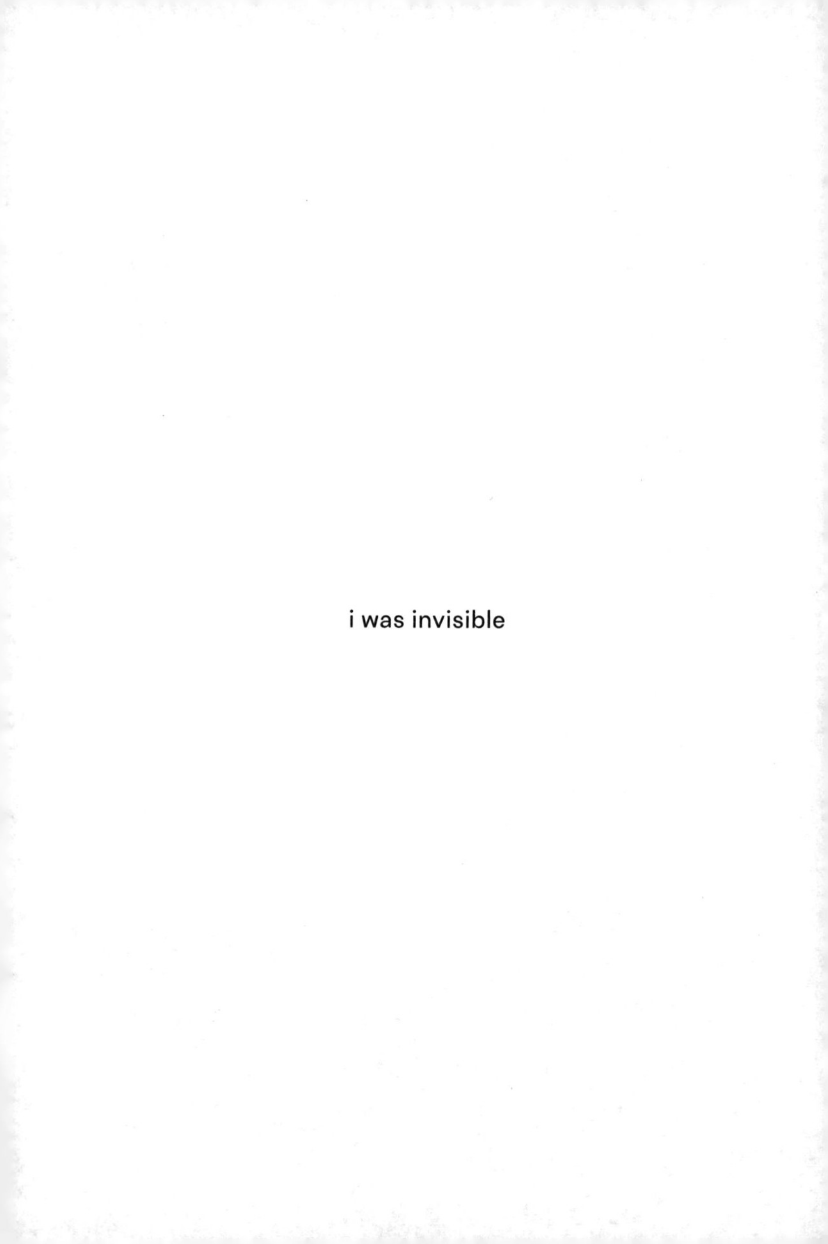

i was invisible

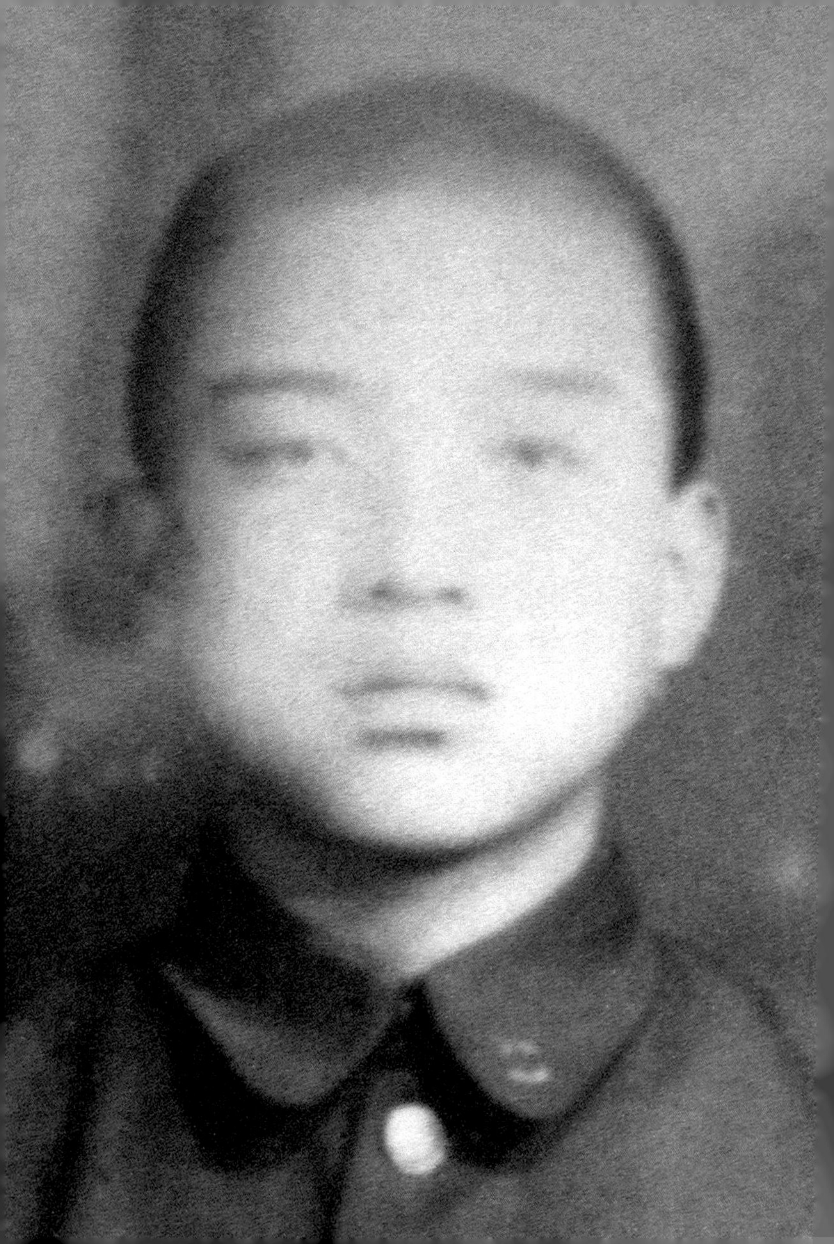

with no one close by

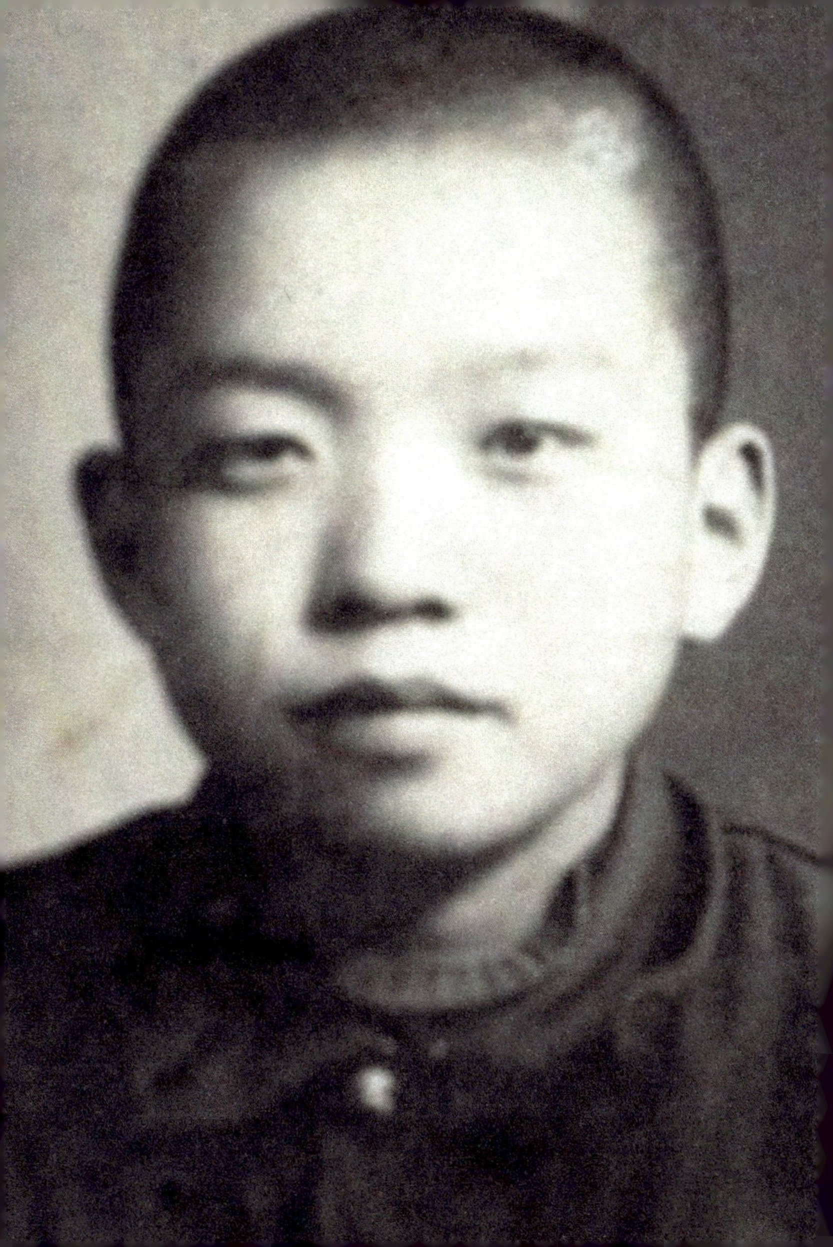

i was alone

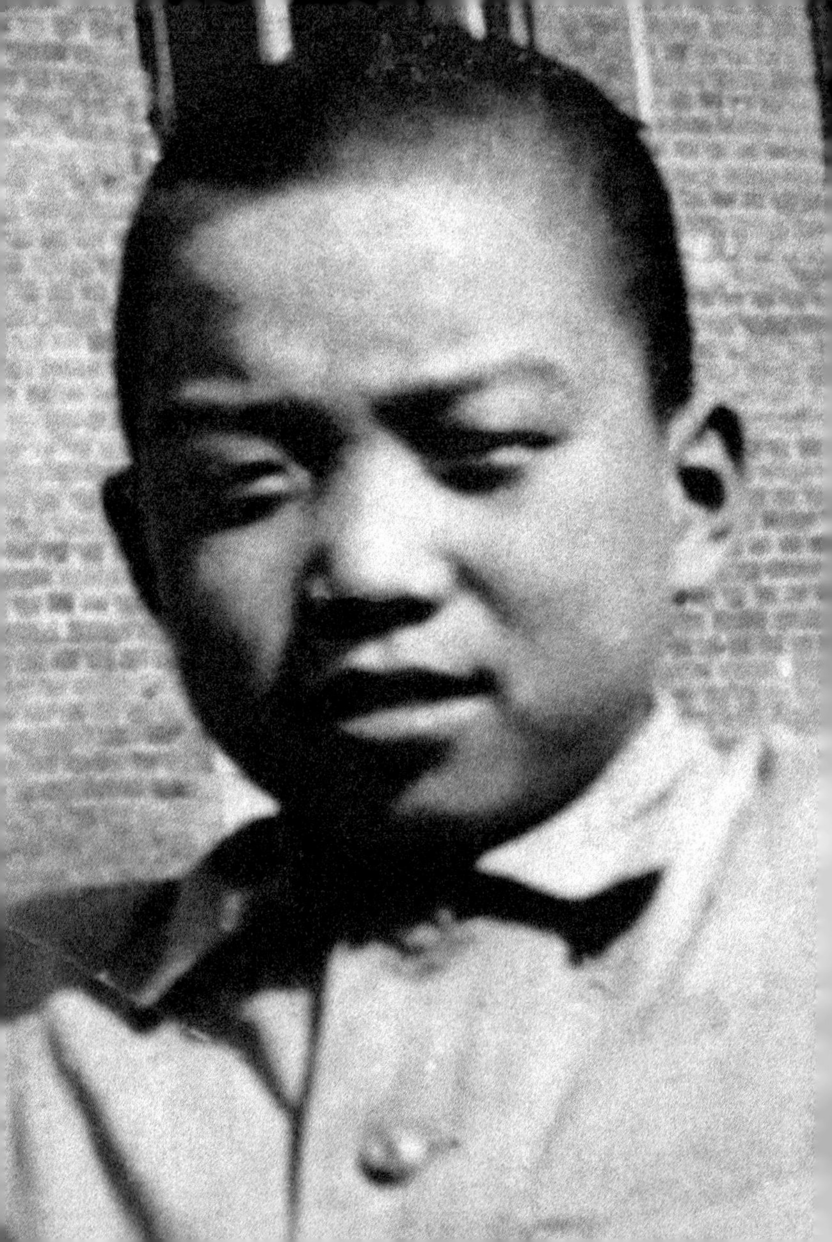

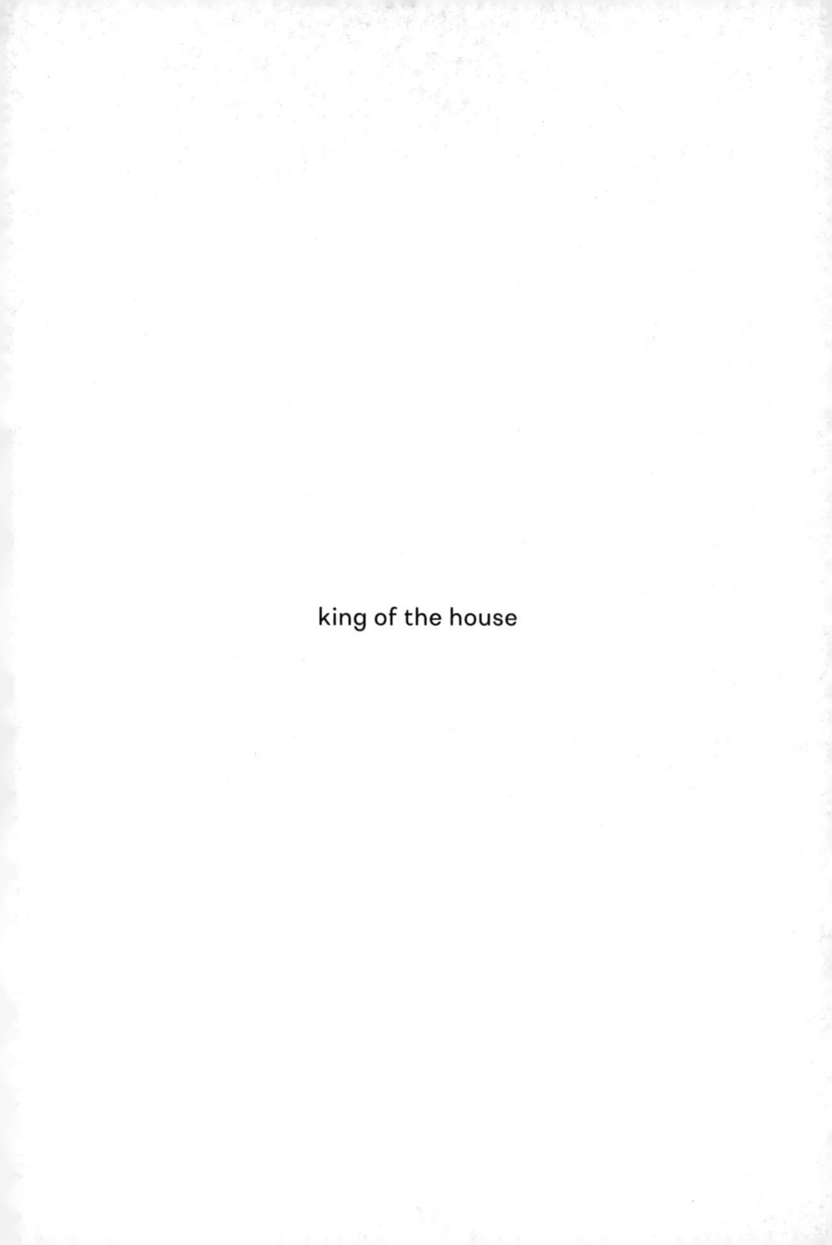

king of the house

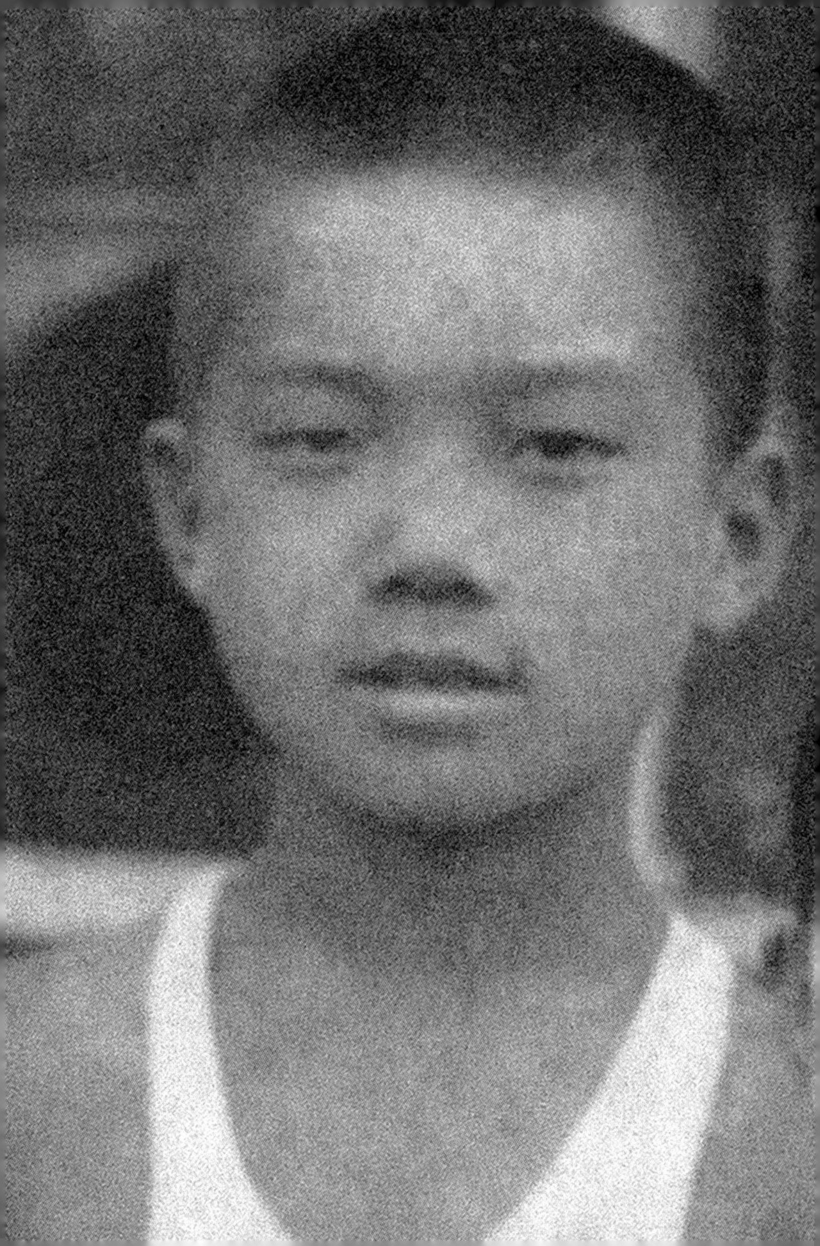

but not the first one

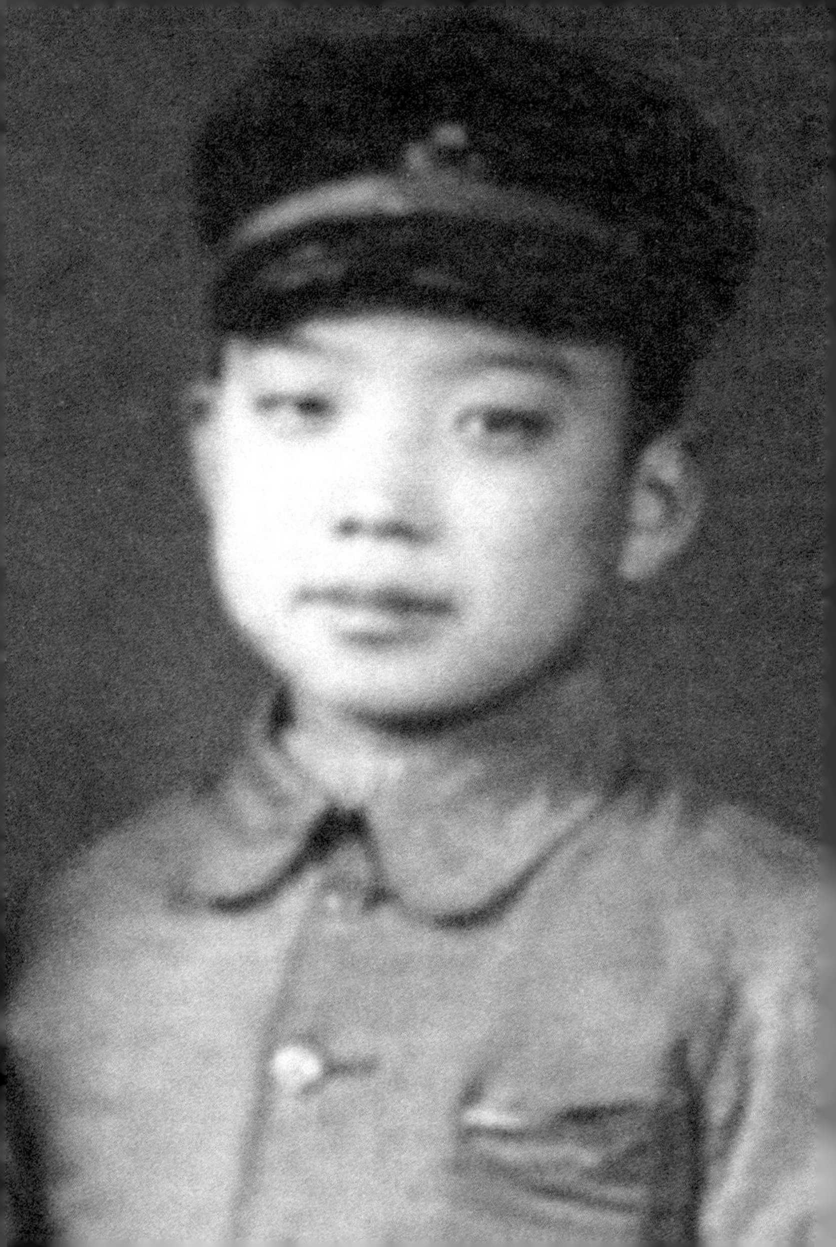

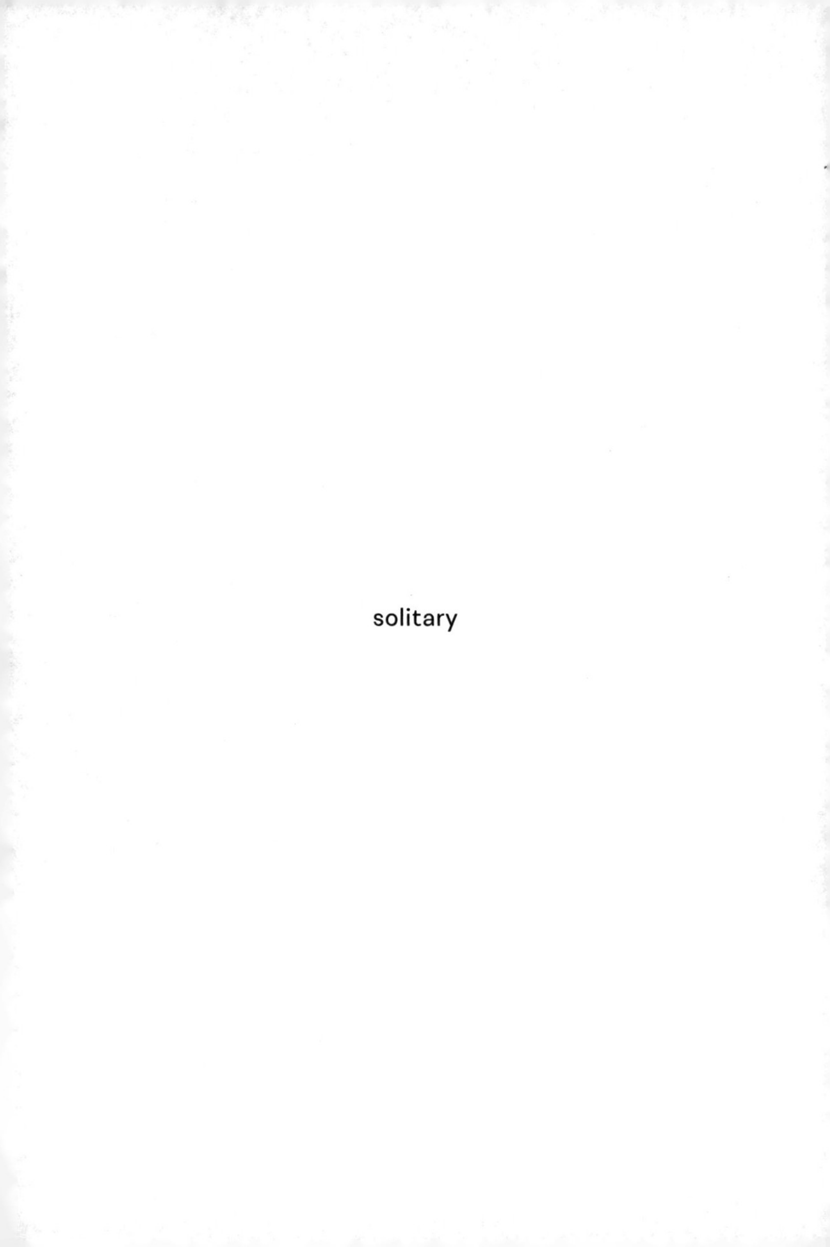

solitary

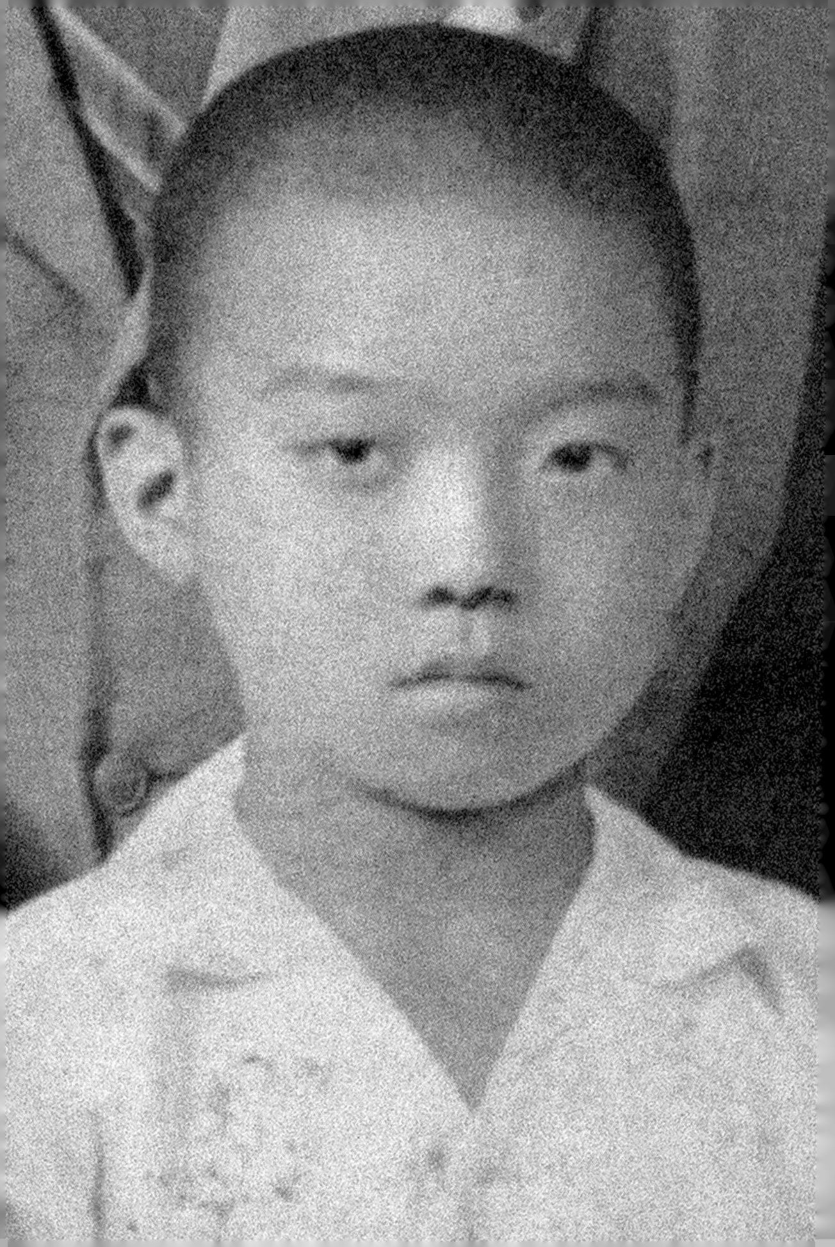

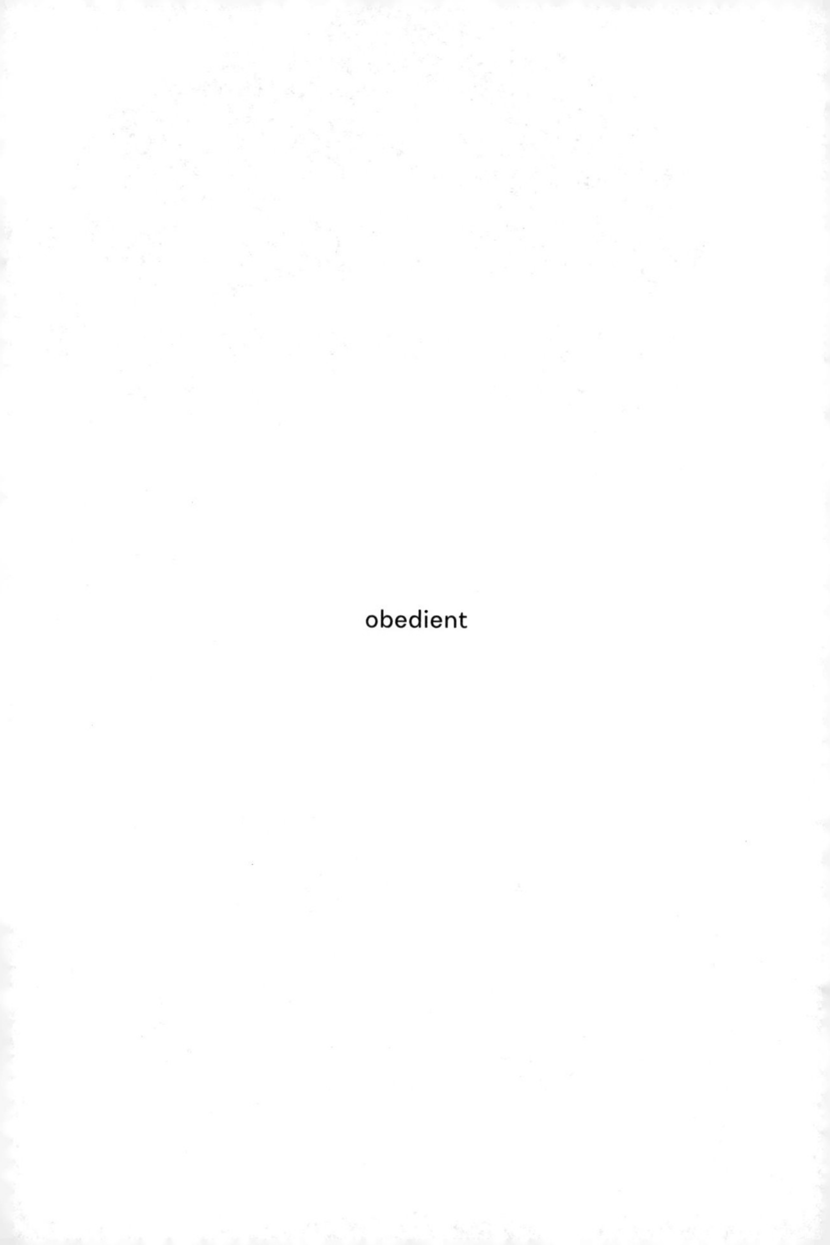
obedient

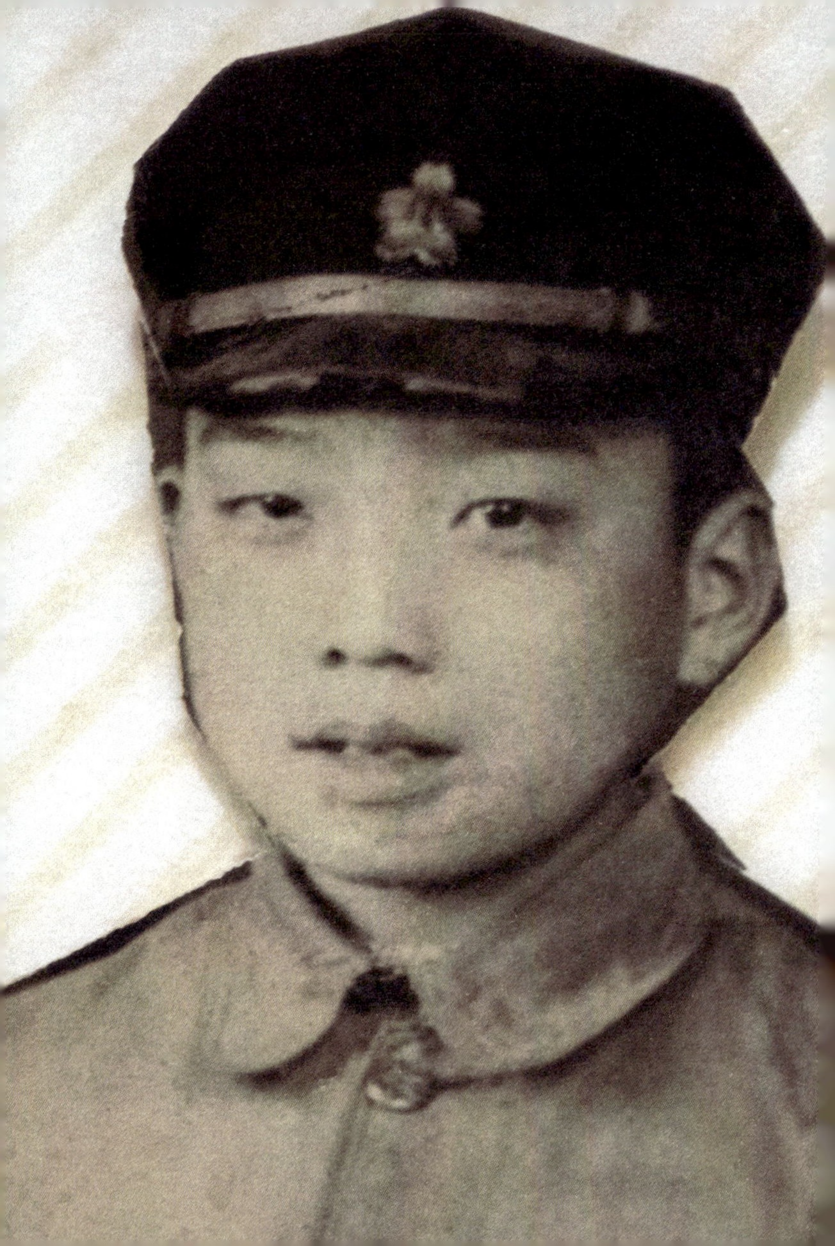

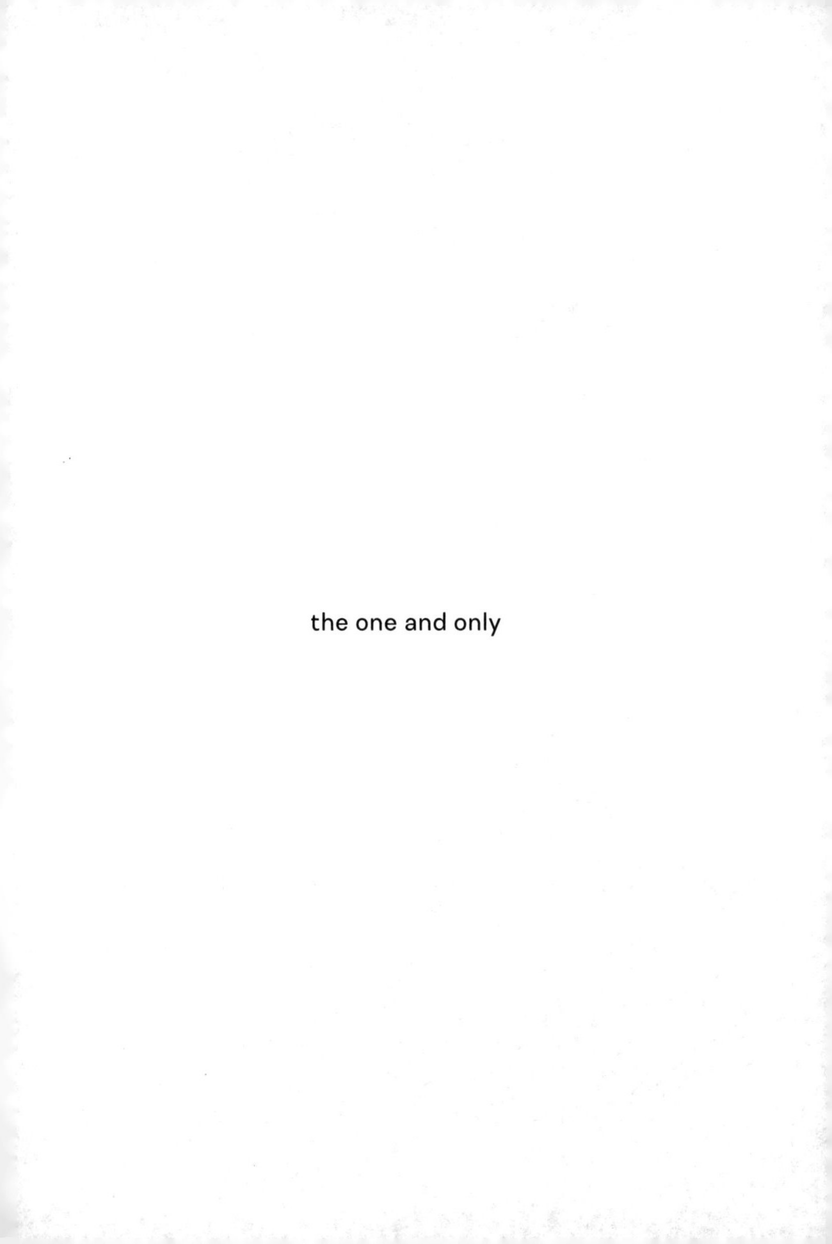

the one and only

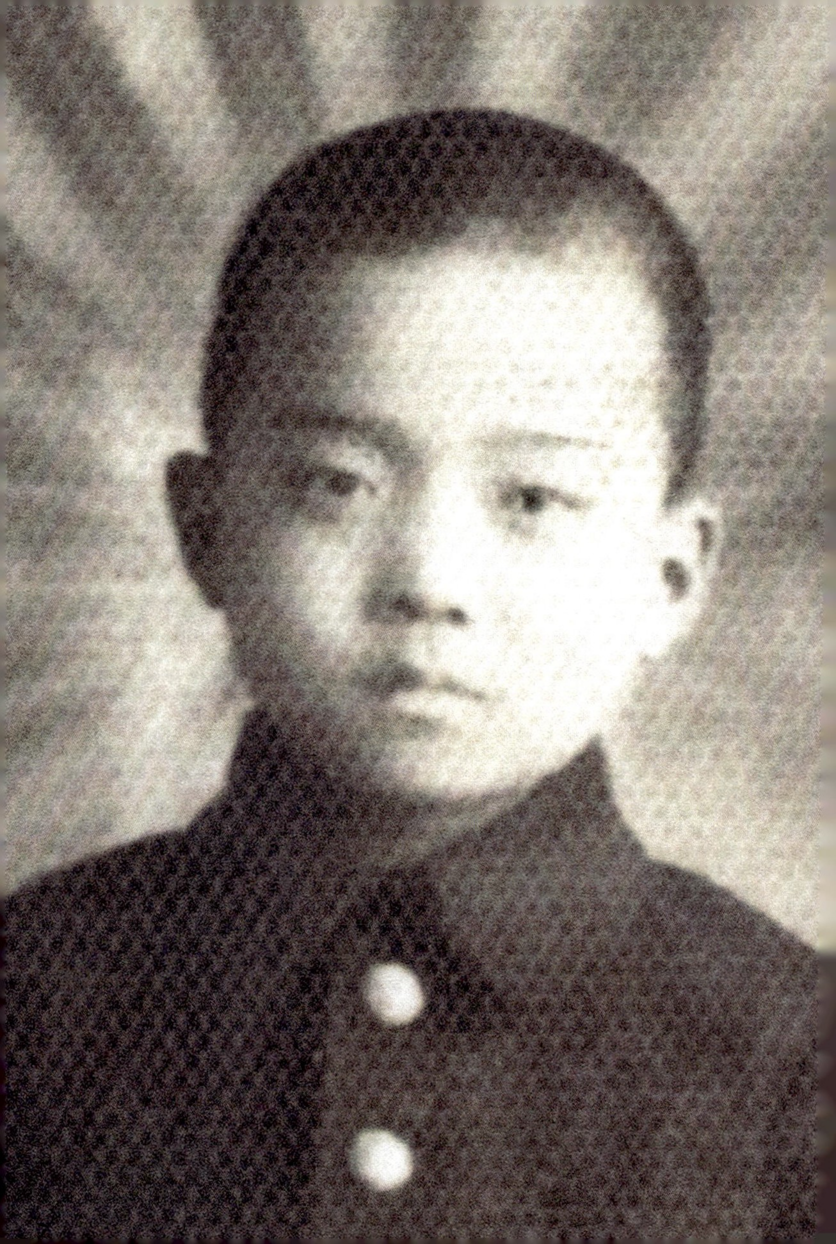

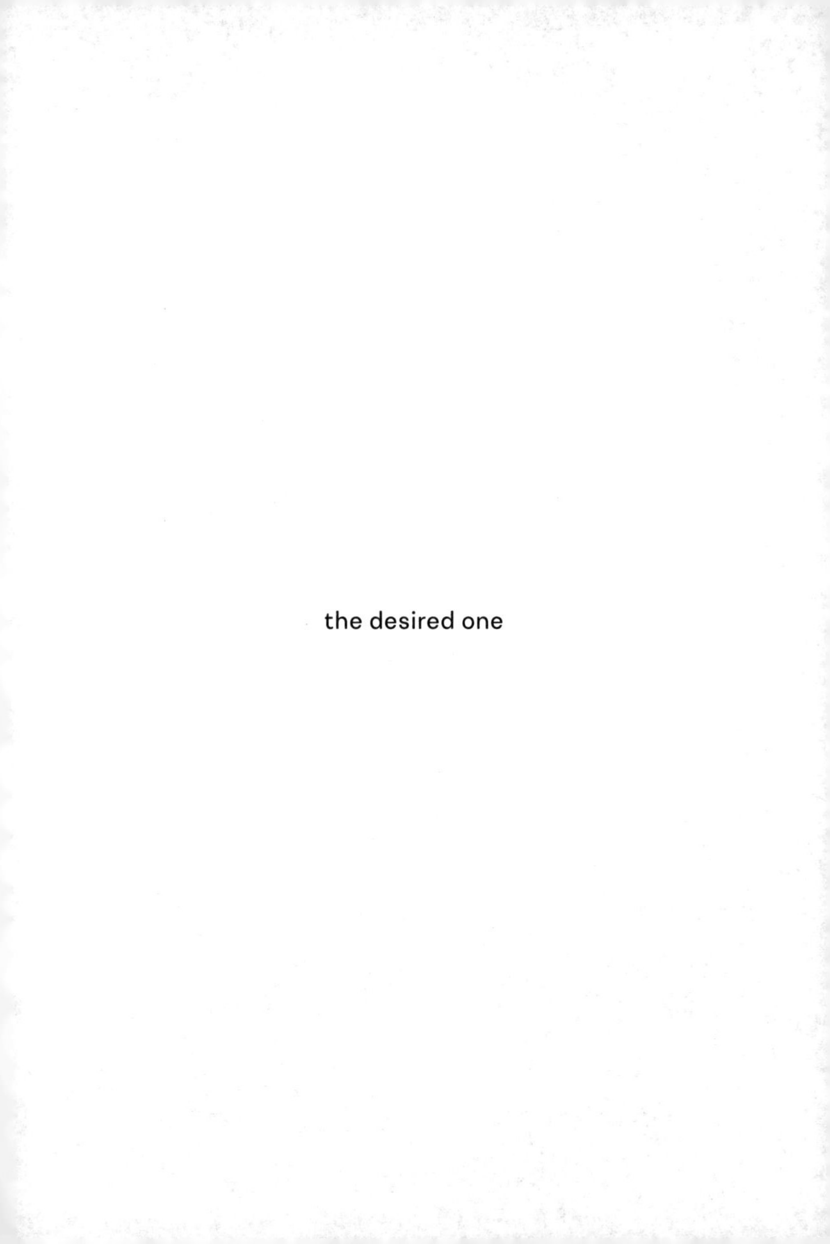

the desired one

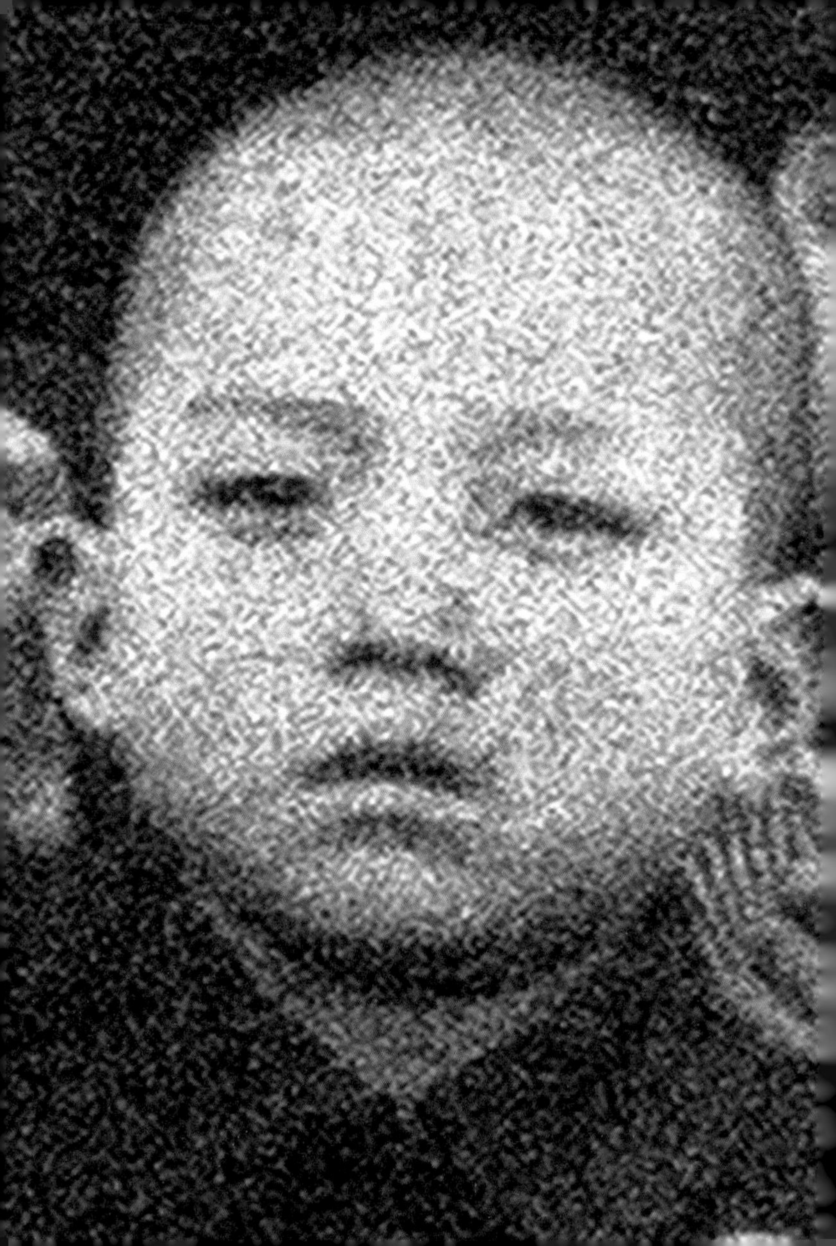

the heir

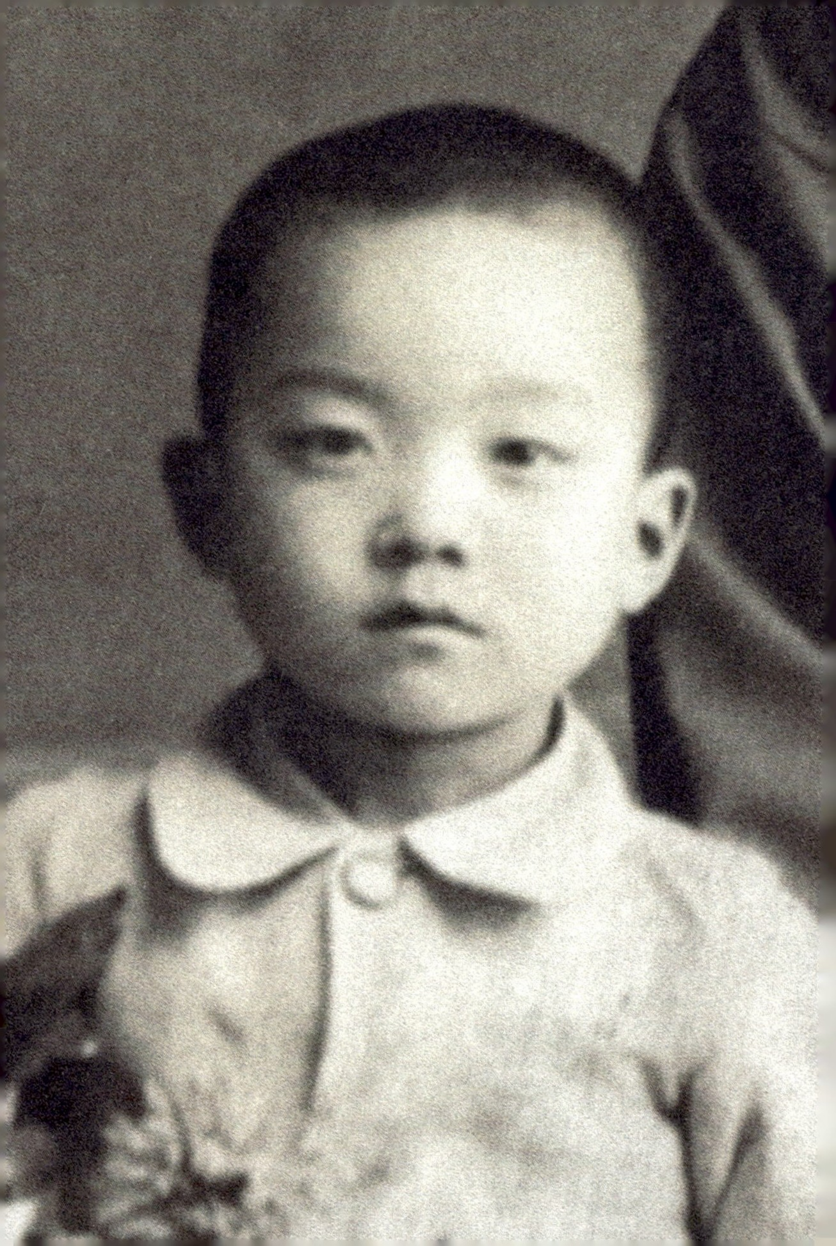

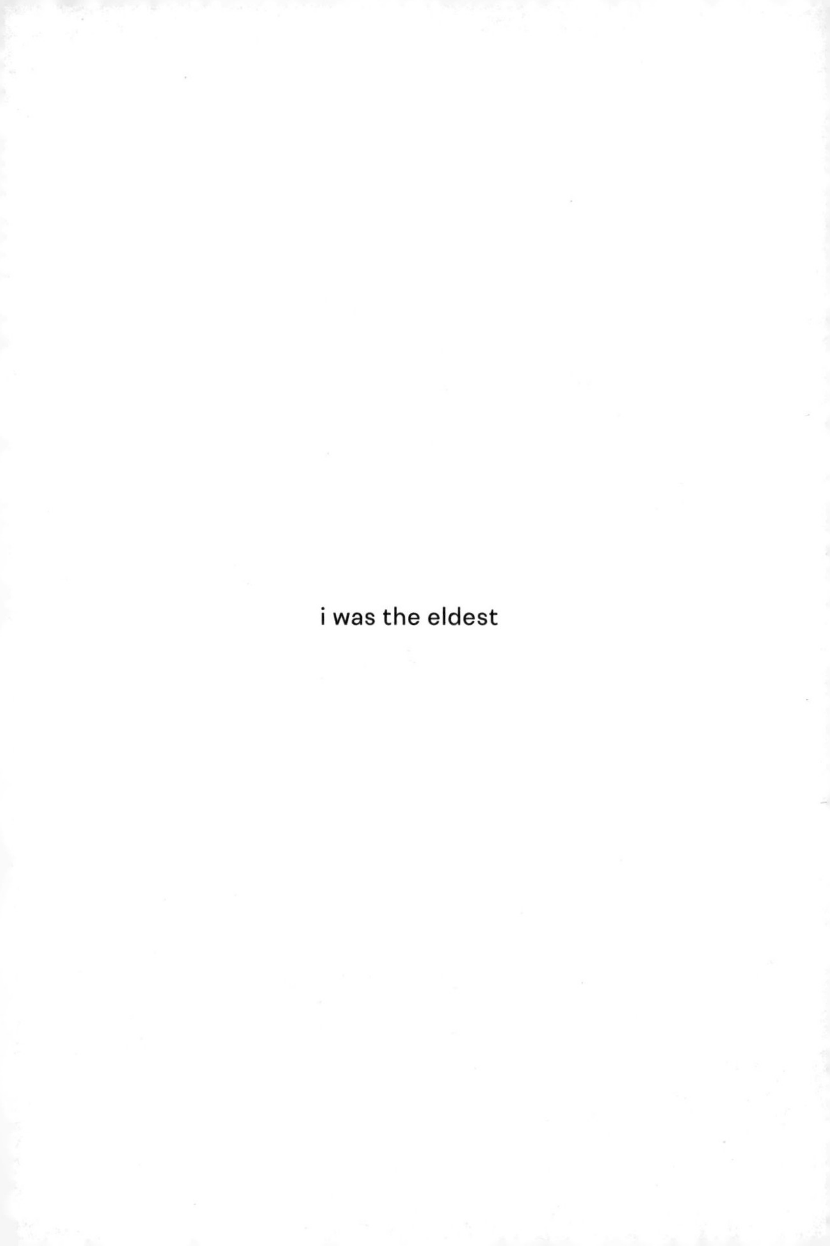

i was the eldest

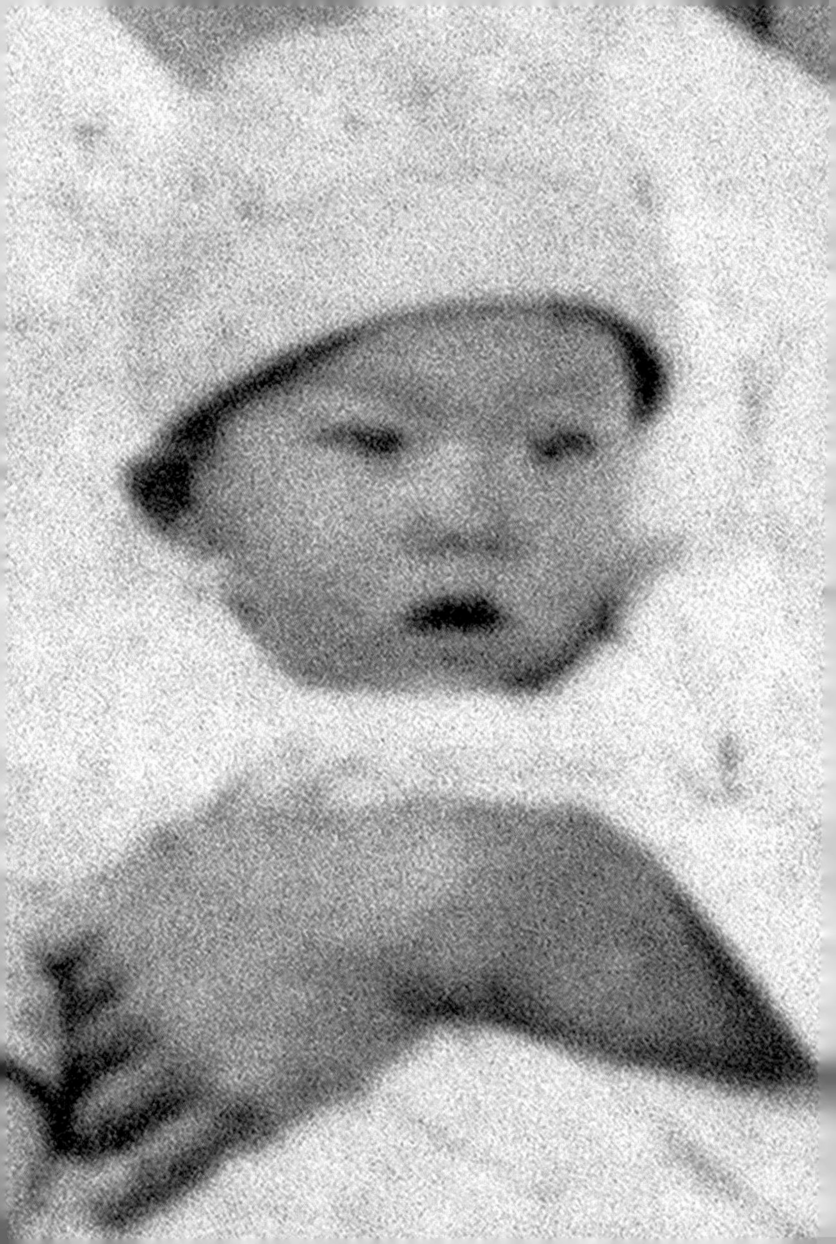

when i was little

Mr